THE INSTITUTIONALIST MOVEMENT IN
AMERICAN ECONOMICS, 1918–1947

This book provides a detailed picture of the institutionalist movement in American economics, concentrating on the period between the two world wars. The discussion brings a new emphasis on the leading role of Walton Hamilton in the formation of institutionalism, on the special importance of the ideals of "science" and "social control" embodied within the movement, on the large and close network of individuals involved, on the educational programs and research organizations created by institutionalists, and on the significant place of the movement within the mainstream of interwar American economics. In these ways, the book focuses on the group most closely involved in the active promotion of the movement, on how they themselves constructed it, on its original intellectual appeal and promise, and on its institutional supports and sources of funding. The reasons for the movement's loss of appeal in the years around the end of World War II are also discussed, particularly in terms of the arrival of Keynesian economics, econometrics, and new definitions of "science" as applied to economics.

Malcolm Rutherford is Professor of Economics at the University of Victoria, British Columbia, Canada, and the leading authority on the history of American institutional economics. He has published widely on this topic in *History of Political Economy*, *Journal of the History of Economic Thought*, *European Journal of the History of Economic Thought*, *Journal of Economic Perspectives*, and *Labor History*. He is the author of *Institutions in Economics: The Old and the New Institutionalism* (Cambridge University Press, 1994). Professor Rutherford has served as President of the History of Economics Society and the Association for Evolutionary Economics.

HISTORICAL PERSPECTIVES ON MODERN ECONOMICS

General Editor: Craufurd D. Goodwin, Duke University

This series contains original works that challenge and enlighten historians of economics. For the profession as a whole, it promotes better understanding of the origin and content of modern economics.

Continued after index

The Institutionalist Movement in American Economics, 1918–1947

Science and Social Control

MALCOLM RUTHERFORD

University of Victoria

CAMBRIDGE
UNIVERSITY PRESS

CAMBRIDGE UNIVERSITY PRESS
Cambridge, New York, Melbourne, Madrid, Cape Town,
Singapore, São Paulo, Delhi, Mexico City

Cambridge University Press
The Edinburgh Building, Cambridge CB2 8RU, UK

Published in the United States of America by Cambridge University Press, New York

www.cambridge.org
Information on this title: www.cambridge.org/9781107626089

© Malcolm Rutherford 2011

First published 2011
Reprinted 2011, 2012
First paperback edition 2013

A catalogue record for this publication is available from the British Library

Library of Congress Cataloguing in Publication Data

Rutherford, Malcolm, 1948–
The institutionalist movement in American economics, 1918–1947:
science and social control / Malcolm Rutherford.
    p. cm. – (Historical perspectives on modern economics)
Includes bibliographical references and index.
ISBN 978-1-107-00699-7
1. Institutional economics – History – 20th century. 2. Economics – United States –
History – 20th century. 3. Hamilton, Walton Hale, 1881–1958. I. Title.
HB99.5.R875 2011
330.15′52–dc22   2010050213

ISBN 978-1-107-00699-7 Hardback
ISBN 978-1-107-62608-9 Paperback

For Margaret

Contents

Tables

Acknowledgments

The production of this book took many years and a great deal of help from many people. The Social Science and Humanities Research Council of Canada supported my research in two multiyear research grants. Without this support, the archival work required for this project could never have been started, never mind completed. I owe thanks to the many archivists who helped me in my research, pointing me to material I would never have found on my own. I benefited tremendously from interviews with John Adams, James Buchanan, Robert Coleberd, Eli Ginzberg, Lowell Harriss, Robert Lipsey, Robert Loube, James Millar, David Penn, Mark Perlman, Warren Samuels, Anna Schwartz, Harry Trebing, and Aaron Warner, and from correspondence with Mark Blaug, Robert Fogel, Milton Friedman, Daniel Fusfeld, Lawrence Klein, Anne Mayhew, Terry Neale, and Mark Perlman. Valuable advice and criticism were given to me by my colleagues in the history of economic thought community, especially by Perry Mehrling, Phil Mirowski, and Mary Morgan, but also by many others too numerous to list here. I would also like to specifically mention the importance to me of the recent work done on the history of institutionalism by Luca Fiorito, Geoff Hodgson, and Yuval Yonay.

The material in this book relies heavily on articles I have previously published in *History of Political Economy*, *Journal of the History of Economic Thought*, *Labor History*, *Cambridge Journal of Economics*, *Research in the History of Economic Thought and Methodology*, and edited volumes published by Edward Elgar. Parts of Chapter 1 are taken from "American Institutionalism and the History of Economic Thought," *Journal of the History of Economic Thought* 19 (Fall 1997): 178–195; parts of Chapter 2 are taken from "Understanding Institutional Economics: 1918–1929," *Journal of the History of Economic Thought*, 22 (September 2000): 277–308, and from "Institutionalism as 'Scientific' Economics," in Roger Backhouse and John Creedy, eds., *From Classical Economics to the Theory of the Firm: Essays in Honour of D. P. O'Brien*, Cheltenham: Edward Elgar (1999), pp. 223–242; Chapter 3 is based on "Walton H. Hamilton and the Public Control of Business," in Steven Medema and Peter Boettke, eds., *The Role of Government in the History of Political Economy*, Supplement to volume 37, *History of Political Economy*, Durham, NC: Duke University Press (2005), pp. 234–273; Chapter 4 is based on "Morris A. Copeland: A Case Study in the History of Institutional Economics," *Journal of the History of Economic Thought* 24 (September 2002): 261–290; Chapter 5 utilizes parts of "Chicago Economics and Institutionalism," in Ross Emmett, ed., *The Elgar Companion to the Chicago School of Economics*, Cheltenham: Edward Elgar (2010), pp. 25–39, and parts of "Thorstein Veblen's Evolutionary Programme: A Promise Unfulfilled, *Cambridge Journal of Economics* 22 (July 1998): 463–477; Chapter 6 is based on "On the Economic Frontier: Walton Hamilton, Institutional Economics, and Education," *History of Political Economy* 35 (Winter 2003): 611–653; Chapter 7 is based on "Wisconsin Institutionalism: John R. Commons and His Students," *Labor History* 47 (May 2006): 161–188; Chapter 8 is based on "Institutional Economics at Columbia University," *History of Political Economy* 36 (Spring 2004): 31–78; Chapter 9 utilizes parts of "'Who's Afraid of Arthur Burns?' The NBER and the Foundations," *Journal of the History of Economic Thought* 27 (June 2005): 109–139; Chapter 10 is based on "The Institutionalist Reaction to Keynesian Economics" (with Tyler DesRoches), *Journal of the History of Economic Thought* 30 (March 2008): 29–48; Chapter 11 utilizes sections from both "'Who's Afraid of Arthur Burns?' The NBER and the Foundations," *Journal of the History of Economic Thought* 27 (June 2005): 109–139, and "Chicago Economics and Institutionalism," in Ross Emmett, ed., *The Elgar Companion to the Chicago School of Economics*, Cheltenham: Edward Elgar (2010), pp. 25–39; and Chapter 12 utilizes a section from "Institutional Economics: The Term and Its Meanings," *Research in the History of Economic Thought and Methodology* 22-A (2004): 179–184. I thank the publishers for permission to make use of this material.

PART ONE

INTRODUCTION

1

American Institutionalism in the History of Economics

The arrival of institutionalism as a self-identified and self-proclaimed movement in American economics can be dated quite precisely to December 1918 and to a much anticipated American Economic Association (AEA) conference session on economic theory, featuring papers by Walton Hamilton, J. M. Clark, and William Ogburn (a sociologist), and with Hamilton's colleague, Walter Stewart, as chair. Hamilton's paper, "The Institutional Approach to Economic Theory" (Hamilton 1919a), introduced the term "institutional economics" to the literature, and from that time on, there has been discussion and debate over the nature of institutional economics, its methods, its content, and its significance.

THE STANDARD VIEW

What might be called the standard view of American institutional economics can be easily found in textbooks on the history of economic thought.[1] There are a number of evident characteristics in these treatments. The first is that institutionalism is presented as an aside to the main story. This is not difficult to understand because these books are quite explicitly designed to follow what is seen as the main line of development of the discipline from classical economics to modern neoclassicism. From this perspective, it is easy to present institutionalism as ancillary to the main narrative.

Second, the discussions reflect an unresolved difficulty in the definition of the institutionalist movement. Thorstein Veblen is always a major component of the treatments, but there are surprising differences

---

[1] What follows is a composite view that does not apply in all particulars to all textbooks. The texts I looked at most closely were Blaug (1978); Oser and Brue (1988); Ekelund and Hebert (1990); Landreth and Colander (1994); and Rima (1996).

among the coverage provided to other institutionalists, and all the books grapple uncomfortably with the obvious divergences among many of the leading figures. Even if one only considers the three people usually presented as the major figures – Thorstein Veblen, Wesley Mitchell, and John R. Commons – the difficulties are immediately clear. Veblen is associated with an evolutionary approach based on efficient cause, a key distinction between pecuniary, or business, institutions and technological, or industrial, requirements, and a biting critique of both neoclassical theory and real-world business practices; Mitchell is known for quantitative methods and detailed research on business cycles, an approach he established at the National Bureau of Economic Research (NBER); and Commons is associated with trade union histories, labor legislation, public utility regulation, and an analytical scheme emphasizing the evolution of legal institutions and processes of dispute resolution. Matters are not improved if the discussion includes others such as J. M. Clark and Clarence Ayres.

This problem of definition gives rise to the treatment of institutionalism as primarily a species of "dissent," because dissent from neoclassicism is indeed a shared characteristic (Landreth and Colander 1994; Rima 1996). George Stigler claimed that institutionalism has "no positive agenda of research," "no set of problems or new methods," and nothing but "a stance of hostility to the standard theoretical tradition" (quoted in Kitch 1983, p. 170). Likewise, Mark Blaug has stated that institutionalism "was never more than a tenuous inclination to dissent from orthodox economics" (1978, p. 712). This view still finds currency. For example, Oliver Williamson argues, "unable or unwilling to offer a rival research agenda, the older institutional economics was given over to methodological objections to orthodoxy" (Williamson 1998b, p. 24; see also 1998a).

Third, this emphasis on dissent from neoclassical theory reinforces the idea that institutionalism is to be placed on the fringes of the discipline. In the textbook treatments, there is usually little description of the overall character of American economics of the time (Ekelund and Hebert 1990 is a partial exception here), and often no mention at all of the fact that institutionalism was a major part of American economics in the interwar period. After all, if institutionalism was mainly dissent, how could it have been a significant part of the mainstream of economics or have contributed anything to it?

Finally, the decline of institutionalism in the post–World War II period tends to be discussed briefly and almost exclusively in terms of institutionalism failing to produce a "viable" alternative to neoclassicism in the form of a "single, cohesive, and consistent body of thought" (Ekelund and Hebert

1990, p. 478). This is an argument that, in various forms, one finds repeated throughout the literature. It holds that institutionalism failed because it was too descriptive and did not produce "theory," or at least a sufficiently well-specified theory. Examples of this argument range from Paul Homan's complaint that "the supposed existence of a distinguishable body of economic knowledge or theory properly to be called institutional is an intellectual fiction" (Homan 1932, p. 10) to Ronald Coase's dismissive comment that "American institutionalists were not theoretical but anti-theoretical. ... Without a theory they had nothing to pass on except a mass of descriptive material waiting for a theory or a fire" (Coase 1984, p. 230).[2] This lack of systematic theory is taken as such an obvious reason for the failure of institutionalism that no further examination or comment is offered.

Thus, the standard view presents institutionalism as a minor, passing phase in the history of economics – as a movement with little coherence other than a shared disdain for orthodox theory, which, having had little impact on mainstream economic thinking, finally passed away because it was overly descriptive and produced no consistent body of thought.

AN OUTLINE OF A REVISIONIST VIEW

The primary argument in this book is that the picture of institutionalism given in this standard view is a highly misleading one. There are a number of aspects to this argument, but the general point is that understanding institutionalism requires understanding the character of American economics in the period from about 1890 through to the end of the 1940s. In many discussions of American economics, it is assumed that the work of J. B. Clark resulted in a consolidation of neoclassical economics in America (Persky 2000),[3] but this is far from correct. If we look first at the period from the late 1880s to World War I, American economics was highly unsettled in nature. Although American economics was professionalizing, there was no authoritative figure such as Alfred Marshall in England, and Marshallian economics did not dominate the American discourse. Marginalist, Austrian,

---

[2] Despite this criticism, Coase has made numerous remarks that would seem to place him close to the institutionalist position. Taylor (2010, p. 257) quotes Coase as saying "firms never calculate marginal costs ... I think we ought to study directly how firms operate and develop our theory accordingly."

[3] Persky also seems to think that a well-defined institutionalist school existed in 1899. Persky seems to be talking about Veblen and a number of "New School" writers such as H. C. Adams and Richard Ely. I would rather see these writers as people who produced work that was incorporated, to a greater or lesser extent, in the institutionalist movement as it coalesced around 1918.

institutional, historicist, and various evolutionary ideas all contended and were variously intermixed. The German historical tradition had considerable influence in America due to the large numbers of economists who went to Germany for graduate training and who populated the expanding American university system (Herbst 1965; Parrish 1967).

In the 1890s, the American economics profession was diverse both in terms of a spectrum of opinion running from William Graham Sumner to F. W. Taussig and from J. B. Clark to Thorstein Veblen, and in terms of the eclecticism of many individuals. Two good examples of this eclecticism are A. T. Hadley and H. J. Davenport. Hadley was politically conservative. He sought to combine marginalist and evolutionary ideas, and his economics included a clear appreciation of the role of property rights and institutions, as well as recognition of the problems created by competition in industries with high overheads, such as railroads (Davidson and Ekelund 1994). Davenport worked in the Austrian tradition and made important contributions to the concept of subjective or opportunity cost and to the concept of entrepreneurial action (Gunning 1998), but he was also a firm friend of Veblen and much influenced by Veblen's critique of financial predation and exploitation. To be sure, economists such as R. T. Ely and H. C. Adams, among others, faced challenges to their academic careers due to their supposed socialism, and the breadth of the American academy had its limits, but it remains true that American economics was of a broad and unsettled character.

Writing from the perspective of later neoclassical dominance, it is easy to overstate the position of American neoclassicism in this period. If one had to define what "marginalist" or "neoclassical"[4] economics meant to American economists circa 1900, it would probably have been thought of in terms of the work of J. B. Clark and Irving Fisher, which argued for a theory of value based on marginal utility, a marginal productivity theory of distribution, and a theory of competitive markets. But there was much discussion and disagreement over the adequacy of this "static" theory, a frequently expressed desire for some type of dynamic theory (a desire shared by J. B. Clark himself), and many doubts concerning the adequacy of economic theory and the market mechanism itself, in the face of the new economic developments and social conflicts being brought about by American industrialization. At the end of World War I, institutionalism emerged as a movement at one end of the spectrum of American

---

[4]   The term "neoclassical" appears to have been invented only in 1900 by Thorstein Veblen in his discussion of Marshall (Veblen 1899/1900).

economics. Slightly later, in the 1920s and 1930s, American neoclassicism also developed considerably, particularly in the hands of Frank Knight and Jacob Viner, but American economics remained relatively pluralistic throughout the interwar period (Morgan and Rutherford 1998), and was not dominated by a single perspective, either institutionalist or neoclassical.[5]

In addition to this pluralism, it is vital to observe that in the period between the wars, institutionalism was far from marginalized. Institutionalists published regularly in the leading journals of economics, held positions in major research universities (dominating the faculty at two of the top four PhD-granting universities in the country),[6] were highly active in the creation of institutions for research and education in the social sciences, had excellent links to funding agencies, were deeply involved in economic policy making, and became presidents of the American Economic Association and American Statistical Association.[7] In other words, institutionalism was fully a part of the *mainstream* of American economics. The idea of institutionalism as nothing but dissent makes this impossible to understand. This observation leads, in turn, to another crucially important point: institutionalism must have been seen to be offering something positive (potential or actual) to have attracted adherents and have gained the professional and organizational position it had. The question that arises is one of what institutionalism meant to those who were a part of the movement and actively engaged in its development.

---

[5] Hodgson has claimed that institutionalism was the mainstream, but this is an overstatement (Hodgson 2004, p. 4). Hodgson and I are in agreement on many aspects of the "revisionist view" presented here, and Hodgson's book, *The Evolution of Institutional Economics* (2004) is an important contribution. The focus of Hodgson's work, however, is very much on the development of Veblen's specific evolutionary theory, its later abandonment by institutionalists, and on general problems of agency and structure in evolutionary explanation. The present work is centered on the nature of interwar institutionalism, its programs, institutional supports, and place in American economics.

[6] The leading four PhD-granting institutions in economics in the 1920s and 1930s were Columbia, Harvard, Chicago, and Wisconsin, with Columbia being by far the largest in terms of numbers of candidates reported and Harvard granting the largest number of degrees (Froman 1942). Institutionalist faculty dominated at Columbia and at Wisconsin. Chicago had a significant but by no means dominant institutionalist complement until about 1926. Harvard Business School included Edwin Gay and W. Z. Ripley, who had clear institutionalist sympathies. Neoclassical economics was poorly represented at both Columbia and Wisconsin.

[7] Institutionalist Presidents of the American Economic Association include John R. Commons (1917), Wesley C. Mitchell (1924), J. M. Clark (1935), F. C. Mills (1940), Sumner Slichter (1941), Edwin Nourse (1942), E. E. Witte (1956), and Morris A. Copeland (1957). Presidents of the American Statistical Association included Wesley C. Mitchell (1918), F. C. Mills (1934), Winfield Riefler (1941), Isador Lubin (1946), and Willard Thorp (1947).

This issue will be dealt with in much more detail in later chapters, but at this stage it is useful to make a few observations concerning the nature of institutionalism in its early years. Two related characteristics stand out. The first of these is a shared notion of science as involving some form of empirical "realism," and the second is a view of economic and social arrangements or institutions as in need of significant reform. In Dorothy Ross's words, "what fuelled the institutionalist ambition was an overflow of realism and new liberal idealism that could not be contained by neoclassical practice" (Ross 1991, p. 411; Rutherford 1997).

Realism seems to have meant a number of things to institutionalists. It certainly meant an empirical and *investigative* view of science, one that was thought of as modeled on the natural sciences. The emphasis that one finds in this literature on the application of natural science methods to economics is striking indeed. One aspect of this was Wesley Mitchell's advocacy of quantitative methods – Mitchell saw the statistical laboratory as the closest approach to the methods of the physical sciences that was possible to achieve in the social sciences – but it was by no means confined to that. Institutionalists as a group saw the scientific method as one that emphasized empirical investigation, the development of theories based on assumptions that conformed to real-world conditions, and the critical examination of theories on the basis of empirical findings. In this light, much neoclassical theory was seen as too abstract, based on assumptions not met in the real world, and frequently untested or untestable.

Beyond this empiricism, realism also meant being consistent with the state of scientific knowledge in other, related fields, particularly psychology, sociology, and law. This desire for consistency with other fields not only ruled out hedonism as a psychological foundation for economics, but was also taken as pointing to the social-psychological foundation of institutions and economic behavior. Realism also meant an emphasis on the institutional (as opposed to natural) character of the economic system, and this in turn implied that the economy was not determined by given and unchanging natural laws, but by social and legal norms and conventions that changed (and could be changed) over time.

This last aspect was explicitly linked to the issue of relevance, in the sense of relevance for the solution of pressing social problems. Problems such as labor unrest, business cycles, unemployment, poverty, externalities of various kinds, monopoly, manipulation of consumer wants, sharp practice, resource depletion, and waste and inefficiency were all attributed to a failure of markets, or "pecuniary institutions" more generally, to control or direct economic activity in a manner consistent with the public interest.

The notion of an economics "relevant to the problem of control" (Hamilton 1919a) recurs repeatedly in the literature. This idea of "social control" as government intervention and regulation designed to guide the economy in socially desirable directions became a key part of the institutionalist creed (Everett, 1931).[8] The phrase "social control" became almost a mantra for the institutionalists of the time.

Whereas these elements and others provided common ground among institutionalists, there were differences between them, too: in the particular forms their empiricism took, in the extent to which they thought standard theory would have to be replaced (as opposed to supplemented), in the extent of their dissatisfaction with the market as an instrument of control, and in their specific proposals for reform and the degree of statism involved. The combination of scientism and reformism also created tensions that different individuals solved in different ways. Institutionalism did not consist of a well-defined "school" of economics, but as a *movement* held together by some fairly general methodological, theoretical, and ideological commitments.[9] Nevertheless, the movement can hardly be described as incoherent or without a positive program of its own.

The claim that interwar institutionalism was a part of the mainstream of economics leads directly to another argument, namely that institutionalism only later *became* a dissenting heterodoxy lying outside of the mainstream of American economics. As we move from the interwar to the post–World War II period, the marginalization of institutionalism occurred gradually in a process that coincided with the rise to dominance of neoclassical and Keynesian economics. These events are linked and are of obvious importance in the history of American economics. Understanding the relative decline of institutionalism is a necessary part of understanding the character of post-1945 American economics more generally. Here, my argument is that the story of institutionalism's relative decline is a complex one, involving a number of factors that together greatly weakened its appeal. A part of this story is that institutionalism increasingly came to be seen as insufficiently theoretical, but simply leaving the argument there fails to get to the heart of the matter. Institutionalists were certainly not enamored of the highly abstract and speculative nature of much neoclassical theory, but they

---

[8] Helen Everett had been a student of Walton Hamilton's at the Brookings Graduate School.

[9] This idea of institutionalism as an intellectual and sociological movement may have some connections to the concept of a "creative community." This concept has been explored recently at a conference at Duke University and will be the subject of a forthcoming special issue of *History of Political Economy*.

were not antitheoretical. They argued for a different conception of economic inquiry and theory. The standard view avoids the key question by implicitly adopting neoclassical criteria of theoretical adequacy. The real question is how and why such criteria came to dominate. Think for a moment about all the other social sciences, none of which developed in the same fashion as economics. Keep in mind, also, that Wesley Mitchell's research program as embodied in the NBER was based on an analogy with the physical sciences, and was one that had considerable respect, prestige, and Rockefeller Foundation funding. Indeed, in the interwar period it was the institutionalists, not the neoclassicals, who were most successfully claiming the mantle of modernism and "science" (Rutherford 1999). Somehow these positions reversed themselves.

PLAN OF THE WORK

This book seeks to give a detailed picture of institutionalism as an important part of American economics between the wars. This will involve not only a discussion of the ideas of institutionalists but a depiction of institutionalism as a movement – a network of people and institutional supports that occupied a significant place in the profession of economics. The primary focus will be on the years from 1918 to 1947, the years of institutionalism's greatest prominence and success, but events prior to and immediately after those dates will not be ignored. The discussion of the factors leading up to the development of institutionalism goes back to the 1880s and 1890s. There are treatments of developments somewhat beyond 1947 in a number of places, and the changing position of institutionalism in the post–World War II period is dealt with in Part Four of the book. Nevertheless, the primary focus is on the period between 1918 and 1947. I have chosen 1918 as the starting point because that was the year of Hamilton's original institutionalist manifesto. I have chosen 1947 as the end date because that was when the major universities resumed hiring after the Depression and World War II and conspicuously failed to hire institutionalists, indicating that an important change in academic status had occurred. It is also the date of the Cowles Commission's attack on the NBER (Koopmans 1947) and the date of the publication of Paul Samuelson's *Foundations of Economic Analysis* (Samuelson 1947).

Part One of this book, consisting of this chapter and the next, is intended to provide an introduction to the institutionalist movement. Most discussions of institutionalism focus on the ideas developed by a small number of key individuals including Thorstein Veblen, Wesley Mitchell, and John R. Commons. These three writers are usually presented as the three "founding fathers" of institutionalism, but that is not the way that the movement was represented at its beginning. Rather, that conventional conceptualization turns out, on examination, to be a later artifact, produced by commentators such as Joseph Dorfman (Dorfman 1959, 1963).[10]

The next chapter elaborates on many of the themes introduced earlier and provides an overview of interwar institutionalism. The first three sections of the chapter deal with the initial development and promotion of the idea of a definable institutional approach to economics that was undertaken between 1918 and 1927 by Walton Hamilton and others. The point will be to see who was involved in the initial promotion of the institutionalist idea, how they themselves defined the institutional approach, how they related themselves to the rest of the discipline, and the broader network of people involved and their institutional affiliations. All this involves focusing on how the promoters of the institutionalist movement constructed it *themselves*. The next two sections will discuss the background of institutionalism in terms of its sources and inspirations. Who were seen as the precursors and current contributors to the institutional approach? What role did Veblen play? What parts of the Veblenian canon were taken into institutionalism and which were not? To what extent did they draw on the ideas of the earlier generation of progressive-era economists such as R. T. Ely and H. C. Adams, and how did they differ from them? What factors led to the movement coalescing exactly when it did, in the period during and immediately after World War I? The last section will briefly sketch the content and contributions of interwar institutional economics. This involves indicating some of the

---

[10] Yonay (1998, pp. 71, 110) states that the term institutionalism "originally ... was coined as a label to describe the work of Thorstein Veblen only," but he gives no reference or citation for this usage, and it is clearly not correct. Allan Gruchy's 1947 book restricts the use of the term "institutional economics" to Veblen on the grounds that it was *then* the standard usage, a claim that may be correct (Gruchy 1947, p. 4). Paul Homan in his "An Appraisal of Institutional Economics" (Homan 1932, p. 10) states that it is "the contention of Mr. Dorfman, Veblen's biographer, that Veblen alone may be properly classified under the category of institutional economics." Homan gives no citation for this statement about Dorfman. Dorfman's biography of Veblen did not appear until 1934, and the terms institutionalism or institutional economics do not appear in the index. In his *Economic Mind in American Civilization* (1959, p. 353), Dorfman mentions Hamilton's first published use of "institutional economics" and states that the term "institutionalism," referring to a movement, "gained wide currency in the 20s and 30s." He goes on to say that the roots of this movement reach farther back and that "the 'founding father' of the movement was Thorstein Veblen; and after him Wesley C. Mitchell and John R. Commons." In a slightly later essay on "The Background of Institutional Economics," Dorfman simply talks of "the three founders of institutionalism: Thorstein Veblen, John R. Commons, and Wesley C. Mitchell" (Dorfman 1963, p. 1).

major institutionalist research programs, the institutionalist involvement in economic policy, and their role in developing institutions of education and research in economics. It will be seen that the range and quantity of work produced is such as to refute the idea that institutionalism was merely dissent. Overall, the chapter will provide insight into what it was about institutionalism that was appealing to young economists at the time.

The next two chapters form Part Two of the book and focus on the careers of two individuals, Walton Hamilton and Morris Copeland. This is a major departure from the usual discussions that focus on Veblen, Mitchell, and Commons. Hamilton is chosen for close examination because he was the chief promoter of the institutionalist concept in its early years and played a key role in inspiring many younger economists to join the movement. He was closely involved with important centers of institutionalist education at Amherst and at the Brookings Graduate School, and was also involved in many aspects of the New Deal. His work on law and economics, industrial organization, and the social control of industry illuminates one of the most important lines of institutionalist work. Copeland is a less obvious candidate for detailed treatment. It is not claimed that his contributions to institutionalist ideas rank him with Veblen, Mitchell, Clark, Hamilton, and Commons, but he was one of the most important of the second generation of institutionalists, the generation who were taught by members of the founding group, and his career is particularly revealing of the character of interwar institutionalism. He was a student at both Amherst and Chicago, and studied under Walter Stewart, Walton Hamilton, and J. M. Clark. He was an admirer of Wesley Mitchell and much of his work involved issues relating to measurement, but whereas Mitchell was largely occupied with work on business cycles at the NBER, Copeland's career spanned a broader range of topics and involved both academic and government work. Copeland also had close contacts with Clarence Ayres and many others in the institutionalist movement. Ayres was of the same generation as Copeland, but his career was much less typical of interwar institutionalists. Together, these chapters provide insight into both the founding group and their students, and into both the quantitative and qualitative wings of the institutionalist movement.

Part Three represents the core of the book and is intended to build up a detailed picture of the personal, institutional, and programmatic bases of the institutionalist movement in the interwar period. The first chapter deals with the Chicago department, dealing primarily with the period from the time of Veblen's presence there until the departure of J. M. Clark in 1926. Chicago has a claim to be the place where institutionalist ideas first began to coalesce. Veblen's later periods at Stanford and Missouri, and Mitchell's period at Berkeley are also included. The next chapter will deal briefly with Michigan, where H. C. Adams and C. H. Cooley trained Walton Hamilton and Walter Stewart, and with the further development of Hamilton's institutionalist programs at Amherst (where Stewart and Clarence Ayres also taught) and at the Brookings Graduate School. The focus here will be on the educational programs and the students involved. The third chapter in this section deals with Wisconsin and with John R. Commons and his students. This will include details of the Wisconsin program, the work on labor economics and labor legislation, the development of Commons's institutional economics, and the careers of his students both in academia and in the New Deal, particularly in the area of Social Security. The fourth chapter will pick up the story of Wesley Mitchell from the time he moved from Berkeley to Columbia and the subsequent development of the large institutionalist component at Columbia, including J. M. Clark and many others. The founding of the New School for Social Research will be dealt with briefly, as will the interactions between law and economics at Columbia, the role of Columbia faculty in the Social Science Research Council, and the Columbia involvement in the New Deal, in the persons of Rexford Tugwell, A. A. Berle, and Gardiner Means. The last chapter in this section deals with the institutionalist involvement with the NBER. A great deal of the earlier work of the NBER related to Mitchell's research program on business cycles and had a clearly institutionalist character. The NBER received funding from Rockefeller and other major foundations, and the history of this relationship gives a great deal of insight into how institutionalist ideas of science and social control initially meshed closely with those of the major foundations. Later, the ideals of empirical social science embedded in the NBER program became out of step with the more econometrically based ideas held in the profession more broadly, resulting in conflicts and eventual changes in the NBER.

Part Four of the book deals with the decline of institutionalism to a more marginalized position. The question here becomes one of why it became a program much less attractive to the new post–World War II generation of economists. There are many parts to this story: the rise of Keynesian economics, the development of econometrics, new concepts of "scientific" work in economics, failures within certain key institutionalist research programs, a loss of interdisciplinary connections, and a shift of some of the content of institutional economics to new professional schools of industrial relations and public administration. The sum of these factors had the effect of narrowing the discipline of economics and focusing it on a "model building" approach that was quite alien to interwar institutionalist notions of science.

The first chapter in this part deals with the impact of Keynesian economics on institutionalist research programs dealing with depression and unemployment. Keynesian economics had a major impact and displaced a number of institutionalist research agendas. This is not to say that Keynesian economics was simply adopted without question by institutionalists, because it was not. Institutionalists made a number of penetrating criticisms of Keynesian economics. The second chapter in this section seeks to pull together a discussion of the increasing challenges that institutionalism was facing from a developing neoclassical economics, from new research programs in industrial organization and labor economics, from a variety of new methodological ideas, and from ideological opposition to the expansive role for government implied in institutionalist notions of social control. Clarence Ayres attempted to provide a restatement of institutionalism in response to the charge that institutionalism lacked theory, but his *Theory of Economic Progress* (1944) failed to maintain a presence for institutionalism in the mainstream of the profession. Although Ayres's charismatic personality attracted followers among his own students, by the late 1940s institutionalism no longer held the more general appeal it had once had.

The last part of the book contains a conclusion that will draw together the main themes and arguments, locate those elements that gave coherence to the institutionalist movement over the period studied, and provide a view of the movement's strengths, weaknesses, successes, and failures. The narrative provided here will also be placed in the context of the work that has been done on the development of modern neoclassical economics.

2

Understanding Institutional Economics

If institutionalism today is associated with a single figure, it is with Thorstein Veblen, but the terms "institutional economics" or "institutionalism" to denote an identifiable movement within American economics did not come into common use until the interwar period. Veblen's most substantial and influential writing appeared in the years between 1898 and 1914, and although Veblen was far from uninvolved, it was those influenced by Veblen's ideas, such as Walton Hamilton, Wesley Mitchell, and J. M. Clark, rather than Veblen himself, who played the major role in defining and promoting what became known as institutional economics (Rutherford 2000a, 2000b).

"INSTITUTIONAL ECONOMICS"

The very first mention of the term "institutional economics" in print occurs in a footnote in Walton Hamilton's 1916 article dealing with the work of Robert Hoxie (Hamilton 1916a, p. 863, n.5). Hoxie and Hamilton were colleagues for a short time at Chicago, and Hamilton claims that Hoxie called himself an "institutional economist." Hoxie had been a student of Veblen's at Chicago and was initially much influenced by Veblen's ideas on the effect of the "industrial discipline" on the habits of thought of unionized workers. Hoxie was also a highly regarded investigator of the American labor movement, an influential teacher, and a point of connection between those around Veblen and other students of the labor movement, particularly John R. Commons and some of his students.

An alternative origin story is given by A. B. Wolfe (1936), who claims that the term "institutional economics" was invented "probably by Max S. Handman in a conversation with Thorstein Veblen, about 1916" (Wolfe 1936, p. 192). Handman and Veblen were colleagues at Missouri at that time, Handman teaching sociology and Veblen economics. Handman and Wolfe later became colleagues at the University of Texas. This same story is repeated by Troy Cauley in an obituary of Handman published in the first Bulletin of the Wardman Group[1] (Cauley 1964, p. 2). Cauley states "Handman is given credit for first applying the term 'institutional economics' to the brand of economics developed by Veblen, Mitchell, and their co-workers."

Clearly, the term "institutional economics" was in use by those in some way connected to Veblen by 1916, but, as mentioned earlier, the first real manifesto of this institutional economics was that provided by Walton Hamilton in his 1918 AEA conference paper, "The Institutional Approach to Economic Theory" (Hamilton 1919a). Following Hamilton's paper, the terms "institutional approach" and "institutional economics" came into common use and can be found frequently in published pieces in the 1920s. The terms "institutionalism" and "institutionalist" appear to be of only slightly later origin. The first usage of these terms I have been able to find occur in a PhD thesis completed in 1921 by Morris Copeland. Copeland had been a student of Walton Hamilton and Walter Stewart at Amherst and had gone on to Chicago where J. M. Clark supervised his thesis. By the later 1920s, these terms had become commonplace. In a 1931 AEA Round Table on Institutional Economics, Paul Homan explicitly discussed the origins of the terms institutional economics and institutionalism. He starts with Hamilton's 1918 use of the phrase "institutional approach to economic theory" and goes on: "A little later 'institutional economics' became a current phrase. Then one began to hear of an 'institutional school' and 'institutionalism'" (Homan 1932, p. 11).

THE DEFINITION OF INSTITUTIONAL ECONOMICS

Hamilton's original institutionalist manifesto, and the conference session in which it was given, are worth close examination. The session itself was planned by Walton Hamilton, J. M. Clark, and Harold Moulton. Clark and Moulton were then both at Chicago, Hamilton at Amherst. In preparation for this session, Moulton visited Walter Stewart, Wesley Mitchell,

---

[1]   The Wardman Group was the name originally given to the group of institutionalists who met during the AEA meetings in Washington, DC, in December 1959. This group continued to meet at AEA meetings and developed into the Association for Evolutionary Economics (AFEE) in 1965. The Group produced two Bulletins in 1964. A Bulletin under the AFEE name was produced in 1965. Copies of these are in the possession of the author.

and Thorstein Veblen to speak about the session and their hopes of affecting a "permanent reclamation" of the American Economic Association. It is clear that they sought some significant impact. This was not to be just another conference session; it was to be an attempt to shift the course of American economics. According to Moulton, Veblen referred to Hamilton as a "disturber of otherwise untroubled waters" (Moulton to Hamilton, 13 May 1918, Records of the War Labor Policies Board, Correspondence of Walton Hamilton). The session had Walter Stewart in the chair and, in addition to Hamilton's paper, J. M. Clark spoke on "Economic Theory in an Era of Social Readjustment" (Clark 1919) and William Ogburn on "The Psychological Basis for the Economic Interpretation of History" (Ogburn 1919).[2]

This session did not simply spring out of the blue. It had been preceded by a series of papers by Mitchell critical of hedonistic and rationalistic psychology (Mitchell 1910a, 1910b, 1914) and by a 1915 AEA session on "Tendencies in Economic Theory," in which Mitchell gave his paper "The Role of Money in Economic Theory" (Mitchell 1916). This paper also expressed criticism of accepted economic psychology and the standard interpretation of value theory – criticisms that were strongly supported by Walton Hamilton in his role as discussant (Hamilton 1916b). The year 1918 was also when Hamilton published two important articles in the *Journal of Political Economy*, "The Price System and Social Policy" (Hamilton 1918a) and the two part "The Place of Value Theory in Economics" (Hamilton 1918b), both of which were critical of orthodox value theory and laid out the importance of legal and other social institutions. J. M. Clark too had been active, pursuing his views on the need for a concept of social value in papers in 1915 and 1916, and publishing a very sophisticated critique of the theory of utility maximization in 1918 (Clark 1915; 1916; 1918).

Hamilton opens his paper on the institutional approach by distinguishing between "value economics," concerned with the origin and manifestation of value, and "institutional economics," concerned with the arrangements, customs, and conventions "which determine the nature of our economic system" (Hamilton 1919a, p. 310). Examples of the former are "Boehm Bawerk's *Positive Theory of Capital*, and J. B. Clark's *Distribution of Wealth*." In Hamilton's view, such "value economics" has become so narrow and hedged around with special assumptions that it can no longer claim to be "economic

---

[2] William Ogburn had close contacts with many of the institutionalist group and particularly with Wesley Mitchell. He is best known for his quantitative work, and for his "culture lag" theory of institutional change, which has some similarities to Veblen's.

theory" at all. For Hamilton, economic theory proper has the task of providing a "generalized description of the economic order" and only an institutional economics can meet that demand (Hamilton 1919a, pp. 310–331):

> Its quest must go beyond sale and purchase to the peculiarities of the economic system that allow these things to take place on particular terms and not upon others. It cannot stop short of a study of the conventions, customs, habits of thinking, and modes of doing which make up the scheme of arrangements which we call "the economic order." It must set forth in their relations one to another the institutions which together comprise the organization of modern industrial society. (Hamilton 1919a, p. 311)

Hamilton then presents five "tests" that anything aspiring "to the name of economic theory" should be able to meet (Hamilton 1919a, p. 311). These tests are that economic theory should (1) unify economic science; (2) be relevant to the modern problem of control; (3) relate to institutions; (4) be concerned with matters of "process"; and (5) be based on an acceptable theory of human behavior. According to Hamilton, only institutional economics can meet these tests.

These points all require some elaboration. At the time Hamilton was writing, the lack of connection between economic theory and the various fields of applied economics was quite widely recognized as a problem and was frequently seen as owing to the lack of applicability of the standard value theory and static theories of perfectly competitive markets. Indeed, at this time, very few American economists worked on theoretical issues at all; most were engaged in studies of highly concrete problems such as railroads, utilities, unions, and trusts, and used little abstract theory of any sort (see Backhouse 1998). Even as late as 1927, J. M. Clark could characterize the economics profession as composed of a "relatively small number of 'theorists,' mostly of the older generation, surrounded by specialists in labor problems, corporations and trusts, public service industries, banking and financial institutions, public finance, statistics, socialism, and other branches" (Clark 1927, p. 217). Hamilton's argument was that the existing orthodox "value theory" was not utilized in many studies of particular applied areas, so that "for all the constraints of neo-classical theory, each of these subjects tends to develop an isolated body of thought." In contrast, the institutional approach, by providing a common context within which studies of different topics could be placed, could "unify" economics: "In describing in general terms economic organization it makes clear the kind of industrial world within which such particular things as money, insurance, and corporation finance have their being" (Hamilton 1919a, p. 312). A few years later, the same point was made by Wesley Mitchell:

For many years there has been a notable difference between the way in which economists handled economic theory on the one hand and the way in which they handled such problems as transportation, public finance, tariffs, money, banking, insurance, trusts and labor on the other hand. The monographs made little use of the theoretical treatises, and the treatises drew upon the monographs for little beyond illustration. Text books often had a theoretical part and an applied part held together by nothing more intimate than the binding. When, however, economic theory is made an account of the cumulative change of economic behavior, then all studies of special institutions become organic parts of a single whole. (Mitchell 1924b, p. 24)

The second test, that economics should be relevant to the "modern problem of control," became a very central part of the institutionalist creed. There are a number of meanings attached to this. In Hamilton's own paper, it is linked to an economics that does not deal in hypothetical worlds, but which concerns itself with "gathering facts and formulating principles necessary to an intelligent handling" of contemporary economic problems (Hamilton 1919a, p. 313). It implies a need to respond to the economic and social problems relating to the new industrial world in America, problems that seemed to demand new forms of "social control" to supplement the market. J. M. Clark, in the same 1918 conference session, emphasized this theme in his own paper. Clark argued for an economics "actively relevant to the issues of its time" (Clark 1919). Social control was a major theme in both Hamilton and Clark's work, notably in Clark's *Social Control of Business* (Clark 1926). Other examples are Sumner Slichter's 1924 essay, "The Organization and Control of Economic Activity," that detailed many failings of "free enterprise" and the need for new methods of control (Slichter 1924); Leo Wolman's 1927 essay, "The Frontiers of Social Control," that outlined many areas in pressing need of legislative reform; and Dexter Keezer and Stacy May's *Public Control of Business* (1930), a critical analysis of existing methods of control such as the antitrust laws. Hamilton's student, Helen Everett, was later to define the concept as the "active intelligent guidance of social processes" or "the consciously planned guidance of economic processes," and went on:

In America the institutionalist school of economics, whose outstanding figures are Thorstein Veblen, Wesley C. Mitchell and Walton H. Hamilton, has made important use of the concept of social control. Indeed it is perhaps their central organizing principle. The emphasis of the institutionalists is that economic arrangements are man made and susceptible to almost limitless variation. While for most economists the idea of control is like a mechanical bit of apparatus, for the institutionalists it is more of the nature of the guiding formula itself. (Everett 1931, p. 345)

A notion of "social control" begs the question of social control to what ends. In terms of their own philosophical position, virtually all of the institutionalist group subsequent to Veblen adopted a pragmatic or instrumental position taken from John Dewey, either directly or through others influenced by him, such as Charles Horton Cooley.[3] Hamilton was himself a pragmatist of Deweyan persuasion, although he did not explicitly talk of pragmatism in his 1918 conference paper. Mitchell was also much affected by Dewey's ideas as were numerous others in the institutionalist ranks. One early expression of this is to be found in Morris Copeland's 1921 PhD thesis that contains a lengthy appendix on institutionalism and pragmatism. Following Dewey, Copeland argues that thinking and reasoning are instruments in the solution of problematic situations. Theories are to be seen as instruments for "prediction and control" and should be judged as such. Reasoning, investigation, and appraisal of consequences are also the way in which people construct and reconstruct their values. In this manner, pragmatism is a "protest against the over-rationalized and consequent over-mechanization of human conduct presented in the Utilitarian theory of value" (Copeland 1921, p. Y9.1). Scientific investigation and information are vital to the creation of an informed discourse over both means and ends.

Placing institutions as the central focus is intimately related to the previous point. If economics is to be relevant to the problem of control, it "must relate to the changeable elements in life and the agencies through which they are to be directed" (Hamilton 1919a, p. 313). This involves an understanding of economic institutions as social constructions that are capable of change and of being changed, rather than as natural and immutable. Control is to be exercised though the modification of institutional arrangements. This requires detailed knowledge of institutional arrangements, their interrelations, and of the ramifications of any proposed changes. This is what pragmatists meant by the purposes of science being "prediction and control."

A further aspect of this is the emphasis on "process." This is placed in opposition to an analysis running in terms of equilibrium states. An economic institution is not static, but always in a process of change, both internal and changes brought about by external developments. In Hamilton's words, institutions "refuse to retain a definite content," and this is true of

---

[3]   There are pragmatic and instrumentalist concepts contained in Veblen's "instinct of workmanship," which he does treat as a basic value. Workmanship, however, is concerned with means and not with ends. More importantly, Veblen does not present the process of institutional evolution, or that of changing social values, as consisting of an instrumental appraisal of consequences.

particular institutions and of the "complex of institutions which r
the economic order" (Hamilton 1919a, p. 315). The institutional system has
to be seen as an entity that is always in the process of evolution. Hamilton,
however, does not specify any particular theory of institutional change.

The final element mentioned by Hamilton – that economic theory must
be based on an acceptable theory of human behavior – had a great deal
of resonance at the time. Veblen had provided a damaging criticism of
the hedonistic and rationalistic psychology implicit in marginal utility
theory (Veblen 1898) and pointed to an alternative based on instinct/habit
psychology. Veblen's work on this subject was itself influenced by the psychology of William James (Rutherford 1994a, pp. 56–57), but what was
important was not Veblen's specific formulation, but the impetus he gave
to the idea that economics might be reconstructed on the basis of "modern psychology." Particularly important in this was William McDougall's
An Introduction to Social Psychology (1908) and John B. Watson's earlier
work toward a "behaviorist" approach. Mitchell had also provided lengthy
discussions of McDougall's instinct theories and of the role of rationality
in economics (Mitchell 1910a, 1910b), and Graham Wallas's social psychology, especially as found in his *Human Nature in Politics* (1908) and
The Great Society (1914) (Mitchell 1914). Mitchell wrote to Wallas that
"everyone who is trying to make one of the social sciences more significant by making it take account of man as he actually is owes much to your
leading" (Wesley Mitchell to Graham Wallas, 23 September 1914, Wallas
Papers, 1/57).

Another important contributor to this line of thinking was Carleton
Parker, who took inspiration from Veblen, Wallas, and Ogburn to attempt
to incorporate instincts into a theory of industrial unrest (Parker 1920).[4]
Ogburn himself gave his paper on "The Psychological Basis for the Economic
Interpretation of History" (Ogburn 1919) at the same session as Hamilton's
"Institutional Approach." J. M. Clark had also produced a critique of the
utility-maximizing hypothesis, which anticipated ideas of bounded ratio-
nality (Clark 1918). All of this generated enormous excitement at the time.

---

[4] Carleton Parker is discussed more in Chapter 5. He studied at Harvard (with W. Z. Ripley)
and spent time at the LSE (with the Webbs) and at the University of Heidelberg. He taught
at Berkeley where, in 1915, he had much contact with William Ogburn. This inspired
his work applying psychological theory to labor unrest. Parker was appointed Dean of
Commerce at the University of Washington in 1917. Parker died in the flu epidemic
of 1918. See C. Parker (1920) and his wife Cornelia S. Parker's biography (C. S. Parker
1919). The book of Parker's essays was edited by his wife after his death and is dedicated
to Thorstein Veblen.

F. C. Mills, who studied with Mitchell and Parker at Berkeley before moving
to Columbia, wrote of his experience between 1915 and 1917 as follows:

When I was studying at California and later at Columbia, there was a feeling that
exciting new prospects for economics had been revealed by recent work in psychology. In seminar at California, and to a lesser degree at Columbia, the work of
McDougall in social psychology, John B. Watson on behaviorism, Patrick on the
psychology of relaxation, Trotter on instincts of the herd in peace and war, Crile
and others working in psycho-physiological fields, James Harvey Robinson on the
making of the mind, and of course Freud (but this, it seems in retrospect, only inci-
dentally), struck us with tremendous impact. That stream of thought in some ways
supplemented the one flowing from Peirce, James and Dewey. ... Veblen again,
particularly in raising questions as to why economics was not an evolutionary science, seemed to cut away other pillars. All of this provided a climate thoroughly
opposed to the rationalistic tenets of classical economic thought. (F. C. Mills to
Milton Friedman, 25 June 1951, Milton Friedman Papers, Box 30)

These aspects of the institutionalist program as outlined by Hamilton were
clearly shared by other institutionalists and provide a preliminary basis for
a working definition of the movement. It is noteworthy that Hamilton's
definition can easily incorporate that developed later by J. R. Commons.
Commons (1931) defined institutions as collective action in the control, liberation, and expansion of human action, but there is nothing in Commons's
work incompatible with Hamilton's outline of the key characteristics of
an institutional approach. On the other hand, there are some additional
aspects to institutionalism that Hamilton's manifesto does not bring out as
clearly as it might, and there were several other efforts to define the core of
the institutionalist approach made between 1918 and the later 1920s that
are worthy of examination.

The person who chaired the session at which Hamilton presented his
institutionalist manifesto was Walter Stewart. Stewart was at that time a
colleague of Hamilton at Amherst College and had studied with Veblen at
Missouri. In his remarks from the chair, Stewart also commented on need
to utilize the "most competent thought in the related sciences of psychology
and sociology" and to build an economics "organized around the central
problem of control," but he added some significant comments relating to
the complexity of industrial society and stating his belief that "an adequate
analysis of many of our problems can be made only by a union of the statistical method and the institutional approach" (Stewart 1919, p. 319) – an
obvious reference to his own and to Wesley Mitchell's quantitative work.

Mitchell himself was already associated both with quantitative methods, due
to his outstanding work *Business Cycles* (1913), and with the use of Veblenian
ideas concerning the impact of pecuniary institutions on habits of thought

(Mitchell 1916). His most explicit linking of quantitative and statistical work with an institutional perspective is found in a 1924 paper (Mitchell 1924b) and in his Presidential Address to the AEA in the same year (Mitchell 1925). In these papers, Mitchell, on a social-psychological premise, argued that it is institutions that standardize behavior and create the patterns, regularities, and cycles that are to be observed in the data. The economist studies "mass behavior," "hence the institutions which standardize the behavior of men create most of the openings for valid generalizations" (Mitchell 1924b, p. 27). Because of this, quantitative economists will be drawn to proposing and examining institutional explanations of their observations (Mitchell 1925, pp. 7–8). In his Presidential address, Mitchell even suggested that quantitative methods would transform economics by displacing traditional theory and leading to a much greater stress on institutions, including the Veblenian problem of the relation between making goods and making money (Mitchell 1925, p. 7; see also Mitchell 1923a). Lionel Edie called this address "a genuine manifesto of quantitative and institutional economics," one that stated "the faith of a very large part of the younger generation of economists" (Edie 1927, p. 417). The link between statistical work and institutionalism can also be seen very clearly in Mitchell's own work on business cycles, a phenomenon he always regarded as the result of a particular scheme of monetary or pecuniary institutions (Mitchell 1927, p. 61). Ogburn, too, was a leader in the use of statistics in sociology, and he maintained close ties with Mitchell.

Institutionalism, then, clearly included statistical and quantitative work within its compass, but more than this: The early work on institutional economics is full of the rhetoric of making economics more "scientific." The idea of science contained within the literature of interwar institutionalism is clearly based on the pragmatic ideas of Charles Peirce and John Dewey and can be illuminated in more detail by considering the writing on this subject by J. M. Clark, Lionel Edie, and by many of the contributors to Rexford Tugwell's 1924 volume *The Trend of Economics* (Tugwell 1924b; Yonay 1998). Tugwell's book was not limited to institutionalist contributors, but was heavily institutionalist in content with essays by Wesley Mitchell, J. M. Clark, Morris Copeland, Sumner Slichter, F. C. Mills, George Soule, Robert Hale, A. B. Wolfe, as well as Tugwell himself, and was commonly seen as primarily intended to provide a forum for institutionalist views.[5]

---

[5] There were some contributors representing the "conservative" position, notably Frank Knight. Allyn Young wrote a critical review of the volume (Young 1925), and the Young papers contain a whole folder of correspondence with respect to this review (Young Papers, Box 6). Young had mutual interests with Mitchell concerning statistics and quantitative work. Even though Young admired Veblen's capacity for insight, he did not approve of his emphasis on the "genetic" approach or his overall view of the functioning of the U.S. economy.

J. M. Clark's notion of what constitutes science and a scientific economics is of particular interest because his own work was not heavily quantitative and he made a number of important theoretical and conceptual contributions. One of Clark's earliest statements on the proper nature of economics argued that economics should be "based on a foundation of terms, conceptions, standards of measurement, and assumptions which is sufficiently realistic, comprehensive, and unbiased" to provide a basis for the analysis and discussion of practical issues (Clark 1919, p. 280). Relevance to practical issues, accuracy of data, and comprehensiveness, in the sense of not excluding any evidence relevant to the problem at hand, were the characteristics of a scientific approach to economics that Clark most frequently stressed (Clark 1924, p. 74). Clark certainly thought of theory as playing a key role, but he saw the aim of theorizing as that of forming hypotheses "grounded in experience" for further study and inductive verification, rather than the production of a highly abstract system of laws. Hypotheses must therefore be formulated in terms that allow for empirical verification or refutation (Clark 1924, p. 76):

Economics must come into closer touch with facts and embrace broader ranges of data than "orthodox" economics has hitherto done. It must establish touch with these data, either by becoming more inductive, or by much verification of results, or by taking over the accredited results of specialists in other fields, notably psychology, anthropology, jurisprudence and history. Thus the whole modern movement may be interpreted as a demand for procedure which appears more adequately scientific .... (Clark 1927, p. 221)

As for the relationship between institutionalism and science, Clark argued that the term institutional economics is a term "used by a group of the younger American economists to define a point of view – one might almost make it coextensive with the scientific point of view – in economic study." This point of view "sets up the ideal of studying the interrelations of business and other social institutions as they are and not through the medium of any simplified abstractions such as are employed by classical, static, and marginal economics" (Clark 1927, p. 271).

Lionel Edie can be found saying similar things. He describes institutional economics as "an extension of scientific method in economics," with a special emphasis on the use of recent work in sociology and social psychology to replace the assumption of "independent individual rationality," on the role of empirical investigations of various kinds to verify or disprove theories, modify theories, or suggest new theories "pertinent to the problems confronting us" (Edie 1927, pp. 407–410). In his slightly earlier survey of institutionalist research entitled *Economics, Principles and Problems*

(Edie 1926), Edie outlined the main characteristics of the "new approach" as including the influence of newer historical and anthropological research and the use of psychological presuppositions in line with modern psychology, the rejection of the notion of immutable natural laws and a substitution of a view of economic conduct as governed by institutions, the use of quantitative methods to supplement qualitative, a view of economic generalizations as tentative and of the nature of hypotheses "to be tested by experimental and statistical science," and a "frank ethical concern for welfare and well-being" (Edie 1926, p. viii).

Many of the essays in the Tugwell volume are replete with the language of "science" (Yonay 1998; Rutherford 1999). George Soule contrasts the confidence that is given to scientific knowledge in the realms of physics and chemistry with the lack of authoritative "tested knowledge" in the area of economics. Soule, however, detects a "rapid growth toward maturity" among institutional economists. This is indicated by their awareness of the deficiencies of classical theory and its psychological foundations, and by their desire to "make the science practically useful." This would involve the development of data and the use of quantitative research and statistical methods (Soule 1924, p. 364). In his own essay, Tugwell argues for an "experimental economics," claiming that the "assurance of rightness in science" is to be found in the replication of experimental results. Social science must try to "isolate its problems and to devise and use special tools for dispassionate verification" (Tugwell 1924a, pp. 386–387):

The whole conception of science, then – and the modern world has gone over to science – *is* experimentalism. Scientists have learned to distrust premises and to depend upon consequences. And in social science this is bound to involve social facts as they are to be observed in a going society. These facts are the consequences. Theory must have reference to them if it is to be useful. (Tugwell 1924a, pp. 394–395)

A. B. Wolfe talks of the "younger men" in economics who all "hold that economics ought to be scientific." Wolfe ascribes this growing "demand for a realistic, inductively analytical, non-metaphysical, scientific economics" to the matter-of-fact spirit of the times and a "growing conviction that the older economic theory, whether classical, neo-classical, or marginalistic, is deficient in scientific quality" (Wolfe 1924, p. 447). F. C. Mills's essay "On Measurement in Economics" (Mills 1924a) takes a view similar to that of his teacher, Wesley Mitchell. Mills quotes Lord Kelvin to the effect that without measurement and numerical expression, there cannot be a *science*, and quotes both Clerk Maxwell and Pearson on the statistical view of nature. For Mills, social relationships do not hold universally or with absolute certainty. In the statistical approach, "we forego the searching for sole causes and, instead, seek to measure the degree of association found in experience" (Mills 1924a, pp. 43–44). Furthermore, such relationships are not seen as "final formulations of truth" but in a process of development toward higher degrees of probability. Interestingly, Mills finds the statistical conception "in complete agreement with the views of philosophers of the pragmatic school" such as John Dewey. Mills quotes with approval Dewey's remarks that generalizations are "not fixed rules ... but instrumentalities for ... investigation" and are "hypotheses to be tested and revised by their further working" (Mills 1924a, pp. 45–46). Mills also links a quantitative and statistical economics to the more effective solution of economic problems. Practical problems will be more readily solved "by quantitative study of specific conditions than by the attempt to apply vague generalizations of doubtful validity" (Mills 1924a, p. 70).

In this early literature, then, institutionalists are clearly attempting to associate the movement with what it means to be "scientific." Being "scientific" meant not being satisfied with speculative armchair theorizing based on unreal premises, including an outmoded psychology, and that, in its depiction of perfectly competitive markets, often seemed to act as a apologetic for existing business practice. Being scientific did mean being investigative, exposing hypotheses to critical empirical examination, and bringing economic thinking into line with recent developments in related disciplines such as psychology, sociology, anthropology, law, and philosophy. These ideas were often summed up as a demand that economics become more "realistic," but more than this: It also meant seeing theories and hypotheses as instruments for social control so that the concepts of science and social control merge together. This merging of ideas in the instrumental view of science is stated, in particularly strong terms, in Dewey's own essay "Social Science and Social Control":

It is a complete error to suppose that efforts at social control depend upon the prior existence of a social science. The reverse is the case. The building up of social science, that is, of a body of knowledge in which facts are ascertained in their significant relations, is dependent upon putting social planning into effect.... Physical science did not develop because inquirers piled up a mass of facts about observed phenomena. It came into being when men intentionally experimented, on the basis of ideas and hypotheses, with observed phenomena to modify them and disclose new observations. This process is self-corrective and self-developing. Imperfect and even wrong hypotheses, when acted upon, brought to light significant phenomena which made improved ideas and improved experimentation possible. The change from a passive and accumulative attitude into an active and productive one is the secret revealed by the progress of physical inquiry. (Dewey 1931, p. 277)[6]

The central components of the "institutional approach" outlined here – the adoption of a central focus on institutions, process, social control, new psychological foundations, and empirical and instrumental "scientific" investigation – serve as a reference point to identify the movement and its adherents. Moreover, this set of intellectual commitments, and particularly the combination of the ideal of "science" with the ideal of "social control," produced a program outline of considerable appeal. In Hamilton's words, what institutionalism offered was "an invitation to detailed study" and participation in "the intelligent direction of social change" (Hamilton nda; Hamilton 1926a).

THE INSTITUTIONALIST NETWORK

These efforts to develop and promote an institutional economics were obviously not the independent actions of isolated individuals. There was a close network of contacts between Veblen, Mitchell, Hamilton, Stewart, Clark, Moulton, and a number of others, that is worth outlining in a little detail. Various parts of this network will be discussed in more detail in later chapters.

Veblen was at Chicago from 1892 to 1906, and while there he had a significant direct influence on a number of colleagues and students including Mitchell and Robert Hoxie. Although Veblen left Chicago in 1906, his influence remained, particularly through Hoxie (until Hoxie's suicide in 1916) and J. M. Clark who was there between 1915 and 1926. Harold Moulton was also at Chicago. He completed his PhD in 1914 under Laurence Laughlin (as did Mitchell), but he also admired Veblen (Dorfman 1959). He became an assistant professor at Chicago in the same year. Moulton developed interests in monetary and financial economics.

Mitchell and Veblen kept in close touch when Veblen was at Stanford (1906–1909) and Mitchell at Berkeley (1902–1913), Veblen often spending weekends with Mitchell (Dorfman 1973, p. 251). Mitchell continued to maintain close contact with Veblen, and provided help to him in many ways.[7] After Stanford, Veblen spent several years at the University of Missouri (1911–1918). Walter Stewart went to Missouri as an instructor

---

[6] The relationship between institutionalist thinking on science and social control and the work of John Dewey can be seen very clearly in Dewey's *Quest for Certainty* (Dewey 1929).

[7] Mitchell's help to Veblen included attempting (unsuccessfully) to help Veblen secure Carnegie research funding support in 1910, and, later, contributions to Veblen's salary from the New School. In the first two years, Mitchell contributed a total of $4,500 of

in order to study with Veblen (Dorfman 1959, p. 415). A small group formed around Veblen there, including Max Handman, Walter Stewart, Isador Lubin, and Leon Ardzrooni, among others (Walter Stewart to Joseph Dorfman, 8 November 1951, Joseph Dorfman Papers, Box 4). After Missouri, Veblen spent a short time with the wartime Food Administration, again with Lubin, and in 1919 joined The New School for Social Research where Mitchell also spent the years 1919–1922. Others on the staff at the New School included Leo Wolman.

Hamilton knew Stewart from the time they were both graduate students at Michigan (1912–1913) and absorbed the ideas of H. C. Adams and C. H. Cooley. Hamilton spent a short time in Chicago in 1914–1915 and became friends with Hoxie, who had recommended his appointment. After only a year in Chicago, Hamilton was recruited to Amherst by the new President, Alexander Meiklejohn, and given the Olds Professorship in Social and Economic Institutions. He was joined by Stewart in 1916 and both contributed to formulating Amherst's Program in Economics (Dorfman 1974, p. 7). This program contained a very significant institutionalist orientation, and will be outlined in more detail below. Clarence Ayres also joined the faculty at Amherst as an instructor for Hamilton's course in the 1915–1916 year. Ayres then went to Chicago where he had intended to work with Hoxie, but on Hoxie's death he moved over to philosophy. On completing his PhD in 1917, he taught philosophy at Chicago, but moved to join the faculty at Amherst in 1920. Amherst students included Morris Copeland (who later went to Chicago to complete his PhD under J. M. Clark), Carter Goodrich (who also went on to Chicago), Willard Thorp (who went to Columbia), and Talcott Parsons.[8] Visitors included R. H. Tawney, who cotaught a course

Veblen's salary through a special fund at the New School. In all, Mitchell contributed $8,000 between 1919 and 1929 (Dorfman 1934, p. 450; Dorfman 1973, pp. 196–197, 225). When Veblen was in New York in 1918, his wife became ill. Veblen's stepchildren were sent to the Stewarts and Veblen's affairs were looked after by Ardzrooni. When Ardzrooni had to leave for California, Mitchell allowed Lubin, who was then working for Mitchell at the War Industries Board, to "take his work to New York and look after Veblen" (Dorfman 1934, p. 411). Stewart, Mitchell, and Ardzrooni selected the essays for the collection *The Place of Science in Modern Civilization*, first published in 1919. When Mitchell was organizer of the AEA meetings, he arranged for Veblen to give a paper. The session on "Problems of Economic Theory" included Veblen's paper "Economic Theory in the Calculable Future" (Veblen 1925). Veblen's paper expresses a cynical and pessimistic view of the future of economics and the economics profession. Veblen did not attend the meetings in person. Mitchell was also involved with the move, spearheaded by Paul Douglas, to have Veblen nominated for President of the AEA.

[8]   Talcott Parsons did not often refer to his intellectual debt to Hamilton and Ayres, but on this point, see Camic (1992) and Parsons (1976). See also the discussion of Parsons in Hodgson (2001).

with Hamilton, and Henry Clay, who came to know Hamilton and Stewart extremely well. Hamilton, Ayres, Copeland, and Goodrich all kept in touch with each other throughout their careers (Rutherford 2003).

Veblen and Stewart had become close friends while at Missouri, Veblen living with the Stewarts for a time. After Stewart moved to Amherst, Veblen used to visit them (next door to Hamilton) quite often, and others would sometimes join them. According to Dorfman, in 1917 Veblen had entertained some brief hope of being able to move himself, Stewart, Mitchell, and Hamilton to Clark University, but the plans came to nothing (Dorfman 1934, p. 313). Veblen gave a lecture series at Amherst in May 1918 based on material later published in *The Vested Interests* (Walton Hamilton to Joseph Dorfman, 17 March 1931, Walton H. Hamilton Papers, Box J8, Folder 6), and in July 1919, a group of Veblen, Hamilton, Stewart, Isador Lubin, Leo Wolman, and Robert Duffus formed a weekend conference "for an investigation of the economic order" (Dorfman 1973, p. 214). According to Lubin, this conference was about trying to obtain a research grant from the Inter-Church World Movement for an investigation of the workings of the economic order and "devising a plan for a reorganization of our economic system." The group spent the weekend making plans and "it looked as if Veblen was finally to realize his ambition of getting a group of people around him to look into the vitals of the economic order." The plan, however, came to nothing (Isador Lubin to Joseph Dorfman, 28 January 1932, Isador Lubin Papers, Box 6).

In 1923, the Amherst group itself broke up with the removal of Alexander Meiklejohn as President, an event that prompted a number of resignations, including Hamilton's and Ayres's (Parsons 1976, p. 176). Moulton, who had left Chicago to become the Director of the Institute of Economics, recommended Hamilton to head up the related Brookings Graduate School, where he developed an innovative PhD program. J. A. Hobson visited as a lecturer, as did Graham Wallas and J. R. Commons, and the students included Mordecai Ezekiel and Isador Lubin. Lubin was also on the Staff of the Institute of Economics. Veblen visited too, but did not teach. The Brookings Graduate School was done away with in the reorganization that created the Brookings Institution in 1928, and Hamilton joined Yale Law School (Dorfman 1959, pp. 425–438; Dorfman 1974, pp. 6–7; Rutherford 2003). A number of Hamilton's students from Brookings joined the institutionalist group that formed at Washington Square College of New York University in the late 1920s and early 1930s. They produced a textbook, *Economic Behavior: An Institutional Approach* (Atkins et al. 1931), a project that also involved Clarence Ayres and his sister, Edith Ayres. Another

Brookings graduate was Robert Montgomery who went to the University of Texas, to be joined by Ayres in 1930, who was hired to Texas to replace Max Handman. In the interim, Ayres had worked for the New Republic and taught briefly at Reed College where Joseph Dorfman was a student of his.

J. M. Clark was at Amherst from 1910 to 1915. There he read Veblen, including Veblen's criticisms of his father, J. B. Clark. He felt Veblen's work required reckoning with, but this "didn't mean substituting Veblen for my father" but a "more difficult and discriminating adjustment" (quoted by Shute 1997, p. 12). He also absorbed ideas from Cooley, Ely, Mitchell, and J. A. Hobson. Clark moved to Chicago in 1915, and he, Hamilton, and Moulton coedited *Readings in the Economics of War* (1918). Hamilton and Clark were in close touch with each other, exchanging lists of research topics in 1918 (J. M. Clark to Walton Hamilton, 26 October 1918, Walton H. Hamilton Papers, Box J13, Folder 5).[9] In 1926, Clark moved to Columbia, where he joined Mitchell and became a part of the large Columbia contingent of institutionalists (Rutherford 2004).

Mitchell moved to Columbia from Berkeley in 1913. John Dewey had moved from Chicago to Columbia in 1904. William Ogburn joined the faculty in sociology in 1919. Adolf Berle and later Gardiner Means were associated with the Columbia Law School. During World War I, Mitchell worked on a large series of price indexes, work that also involved Lubin, Wolman, and Stewart. After the war, Mitchell was involved with the founding of the New School for Social Research and helped maintain Veblen's position there.[10] He was also one of the founders of the National Bureau of Economic Research, and served as its Director of Research until his retirement (Dorfman 1959, pp. 438–463). In the 1920s, Columbia became a major center for institutionalism with Mitchell, Clark, Tugwell, F. C. Mills, Robert Hale, James Bonbright, and several others. Carter Goodrich moved from Michigan to Columbia in 1931, and Leo Wolman also moved to Columbia in the same year. Mitchell was the head of the department when they were hired. Mills, Wolman, and Willard Thorp were all

---

[9] This correspondence was connected with the AEA Committee on Cooperation in Economic Research appointed by Irving Fisher to identify the most significant lines of research in the aftermath of the war. Allyn Young was appointed Chair, Hamilton the Secretary. Moulton and David Friday were also members of the Committee (Records of the War Labor Policies Board, Correspondence of Walton Hamilton, American Economic Association Folder).

[10] Mitchell contributed to Veblen's salary through a special fund he set up for the purpose. See note 7 to this chapter.

important members of the NBER research staff. Morris Copeland also did work on a number of NBER projects (Rutherford 2002; 2004).

So far, little has been said about John R. Commons and his students and colleagues at Wisconsin. There is no doubt that Commons was *not* a part of the group of Hamilton, Clark, and Mitchell who actively promoted the institutionalist idea at the beginning. Commons and Veblen had little contact with each other (John R. Commons to Joseph Dorfman, 24 May and 28 September 1932, Joseph Dorfman Papers, Box 61). Nevertheless, there were a number of significant points of contact between Commons, his students, and those members of the institutionalist movement mentioned earlier. Commons made important use of Veblen's notions of intangible property, and the Wisconsin Department also contained the sociologist E. A. Ross who was sympathetic to Veblen's ideas.[11] Other major channels of contact concerned mutual interests in industrial relations, labor economics, and labor legislation. This, of course, was the focus of much of Commons's work, but it led to close contact with Robert Hoxie and with many others. Commons was a commissioner on the U.S. Commission on Industrial Relations (1914–1916). Charles McCarthy of the Wisconsin Legislative Reference Library headed the research staff that included not only many of Commons's students but also Robert Hoxie, Carleton Parker, Paul Brissenden, E. H. Downey, F. C. Mills, Sumner Slichter, and Leo Wolman (Rutherford 2006). A related point of contact was through the American Association for Labor Legislation, which had been founded by Ely and Commons in 1906, and was run by Commons's student, John B. Andrews. The AALL had a wide membership including Commons, many of Commons's students, Hamilton, Mitchell, Leo Wolman, Sumner Slichter, and Carter Goodrich. The New Deal brought about close contact between Isador Lubin, who became commissioner of Labor Statistics, and many of the Wisconsin group.

There were also points of contact between Wisconsin and Hamilton's programs at Amherst and Brookings. Paul Raushenbush and Edward Morehouse were Amherst students who then moved to Wisconsin for graduate work. After Meiklejohn was removed as President at Amherst, he went to Wisconsin to run the new Experimental College between 1927 and

---

[11] The term social control originated with a well-known book, *Social Control*, written by E. A. Ross (1901). Ross was later to join the Department of Economics at Wisconsin. The social control Ross is speaking of is in part the control over behavior exercised by social norms and conventions, but the term social control for Ross clearly indicated deliberative as opposed to spontaneous forms of control. Such forms of control he thought were required in complex societies where spontaneous orders were likely to be insufficient.

1932. Paul Raushenbush taught both at the college and in the economics department. Clarence Ayres and Morris Copeland visited Meikeljohn at Wisconsin and taught at the College during 1928 and 1929.

Hamilton had a central interest in law and economics, and at Brookings his students studied Commons's *Legal Foundations* (1924a) as soon as it appeared. Commons himself visited the Institute of Economics and taught at the Brookings Graduate School when in Washington for the first six months of 1928 (while working on monetary stabilization and the Strong bill). Wisconsin students such as Walter Morton, Elsie Gluck, and Paul Raushenbush all spent at least a year at the school, and many others passed through (Rutherford 2003).

There were, in addition, good contacts between the National Bureau of Economic Research, headed by Wesley Mitchell, and Wisconsin economists. As President of the AEA, Commons had been involved in some of the early discussions concerning the founding of the NBER, and he later served on the Board as the representative from Wisconsin. Wisconsin graduates such as Willford King and Harry Jerome served on the research staff of the Bureau, King working on national income estimates and Jerome on labor migration and business cycles. Jerome was also a faculty member at Wisconsin and maintained strong instruction in statistics there until his death in 1938. It is also worth emphasizing that Mitchell was particularly supportive of Commons's work, and it was Mitchell who first characterized Commons's *Legal Foundations* as a contribution to institutional economics (Mitchell 1924a). *The Legal Foundations* became a work frequently cited by other institutionalists. Mitchell incorporated some of Commons's ideas into his own description of the evolution of the money economy (Mitchell 1927, p 71), and by 1931, Commons was using the term "institutional economics" to characterize his own work (Commons 1931).

CONTRIBUTORS TO INSTITUTIONAL ECONOMICS

Something else that can be gleaned from these early statements concerning the nature of institutional economics is the individuals and pieces of work that were seen as having made contributions to the development of institutional economics up to that time. Hamilton identifies several groups of contributors to "a theory of the economic order." He mentions H. C. Adams and Charles Horton Cooley – his own teachers at Michigan – and Veblen and Mitchell as the "leaders" in America. He also sees contributions coming from a number of English economists including "Webb, Hobson, Cannan, Tawney, and Clay." He further identifies contributions from noneconomists, specifically Graham Wallas (Hamilton 1919a, p. 318). In an early paper, Clarence Ayres talks of the changes occurring in economics and mentions particularly the work of J. M. Clark, Thorstein Veblen, J. A. Hobson, Walton Hamilton, Edwin Cannan, Henry Clay, and forthcoming work by L. C. Marshall (Ayres 1918, pp. 87–89). Rexford Tugwell, in putting together his contributors to his *Trend of Economics*, wrote to Mitchell. In this letter, he talks of Mitchell's "institutional economics" and continues: "I believe this is also the general orientation of J. M. Clark and W. H. Hamilton who I believe to be, with yourself, the most important economists of the present generation" (Rexford G. Tugwell to Wesley Mitchell, 5 January 1923, Wesley Mitchell Papers, Box 13). In 1924, Mitchell classified Commons's *Legal Foundations* as a contribution to institutional economics, and claimed it was also represented "in Germany by Sombart, in England by Mr. and Mrs. Webb, in America by Veblen and many of the younger men." Among these younger men he mentions J. M. Clark, Morris Copeland, Robert Hale, Sumner Slichter, and Rexford Tugwell (Mitchell 1924a, p. 253).

Lionel Edie, writing in 1927 concerning institutionalist contributions, talks of work by Veblen, Mitchell, Commons, Hamilton, J. M. Clark, Hobson, John Dewey, and Harold Moulton. In the same year, J. M. Clark published a survey of economics that devoted considerable space to discussion of Veblen, Hobson, and of institutional economics. In terms of American contributors to institutional economics apart from Veblen, Clark locates C. H. Cooley, R. T. Ely – particularly his *Property and Contract* (Ely 1914) – and John R. Commons as contributors, and then mentions "a group of articles and papers by C. H. Cooley, Walton Hamilton, C. E. Ayes, and W. F. Ogburn, flanked by H. G. Moulton on the more descriptive side, and perhaps supported by Carleton Parker and the 'instinct' school on the psychological side." He goes on to state that Wesley Mitchell has also "contributed powerfully to the general point of view" (Clark 1927, pp. 273–274).

These attempts to name the primary contributors to the institutional approach are interesting because they are being made by those involved in attempting to promote the movement themselves and not by outside or later commentators. Several points can be made. First, Veblen is always mentioned, but never in isolation. It is Veblen and Hobson and Mitchell and various "younger men." As will be argued further, institutionalism as it emerged in the years around World War I was not just Veblenism. Second, Mitchell, J. M. Clark, and Walton Hamilton figure very prominently, and Harold Moulton's name comes up a number of times. Moulton, Clark, and Hamilton had quite a lot to do with each other around the end of World War I, and, as mentioned earlier, it was they who actually organized the

1918 conference session. Moreover, this 1918 session was followed up in 1920 by another AEA session critical of traditional theory and again featuring J. M. Clark who presented his paper, "Soundings in Non-Euclidian Economics" (Clark 1921), a clever critique of a number of standard economic propositions. In 1922, Mitchell gave a paper on the Veblenian theme of "Making Goods and Making Money" to a joint session of the AEA and the American Society of Mechanical Engineers (Mitchell 1923a), and in 1924 he gave his extremely provocative Presidential Address to the AEA, mentioned earlier. Given all of this, it is clear that it was Hamilton, Clark and Mitchell who were the principal active promoters of the idea of an institutional economics. Third, and related to the previous point, Commons becomes explicitly included as a contributor to institutional economics only after 1924 and the publication of his *Legal Foundations of Capitalism* (Commons 1924a). I have not been able to find any reference to Commons as an institutionalist prior to 1924, which is quite surprising given his previous work on trade union history (not dissimilar to that of the Webbs, who are mentioned) and his even earlier series of papers on "A Sociological View of Sovereignty" (Commons 1899–1900). Fourth, there are references back to the earlier generation of American progressive economists, particularly to H. C. Adams and R. T. Ely, and quite a number of references to sociologist Charles Horton Cooley. Finally, there are a number of references to English writers such as the Webbs, J. A. Hobson, Edwin Cannan (because of his work on property rights), Graham Wallas, and Henry Clay. Hamilton in particular had close contacts with Hobson, Tawney, Clay, and Wallas.[12] In contrast, there are only occasional references to German writers such as Werner Sombart, even fewer references to Max Weber,[13] and almost none to earlier members of the German historical school.

It is also pertinent to note the American economists of the time who are *not* named as contributors to institutionalism, for example Allyn Young, Frank Knight, and Alvin Hansen. Both Allyn Young and Alvin Hansen have been placed within the institutionalist tradition (Mehrling 1997), but more because of their Wisconsin backgrounds than any adherence to the institutionalist program as previously outlined. Although Young had close connections with Mitchell, and even admired Veblen's capacity for insight, his own work was much more along orthodox lines. Hansen went from an interest in European cycle theories to Keynesianism, although he

---

[12] For an examination of the connections between American institutionalists and British reform liberals and Fabians, see Rutherford (2007).

[13] Later on Commons would refer to Weber's method of ideal types in his *Institutional Economics* (1934)

always adhered to a Wisconsin style of reformism.[14] Knight has been called a "maverick institutionalist" (Hodgson 2004). Knight had a deep interest in issues of institutional history, but he defended a central analytical role for competitive price theory and rejected the scientism, behaviorism, and reformism that were central parts of the institutionalist program. Although Knight did have close contacts with a number of institutionalists, his role was more that of the perennial critic of the movement.[15]

THE SOURCES OF INSTITUTIONAL ECONOMICS

The picture of Hamilton, Clark, and Mitchell as the major figures in the early interwar development of the institutionalist movement requires some consideration of the role of Veblen. It will be argued here that Veblen played a vital inspirational role. It would be impossible to think of institutionalism without giving Veblen's work a central place, but at the same time he did not uniquely define the research agenda or methodology of what became institutionalism in the interwar period. Also, over the period in question, he cannot be described as other than a marginal presence within the economics profession at large, in contrast to Mitchell, Clark, and Hamilton. Veblen had become increasingly skeptical concerning the prospects for a significant change in economics (Veblen 1925), and it is worth remembering too that by 1918, Veblen was not in particularly good health and was older than his sixty-one years. Moulton, writing to Hamilton after a meeting with Veblen in May 1918, called him "the old boy" (Harold Moulton to Walton Hamilton, 13 May 1918, Records of the War Labor Policies Board, Correspondence of Walton Hamilton), and that was likely a common attitude.

Nevertheless, Veblen's influence, whether direct or indirect, was one of the major elements providing a commonality and a bond between the members of the institutionalist movement mentioned earlier. Veblen was important in a number of crucial respects. He provided a strong criticism of hedonism, including marginal utility theory, satirizing its conception of man as a "lightning calculator of pleasures and pains" (Veblen 1898, p. 389), and arguing that economics should look to more modern social-psychological theories of behavior based on instinct and habit. As mentioned previously, this was a theme actively pursued by Mitchell, Clark, and numerous others.

---

[14] Others, such as Paul Douglas and Alvin Johnson, were of reform liberal persuasion and had contact with the institutionalist group along those dimensions, but their own economic work was significantly more neoclassical in nature. The set of reform-minded liberals and the set of institutionalists had much overlap but were not identical.

[15] Knight is discussed in more detail in Chapter 5 of this book.

Veblen's overall evolutionary framework was one that stressed the cumulative and path-dependent nature of institutional change, the role of new technology in bringing about institutional change (by changing the underlying, habitual ways of living and thinking), and the predominantly "pecuniary" character of the existing set of American institutions (that is, expressing the "business" values of pecuniary success and individual gain by money making, to the virtual exclusion of all other values). For Veblen, as for other institutionalists, institutions were more than merely constraints on individual action, but embodied generally accepted ways of thinking and behaving, and worked to mold the preferences and values of individuals brought up under their sway. Within this framework, Veblen developed his analyses of "conspicuous consumption" and consumption norms; the effect of corporate finance on the ownership and control of firms; the role of intangible property and the ability to capitalize intangibles; business and financial strategies for profit making, salesmanship and advertising; the emergence of a specialist managerial class; business fluctuations; and many other topics (Veblen 1899; 1904).

Veblen did not think of existing institutions as necessarily functioning to promote the social benefit – in fact, rather the opposite. Existing institutions, due both to the inertia inherent in any established scheme and to the defensive activities of vested interests, tended to become out of step with new technological means and with the economic issues and social problems they generated. Thus, for Veblen, the existing legal and social institutions of his America were outmoded and inadequate to the task of the social control of modern large-scale industry. In Walton Hamilton's rendition, this became "a fault line – I don't like the word lag – between the industrial arts with which we carry on and the antiquated social organization with which we attempt to harness them" (Walton Hamilton to Clarence Ayres, 15 May no year, Clarence Ayres Papers, Box 3F288).

Veblen was pointing to what he perceived as a systemic failure of "business" institutions to channel private economic activity in ways consistent with the public interest. For Veblen, the "invisible hand" notion of the market may have been applicable to conditions of small-scale manufacturing, but not to conditions of large-scale production, corporate finance, and salesmanship. Veblen was particularly harsh in his attack on the manipulative, restrictive, and unproductive tactics used by business to generate income (including consolidations, control via holding companies, and interlocking directorates, financial manipulation, insider dealing, sharp practices of various kinds, and unscrupulous salesmanship), and on the "waste" generated by monopoly restriction, business cycles, unemployment, and competitive advertising. Veblen held out little hope of change short of a complete rejection of "business" principles (Veblen 1904; 1921).

Many of these aspects of Veblen's thinking had significant influence on other institutionalists and can easily be found displayed in the work of Hamilton, Mitchell, Clark, and others. Even Commons, who took less from Veblen than most other institutionalists, gave central importance to his analysis of intangible property and spent considerable space discussing his ideas (Commons 1934a, pp. 649–677).

Not all aspects of Veblen's work, however, were adopted by interwar institutionalists, and it is not difficult to find criticisms of Veblen's methodology and of some of his specific theories. As mentioned earlier, institutional economics was frequently and explicitly linked to quantitative and other forms of empirical research. Veblen's own research agenda was one of providing sweeping dissections of existing institutional arrangements, but often without the careful investigation or close consideration of factual evidence that might seem to have been implied by his own many references to the "matter of fact" approach of "modern science" (Veblen 1906). Many later institutionalists, including Hamilton, Mitchell, Clark, and Tugwell, commented adversely on Veblen's lack of attention to what they considered proper scientific methodology (Rutherford 1999). For Hamilton, Veblen was an "emancipator," someone who inspired but who could not have done the detailed empirical work of Hoxie, Stewart, or Mitchell (Hamilton 1958, pp. 21–22). For Clark, Veblen provided "orientation," a "conception of the problem," but neglected "scientific procedure" (Clark 1927, pp. 248–249). Similarly, Tugwell argued that Veblen "had discredited orthodox economics and had undermined the business culture," but that "all the constructive work remained to be done" (Tugwell 1937, p. 239). For Mitchell, Veblen's conceptions of human nature were "a vast improvement" and he had "uncanny insights" (Mitchell 1928a, p. 412), but "like other intrepid explorers of new lands, Veblen made hasty traverses" and his "sketch maps" were "not accurate in detail" (Mitchell 1929b, p. 68). As early as 1910, Mitchell had attempted to persuade Veblen to turn away from criticism and speculation toward more constructive and scientific work (Dorfman 1973, p. 197). Mitchell was highly suspicious of "speculative" approaches and included applications of Darwinian theory to social evolution in that category. For Mitchell, the path of progress in social science lay in the methods of physics and chemistry: "They had been built up not in grand systems like soap bubbles; but by the patient processes of observation and testing – always critical testing – of the relations between the working hypotheses and the processes observed" (Mitchell 1928a, p. 413).

In addition, Veblen's overall evolutionary scheme was found to have more specific problems. Veblen's theory of institutional evolution emphasized the role of new technology bringing about institutional change via a causal process of habituation to new "disciplines" of life. Here rational appraisal of consequences plays no significant role, the process being one whereby new ways of thinking are somehow induced by new patterns of life. In the early years of the twentieth century, both Mitchell and Hoxie attempted to apply Veblen's theory, but each ran into difficulty. Mitchell's work on the development of the "money economy" found many more factors at work in institutional evolution than Veblen suggested, and Hoxie came to reject Veblen's hypothesis, expressed in *Business Enterprise* (Veblen 1904, pp. 306–360), that the discipline of machine industry would tend to turn the habits of thought of unionized workers in a socialistic direction (Rutherford 1998; see Chapter 5 in this book).

Institutionalists in the interwar period obviously did share Veblen's conception of the institutional scheme as evolving over time, of institutions establishing the context within which economic activity takes place and is to be explained, and of the "pecuniary" nature of existing economic institutions, but they did not pursue the development of Veblen's specific theory of institutional evolution. Indeed, for most institutionalists the issues of the current performance of economic institutions, and matters of immediate social concern took center stage while issues of longer-term institutional change were largely left aside.[16] The major exception to this is the later work of J. R. Commons, but Commons explicitly rejected Veblen's basic dichotomization of industry and business (or technology and institutions), and his own theory of institutional evolution stressed processes of legal evolution through courts, legislatures, and processes of conflict resolution.

Furthermore, institutionalists were influenced by the earlier generation of American progressive economists and social theorists such as Richard T. Ely, H. C. Adams, C. H. Cooley, and, to a slightly lesser extent, Simon N. Patten. Writers such as these were also concerned with institutions and institutional change, but they did not share Veblen's radicalism and imparted a much more reformist position to their students. Although Veblen is often included as a part of American progressivism, along with people such as Ely, H. C. Adams, and pragmatist philosophers such as John Dewey, Veblen's evolutionary theory gives little room for deliberative social

---

[16] My archival research did turn up a number of unfinished manuscripts attempting to provide discussions of institutional evolution or of the economic order. That these were never completed attests to the difficulty of the task.

guidance and legislative reform (Ross 1991, p. 213), and his work did not focus on issues such as labor law or business regulation that held a central place in the progressive literature more generally.

A key part of this difference relates to the significance place given to legal evolution and the ability of the law to respond to new circumstances, either through the courts or through legislatures. Many institutionalists, including Hamilton, J. M. Clark, Commons, and Robert L. Hale, placed a much greater emphasis on the evolution of legal institutions than did Veblen. Both Hamilton and Hale moved into law schools and had close connections with legal scholars of the realist school. The major sources of this emphasis on legal institutions were Richard Ely (who taught Commons) and H. C. Adams (who taught Hamilton). This greater emphasis on law and on legal evolution helped shift the character of institutionalism away from Veblen's radicalism and connect it to a reformist and pragmatic philosophy that looked to legislative and legal reform concerning such issues such as business regulation, labor law, collective bargaining, health and safety regulations, and consumer protection. Thus, in the hands of institutionalists such as Hamilton, Clark, Mitchell, and Commons, the problem became one of supplementing (rather than replacing) the market with other forms of "social control" or one of "how to make production for profit turn out a larger supply of useful goods under conditions more conducive to welfare" (Mitchell 1923a, p. 148). Although Veblen's influence made institutionalists somewhat more critical of existing institutions than many of the previous generation of progressives, it does have to be understood that it was not Veblen alone who was the fountainhead for interwar institutionalism, but rather Veblen moderated by pragmatic and progressive views of science and social reform.

On the other hand, this is not to say that institutionalism was simply a continuation of the work of the generation of German-trained economists who had brought historicist ideas and a progressive reform agenda to American economics in the 1880s. This issue was raised by R. T. Ely in a 1931 AEA discussion of institutional economics. Ely argued that institutional economics contained nothing new, that it had all been said before in the 1880s by the German influenced scholars who founded the AEA, such as himself, H. C. Adams, and J. B. Clark (at least in J. B. Clark's earlier work). Ely also criticized the effect of Veblen's influence on Commons (Ely 1932, pp. 114–115). Institutionalists certainly claimed H. C. Adams and R. T. Ely as predecessors. Particularly important in this respect was Adams's essay "The Relation of the State to Industrial Action" (1887) and Ely's book *Property and Contract* (1914). Institutionalists also looked back to the reformism that was embedded in the original founding constitution of the AEA (Coats 1960). This is clear in the comments quoted earlier concerning their desire to undertake a "reclamation" of the AEA. In doing this, they were placing themselves in this longer American tradition that stretched back to the 1880s. It is also noteworthy that the combination of quantitative and statistical research with progressive reformism that formed such a significant part of institutionalism had its roots in the work of German economists such as Ernest Engel and others (Grimmer-Solem 2003, pp. 127–168). However, institutionalists saw themselves not merely as continuing that tradition, but as significantly updating, modernizing, and revitalizing it in a number of ways.

Institutionalists, following Veblen's opinion of Schmoller (Veblen 1901), tended to be critical of German historicism for its tendency to descriptivism, and it is very noticeable that institutionalists did not usually refer to German historicists as predecessors.[17] Veblen thought of himself as providing a more theoretical approach to institutions, and the Veblenian influence on institutionalism is an important element that separates institutionalists from the previous generation of American progressive economists. Another important difference is to be found in the Social Christianity of Ely, Adams, J. B. Clark, and the younger Commons. The institutionalist literature is thoroughly secular with no important reference to the church or to Christian morality as important agents of reform (Bateman 1998). The references instead are to science, pragmatic philosophy, and to the actions of the state. Another difference is that many of the German-trained economists had subsequently made an accommodation with marginalism (Yonay 1998, pp. 39–46). This can be seen especially in the later editions of Ely's introductory text book (Ely et al. 1908),[18] in J. B. Clark's work on marginal productivity theory, and also in the work done by Seligman and many others. Institutionalists largely rejected this accommodation. Finally, some of the progressives of the previous generation had become increasingly conservative; Ely certainly had become so. The Veblenian critique of business institutions and marginalist economics, placed together with the ideas of empirical science and Dewey's

[17] Veblen did translate Gustav Cohn's *Science of Finance*. Cohn was regarded as someone who charted a middle way between the descriptivism of some historicists and the deductivism of English economics. See Camic (forthcoming) for a fascinating analysis of this part of Veblen's career.
[18] The later editions of Ely's text included T. S. Adams, Max Lorenz, and Allyn Young as coauthors. Young was particularly involved. The text included both marginal utility and marginal productivity theory.

pragmatic reformism, worked to refocus and reenergize the progressive impulse.

One final source of inspiration that needs to be mentioned is the part played by many of those involved in the formation of institutionalism in the economic planning developed as a part of World War I. The war brought economists into government agencies in an unprecedented fashion. H. C. Adams wrote to his wife from Washington, DC, about the "college professors that swarm" in this city, and observing that "applied economics and political science will, at the close of the war, either have made or blasted its reputation for scientific and expert knowledge" (H. C. Adams to Bertha Adams, 15 August 1918, H. C. Adams Papers, Box 11). As previously noted, Mitchell headed the Prices Section of the War Industries Board (WIB) and worked on a large study of prices during the war – work that also involved Isador Lubin, Leo Wolman, and Walter Stewart. The WIB was chaired by Robert Brookings, and its statistical work has been described by Wolman (1919). Brookings's endowment of research agencies in public administration and economics was inspired by his wartime experience, and Mitchell's concern with statistical and factual knowledge, and the need for improved research in the social sciences, was given special urgency by his experience of wartime administration. In 1918, Mitchell became President of the American Statistical Association. His Presidential Address, "Statistics and Government" (Mitchell 1919) specifically related his war experience to the need for more work on "social statistics." William Ogburn had similar experiences. During the war, when he had the help of the staff of the War Labor Board and Bureau of Labour Statistics, he could complete ten or twelve empirical studies a year, compared with only one prior to that (Frank 1923a, p. 30). Hamilton and Moulton worked with the War Labor Policies Board, chaired by Felix Frankfurter, as economic experts dealing mainly with reconstruction issues. All three were keen to see some of the wartime planning apparatus retained to manage the period of reconstruction, and Hamilton seems to have been enthused by the opportunities for economic research and policy formation in the context of reconstruction.[19]

---

[19] Records of the War Labor Policies Board, RG 1.2, Entry 5, Box 1, Correspondence of Walton Hamilton. The war also saw Allyn Young concerned about the available statistical data (Young 1918). Young was to become centrally involved in the research into economic conditions in Europe in preparation for the peace negotiations, a project called "The Inquiry" (Blitch 1983). Young's correspondence with respect to "The Inquiry" is interesting as he was in favor of involving Veblen to work on the "the bearing of the terms of the peace of the possible extension of the revolutionary situation in Europe and its possible development in the United States" (Allyn Young to Sidney Mezes, 7 February,

That economists both could and should share in fixing the "foundations of a new economic organization" was the theme of Irving Fisher's 1918 Presidential Address to the AEA (Fisher 1919, p. 21). Economics had established itself as an important tool for government policy formation, and the possibilities for the discipline seemed immense. This provided a critical impetus to the ideals of scientific investigation and social control that were so apparent in Hamilton's manifesto and the conference session of which it was a part.

THE INSTITUTIONALIST PROGRAM

Many of the early articles and conference papers written by Hamilton, Clark, and Mitchell in their efforts to establish an institutional economics were of a critical and polemical nature. This may have contributed to the idea of institutionalism as little more than a tradition of dissent with no positive program of its own, but such a view of institutionalism does not stand up to a closer examination of the literature produced by institutionalists. What follows is an attempt to provide a brief composite overview of the positive aspects of the institutionalist program in the interwar period. Many parts of this program will be discussed in more detail in later chapters, so what follows here is merely indicative. The materials referred to will include, without being limited to, the books most often mentioned as paradigms of institutionalist research in the literature of the period, and the many institutionalist textbooks that were produced in the 1920s and 1930s. In the former category are Wesley Mitchell's *Business Cycles* (1913) and *Business Cycles: The Problem and its Setting* (1927), J. M. Clark's *Overhead Costs* (1923) and *Social Control of Business* (1926), Hamilton and Stacy May's *The Control of Wages* (1923), Hamilton and Helen R. Wright's *The Case of Bituminous Coal* (1925), Commons's *Legal Foundations* (1924a) and *Institutional Economics* (1934a), and A. A. Berle and Gardiner Means's *The Modern Corporation and Private Property* (1932). In the latter category are Hamilton's *Current Economic Problems* (1919b), Lionel Edie's *Principles of the New Economics* (1922) and *Economic Principles and Problems* (1926), Rexford Tugwell, Thomas Munroe, and Roy Stryker's *American Economic Life and the Means of Its Improvement* (1925), Willard L. Thorp's *Economic Institutions* (1928), Sumner Slichter's *Modern Economic Society* (1931), Willard Atkins and colleagues' *Economic Behavior: An Institutional Approach* (1931), Tugwell and

---

1918, Allyn Young Papers, Box 2). This interest related to Veblen's work *An Inquiry into the Nature of Peace* (Veblen 1917). Veblen did write two memoranda for The Inquiry but was not given a permanent place in it (Dorfman 1934, pp. 373–380).

Howard C. Hill's *Our Economic Society and its Problems* (1935), and Horace Taylor and colleagues' *Contemporary Economic Problems and Trends* (Taylor 1938). For "classroom purposes," Clark explicitly suggested that his *Social Control of Business* be used in connection with Hamilton's *Current Economic Problems* (Clark 1926, pp. xiv–xv). For an overview of interwar institutionalism, one could do a lot worse.[20]

First, in all of these works, institutions are placed at the center of the analysis. As argued earlier, institutionalists in the interwar period did not pursue the development of Veblen's specific theory of institutional evolution, but they held fast to the importance of institutions and institutional change. Examples of this institutional contextualization of economic issues and problems, and particularly of the idea of the modern economy being dominated by "pecuniary institutions," can be found in abundance in the various books mentioned previously. Hamilton's *Current Economic Problems* (1919b) contains lengthy sections on "The Antecedents of Modern Industrialism" and "The Industrial Revolution" (containing selections from Ashley, Bucher, Toynbee, Cunningham, Veblen, as well as many pieces written by himself), followed by a section entitled "The Pecuniary Basis of Economic Organization," with subsections dealing with "Price as an Organizing Force," "The Organization of Prices," "Pecuniary Competition," "Price Fixing by Authority," "Speculation," "The Corporation," and including selections of writing from H.C. Adams, Cooley, J. M. Clark, Mitchell, and J. A. Hobson, among others. This is followed by sections dealing with specific problems such as business cycles, trade and protection, railway regulation, monopoly, immigration, unemployment and health and safety, unionism, and wage contracts. The book finishes with sections on the control of industry and social reform.

Very similarly, Thorp's *Economic Institutions* (1928) opens with a section dealing with the historical background and main elements of the American economic order, including a definition of an institution as a "*social* habit of thought or action" (Thorp 1928, p.12). This is followed by a section on "The Institution of Machine Technique," detailing the impact of mechanization on particular industries and on society more broadly, and sections on "The Institution of the Price System," "The Institution of Private Property," and "The Institution of Business Enterprise." The concluding section deals with various proposals for institutional reform. References can be found in work by Cooley, Veblen, Hamilton, Moulton, Tugwell, F. C. Mills, and Mitchell.

---

[20] It is not often appreciated how many institutionalist texts were written or what a high proportion of the total number they accounted for. For a survey of textbooks of the period, see Ise (1932).

Economic Behavior: An Institutional Approach (Atkins et al. 1931) opens
with "Book One: The Pecuniary Basis of Industrial Society," which discusses the institutional element in economic behavior, the rise of modern
industrialism, the development of money and "profit-seeking enterprise,"
the corporation, and recent tendencies in ownership. Book Two discusses
financial and money markets, Book Three discusses goods markets, including the various types of competition, problems of too much competition
in oil and excess capacity in coal, changing forms of competition using
the automobile industry as an example, and business cycles. Books Four,
Five, and Six discuss consumers (including income and income distribution), labor and unions, and the need for "change and control" respectively.
Another textbook, Slichter's *Modern Economic Society* (1931), contains a
little less economic history but is otherwise not dissimilar in structure. It
opens with a characterization of the existing economic order focusing on
capitalistic organization, machine industry, large business units and modern business organization, the organization of labor, speculative production, and the credit economy. The book goes on to discuss problems of price
determination and stability, monopoly, public utilities, the business cycle,
the position of consumers, the labor bargain, international trade and monetary problems, and closes with suggestions for reform.

Even books not designed as general texts, but as works on particular topics,
share the explicit presentation of this institutional context. J. R. Commons's
Legal Foundations (1924a) is an examination of the most basic legal institutions of capitalism, their historical development and economic importance.
J. M. Clark's *Social Control of Business* (1926) opens with chapters devoted to
providing an institutionalist frame with discussions of the nature of "business" institutions and the rules that govern the "game" of business, and of
the history of the various types of institutional rules that constitute systems
of "control" of business activity. These first two chapters make reference to
Beard, Bucher, Cunningham, Commons, Cooley, Hamilton, Hobson, Ross,
Tawney, and Veblen. Mitchell's *Business Cycles: The Problem and Its Setting*
(1927) devotes the whole of chapter two – some 125 pages – to a discussion
of the historical connection between business cycles and the use of money,
the evolution of the pecuniary or "business" economy, the modern organization for making money (including business enterprises, their size and
interdependence, and profit-seeking behavior), the system of prices, monetary mechanisms, and the "guidance of economic activity."

Second, and following from their view of science, institutionalists took
the issue of improving economic measurement seriously. This is perhaps
most obvious in the work of Wesley Mitchell and the NBER. The NBER not

only produced many empirical studies relating to business cycles, labor, and price movements, but also played a vital role in the development of national income accounting, particularly through the work of Mitchell's student, Simon Kuznets. In conjunction with the Federal Reserve, the NBER also did much to develop monetary and financial data. Moreover, during the New Deal, institutionalists such as Morris Copeland were heavily involved in the effort to improve the statistical work of government agencies (Rutherford 2002). Textbooks such as Edie (1926) and Thorp (1928) made a point of the presentation of statistical data.

Again, following their view of science, institutionalists did engage in various types of "testing" of theories. Testing was done by comparing the implications of theories with the results of empirical and statistical investigations in a variety of ways. Mitchell, in the course of his statistical examinations of the course of business cycles, frequently remarked on the consistency or inconsistency of his finding with various business cycle theories (Mitchell 1913). Morris Copeland tested different views of the quantity theory (pro and con) by drawing out the implications for the leads and lags one would expect to find and then examining the data (Copeland 1929). Hamilton's work on the bituminous coal industry found many buyers and sellers and a relatively homogeneous product, but an industry characterized by "chaos" and not by a stable competitive equilibrium (Hamilton and Wright 1925). Clark examined the effect of overhead costs of the pricing policy of firms, concluding that they resulted in departures from the standard models, and provided an explanation for such observed phenomena as price discrimination and cutthroat pricing (Clark 1923). Examples such as these could be multiplied.

Third, institutionalists made contributions to a number of key debates in economics on issues such as psychology and economics, the economics of the household, the pricing behavior of firms, ownership and control of corporations, monopoly and competition, unions and labor markets, public utilities and regulation, law and economics, various types of market failures, and business cycles and depressions.

As noted earlier, one of the most often repeated claims among institutionalists was that a "scientific" economics would have to be consistent with "modern" psychology. A typical argument was that economics "is a science of human behavior," and any conception of human behavior that the economist may adopt "is a matter of psychology" (Clark 1918, p. 4). J. M. Clark made one of the most interesting efforts to develop the psychological basis of institutional economics in a paper published in 1918. Building on William James and Cooley, he argues that the "effort of decision" is an important cost. Clark here is considering both the costs of information gathering and of calculation. Taking into account such decision costs would mean that even a perfect hedonist "would stop calculating when it seemed likely to involve more trouble than it was worth" (Clark 1918, p. 25). This point cannot be determined with exactness, so that information and decision costs provide an explanation and an economic function for custom and habit. Custom and habit are methods of economizing on decision costs, but habits and customs are "quasi-static" and slow down the responses of consumers to changes in prices or quality. In a rapidly changing world, habit and custom can quickly become outmoded (Clark 1918, p. 30). Clark's work clearly anticipates modern bounded rationality arguments.

Many others contributed to the institutionalist literature on psychology and economics, including Tugwell (1922b; 1930), Florence (1927), Copeland (1930), and Ayres (1918; 1921a; 1921b; 1936). Lionel Edie's 1922 textbook also made copious reference to new psychological foundations (Edie 1922). He starts with a lengthy discussion of a wide range of instincts taken from Veblen, James, McDougall, and others, followed by a discussion of the expression of the instincts through habits, imitation, sympathy, and suggestion. Habit "facilitates the established process of economics, and serves to link the instincts in stabilized and settled ways to the methods of the economic order" (Edie 1922, pp. 42–43). New economic processes and ideas require "not only the breaking of old habits, but the laborious and difficult task of forming new ones in their place" (Edie 1922, p. 43).

Most of the items written before the mid-1920s utilize instinct/habit psychology (Ayres is an exception). Later work made more use of behaviorism with particular reference to its focus on measurement, observable behavior, and its "natural science" character (Asso and Fiorito 2004a). In 1924, Mitchell argued that psychology was "moving rapidly toward an objective conception and a quantitative treatment of their problem," and that the psychologist's emphasis on stimulus and response, conditioned reflexes, performance tests, and experimental method favor the spread of the conception that all the social sciences have common aims, methods, and aspirations (Mitchell 1925, p. 6). Similar views were expressed by Copeland (1930). The shift to behaviorism changed psychology dramatically (Curti 1980; Degler 1991). Among institutionalists, however, behaviorist ideas were used more in the making of methodological points relating to the importance of measurement than in any detailed way in the discussion of economic behavior. Indeed, the pragmatic concept of mind militated against any such use, and the institutionalist notion of behaviorism often involved little more than the general idea of social conditioning and education to prevailing cultural norms.

Related to the work on psychology and economics were the economics of consumption and of the household. This work developed largely from Veblen's *Theory of the Leisure Class* (1899) and Wesley Mitchell's essay, "The Backward Art of Spending Money" (1912), which contrasted the developed business art of making money with the largely conventional nature of consumption behavior. The institutionalist approach to consumption was always critical of marginal utility theory as a basis for a theory of consumption, and emphasized the social nature of the formation of consumption habits and on socially defined "standards of living." This line of work was pursued further by Hazel Kyrk in her *Theory of Consumption* (1923) and her *Economic Problems of the Family* (1933), and by Theresa McMahon in her *Social and Economic Standards of Living* (1925). McMahon made use of Veblen's conception of emulation in consumption, whereas Kyrk adopted Mitchell's view that notions of rationality derived from business calculation of profit cannot be applied to households controlled by other standards (1923, p. 144). Kyrk undertook to measure and critically analyze existing standards of living, and to create policy to help achieve higher standards of living. Others, such as Jessica Peixotto (1927) also contributed to this literature (Dorfman 1959, pp. 570–578; Hirschfeld 1998). Institutionalist texts commonly contained sections on consumption behavior based on similar ideas.

Following from the institutionalist conception of the industrial economy as dominated by pecuniary or business institutions, a great deal of work was conducted by institutionalists on the behavior of business firms and of the functioning of markets. To a large extent this work derived from Veblen's ideas on the nature of business enterprise, and there was considerable interest in issues of the ownership and control of corporations, corporate finance and speculation, monopoly, and pricing. Hamilton's *Current Economic Problems* (1919b) contains subsections on the price system, pecuniary competition, the corporation, and on speculation as well a section devoted to the problem of "capitalistic monopoly." In this book and in others such as the texts by Thorp (1928), Slichter (1931), and Atkins (Atkins et al. 1931), there is a great deal of material on "modern business organizations," corporation finance, the advance of mechanization, and the impact of technological change, unfair or cutthroat competition, and business practices designed to reduce or limit competition and gain market power.

An important line of argument came from J. M. Clark's *Overhead Costs* (1923). More capital-intensive methods of production had given rise to much higher overhead costs. This could result in marginal costs below average total costs. Although overhead or fixed costs have to be covered in the long run, they need not be covered in the short term, and the share of the overhead to be borne by any given part of the business is a matter of business policy. For Clark, high overhead costs could result in cutthroat competition, price discrimination, or an extension of monopoly. The discussion of the inadequacy of the standard models of perfect competition and pure monopoly was also backed up by numerous industry case studies (Hamilton and Associates, 1938). The coal industry received much attention. In that industry, Hamilton and Wright (1925) found little that corresponded to the ideal of a competitive industry. Hamilton's argument was that, particularly under modern conditions of technological advance and high overheads, competition could lead to disorder and inefficiency rather than to order and efficiency. Beyond the coal industry, George Stocking's (1925) Columbia Ph.D. thesis dealt with common pool problems in the oil industry, and Mordecai Ezekiel (1938) worked on agricultural pricing, including the cobweb model and its implications for the orthodox view of "self regulating" markets.

On issues of corporate finance and ownership, Bonbright and Means (1932) coauthored *The Holding Company*, and Berle and Means (1932) *The Modern Corporation and Private Property*. These works much extended Veblen's earlier discussions of corporate consolidation and the separation of ownership and control (Veblen 1904). Berle and Means's work raised important issues of agency and whether managers would maximize profits. A related theme, deriving from J. M. Clark's work on overheads, was that technological change had altered the structure of costs faced by firms and had resulted in an increase in price inflexibility over the cycle. F. C. Mills conducted empirical work on price flexibility for the NBER, and Gardiner Means (1935) generated his theory of administered pricing that sparked a vast literature on relative price inflexibility.

On labor market issues, institutionalists concerned themselves with studying unions and the history of the labor movement (Commons et al. 1918), developing in the process both classifications of unions and explanations for the particular pattern of trade union development in America (Commons 1909; Perlman 1928). Mitchell's National Bureau also sponsored studies on the growth of trade unions (Wolman 1924) and on many other labor issues. Wage determination was also a problem that attracted the attention of institutionalists. Walton Hamilton's 1922 article on wages and 1923 book, *The Control of Wages* (with Stacy May), attempted to outline the various factors that contributed to the determination of wages, and provide what he called a "functional theory of wages" (Hamilton and May 1923, p. 112). Discussions of "the wage bargain" or "the labor bargain" were provided by other institutional labor economists such as Commons (1924a) and Sumner Slichter (1931). In this work, much attention was given to issues of collective bargaining and systems of conciliation and mediation. The work of Commons and his students on labor issues and labor legislation was well known, contributing hugely to the development of industrial relations in both its academic and applied aspects (Kaufman 1993). The importance attached to these issues is also apparent in the textbooks. Slichter's text (1931) contains chapters on the organization of labor and three separate chapters on the labor bargain (wages as an incentive, the determination of wages, and the control of work and working conditions). The Atkins text (Atkins et al. 1931) devotes about a sixth of the book to a discussion of unions and labor issues.

Public utilities, including issues relating to the valuation of utility property and the proper basis for rate regulation, were major areas of institutionalist research. Concepts of intangible property and of goodwill were developed within this discussion, again deriving from Veblen. Clark devoted several chapters in *The Social Control of Business* (1926) to the topic, whereas Commons devoted considerable space to the concept of intangible property, goodwill, and valuation issues in his *Legal Foundations* (Commons 1924a, pp. 157–215). Bonbright's (1937) *Valuation of Property* dealt with the difference between commercial and social valuation, with a special emphasis on issues of the valuation of public utilities. Commons (1907; 1910), Bonbright (1937), Hale (1921), and Glaeser (1927) all wrote extensively on issues of public utility regulation.

In his *Social Control of Business*, Clark argues that business cannot be regarded as a purely private affair. In Clark's words, "it is sufficiently clear that industry is essentially a matter of public concern, and that the stake which the public has in its processes is not adequately protected by the safeguards which individualism affords" (Clark 1926, p. 50). This idea of private business being broadly "affected with a public interest" was absolutely central to the institutionalist literature of this period and to the theme of social control. It was a key issue in the legal economic work of Robert Hale. For Hale, any business affected the public in numerous ways, so that to limit state regulation to those businesses "affected with a public interest" was no more limiting than the "notion of 'public welfare' itself" (Fried 1998, p. 106). Clark expresses the same idea in his claim that "every business is 'affected with a public interest' of one sort or another" (Clark 1926, p. 185), and the argument reappears in Tugwell's "The Economic Basis for Business Regulation" (Tugwell 1921), and *The Economic Basis of Public Interest* (Tugwell 1922a), in Walton Hamilton's "Affectation With Public Interest"

(Hamilton 1930b), and in Dexter Keezer and Stacy May's *Public Control of Business* (1930), as well as in other literature. These ideas provided the foundation for the institutionalist support of further regulation of business activity in the public interest. The rhetoric of social control also appears in the textbooks as "the control of economic activity" (Slichter 1924; 1931), "change and control" (Atkins et al. 1931), and "economic control" (Edie 1926).

More general interconnections between law and economics and the operation of markets were addressed by Hamilton (1938c), Hale (1923; Samuels 1973), and Commons (1924a; 1934a). Commons's approach was the most developed and was built on his notions of the pervasiveness of distributional conflicts, of legislatures and courts as attempting to resolve conflicts (at least between those interest groups with representation), and of the evolution of the law as the outcome of these ongoing processes of conflict resolution – a process he described as "artificial selection." He developed his concept of the "transaction" as the basic unit of analysis. In turn, the terms of transactions were determined by the structure of "working rules," including legal rights, duties, liberties, and exposures, and by economic (bargaining) power. Market transactions were conceived of as a transfer of rights that took place in a context of legal and economic power, and always involving some degree of "coercion," in the sense of some degree of restriction upon alternatives (Commons 1932; see also Hale 1923). He also provided a theory of the behavior of legislatures based on "log-rolling," and a theory of judicial decision making based on the concept of "reasonableness," a concept that included, but was not limited to, a concern with efficiency (Commons, 1932, pp. 24–25; 1934a, pp. 751–755).

The institutionalist program dealing with business cycles, within the period before the Great Depression, was centered on Wesley Mitchell's work and that he promoted through the NBER. Mitchell explicitly placed his work on business cycles within an institutional context by associating cycles with the functioning of the system of pecuniary institutions. Mitchell's 1913 volume, *Business Cycles*, with its discussion of the four-phase cycle driven by an interaction of factors such as the behavior of profit-seeking firms, the behavior of banks, and the leads and lags in the adjustment of prices and wages, became the standard institutionalist reference. Mitchell's work featured prominently in Hamilton's section on business cycles in his *Current Economic Problems*, in the chapter on cycles in Slichter's *Modern Economic Society* (1931), and in the chapters on cycles in Edie (1926) and Thorp (1928). In the Atkins text, Mitchell's work is quoted directly for more than six full pages (Atkins et al. 1931, pp. 529–536).

Institutionalist work on business cycles, however, did not end, but only really began, with Mitchell's 1913 volume. At the NBER, Mitchell focused heavily on promoting work that would add to the understanding of business cycles, generating a stream of research studies far too long to list here, but contributing to the development of national income measures, business cycle indicators, and much more. In addition, J. M. Clark developed his concept of the accelerator out of his study of Mitchell's 1913 work, and the accelerator mechanism soon became a standard part of cycle theory (Clark 1917). Clark's *Overhead Costs* (1923) also contributed to the discussion of cycles. This book contained one of the earliest suggestions that large, capital-intensive firms may display less price flexibility over the course of a cycle and thus exacerbate the fluctuation of output and employment. This was a point that found an empirical counterpart in Willford King's NBER study on employment in large and small firms (King 1923), and in the work of F. C. Mills, again for the NBER, on price movements (Mills 1927, 1929). Arguments about the role of price inflexibility were to play an important part in later institutionalist work on cycles and depressions by Tugwell (1931, 1932a), Gardiner Means (1935), and others (see Rutherford 1994b; Woirol 1999). Clark was to make many further contributions to business cycle research in the 1930s (Clark 1934; 1935b). Mitchell's work was not the only approach to business cycles to be found within institutionalism. Many institutionalists, including Hamilton, had an interest in the work of J. A. Hobson, and Hobson's underconsumptionism became popular among institutionalists in the 1930s (Rutherford and DesRoches 2008).

Fourth, and intimately related to the previously discussed, institutionalists made important contributions to policy in their roles in the development of instruments of social control such as unemployment insurance, workmen's compensation, social security, labor legislation, public utility regulation, agricultural price support programs, and in the promotion of public works programs and various forms of government "planning" to create high and stable levels of output. Commons pioneered public utility regulation, unemployment insurance, and workmen's compensation in Wisconsin, and the Wisconsin model was widely influential. Many institutionalists were active members of the American Association for Labor Legislation, and the AALL promoted many reforms to labor legislation. Medical insurance programs were also pursued by the AALL (Chasse 1994) and also by the Committee on the Costs of Medical Care, which involved both Hamilton and Mitchell.

Institutionalists also had significant influence within the New Deal. Commons's students, such as Witte, Arthur J. Altmeyer, and Wilbur Cohen, played leading roles in the development of federal social security programs. Berle and Tugwell were two of Roosevelt's original "Brains Trust," and Tugwell, Means, and Ezekiel were the leading advocates of the "structuralist" or planning approach that had influence in the early part of the New Deal (Barber 1996). Tugwell was Assistant Secretary of Agriculture, and Ezekiel became an economic adviser to the Secretary of Agriculture and played a prominent role in the design of agricultural policy. Means also worked as an economic adviser in the Department of Agriculture, and later led the industrial research group of the National Resources Committee, which also included Lubin, Ezekiel, and Thorp. Hamilton served in a variety of capacities, primarily in the Consumers' Division of the NRA. Thorp served as Consumers' Division Director of the National Emergency Council and Chairman of the Advisory Council of the National Recovery Administration, and Lubin became Commissioner of Labor Statistics.

There are distinctions to be made between those institutionalists who favored commissions and other similar devices, and those in favor of more comprehensive types of planning (Barber 1994). The greatest emphasis on planning came largely in the context of the Great Depression and from Tugwell, Means, and Ezekiel. Clark argued for countercyclical public works programs, and Mitchell for more modest indicative planning. Such disagreements over specific policy instruments, however, could be accommodated within the general ideal of a pragmatic and experimental approach to social control. Hamilton's approach to policy experiments within the New Deal, discussed in the next chapter, is particularly instructive in this respect.

Finally, institutionalists were active in the development of institutions of education and research in economics. Institutionalists were not only associated with the NBER, but also with the Institute of Economics, The New School for Social Research, the Brookings Graduate School, the Social Science Research Council, and with other programs of education and research. In these endeavors, institutionalists were able to gain the substantial support of Foundations such as Rockefeller.

Not all elements of this institutionalist program were pursued successfully, but there can be no doubt that institutionalists did make important positive contributions to economics in the interwar period – in empirical, theoretical, policy, and institutional terms. Although it can be argued that institutionalists did not develop a *systematic* body of theory, it cannot be argued that the institutionalist literature lacked theories or was purely descriptive in nature. Indeed the institutionalist literature contains all kinds of theories, including theories of individual decision making (Clark), theories of consumption (Kyrk), theories of the pricing decisions of firms (Clark, Means), theories of corporate finance and agency (Berle and Means), theories of wages (Hamilton and May), theories of trade union behavior (Commons, Perlman), various theories of types of market failure (Hamilton, Clark), theories of agricultural markets (Ezekiel), theories of the business cycle (Clark, Mitchell, Tugwell, and others), and theories of the decisions of courts and legislatures (Commons).

CONCLUSION

The emergence of institutionalism as a defined and self-aware movement in American economics can be dated to the period around the end of World War I. Hamilton's essay and other early works provide a characterization of the movement as the participants themselves saw it, including their major intellectual commitments (ontological, methodological, theoretical, and ideological) and their view of the predecessors and current contributors to the institutionalist literature. An examination of the contacts between those involved indicates clearly that institutionalism existed in a sociological sense as well as an intellectual one; this was a functioning network of individuals. Veblen was involved in that network without question, but he was not the most active party, and institutionalism was not defined exclusively in Veblenian terms. Furthermore, it is obvious that institutionalists themselves conceived of their program as a positive one, not merely one of dissent, and that the program did in fact have a great deal of positive content.

The institutionalist literature discussed above is littered with terms such as "new," "modern," "current," "trend," "prospect," "tendencies," and "scientific." This powerful rhetoric of newness, modernity, and of science was clearly appealing to the upcoming generation of economists and attracted them to the institutionalist cause. To a young aspiring economist in the mid-1920s, institutionalism would have meant something to do with the ideas of Thorstein Veblen, but it would not have meant Veblenism, or a Darwinian style of evolutionary theory, or biological analogy. It would also have meant something to do with people such as Mitchell, Clark, Hamilton, and Commons, but it would not have meant descriptivism or measurement without theory, or mere criticism of orthodox theory with no positive research program of its own. It would have meant the critical study of the functioning of the existing set of pecuniary or business institutions and an active and pragmatic liberal reformism. The institutionalist program would have appeared to be something new and modern, promising critical realism, scientific investigation of economic issues, consistency with the latest in related areas of social science, law, and philosophy, and involvement in important issues of social reform.

Whatever the justice of these claims, the point is that institutionalism would not have appeared as merely "a tenuous inclination to dissent from orthodox economics" (Blaug 1978, p. 712), but could easily have been seen as an attractive and exciting research program. Moreover, institutionalism established itself at leading universities and research institutes, with good connections to funding agencies and the policy activities of government. In the 1920s and 1930s, this program was successful in its appeal, and many young American economists associated themselves with institutionalism. The following chapters detail two outstanding institutionalist careers and then proceed to an examination of the institutional and programmatic foundations of the movement.

PART TWO

INSTITUTIONALIST CAREERS

3

Walton Hamilton

Institutionalism and the Public Control
of Business

As has already been argued, Walton Hamilton was one of the leading promoters, if not the leading promoter, of the institutionalist approach to economics at the time of the movement's formation. Despite this, Hamilton's career has been the subject of remarkably little commentary in the secondary literature (but see Dorfman 1974). The reason for this neglect can only be the subsequent focus on Veblen, Mitchell, and Commons. It certainly cannot be because Hamilton's career lacked importance for the institutionalist movement – quite the opposite is true. Hamilton's books on wages (Hamilton and May 1923) and the coal industry (Hamilton and Wright 1925) were frequently held up as models of institutional analysis at the time; his work on law and economics and on the regulation of business contributed greatly to one of the central themes of the institutionalist literature; he was much involved with the New Deal and with other reform efforts; and the programs of education he led at Amherst College and at the Brookings Graduate School were both innovative and trained a large number of young institutionalists (see Chapter 6). Some contemporary observers, such as Herbert Davenport, thought that it would be Hamilton, if anyone, who would provide a systematic statement of institutional economics.[1]

HAMILTON'S CAREER IN OUTLINE

Walton Hamilton was born in 1881 in Hiwassee College, Tennessee, the son of an itinerant Methodist minister. He attended the Webb School in Bell Buckle, Tennessee, and between 1901 and 1903 he attended Vanderbilt University. Later, he moved to the University of Texas where he graduated

---

[1] This was Davenport's view in a 1930 conversation with Clarence Ayres (Clarence Ayres to Allan Gruchy, 11 February 1968, Clarence Ayres Papers, Box 3F288).

in 1907. He then taught English and the classics in public schools for two years before returning to the University of Texas as an instructor in medieval history and for graduate level work. It was there that Hamilton took a seminar in economics from Alvin Johnson. In his autobiography, Johnson remarks that Hamilton was the best student he ever had (Johnson 1952), and they became lifelong friends. Johnson encouraged Hamilton to go to the University of Michigan for graduate training in economics, which Hamilton did in 1910.

Johnson's recommendation of Michigan (as opposed to, say, Columbia or Chicago) may seem strange, but at that time, the Michigan Economics Department contained a particularly interesting and diverse faculty, including Fred M. Taylor, Henry Carter Adams, and the sociologist Charles Horton Cooley. Taylor had a reputation for providing an extremely thorough and rigorous training in neoclassical economics. In contrast, Adams had been profoundly influenced by his exposure to German historicism, was a pioneer in the area of law and economics, and a champion of the role of government in the regulation of industry (Adams 1887). For Adams, standards and regulations were required to prevent competition from becoming a race to the bottom, to define what he called the "plane of competition," and to constrain the market power of monopolies and large corporations. In a passage that foreshadows Hamilton's views, Adams argued that "corporations assert for themselves most of the rights conferred on individuals by the law of private property, and apply to themselves a social philosophy true only of a society composed of individuals who are industrial competitors" (quoted in Dorfman 1949, p. 170).[2]

Cooley had been a graduate student of John Dewey's when Dewey was at Michigan, and he maintained a Deweyan emphasis on society as an organism and on the social construction of the mind. Cooley began teaching sociology in 1894, but he remained a part of the Department of Economics (Sociology did not become a separate department at Michigan until 1924). Cooley's work in the period between 1912 and 1915 is of special interest because it concerned issues of "pecuniary valuation." For Cooley, the market – meaning "the system of pecuniary transactions" – is to be seen in institutional terms, as "a vast and complicated social system, rooted in the past, though grown enormously in recent times, wielding incalculable

---

[2] Adams also established the Statistical Bureau for the Interstate Commerce Commission and became deeply involved in issues of railway accounting and regulation. Adams is commonly given much significance in the formation of American "reform" or "new" liberalism. See Furner 2005.

prestige, and, though manned by individuals like other institutions, by no means to be understood from a merely individual point of view" (Cooley 1913, p. 546). For Cooley, the usual treatment of valuation in economics was severely insufficient because it failed to go back to the individual's given wants, "it being assumed, apparently, that these wants spring from the inscrutable depths of the private mind," and not usually recognized that "they are the expressions of institutional development." Individual preferences are "molded by the market;" the market "is a continuous institution in which the individual lives and which is ever forming his ideas" (Cooley 1913, pp. 546–547). Cooley also regarded public control as a "normal and inseparable part of the economic process" (Dorfman 1949, p. 404).

At Michigan, Hamilton became one of Taylor's teaching assistants whose job was to act as "drill sergeants," charged with making "marginal utility in all its ramifications clear to the sophomores" (Hamilton 1929a, p. 183). He also took Taylor's course in theory, courses from Adams when available, and Cooley's seminar. Adams's influence can be seen in Hamilton's lifelong interest in the intersection of law and economics, but Cooley's influence was also profound:

He helped us see the industrial system, not as an automatic self-regulating mechanism, but as a complex of institutions in process of development. He may never had said so, but from him we eventually learned that business, as well as the state, is a scheme of arrangements, and that our choice is not between regulation and letting things alone, but between one scheme of control and another. In some way he forced us to give up our common sense notions, led us away from an atomic individualism, made us see "life as an organic whole." and revealed to us "the individual" and "society" remaking each other in an endless process of change. (Hamilton 1929a, p. 185)

Hamilton completed his doctoral dissertation, "Medieval Ideals of Authoritative Control," and became an assistant professor at Michigan in 1913. As mentioned earlier, he was recruited to the University of Chicago in 1914 on the recommendation of Robert Hoxie. There he became friendly with Hoxie and with Harold Moulton, but he only stayed for a year before being hired away to Amherst. Hamilton resigned in 1923 to protest Alexander Meiklejohn's removal as College president, and went on to head the new Bookings Graduate School for Economics and Political Science. In 1928, he joined the Law School at Yale.

Hamilton was a member of the American Association for Labor Legislation, a supporter of workers education, and a keen student of "the labor problem." This led to his wartime position with the War Labor Policies Board and his book *The Control of Wages* (Hamilton and May 1923).

His interest in labor problems continued and in 1935, Hamilton served as U.S. representative to the meeting of the International Labour Organization (ILO) in Geneva (the first occasion the United States was officially represented). Outside of labor issues, Hamilton was a member of the Committee on the Costs of Medical Care (CCMC) that functioned between and 1927 and 1932. Hamilton also had an interest in the particular problems of the bituminous coal industry, and in two books, he and his Brookings colleague, Helen R. Wright, analyzed the problems of the industry and made proposals for substantial reform (Hamilton and Wright 1925; 1928). Hamilton remained concerned with the problems of the coal industry through to the early 1940s.

At Brookings and Yale, Hamilton developed his interest in law and economics, particularly with Supreme Court decisions and the judicial control of industry. Hamilton was a legal realist, opposed to legal formalisms, and became a powerful critic of the more "conservative" of the Supreme Court Justices who sought to interpret the constitution in ways limiting to social and economic legislation. Several of his students wrote on similar issues in law journals and in books.

Hamilton played a number of roles in the New Deal. He joined the National Recovery Administration (NRA) in 1933 as a member of the Consumers' Advisory Board (CAB).[3] With the successive changes to the organization of the NRA, Hamilton became Chairman of the Advisory Council of the NRA and then a member of the National Industrial Recovery Board. The internal debates over the NRA codes and price policy led, in 1934, to the formation of a Cabinet Committee on Price Policy (which also included Lubin as Chairman, Means, Thorp, and Leon Henderson). Hamilton was appointed as Director of Studies, and the 1938 book, *Price and Price Policies* (Hamilton and Associates 1938) contains a selection of these price studies. In July 1935, he was appointed Director of the Consumers' Division of the NRA. In this capacity, he was also a member of the National Emergency Council. His positions in the NRA also led to him being appointed a member of the Technical Board of the Committee on Economic Security, and late in 1935, he was appointed by John G. Winant, the first Chairman of the Social Security Board, as Director of the Division of Economic Research of the Social Security Board, his mandate being to assemble the research staff. Ewan Clague replaced Hamilton in this position in 1936. Later, from 1938 to

---

[3]   Other social scientists who were members of the CAB at various times included William Ogburn, Dexter Keezer, Robert Lynd, Gardiner Means, and George Stocking (Campbell 1940; Donohue 2003, pp. 226–229).

1945, Hamilton became Special Assistant to the Attorney General, working closely with his former Yale colleague Thurman Arnold on issues of antitrust and patents. Hamilton's involvement with the New Deal thus spanned many of its different aspects and manifestations. In 1948, he retired from Yale and joined the Washington law firm of Arnold, Fortas, and Porter. He continued to write extensively on issues of trade practice, antitrust, patents, judicial decision making, and the ongoing, and ever-changing, problem of the control of industry.

HAMILTON'S INSTITUTIONALISM

Hamilton's particular version of "the institutional approach" to economics was one that was highly problem-centered and consistently stressed the need to develop new programs of control. In all of his educational work, his aim was to "teach the art of handling problems" and to produce people who could make "contributions to an intelligent direction of social change" (Hamilton 1926a). Perhaps the most central of Hamilton's arguments is that economics "should be relevant to the modern problem of control" (Hamilton 1919a, pp. 312–313). This "modern problem" had arisen out of new economic circumstances creating new social and economic problems and a growing demand for regulation. In order to have relevance to this problem of control, economics must relate to institutional arrangements. Control is exercised by "modifying the arrangements which make up our scheme of economic life," but any such "control of the development of industrial society is contingent upon a knowledge of the bundle of conventions and arrangements which make it up." The type of knowledge Hamilton considers necessary is of a detailed nature. For example: "If one would understand the corporation problem, he must learn the peculiar features of this form of business, the various devices that together make up its organization, and the place which it takes in industrial society" (Hamilton 1919a, p. 314). Moreover, institutional arrangements are in a constant process of change both from within and from outside developments (Hamilton 1919a, p. 315). What is required, then, is to analyze a problem in terms of how the current reality came to be, how it came out of the past, how it is changing, and how that change might be directed so as to better serve the end of human welfare. For Hamilton, institutional economics had as its basis a long-term view of development, a control of process, and an instrumental view of society and social institutions (Hamilton nda).

On a more specific level, Hamilton's institutionalism borrowed heavily from both Veblen and Cooley. A great deal of what Hamilton taught in his courses at Amherst and Brookings began with a discussion of the development of "modern industrialism" from the precapitalist manorial system. This process included both the development of technology, culminating ultimately in the widespread adoption of large-scale machine methods of production, and a complex of institutional developments relating to property and contract, the rise of markets, the adoption of pecuniary goals and incentives, the corporate form of organization, and to the rise of what Hamilton called at various times the system of "business control" or "the pecuniary order."[4] This scheme of control developed out of elements "long in existence;" the instrumentalities it employs are "the corporation, the pecuniary calculus, and profit making." It grew partly out of tradition, partly as a result of conscious policy, but mostly as an unintended consequence of "judgments made with other ends in view." The system of business control is dominant, but Hamilton never forgets there are significant areas of economic life controlled by other institutions such as the family, professional organizations that may or may not have entirely adopted the values of business, and, of course, government. Government imposes limitations on "almost all forms of industrial activity, and controls some of them quite directly" (Hamilton ndb).

The key issue, of course, is the adequacy of this system of control. In the economics textbooks, it is competition that is supposed to operate to reconcile the individual pursuit of pecuniary gain with community welfare, but Hamilton consistently argues that competitive theory and the policies it suggests apply only to an economy of "petty trade," and thus fail to provide an adequate analytical foundation for the understanding or control of large-scale industry and "big business." The basis of the competitive system is to be found in two pairs of institutions: private property and contract; and profit making and freedom of a trade:

Yet in no industry is competition as simple, mechanical, or articulate as this. Each of the four institutions is a compound of many usages. The right to property is a bundle of equities, such as a voice in control, an interest in disposition, and a claim to income, which may be put together into many permutations.... The right of contract, once thought of as a voluntary agreement between equals, is a changing thing; it has been remade by the rise of the corporation, the coming of business and the growth of large scale production.... The profit motive appears in many forms; the corn grower and the automobile manufacturer, the baron of steel and the baronet of

---

[4]   From his notes and teaching materials available in the Hamilton papers, it is clear that Hamilton knew a great deal both about the history of technology and about the history of legal and economic institutions (see Hamilton Papers Box J3, Folder 3; J4, Folder 7; J22, Folder 1; J30, Folder 4).

coal, may be equally devoted to their own pecuniary interests, but the arts of money making which they practice are very different. All trades at law may be equally open, but in fact they are buttressed about by very different barriers against the intruder. (Hamilton 1931a)

For Hamilton "the fundamental issue stands out in clear-cut relief": There is a lack of harmony between the technology of industry and the form of its organization and control. "An economic order in which the productive processes belong to big business and the arrangements for its control to petty trade cannot abide." The task is to "devise a scheme adequate to the direction of great industry. In a world of change a society cannot live on a wisdom borrowed from our fathers" (Hamilton 1932a, p. 593).

SOME PROPOSALS FOR CONTROL, 1918–1932

An important source of Hamilton's early ideas concerning forms of social control was his experience of wartime planning in 1918. Hamilton's major concern was to make the transition to a peacetime economy while maintaining output, employment, and the gains made by labor during the war. To this end, he favored the maintenance of some of the wartime planning apparatus in order to control the pace of demobilization and displacement of labor out of war industries (Hamilton 1919c). More generally, Hamilton, as many others, was struck by the substantial increase in output generated during the war. Full use of resources had meant an increase in output of some 25–30 percent over prewar levels, and this despite the diversion of manpower to war. Such observations seemed to confirm the "waste," in terms of loss of potential output, generated by the "unplanned" system of private business enterprise (see Friday 1919; Chase 1925, pp. 3–12), and held out the possibility of providing a modest standard of living for all if only such wastes could be eliminated.

Hamilton proposed the formation of a "national economic council" or commission that could formulate programs related to the transition to the peacetime economy and make recommendations to government. The commission would consist of prominent people representative of different industries and interests, and could call on the best scientific research (Dorfman 1974, pp. 8–9).[5] The problems they would face would include how the industrial system might be organized to provide full employment

---

[5] A number of Hamilton's wartime memoranda on reconstruction and demobilization issues are available in the Walton Hamilton File in the Papers of the War Labor Policies Board. See also Hamilton 1919c. Hamilton, in addition, concerned himself with food policy during the war (Hamilton 1918c).

of resources, the terms on which labor and capital should "combine their efforts in supplying society with the comforts and vanities of life," and the use that society should make of the "surplus of wealth which it produces over and above the necessities of its members." These problems "cannot be solved, even for the moment, by a return to the pre-war scheme of things," they require "the conscious guidance of social and industrial development" (Hamilton 1919b, pp. 303–305). Of course, Hamilton was disappointed in his expectations, and the wartime planning system was rapidly dismantled. This Hamilton criticized as an unfortunate "lapse to laissez-faire," arguing that "ordinary business practice" could not be depended on either to "secure full employment of productive resources" or to "secure within the demobilization period a proper distribution of men and materials among different industries" (Hamilton 1919d).

Hamilton's interest in labor issues continued. He, along with his student Stacy May, became particularly interested in workers' education. Both were involved in the development of Brookwood Labor College (established in 1921), Hamilton serving as a member of its Educational Committee.[6] In Hamilton's view, a labor college could do "much to stimulate and direct the labor movement." It must be established "in the belief that our economic order and its institutions are mere instruments; that at present they very imperfectly serve their purpose; and that, through the intelligent effort of the laborers of the country a new economic and social order can be eventually realized" (Hamilton 1924). Hamilton also believed the College should posses a research department to investigate and appraise programs of reform and to draft legislative bills and briefs.

Hamilton was a critic of the craft unionism of Samuel Gompers and of the American Federation of Labor, much more so than Commons. In a review of Gompers's essays, Hamilton argued that Gompers provided no overall vision or program for labor. Gompers's focus on "the acquisitive efficiency of the business agent of the craft union" resulted in a rejection of both

---

[6] Other members of the Educational Committee included William Ogburn, Joseph Willits, and Leo Wolman. Stacy May taught workers education classes through Amherst College in 1920–1922 and at Brookwood College in 1922–1923. May was a student of Hamilton's at Amherst and at Brookings. Another faculty member at Brookwood was David Saposs, a John R. Commons student, who taught there between 1922 and 1933. Bookwood's public support of industrial unionism led to a split with the AFL in 1928. It seems likely that it was through their mutual interest in workers education that Hamilton first came into personal contact with the English economist Henry Clay. Clay visited the United States for the first time in the summer of 1921 and taught at the first Summer School for Women Workers in Industry at Bryn Mawr. There is a lengthy dedication to Henry Clay in Hamilton and May (1923).

industrial unionism and political action and left labor without the weapons to attack "the larger issues upon which the welfare of labor depends." Gompers's work provided "not a single constructive suggestion for raising the real wages of the whole group of industrial laborers," nor even the "semblance of an articulate plan for fighting unemployment" (Hamilton 1921, p. 328). Shortly thereafter, Hamilton himself sought to provide such constructive suggestions for the raising of real wages.

Hamilton's 1922 article on wages and 1923 book *The Control of Wages* (with Stacy May) attempted to outline the various factors that contributed to the determination of wages and provide what he called a "functional theory of wages" (Hamilton and May 1923, p. 112). J. M. Clark, in his 1927 survey, used Hamilton's work as an "example of what the institutional point of view does when it enters the field of the theory of value and distribution." This is not to provide an "abstract formulation of the characteristic outcome" but a "directory of the forces to be studied" in any particular case. Such studies are a "proper sequel to orthodox laws of supply and demand" (Clark 1927, pp. 276–277). Mitchell was also complimentary, writing to Hamilton that his outline of the many factors that might affect wages provided the "clear preliminary conception of the problem" that was a prerequisite for quantitative investigation (Wesley Mitchell to Walton Hamilton, 14 February 1922, Walton H. Hamilton Papers, Box J5, Folder 5).

As the title suggests, *The Control of Wages* is addressed to the problem of controlling wages in the sense of increasing the regularity of employment and of raising real wages to levels "as nearly adequate as may be" (Hamilton and May 1923, pp. 18–19). As might be expected, the argument places considerable stress on raising the productivity of labor, improving management, introducing new technology and equipment, improving organization, and eliminating various "wastes." There is, however, an equal emphasis on the improvement of the "economic arts," in particular policies to reduce business cycles and unemployment, including the introduction of a tax "assessed against irregularities in the volume of employment," with the receipts "disbursed as unemployment benefits" (Hamilton and May 1923, p. 66) – a proposal similar in many ways to those produced previously by Commons and some of his students.[7] Hamilton also advocated collective

---

[7] Hamilton does not make it clear whether he is supporting pooled reserves or individual employer reserves, but the emphasis he places on penalizing employers for their particular contribution to unemployment and on the prevention of unemployment are more suggestive of what became the "Wisconsin plan" rather than the alternative "Ohio plan" formulated by William Leiserson, based on pooled reserves and insurance against risk principles. See Eisner (1967) and Schlabach (1969).

bargaining by industrial unions and stressed the importance of spreading the gains achieved in the form of lower prices rather than as increased nominal wages. Unions need to give "constant attention to their interests as consumers" (Hamilton and May 1923, p. 90).

Interestingly, Hamilton argued that an important element in the real wage consists of the nonmonetary benefits provided by employers and the public goods provided by the state. On the latter, Hamilton notes the extension of the role of the state in areas such as compensation for industrial accident and the provision of "an elaborate health service," educational institutions, and facilities for recreation. In the very near future, the state may provide "some sort of guarantee of regular employment" (Hamilton and May 1923, p. 100).

More radically, Hamilton proposed "a plan for the eventual 'liquidation of ownership' in natural elements, intangible assets, and other corporate property." The plan involved recalling all outstanding securities and replacing them with terminable annuities (of, say, fifty years) of equal value. This would effectively buy out "all the returns due to ownership fifty or more years from now" (Hamilton and May 1923, p. 68–70), and provide for future increases in wages.[8] Other institutional adjustments Hamilton and May discuss include collective marketing, collective research organizations, and the economies that might be generated through various schemes for the "unification of industry." This last possibility is discussed in tentative terms, pointing out the problems of private monopoly power, the unsettled state of the debate over the nationalization of industries, and the preliminary nature of various other proposals for the unification of industry under the control of management representatives and workers, "of workers and consumers, or of workers alone" (Hamilton and May 1923, pp. 75–79).

A number of the key themes in Hamilton's work on wages reappear in his investigation of and recommendations for the coal industry. Hamilton and Wright's first book characterized the bituminous coal industry as beset by persistent excess capacity, irregular operation, low wages, unsafe working conditions, strikes, and labor unrest. This state of affairs is contrasted with that suggested by the theory of competitive markets. The institutions of competitive free enterprise are supposed to ensure efficient operation, protection of the consumer, and conditions of work "as good as circumstances will permit" (Hamilton 1926b). Instead none of these conditions

---

[8]   Hamilton mentions that this scheme is to be elaborated in a forthcoming article by himself and Willard L. Thorp, entitled "The Liquidation of Ownership" (Hamilton and May 1923, p. 180). A search of indexes failed to turn up any such publication.

pertain. Building on J. M. Clark's work on overhead costs, Hamilton locates the basic problem in technological advance increasing capacity and creating a cost structure with high overheads and deceasing costs. Under these conditions, competition leads to price cutting, low or even negative profits, and low wages. This is combined with uncoordinated investment decisions and bankruptcy laws that allow for reorganizations that retain the mining capacity in the industry.[9] The industry is characterized more by "chaos" than by an orderly state of normal profits and capacity matched to demand. The economic organization of the industry is "backward"; there is a "lag" between the technical development of the industry and its economic organization; the "scheme of arrangements" surrounding the production of coal fails to adequately serve the ends of consumers or workers.

Hamilton concluded that the coal industry was chaotic not as a result of bad intentions but because of its institutional and cost structures. It is a system within which each individual tries to do good, but "evil" comes of it (Hamilton and Wright 1925, p. 256; Hamilton 1926, pp. 225–226; Hamilton 1928a). Clarence Ayres wrote to Hamilton after reading the book describing exactly this argument as "more pregnant in meaning" than Veblen's maxims of business "baulking" industry because it is more impersonal. It makes "confusion a misfortune of a confused transition rather than a conspiracy of malevolent freebooters." Ayres wondered if this could not be the real "point of departure for institutional economics" (Clarence Ayres to Walton Hamilton, 3 May no year, Hamilton Papers, Box J45, Folder 1).

Hamilton and Wright's second book (1928) put forward a controversial proposal for the reorganization of the industry. The book contains two dissenting opinions written by other members of the Institute of Economics, something unique in Institute publications. The proposal is a modified version of one made by Henry Clay in 1919 for the British coal industry, and Clay's original memoranda are contained in an appendix to the book.[10] In the form given it by Hamilton and Wright, the proposal calls for the merger of all coal companies into a single enterprise of a corporate form but under

---

[9] There is a strong resemblance between Hamilton's analysis of the coal industry and Veblen's 1904 discussion of chronic excess capacity created by continuing technological change. See Veblen (1904, pp. 217–255). Hamilton did not, however, apply the argument as generally as did Veblen.

[10] Hamilton and Clay had come to know each other well and corresponded on this and other issues. Clay sent his proposal to the British Coal Commission as an alternative to nationalization of the coal industry under a government ministry on the one hand and unrestricted private enterprise on the other. R. H. Tawney, a member of the Commission, responded with the question "where does the State come in?" (Henry Clay to Walton Hamilton, 24 January 1928, Walton Hamilton Papers, Box J5, Folder 5).

the joint control of workers and consumers. The right to income from investment and the right to "a voice in control" are to be separated.

In this new company, the existing ownership equities are to be exchanged by an issue of debentures on "the basis of an equivalence of values," the interest payments on these debentures being a first charge on the new company. Control is to be given by a small number of shares of common stock, which entitle the various classes of holders to participate in the election of members of the Board of Directors. These shares pay no dividends. Class A shares give a right to one vote in the election of a voting member of the board. These shares are to be defined as belonging to specific blocks that represent the right to fill "a specified seat at the board." Half the shares are to be allocated to workers in the form of a general association, "of which every employee of the company is to be a member," and half to consumers in the form of trade associations or other representative bodies. These shares are to be divided among consumers in proportion to their consumption. As domestic consumers have no representative body, their shares will be held in trust by the President of the United States. An even smaller number of Class B shares are to be issued, again in blocks, with each block representing a nonvoting seat on the board. These shares are to be distributed to administrative and technical staff, their representatives on the board to provide advice, information, and criticism. The board is fourteen members (ten voting) plus a nonvoting Chairman to be selected from without (Hamilton and Wright 1928, pp. 166–173).

Hamilton was clearly very pleased with his proposal, and it is mentioned as an example of an inventive scheme of control in a number of his courses and published papers.[11] His suggestions do not seem to have had the impact he hoped for, but Hamilton was involved in discussions concerning the regulation of the coal industry, both immediately before and during the New Deal, and it is quite likely that his involvement did result in the specific inclusion of representation of the consumer interest, which is a notable feature of the 1935 Bituminous Coal Conservation Act (Guffey Coal Act).[12]

[11] The course outline for "Control of Industrial Development" given at Brookings in 1925 contains significant discussion of Hamilton's scheme. This indicates that the scheme, at least in a basic form, had been worked out well before the publication of the second coal book in 1928. Here Hamilton calls his ideas "a pretty way out of a pretty mess" (Walton Hamilton Papers, Box J6, Folder 1). Hamilton also discusses his scheme in Hamilton (1932b).

[12] See Norman Myers to Walton Hamilton 27 April 1933; and Nathan Margold to Walton Hamilton, 27 April 1933, Hamilton Papers, Box J5, Folder 5. See also Walton Hamilton to Norman Myers, 23 May 1933, Walton Hamilton Papers, Box J46, Folder 3, and a letter to Hamilton from an unknown correspondent (second page of the letter is missing) at Yale

Hamilton's proposals for the unification of the coal industry would, of course, run afoul of the antitrust laws, and Hamilton was an active participant in the debates over antitrust, which developed in the late 1920s and early 1930s out of the 1926 proposals of the Committee on Revision of the Anti-Trust Laws of the American Bar Association, and the Swope plan of 1931, with its suggestion for industrial control and price fixing by trade associations (Fetter 1932; Barber 1988 p.121; Mayhew 1998, pp. 193–195). In this period of his thinking, Hamilton was sharply critical of the antitrust laws. The Sherman and Clayton Acts and the Federal Trade Commission were attempts by the state to enforce competition based on the textbook model of competitive markets. But that model is one that applies to a world of petty trade and not to a world of modern technology and big business. The antitrust laws, in their attempt to "stay the development of large scale enterprise and to make big business behave as if it were petty trade," embody and "express the common sense of another age" (Hamilton 1932a, pp. 591–592).

Hamilton also points out the difficulties in translating economic concepts into legal categories such as that of "conspiracies in restraint of trade"; the clumsy and often inappropriate nature of cases at law in deciding issues of trade practice; the business tactics of delay and invention of new and alternative practices; the decisions made in one case sometimes becoming unfortunate and limiting precedents in others; and the highly uneven record of enforcement (Hamilton 1932a; 1932b; 1932c). But, for Hamilton, the most fundamental problem is that in many industries, such as bituminous coal, lack of competition is not the problem, and an enforced competition would simply lead to more "waste and disorder." Isolated judgments by "the executives of rival businesses" do not necessarily "exorcise plant waste, eliminate surplus capacity, and articulate neat establishments into an orderly industry." The "tyranny" of overhead costs and excess capacity can lead to an "overdone competition" with unprofitable prices, low wages, and irregular production (Hamilton 1932c, p. 167). Nevertheless, the danger of monopoly control means that the antitrust acts cannot simply be repealed; they must be replaced by some other form of control.

Hamilton suggests that "order" might be achieved along one of three lines. First, competition could be retained but regulated to "escape the evils which attend it." Echoing H. C. Adams, Hamilton argues the "plane of competition" could be established by law, and new devices invented to "take up

Law School, 19 May 1933, Hamilton Papers Box J4, Folder 5. This last refers to "Hamilton's Coal Bill" and the use of a rebate of tax to obtain the assent of the operators.

the shock of competition." A body could be established to pass "in advance upon the practices of trade." Second, some industries could be recognized as monopolistic in nature and regulated through commissions. Such commissions are supposed to protect the public interest, and Hamilton notes the popularity of this form of regulation. All the same, he argues that the "dual control" inherent in most commissions means in effect that "private interests are able to do as they please, subject to the delayed approval or disapproval of the commission," and disagreements are likely to end up in court. Third, there "is at least a possibility of contriving for certain industries a control from within," but it is essential here that control of the industry not be limited to those who make profits from it, but also include labor and consumer interests (Hamilton 1932b, pp.11–12). What is needed is "an intellectual and experimental attitude" (Hamilton 1932b, p. 21).

This attitude is also apparent in Hamilton's work on the provision of medical care. Interest in medical care and health insurance has a considerable history among American progressives. Indeed, the American Association for Labor Legislation (AALL) had begun studying compulsory health insurance (along the lines of European schemes) as early as 1912, and by 1915 was actively promoting a model bill (Chasse 1994; Ross 2002). Despite initial support, the efforts of the AALL ultimately failed, but the pursuit of the issue was revived in the late 1920s due to increasing concern over the rising costs of medical care – costs that were leaving even those of reasonable means unable to pay for medical services. Technical developments in medicine, advances in surgery, and higher physician's fees were all partly responsible. In 1926, a small group, "The Committee of Five," including Walton Hamilton, was formed to discuss a possible reorganization of medicine. Out of this came the CCMC that set about a five-year study of the economics of health care. Hamilton was an important member of this Committee.[13]

The final report of the Committee was issued in 1932. It contained a set of majority recommendation, two sets of minority recommendations, and

---

[13] The Committee eventually grew to forty-eight members. Wesley Mitchell was a member, although less involved in the Committee's work than Hamilton. The research staff of the Committee included three of Hamilton's students from Brookings, and one, Harry H. Moore, was the Director of Research and wrote *American Medicine and the Peoples' Health* (1927), and the chapter on health, "Health and Medical Practice," in *Recent Social Trends* (1933). Hamilton planned to write a book on the economics of health, initially with Helen Wright as a coauthor. Some drafts were written, but no book was ever published (Helen Wright to Walton Hamilton, 18 November no year, Hamilton Papers, Box J4, Folder 5; and the drafts of "Medicine in the Making," Hamilton Papers, Box J12, Folder 1 and Box J41, Folder 4).

two individual statements of dissent, one written by Hamilton. The majority report favored group practice and the extension of basic public health services to the whole population, but even though it recommended group payment schemes of various possible types, it stopped short of compulsory health insurance. The first minority report opposed group practice and any government involvement other than in the care of the indigent, and even opposed voluntary insurance unless professionally controlled. This was the position adopted by the American Medical Association (AMA). Hamilton occupied the other extreme of the opinions expressed. For him, the majority report failed to go far enough and should have made a clear-cut recommendation for compulsory medical insurance[14] and outlined a well-defined organizational alternative. As it stood, the majority report failed to keep the distinction between the technology of medicine and its organization clearly in mind, failed to place the problem in its proper social and historical setting, and failed to realize the essentially "instrumental character of the agencies which we employ toward health" (Hamilton 1932d, p.190).

What Hamilton saw in the case of medicine was an older ideal of professional practice becoming converted into "a system of individual business competition" (Hamilton 1932d, p. 193). But in medicine, the market mechanism suffers from a number of deficiencies. The patient has insufficient knowledge to judge the quality of the service given; medical charges can vary substantially between doctors and are often not known in advance; medical costs can be high, come unexpectedly, and be difficult or impossible to meet out of current income; and the incentives of money making may be inconsistent with professional standards and ethics. At the same time, the technical advances in medicine were making medicine an increasingly complex "network of interlocking services" (Hamilton 1930a; Hamilton 1932d, pp. 193–194). Hamilton's solution was compulsory insurance, group practice, and the removal of "the aims and the arrangements for profit making" from the practice of medicine (Hamilton 1932d, p. 195). This last was to be accomplished by making each group practice a nonprofit corporation with a board of trustees made up of lay people, none of whom should have any commercial interest in the venture. The professional staff should be paid by salary and promotion based on medical competence. The corporation could set aside reserves, establish pension funds, but it should not pay

---

[14] Eight signers of the majority report dissented on the issue of compulsory insurance alone. These included Wesley Mitchell. The authors of the first minority report were eight private practitioners and one representative of the Catholic hospitals (Chasse 1994, p. 1070; Ross 2002, p. 132).

out dividends or engage in profit making. Hamilton's model was the university: "In its larger outlines this scheme of organization is not a novelty; it is adapted to a profession engaged in public service; its value has been attested by its employment in education" (Hamilton 1932d, p. 197). The involvement of the state "must be invoked to make membership compulsory," to ensure the collection of the premiums or taxes involved, and to make financial redistributions between centers, if required, but it "is to be hoped that the concern of the state in the venture can be limited to a use of its power of compulsion in financial matters" (Hamilton 1932d, p. 198).

The majority recommendations of the CCMC failed to withstand the organized opposition of the AMA, and Hamilton's more radical proposals fared even worse. Hamilton did remain involved in health issues, and compulsory health insurance was discussed for inclusion in the Social Security Act. Continued opposition from the medical profession, however, resulted in Edwin Witte removing medical insurance from the bill in order not to endanger the main provisions with respect to unemployment insurance and old-age pensions (Schlabach 1969, p. 114; Hirshfeld 1970, pp. 45–59).[15]

THE JUDICIAL CONTROL OF INDUSTRY

Hamilton's interests had always spanned the disciplines of law and economics, but in the last two years he was at the Brookings Graduate School and then during his long tenure at Yale Law School, he very much refined and developed his interest. In 1928, Hamilton began publishing regularly in law journals and quickly established a reputation for penetrating critiques of particular Supreme Court decisions and fascinating historical analyses of the changing judicial interpretation of key legal terms and doctrines.

In the period from the early 1920s through to the mid 1930s, many of the attempts to further develop regulation and intervention in the economy had run into particular problems in the courts. Legislation was frequently struck down or circumscribed by court decisions and interpretations. Legislation involving minimum wages, regulation of hours of work, regulation of prices, workmen's compensation, and unemployment insurance all ran into difficulty. This problem had much to do with the institutionalist interest in

---

[15] The Social Security Act did provide federal grants to the states for public health programs, and in 1937, the movement for voluntary group prepayment of hospital costs resulted in the Blue Cross program. A leading figure in this was C. Rufus Rorem, who had been a member of the CCMC research staff (Chasse1994; Ross 2002). For further information on the CCMC and the later campaign for compulsory medical insurance, see Perkins (1998) and Hirshfeld (1970).

law and economics, an interest that also involved John R. Commons, J. M. Clark, Robert Hale, and others. Leo Wolman, writing in 1927, lamented the retreat from social control that had occurred since World War I, and the increasing resistance to even "modest programs of reform" (Wolman 1927). Hamilton's main concern was with the Court interpreting the Constitution in ways overly limiting to the exercise of the police power of the state. The underlying question is "the kind of thing the Constitution is": is it "a fetish which must be served whatever be the resulting inability of the State to look after its own affairs," or is it "an instrument of government" and an "instrument of public welfare" (Hamilton 1928b; 1936b). Hamilton's special target for criticism was Justice Sutherland who often spoke for the conservative majority of the Court,[16] while his sympathies were more with the opinions of the "liberal" contingent of Justices Holmes, Stone, Brandeis, and Cardozo (after he replaced Holmes).[17] For Hamilton, the coming of industrialism had created a host of new economic and social problems that demanded some response in the form of state regulation, including the regulation of prices, and in his view, there was nothing in the Constitution that prevented the use of the police power of the state in the cause of public welfare. Such prohibitions as Justice Sutherland discovered were not to be found plainly in the text of the Constitution, but were the result of attaching new meanings and constructions to words, and to a reading into the Constitution of meanings and economic philosophies quite alien to the minds of those who had first constructed it (Hamilton 1936b; Hamilton and Adair 1937).

An example of the type of critical analysis of judicial decisions Hamilton's work provides can be found in his article, "The Regulation of Employment Agencies" (Hamilton 1928b). The majority of the Court had denied to the state of New Jersey the right to regulate the fees charged by private employment agencies. The majority opinion written by Justice Sutherland is presented in the form of a syllogism:

The major premise comes easily: if a business is "not affected with a public interest," the fixing of prices by the state is "a deprivation of property" without "due process of law." The minor premise presents more difficulty and is achieved only through a series of steps. They are in order: (1) the business of dealing in theatre tickets has

---

[16]   The four most consistently conservative justices, Sutherland, Butler, McReynolds, and Van Devanter, were popularly known as "the four horsemen."

[17]   Hamilton was quite aware of the differences in approach of Justices such as Holmes, Brandeis, and Cardozo. He was also not unaware of their failings. On Holmes and Brandeis, see Hamilton (1931d; 1941b); on Cardozo, see Hamilton (1938b). Hamilton also "previewed" Felix Frankfurter when he became a Supreme Court Justice (Hamilton 1939a).

been held to be not "affected with a public interest;" (2) therefore the work of "a broker, that is of an intermediary" is not "affected with a public interest;" (3) "the business of securing employment for those seeking work and employees for those seeking workers is essentially that of a broker;" and (4) therefore, the business of running an employment agency is not affected with a public interest. (Hamilton 1928b, p. 231)

The questions Hamilton raises are many. Does the regulation of fees amount to price fixing? Why is the statute not valid under the police power, as a regulation designed to correct a persistent and well-recognized evil? Why does the concept of "public interest" have to be employed in the cases involving regulation of price when it does not have to be so used to justify many other forms of government regulation? What exactly is the basis for "affectation with a public interest" if not a need for regulation evidenced by the importance of the business to the public and the failure of the competitive system to protect the public interest? Where does the category of "brokers" come from, all of whose business is not affected with a public interest? Why does the basis of distinction lie in a mere stage of a marketing process with no connection to the issues of evils, regulation, or government control? Hamilton makes a contrast with the dissenting opinion written by Justice Stone (and supported by Holmes and Brandeis) that is "simple, clear cut, and direct." As the issue is the validity of an act of regulation, he "looks to see whether there was warrant for the specific exercise of power." He is interested in whether evils exist, whether they are grave and persistent and with adverse consequences for the public. He asks whether the regulation is suited to its purpose. He has no difficulty distinguishing ticket brokers from employment agencies in terms of their importance to the public. He sees the action of the legislature "as a proper regulation" designed to remedy a public evil. Hamilton sees the minority position being in accord with the longer legal tradition; it is Sutherland and the "conservative" majority who are providing the "radical innovations" and who "read into the Constitution of the United States the original ideas of ingenious attorneys for plaintiffs in error" (Hamilton 1928b, pp. 233–234).[18]

Analyses such as this led Hamilton to inquire more deeply into the beginnings and subsequent histories of interpretation of a number of key

---

[18] Other decisions analyzed by Hamilton include a 1929 decision unfavorable to farmers' cooperatives written by Justice Sutherland (Hamilton 1929b), a 1931 decision favorable to the regulation of commissions paid by insurance companies to agents and written by Justice Brandeis (Hamilton 1931b), and a decision written by Justice Roberts allowing a political party, as a voluntary association, to exclude blacks from voting in primaries (Hamilton 1935a). He also wrote on a number of the decisions concerning New Deal legislation, which will be dealt with further in the chapter.

legal concepts and doctrines. Most significant are his investigations of "affectation with a public interest" (Hamilton 1930b) and the "due process" and "equal protection" clauses of the Fourteenth Amendment (Hamilton 1938a).[19] "Affectation with a public interest" is a term lifted from a decision of Lord Hale in England in 1676 concerning the regulation of charges at a public wharf. The term is not stressed and it is not made a test for the right of the state to regulate prices. At that time, the regulation of prices was commonplace, and in England, "even to this day Parliament decides for itself how far it may go in the control of industry" (Hamilton 1930b, p. 1094). The term came into American law in the famous case of *Mun* v. *Illinois* in 1877, concerning the regulation of charges by grain elevators. Here the representatives of the elevator operators argued the principle to be a limitation of legislative action to only those businesses affected with a public interest. They lost the case, but the opinion of the Court accepted the principle. In successive decisions, the principle went through some changes in definition that extended the concept but narrowed its meaning. It was used to allow regulation of railway rates on the grounds of "public use." The concept was later translated back to a broader "public concern" with a business, and by 1914, the principle had become "a general, if indefinite, invitation to the legislature to extend price control where the public concern demands it" (Hamilton 1930b, p. 1099). In the 1920s, a number of institutionalist writers explicitly looked to the principle to provide a legal basis for the regulation of business.[20]

Legal interpretations, however, began to change with the Supreme Court of 1921–1923. The work of this Court was marked by the formal recognition of "affectation with a public interest" as a "definite test of constitutionality of price fixing regulation" (at least by the majority), but the same Court sought to narrow its range. Throughout the 1920s "a phrase brought into constitutional law to sanction price fixing" was "consistently used to outlaw

[19] Hamilton also wrote pieces on the history of caveat emptor (Hamilton 1931c), of the concept of property (Hamilton 1932e), the treatment of small debtors (Hamilton 1933a), of the law surrounding compensation for workplace accident (Hamilton 1937), and antitrust (Hamilton 1940a). Hamilton's former teacher and friend, Alvin Johnson, asked Hamilton to write the entries for the *Encyclopaedia of the Social Sciences* on accumulation, acquisition, affectation with public interest, caveat emptor, celibacy, collective bargaining, collectivism, competition, constitutionalism, Charles Horton Cooley, damages, freedom of contract, institution, judicial process, John Stuart Mill, organization–economic, police power, and property.

[20] See particularly Tugwell (1922). For a more sanguine view, see Clark (1926). Hamilton's students Dexter Keezer and Stacy May (1930) also discuss the principle in detail. See Chapters 6 and 8 in this book.

price fixing" (Hamilton 1930b, p. 1100). The principle became a barrier to the ability of states to respond to public concerns via price regulation; the constitutional "test" of affectation being substituted for a recognition of police power and an appraisal of the need for and reasonableness of the regulation in question.

The injunction that "no person shall be deprived of life, liberty or property without due process of law" was contained in the Fifth Amendment, but until after the Civil War was regarded as a procedural concern only. After the Civil War, the Fourteenth Amendment was passed to ensure the rights of the newly enfranchised blacks. The key phrases in the Amendment are "all persons born or naturalized in the United States, and subject to the jurisdiction thereof, are citizens of the United Sates and of the state wherein they reside," and "no State shall make or enforce any law which shall abridge the privileges or immunities of citizens of the United States; nor shall any State deprive any person of life, liberty, or property without due process of law; nor deny to any person within its jurisdiction the equal protection of the laws" (Hamilton 1938a, p. 271). Hamilton traces the history of the attempts to read substantive rights into the due process clause. The first of these occurred with the well-known "slaughterhouse cases" of the 1880s. Initially a corporation was given a monopoly on slaughtering, and the legal representative of independent slaughtermen attempted to argue that a property – the right to follow their trade – had been removed without due process.[21] The argument failed, but a few years later, when the monopoly privilege was revoked, the corporation attempted the same line of argument. That too failed, but in a concurring opinion, two justices effectively revisited the original case and argued that the original grant of the monopoly privilege was indeed unconstitutional and should never have been given in the first place. Thus, despite the losses to the older doctrine of police power, the argument remained in use acquiring "a momentum and an enhancing repute in the opinions in dissent." It was strengthened by a 1886 recognition that the term "person" included corporations, which extended to them the protection of due process and equal protection (Hamilton 1938a, p. 284–286). In the 1890s, rulings on the ability of the Railroad Commission to set rates created, in the name of due process, a "judicial overlordship over

---

[21] John R. Commons also discusses this sequence of cases concerning the liberty, property, and due process clauses of the Fourteenth Amendment, but more with an eye to the shift in the property concept from tangible to intangible. See Commons (1924a, pp. 11–21). These cases were also important in the area of public utility regulation and were discussed in that context by Commons, James Bonbright, and Robert Hale, as well as by Hamilton. For Hamilton's contribution, see (Hamilton 1938c).

what up to that moment been set down as the province of the legislature." In later decisions, the word "liberty" became defined to encompass "freedom of contract," but it was only in 1905 and the case of *Lochner* v. *New York* that "due process first won in a clean-cut combat with the police power" (Hamilton 1938a, pp. 287–290).

The *Lochner* case concerned the regulation of the hours of work of bakers, purportedly on grounds of public health. The majority opinion of the Court found freedom of contract an aspect of liberty and property that "a state may not abridge without due process of law." The opinion of the court was "intended to be an apostolic letter to the many legislatures in the land appointing limits to their police power and laying a ban on social legislation" (Hamilton 1938a, pp. 291–292). The case, however, also occasioned Justice Holmes's famous dissent where he argued that the relation of the hours of bakers to public health was one of fact, that "general propositions do not decide concrete cases," that the liberty of the citizen "is interfered with by school laws, by the Post Office, by every state or municipal institution which takes his money for purposes thought desirable," and that "the Fourteenth Amendment does not enact Mr. Herbert Spencer's *Social Statics*" (http://laws.findlaw.com/us/198/45.html). Hamilton argues that whereas it "is common for latter-day liberals to set this down as the first blast of the trumpet in behalf of social oversight of human rights," the historian is more likely to see it "as a lance worthily broken in behalf of an ancient cause now in retreat" (Hamilton 1938a, p. 292):

A constitutional doctrine contrived to protect the natural rights of men against corporate monopoly was little by little commuted into a formula for safeguarding the domain of business against the regulatory power of the state. The chartered privileges of the corporation became rights which could be pleaded in equity and at law against the government which created them. In a litigious procedure in which private right was balanced against the general good the ultimate word was given to the judiciary. (Hamilton 1938a, p. 293)

THE NEW DEAL: CONSUMERS, CODES, AND PRICE POLICY

The coming of the Depression, its persistence, and the obvious dislocation of the "economic order" only confirmed for Hamilton the pressing need for new forms of control. In a 1931 discussion of "ways out," he emphasized, as did many institutionalists, the paradox of a vast capacity to produce in excess of current production together with and an equally large capacity to use in excess of current consumption, and argued for some form of "centralized control of the conditions upon which the general welfare of the people in an industry rests." The solution lay in a system where decentralized decision making in business was combined with a social control that recognized the public interest in the performance of business and industry (Hamilton 1931e).

Two years later, and exactly as the National Industrial Recovery Act (NIRA) was being passed, Hamilton reviewed Rexford Tugwell's plea for a more planned economy, *The Industrial Discipline and the Governmental Arts* (Hamilton 1933b; Tugwell 1933). As Hamilton points out, the book lacks a detailed discussion of devices for control, but Tugwell's notions of the "governmental arts" certainly include the encouragement of industrial integration (to increase efficiency), control over the allocation of capital, and price controls to protect consumers. Despite the lack of detail, Hamilton welcomes the book as an opportune "credo for a grand adventure into social experimentation." It is a philosophy or a charter "for a purposive and orderly industrial system," "an exposition of the storm centres in our industrial culture, a revelation of the potentialities in our social resources and the grandest sort of sermon to clear the way for the [N]ational Industrial Recovery Act" (Hamilton 1933b, p. 185).

The NIRA was passed in the summer of 1933, along with much other legislation. Title I of the NIRA declared a national emergency and stated the policy of Congress to promote the organization of industry for the purpose of cooperative action among trade groups, to "induce and maintain united action of labor and management," to "eliminate unfair competitive practices," to promote the full use of resources, to increase consumption by increasing purchasing power, to reduce and relieve unemployment, to improve standards of labor, and to rehabilitate industry and conserve natural resources (Lyon et al. 1935, pp. 15–16). The act established the National Recovery Administration (NRA) that was to be the vehicle to administer this policy through a set of industrial "codes," under which an industry agreeing to minimum wages and certain other labor conditions could establish trade practices to eliminate "unfair competition" and receive immunity from prosecution under the antitrust laws.

The original administrative structure of the NRA created three advisory boards, an Industrial Advisory Board, a Labor Advisory Board, and a Consumers' Advisory Board, to advise the Recovery Administrator (General H. Johnson) on the codes. Even at that time, it was recognized that the CAB worked under the handicap of having no organized pressure group behind it. Moreover, General Johnson tended to identify "business prosperity" with the public interest, so that in the early days of the NRA, there was "a general impatience with 'consumer interruption'" and a tendency to see the CAB as an "annoying and unnecessary fifth wheel calculated to slow up the recovery procession" (Lynd 1934, p. 221; Lyon et al. 1935, pp. 123–129; Campbell 1940, p. 31). Nevertheless, it was also recognized that the explicit inclusion of consumer representation in the NRA (and even more so in the AAA) represented a significant development in the area of business regulation.[22] As stated by Robert Lynd: "The recovery machinery officially recognizes for the first time that the consumer is sitting in on the game, and that the rules and procedures built up over decades of federal coaching to help business do not automatically afford equal aid to the consumer across the table" (Lynd 1934, p. 220).

The first Executive Director of the CAB was William Ogburn, but he resigned in August of 1933 and was replaced by Dexter Keezer, a former Brookings student. Keezer recruited Walton Hamilton to the CAB in October 1933. The CAB also created a "Price Section" to undertake research on prices and price policies, a "Standards Unit" that attempted to develop standard grades and other quality standards and have them established in the codes, and a "Bureau of Economic Education" that was to work on establishing "consumers' councils" to provide a consumer organization.[23] The overall concern of the CAB, however, was that the code-making machinery was being used to advance business interests by establishing minimum prices or some degree of price fixing, effectively raising prices at the expense of consumers. As argued by Gardiner Means, the codes were being used to raise prices to a point "where they yield a profit which could be justified only on a very much larger volume of business" (Means 1934). The CAB's strategy in response was to undertake as much careful study of proposed codes as they could and to present well-documented arguments against provisions they felt were unreasonable. A model for these studies was provided by the submission made late in 1933, objecting to the price provisions for the petroleum industry. This submission was produced by the Price Section together

---

[22] For discussion of consumer representation in the AAA, see Campbell (1940). The AAA included an office of Consumers' Counsel with a significant staff. For further discussion of consumers' representation in the New Deal, see Lynd (1936), Keezer (1934), Tugwell (1935a), and Douglas (1934a).

[23] Corwin Edwards headed the Price Section, which was absorbed into the Research and Planning Division of the NRA in April 1934. Robert Brady headed the Standards Unit and Paul Douglas, the Educational Section. Douglas resigned in April 1934. Opposition to the original CAB plan to set up some 3,000 consumers' councils resulted in only about 150 being established. Brady left in the early summer of 1934, frustrated by lack of resources, but remained involved with issues of industrial standardization (Campbell 1940, pp. 48–53; Donohue 2003, p. 240). Keezer left the CAB to take up the Presidency of Reed College in July 1934.

with Board members George Stocking and Walton Hamilton. Shortly after, Hamilton produced a published version (Hamilton 1934).

The main argument concerning the petroleum code was that it proposed to establish prices much higher than those then existing, with serious adverse consequences for consumer purchasing power. Control of output was suggested as an alternative and preferable way to bring some "order" into the industry, provided that the control was supervised by all the interests concerned and not just by producers. The brief also contained a more general argument in which Hamilton discussed the difficulties in transferring control of prices to an administrative board. In this part, it becomes clear that Hamilton's reservations about the commission form of control had grown. He argues that commissions do not contain real consumer representation. The personnel with authority are government appointees "and all of the indirection, exigency and pressure which we associate with the word 'politics' find expression in appointments and in judgment":

The powers possessed by a commission to create or destroy property values and to divert income from one economic group to another make a commission a prize worthy of political capture. The system of regulation has put public utilities into politics; and a small compact group is usually, if not always, more powerful than a larger and unorganized host. (Hamilton 1934, p. 78)

Thus, any board or agency set up to control prices must have proper representation of consumers and not be dominated by the producer interest. It must also have available to it objectively determined (by independent technical staff) information concerning the "necessary social costs of production" that the prices charged would have to cover. In Hamilton's mind this involved not merely an accounting of actual business costs, but a social accounting based on benchmark operating standards and standards of living (Hamilton 1934, p. 96).

The early months of 1934 saw a large amount of criticism of the NRA codes from sources both inside and outside of the NRA.[24] Two results of this debate are relevant here. In May 1934, an Advisory Council of the NRA was established to reconcile differences of opinion between the three advisory boards. Walton Hamilton was the first Chairman of this Council and appears to have created a less charged atmosphere within which proposals

---

[24] The NRA held a series of price hearings in January; there was a Senate debate on price and production policy under the NRA also in January and a conference for code authorities was held in March, and in May, the Darrow report on the NRA codes was released. Objections to the codes also came from the Department of Agriculture due to the effects on farm incomes, from the CAB, and from elsewhere within government. See Hawley (1966, pp. 79–97).

could be discussed and such evidence as was available assessed (Campbell 1940, p. 75). Given this, and the equal representation given to the three boards, the consumer point of view began to fare somewhat better. At the same time, and apparently in response to George Terborgh's critical analysis *Price Control Devices in NRA Codes* (Terborgh 1934),[25] a Cabinet Committee on Price Policy was established. Isador Lubin, then Commissioner of Labor Statistics, became Chair of this committee, and Walton Hamilton was placed in charge of a study into prices and price policies. This study became Hamilton's greatest interest, and he clearly hoped much would come of it.

The study as planned contained a number of "lines of investigation": first a discussion of the price system in genetic, descriptive, and analytical terms, with the ultimate goal of outlining the structure of the price system and "the adequacy with which it performs its function"; second, a quantitative study of the behavior of prices under the NRA and a comparison of code and precode prices; third, a series of case studies of price formation in particular industries; and fourth, a series of studies on particular policy problems, including a study of the NRA codes, the cost formula for price, the general problems of price control, and the operation of the antitrust laws. The case studies formed the core of the project and were presented as attempts "to discern the sources of order, and to diagnose the disorders, of various industries." The industries to be studied were chosen on the basis of availability of data, public interest in the industry, and the contribution that the study would make to "a general account of the price system." In some places Hamilton suggests that the industries were chosen as representing items important in determining "the standard of living" (Hamilton 1936a). Included were automobiles, tires, gasoline, cottonseed, milk, whiskey, women's dresses, paper, wastepaper, razor blades, cigarettes, ice, and several others.[26] The goal was to complete a minimum of twenty case studies in order "to secure a picture of the broader aspects of the price system and to reveal those factors which any price policy on the part of the Federal Government must take into consideration" (Walton Hamilton to

---

[25] George Terborgh had been a student of Hamilton's at the Brookings Graduate School. The reference to his book prompting the formation of the Cabinet Committee on Prices comes from a memo written by Leon Henderson to Miss F. M. Robinson, 11 May 1934 (Leon Henderson Papers, NRA Papers, Prices, Cabinet Committee Folder).

[26] Industries such as coal, movies, and sugar are mentioned in some places. The first of the studies were completed in 1934, the last in 1936. They were confidential and not circulated. Hamilton even had a study of the market for art done by an artist Robert Hallowell. Hamilton gave the piece to Mark Adams to revise. Adams eventually produced an essay "The Price of Art" in 1951 (Walton Hamilton to Mark Adams, 11 August 1951, Walton Hamilton Papers, Box J26, Folder 1). Irene Till wrote several of the studies. Her study of

Isador Lubin, 8 October 1934, Leon Henderson Papers, Series: NRA Papers, Folder: Price, Cabinet Committee; Minutes of Meeting of Committee on Prices, 22 October 1934, Gardiner Means Papers, Series I, Folder: Price Fixing). Plan was never to be carried out entirely as the Supreme Court decision declaring the code system unconstitutional came down in May 1935, resulting in the fairly rapid demise of the whole NRA organization. The price studies were first transferred to the Consumers' Division of the NRA (which also absorbed the Consumers' Advisory Board and the Consumers' Division of the National Emergency Council). Hamilton was named Adviser on Consumers' Problems and Director of the Consumers' Division,[27] but by the end of 1935, Hamilton had left to for the Division of Economic Research of the Social Security Board, the Consumers' Division had been transferred to the Department of Labor, and in February 1936 was reduced to the "Consumers' Project" within the Department of Labor and funded by the Works Progress Administration. Clarence Ayres took over the Consumers' Project and continued the price studies through to November 1936 when he resigned.[28]

A selection of the price studies (the case studies on automobiles, tires, gasoline, cottonseed, dresses, whiskey, and milk), together with an introductory and concluding chapter by Hamilton, were eventually published in 1938 (Hamilton and Associates 1938).[29] Given the highly concrete nature of these case studies, it is hard to summarize them or make generalizations – but this was a significant part of Hamilton's point. Here and elsewhere, Hamilton repeatedly argues that industries are not alike; they have their own particular sets of practices and conventions that have grown up within the trade; they differ in scale of enterprise and in the number of

---

the milk industry also became her 1937 PhD thesis in political science from Columbia. She became Hamilton's second wife.

[27] Campbell argues that in this capacity, Hamilton did a poor job of promoting and ensuring some continued basis for the representation of the consumer interest. There is no doubt that Hamilton's major focus at this point was on the price studies. See Campbell (1940, p. 84) and Hamilton (1935b).

[28] Ayres visited Washington to spend a month with Hamilton's group in the summer of 1935. This period and his time in charge of the Consumers' Project was his only employment with the federal government. According to Campbell, Ayres did not agree with Hamilton's ideas concerning the "functional representation of economic interests" in the form of industry, labor, and the consumer. Ayres thought this was likely to lead to "fascism" (Campbell 1940, pp.86–87). He also had arguments with Robert Brady about standards for automobiles (Clarence Ayres Papers, Box 3F285, Robert Brady Folder and Box 3F288, Walton Hamilton Folder).

[29] The quantitative aspect of the study, "Recent Price Behavior," was completed by Willard Thorp (with a number of assistants) in 1934 but not included in the published selection. A copy is available in the Columbia Law Library.

competitors; in the structure of costs and the existence of joint products; in the arrangements made with suppliers and distributors; in the impacts of new technology or of new regulations; in advertising and packaging; and in the ability, and the exact methods used, to confine or limit competition. Each industry's particular pattern is also undergoing continuous change (Hamilton and Associates 1938; Hamilton 1940b). There is no sharp line of demarcation between competition and monopoly, nor even a line running from perfect competition through monopolistic competition, oligopoly, duopoly, to pure monopoly on which particular cases may be set down. To do so "is to make hypothetical economic phenomena the subject of mathematical exercises." The "trick may be pulled off; but the result is not a picture of the pragmatic reality called industry" (Hamilton and Associates 1938, p. 23).[30]

For Hamilton, to understand the variety of industrial practice, to get behind the abstractions of demand and supply, and to come to understand why a price is what it is could serve two important purposes. The first has to do with understanding what, if any, barriers stand in the way of improving the American standard of life: of bringing "the good things of life within the reach of the great mass of people" (Hamilton 1936a, p. 7). Here, the point of attack of the price studies "is what lies back of a price – to make it high or low – to restrict or enlarge supply – to bring it within the reach of the few or the many." They are thus part of a campaign against waste, disorder, and restriction, and for greater abundance and higher living standards (Hamilton 1936a, p. 9). This is entirely of a piece with Hamilton's earlier work on the costs of medical care. The second function has to do with the design of business regulation and programs for control. Business interests and the mechanism of price do not necessarily lead to an industry functioning in a way compatible with the public interest, but any system of control has to be sensitive to particulars:

The road towards industrial government runs by way of authority and the particular. A proper freedom of collective action, within strict limits of public interest, must be accorded the agencies of business. The state in formulating public policy, must have a wide discretion, and statutes should be written in the broadest of terms. But a way of order and a program of control can be crowded into no set formula. The general standards of industrial code and legislative standard must be adapted to the shifting circumstances of particular industries. Since usage is

---

[30] Needless to say, Hamilton's price studies did not go down well with more orthodox economists. See the review by Mund (1938) and Hamilton's reply titled "Industrial Inquiry and Sectarian Dogma" (Hamilton 1939b).

forever on the make the exercise of authority must be grounded in a continuing exploration of industrial arrangements. (Hamilton and Associates 1938, p. 555)

Hamilton's involvement with the CAB, his chairmanship of the Advisory Board, and his membership of the National Industrial Recovery Board brought him into close contact with the processes of code making under the NRA. Hamilton gave testimony to the Senate hearings in 1935 considering the continuation of the NRA. Apart from public utilities, Hamilton divided industries into those where competition "works not perfectly but at least reasonably well," those where competition is "underdone" due to restrictive practices of some kind, and those where competition is "overdone," such as in coal and textiles. The last two cases represent areas for intervention, although the problems involved are quite distinct (Hamilton 1935c, p. 2047).

It is clear that Hamilton favored the retention of the NRA, although with modifications. Hamilton wished to see a clear statement that all industry is affected by a public interest, to give the State the right "to break in whenever the State decides that the conduct of the industry is not serving the interests of all who have a stake in it" (Hamilton 1935c, p. 2053); a clear positive affirmation that the codes must be constructed with a view to preventing monopoly, and not merely that they should not encourage monopoly; and that all interest groups, including consumers and workers, have input into the code making. In terms of the administration of codes, if the code controls prices or production, then the code authority must include more than the business interest (Hamilton 1935c, pp. 2046–2050). If the code involves a public interest, then public officials should be involved in its administration; no group "should be in the double position of an interested party and a judge of their actions at the same time" (Hamilton 1935c, p. 2052). Further, the notion of "unfair competition" should be broadened to include unethical business practices that might lower the plane of competition, competition that is unfair to labor, and competition that is unfair to the consumer. The provision of information to the code authorities should also be required.

In terms of the antitrust laws, Hamilton states that he has no quarrel with the ultimate purposes of the acts, but reiterates his view that the mechanism of legal proceeding and criminal prosecution is flawed. The issue is "whether we can devise better mechanisms than the Antitrust Act for accomplishing the same purpose" (Hamilton 1935c, p. 2057). The antitrust laws and the Federal Trade Commission provide only "a measure of protection" of the public interest. Hamilton argues that "it is quite possible through the NRA to add to that another measure of protection and probably a more important measure of protection than has yet been achieved." The antitrust act is only a "tentative answer" to the problem of the control of industry – "it is an instrument, it is a mechanism, and not a final answer to the problem" (Hamilton 1935c, p. 2058):

> I think the NRA can do a constructive job that the Federal Trade Commission and the Department of Justice cannot do, by devising administrative remedies against monopoly. I think they can also address themselves to the job of trying to find out why various industries are not turning out goods in greater abundance and why the American standard of living is as low as it is. That is a long time job; it is not a matter of panacea; it is a matter of detailed treatment. (Hamilton 1935c, p. 2059)

It is no surprise, then, to find Hamilton reacting negatively to the series of Supreme Court decisions that struck down the NRA code-making machinery in 1935, and then the Guffey Coal Act and parts of the AAA in 1936. Hamilton outlines the course of development of Court decisions: in 1934, in the *Nebbia* case, "it was willing to allow remedial legislation to take its course;" in the next year, the Court first began to use "procedural devices" against Federal legislation, but then moved to substantive issues to strike down the industrial codes of the NRA. By the winter, the Court "was ready to pass the death sentence upon the Agricultural Adjustment Act; and in the spring of 1936 it laid on with abandon against all social legislation, state and national" (Hamilton 1938b, p. 17). Fear of the President's power and the "ghost of an imaginary fascism" deflected even Brandeis and Stone from their customary views.

In the NRA case the Court held that the NRA codes represented an unconstitutional delegation of legislative power to the President. Cardozo and Stone in their separate concurring opinion went less far. They also found the delegated powers granted to be too unconstrained, but agreed that Congress itself could not set up standards for regulation for all industries given their variety and number.[31] In retrospect, Hamilton conceded that the NRA should have begun with key industries such as coal, oil, lumber, and textiles where "disorder was notorious." The NRA could have been revised to "surrender its control over local industries" and had its deficiencies repaired by new legislation (Hamilton and Associates 1938, p. 21).[32] The case concerning the AAA was decided by a majority of the Court who ruled

---

[31] In an earlier case concerning the "hot oil" industry, Cardozo had not objected to the delegation of powers as the delegation was "narrow" and what could be done "is closely and clearly circumscribed both as to subject-matter and to occasion." Cardozo was in a minority of one in that opinion. See http://newdeal.feri.org/court/293US388.htm

[32] After the NRA decision, a number of people, including Tugwell, Ezekiel, and Galloway, attempted to gather interest in an "Industrial Expansion Act." This act was modeled on the

the tax on processors to provide revenue to pay farmers to take land out of production – a central part of the program – to be coercive and unconstitutional. Stone, Brandeis and Cardozo dissented on the grounds that the tax was levied in accord with legislation passed by Congress, and "Courts are not the only agency that must be assumed to have capacity to govern" (http://newdeal.feri.org/court/297US1.htm).

The Bituminous Coal Conservation Act (Guffey Coal Act) was passed in 1935 to replace the NRA code and to regulate prices, minimum wages, maximum hours of work, and "fair practices." A tax was levied, but those who complied were given tax refunds. The Act established a National Bituminous Coal Commission, a Coal Labor Board, and a Consumers' Council. In 1936, the Act was declared unconstitutional largely on the grounds that labor conditions were local, within state, and not interstate evils, and therefore did not fall under Federal jurisdiction. Cardozo, Brandeis, and Stone again dissented, taking the view that coal production was an interstate business and that the conditions in the coal industry meant that "Commerce had been choked and burdened; its normal flow had been diverted from one state to another; there had been bankruptcy and waste and ruin alike for capital and for labor. The liberty protected by the Fifth Amendment does not include the right to persist in this anarchic riot" (http://newdeal.feri.org/court/298US238.htm). Hamilton poured scorn on the view that the meaning of interstate commerce was to be narrowly construed to apply only the interstate movement of goods. This interpretation was the one Justice Sutherland claimed was "used in the Constitution," but, as Hamilton argued at length, the Constitution was written by a group consisting in large part of those of a mercantilist mentality for whom "commerce" meant nothing less than the whole of production and trade (Hamilton and Adair 1937). The paradox is that "as industry has become more and more interstate in character, the power of Congress to regulate has been given narrower and narrower interpretation" (Hamilton and Adair 1937, p. 192).

In 1937, after Roosevelt's threat to pack the Court but before any change in membership, the Court began a rapid process of reversing its opposition

ideas contained in Mordecai Ezekiel's book *$2,500 A Year* (Ezekiel 1936), which argued that a moderate standard of living could be attained by all via a planning agency similar in some respects to the AAA. It was also to use a processing tax, the receipts to go to those signing agreements concerning output, price, working conditions, etc. The effort picked up some support and bills were introduced in 1937 (See Hawley 1966, pp. 179–184). A copy of the bill and correspondence between Hamilton and Galloway concerning it can be found in the Walton Hamilton Papers (Box J45, Folder 1). Ezekiel's later *Jobs for All Through Industrial Expansion* (1939a) was a summary version of the industrial expansion plan (Mordecai Ezekiel Papers, Boxes 11, 12, and 19).

to social legislation. The Social Security and National Labor Relations Acts were upheld and "a body of constitutional doctrine, lately overlooked or relegated to dissent, was rediscovered" (Hamilton 1938b, p. 19). A replacement Coal Act was passed in 1937 without the labor conditions, and was upheld.[33] New membership changed the attitude of the court even further (Hamilton and Braden 1941), but the larger NRA experiment would not be revisited, and Hamilton had already turned elsewhere for other possible instruments of control.

ANTITRUST, PATENTS, AND CORPORATE CONTROL

In 1938, Thurman Arnold was appointed head of the Anti-Trust Division of the Department of Justice. In the past, Arnold had been a severe critic of the antitrust laws (Arnold 1937),[34] but he came into his new job determined that the antitrust should be revised so "that the government could strike at market domination, regardless of how the power over prices had been acquired and regardless of motive or intent" (Hawley 1966, p. 411). Arnold had been a long-time colleague of Hamilton's at Yale, and between 1938 and 1945, Hamilton worked as a Special Assistant to the Attorney General working on problems of patents, monopoly, and restraint of trade. For Hamilton, Arnold's approach to antitrust linked to his own. Hamilton wrote to Dexter Keezer that Arnold:

is definitely persuaded that if the Anti-Trust Acts are to serve a constructive purpose, they must come to grips with the web of usage in distinctive industries, so he wants to get a number of industrial studies underway. Each will appear as a memo and in form should be comparable to an opinion of the United States Supreme Court that grapples with the law as public policy and stakes its judgments upon a recitation of industrial fact. (Walton Hamilton to Dexter Keezer, 11 May 1938, Walton Hamilton Papers, Box J9, Folder 8)

---

[33] It is interesting that when this act was due to expire in 1941, Hamilton leapt to the defense of continuing with the "experiment" in control. Eugene Rostow, a Yale Law School colleague of Hamilton's, wrote an article arguing that the 1937 act had been an experiment that failed to work. Conditions had changed, and expansion of the economy and public welfare would be better served by government spending and imaginative enforcement of the antitrust laws (Rostow 1941). Hamilton replied with a defense of the 1937 act, which maintained that all the causes of past "disorder" were still present in the industry, and that both the coal act and deficit spending were "experiments" that would require adjustment as they proceeded (Hamilton 1941c).

[34] In the Hamilton papers, there is an undated piece called "Scattered Thoughts on Thorstein Veblen," written by Hamilton for Thurman Arnold. It ends: "This, I hope, supplies enough material for a bridge from Veblen to Arnold. Once the bridge is half way crossed, Arnold is on his own" (Walton Hamilton Papers, Box J29, Folder 3).

On the same day, Hamilton wrote to the publisher of *Price and Price Policies* that Arnold is insisting that the Department of Justice "get down to concretions" and deal with the "web of industrial usage," and that Arnold's approach "is an application of the approach worked out in 'Price and Price Policies', and I wish we had some way of advertising the fact."[35]

Hamilton's involvement included work on briefs including antitrust suits brought against the AMA for their actions against experiments in group health (Hamilton 1938d), the movie industry for its distribution practices, and many others (Hamilton 1940b). But the major products of Hamilton's time with the Anti-Trust Division were two reports for the TNEC: *Antitrust in Action* (Hamilton and Till 1940a) and *Patents and Free Enterprise* (Hamilton 1941a). In the first of these studies, and in a related paper (Hamilton and Till 1940b), Hamilton repeats many of the concerns he had expressed before concerning the inappropriate nature of legal proceedings, particularly criminal proceedings, for dealing with matters of trade practice, and the problems of some industries being an "overdone" competition rather than a lack of it. In such industries where the problem is an "overplus" of competition – as in bituminous coal, women's dresses, shoe making, and automobile dealerships – any concerted move against "disaster" may run afoul of the law (Hamilton and Till 1940a, p. 19). Hamilton also discusses the development of new forms of restraint involving various forms of tacit collusion, price leadership, delivered price systems, "quality standards," patents and licence agreements, unequal bargaining power as between large manufacturers and their suppliers or distributors, and regulations originally enacted to protect a public interest being turned into a "smoke screen for vested interest" (Hamilton and Till 1940a, pp. 12–19).

Hamilton goes on to suggest two avenues of change, the first involving a "streamlining" of the antitrust acts and the second a move to an administrative rather than a judicial base. Streamlining would involve providing adequate funding, a power of subpoena, a greater use of the equity decree in place of criminal actions, a shift from crime to tort, a penalty equal to twice the total net income gained during the period of wrongdoing, placing the burden of proof on the party that enjoys access to all the facts, and providing the consumer with a cause for action (Hamilton and

---

[35] Walton Hamilton to Hugh Kelly, 11 May 1938, Walton Hamilton Papers, Box J22, Folder 2. The Arnold/Hamilton case-by-case approach did not find favor with all antitrusters. Frank Fetter clearly wanted a more general approach to antitrust policy. Paul Homan wrote to Jerome Frank and Hamilton expressing hope that the disagreements would not work to the detriment of the whole antitrust enterprise (see Paul Homan to Jerome Frank, 14 March 1939, Walton Hamilton Papers, Box J31, Folder 3).

Till 1940a, pp. 101–106). Hamilton, however, regards these reforms as insufficient because they fail to penetrate to "the heart of the difficulty." What is required is a movement that develops the advisory opinion and consent decree of the Department of Justice into an administrative system that can provide for a flexible and timely case-by-case approach. This cannot "come into practice full blown" but must "begin as a cautiously experimental power" (Hamilton and Till 1940a, p. 108). An administrative system would allow for the approval in advance of "a code of industrial behavior," with the government and industry in cooperation spelling out "a line of business activity which is believed to accord with public policy, and in the furtherance of which immunity from prosecution is promised" (Hamilton and Till 1940b, p. 19). This process requires information about the industry to be gathered, analyzed, and kept up to date. Agreements cannot be permanent as conditions change, so that every measure is subject to correction. Agreements require oversight and policing, but with breaches treated as a civil offense and punishable by fines. A "Decree Section" should be established and be concerned with industrial analysis and remedies rather than litigation. Judicial review should be by a "specially constructed industrial court" with five or seven members well versed in the ways of industry.

As a "caveat" to his proposals, Hamilton raises the problem of administrative processes being "captured" by the business interests they are supposed to regulate. Commissions have "closed public utilities to outsiders"; the various agricultural controls have been "sensitive to the plight of the farmers, negligent of farm labor, and indifferent to the general public who must pay the bill"; the NRA "staged a full dress performance of the hazards of the administrative process" in which wide powers were granted only to "become sanctions under which the strategic group could lord it over the industry" (Hamilton and Till 1940b, p. 25). This concern was to become increasingly insistent in Hamilton's work in the years after the Second World War.

The issue of patents and their use in certain industries to maintain privileged market positions came to Hamilton's attention during the price studies. As he continued work on this issue, he came to see it as a preeminently important and particularly difficult policy problem. Knowledge is more important than real property, natural resources are largely what the current state of knowledge makes them, and modern industry is "nothing more than our accumulated technical knowledge" (Hamilton 1949a, p. 339). Abundant production and rising standards of living rest on the advance of knowledge and its dissemination.

Patents have as their purpose the promotion of technological advance, but Hamilton's investigations indicated to him that the existing patent system had numerous failings in achieving that end. Research and invention had become a matter of corporate R&D laboratories. In the hands of corporations, the patent system could easily be used to create control of an industry. A flood of closely related products could be patented, blocking out other competitors; patents could be used to "fence" in an invention, "block" the work of rivals, or "trawl" for information; patent protection could be extended in time by patenting successive modifications; special terms and conditions could be written into patent licences, dividing the market between producers by quota, or territory, or product, and setting prices for various users; patents could be pooled, resulting in a closed and collusive market; and international agreements involving patents provide the basis for trade agreements between firms and international cartels (Hamilton 1941a; Hamilton and Till 1948). With the American involvement in the Second World War, Hamilton also became concerned over Axis control of patents holding up the delivery of strategic materials (Hamilton 1943a).

Hamilton made a number of proposals to improve the patent system. Justice should push forward cases involving restrictive covenants to define more clearly what could and could not be included in a patent licence. An easier and more expeditious method of validation of patents might prevent some pooling of patents, but where pooling was required for efficient production, the pool should be accepted and placed under public authority. Patents not in use should be canceled or compelled to licence. Higher standards for patentability should be established or different types of invention given different types of patent. Here Hamilton wanted to differentiate between genuinely novel and important inventions and mere modifications or variations. For example, applications for reissue or renewal should be prohibited. He also suggested the establishment of a "Public Counsel on Patents" to exercise general oversight of patent grants, of assignments and leases, and of all patent litigation, and with a right to intervene in applications and institute suits in order to protect the public interest (Hamilton 1941a, pp.146–152).

These steps, however, "fall short" of an answer to the problem of accommodating the patent grant "to its corporate and industrial habitat" (Hamilton 1941a, p. 156). If a "fresh slate" were at hand, a system of compulsory licensing might be best, but in the existing circumstances, Hamilton suggests an expert commission of inquiry to consider a more fundamental redesign based on "further study and the formulation of a program" (Hamilton 1941a, p. 163). A National Patent Planning Commission was established in

1942, but produced not a close study or a new program but a skimpy, eleven-page report that "whitewashed" the patent system, ignored the major problems, made proposals that would, if anything, lower the standards of patentability, and suggested extending the time a patent grant could run (Hamilton 1943a).

The conclusion of this work on antitrust and patents was a growing concern on Hamilton's part with the development of what he called "property rights in the market" or "market equities" (Hamilton 1943b). These property rights could take the form of a wide variety of business practices; the requirements of a profession or trade; the control of a strategic ingredient or resource; the protection given to local industries or favored producers by state or national regulations; regulations originally adopted for public benefit turned into barriers to entry; and patents, patent licences, and patent pools used as a basis for the control of markets.[36] Most significantly, corporations have discovered that "regulation is a two edged thing"; controls can be captured and put to uses never intended (Hamilton 1943b, p. 29).

In his work in the late 1940s and 1950s, Hamilton elaborated on this theme and gave it more historical perspective. The failures of the market to properly control business in the public interest had resulted in a move toward regulation. But regulation broke down the older division between state and economy. The most used form of regulatory device, the commission, was particularly susceptible to capture by the interests it was supposed to be regulating, and the campaign for regulation ultimately produced "its own counterrevolution" (Hamilton 1949b; 1957). The "interest to be regulated is compact, organized, mobile," and alert to opportunities. The public interest is general, sluggish, diffused, and "unable to effect a united front or move in time" (Hamilton 1949b, p. 85; 1953, p. 268). The business to be regulated has the initiative, the commission becomes bogged down in detail, staff members that earn a reputation for understanding business can move into a career in industry, routines are established and maintained, and competition from new sources may be stifled to maintain older privileges (Hamilton 1949b, p. 83; 1957).[37] Looking back at the NRA, Hamilton argued that it began as an exercise in price fixing, but as these sanctions

---

[36] Hamilton discusses professional associations such as the AMA, the spread of professional licensing to cover many trades and occupations, the control over news by the Associated Press, international cartels as operating in tin and rubber, Florida regulations concerning the citrus fruit industry, regulations on milk, and patents.

[37] Examples given by Hamilton include the ICC being given the regulation of canals and motor transport, to the advantage of the railroads, and The Civil Aeronautics Board discouraging low-cost carriers.

were toned down or refused, "business gradually lost interest in the NRA." Despite the demise of the NRA, it was "not without its effect on economic structure." Representatives of different companies had been brought together in Washington, and the NRA left many industries "much more tightly organized than they had been before" (Hamilton 1957, p. 97). This move toward a "private government of industry" making use of "the devices and procedures of politics" was much advanced by the Second World War. The War Production Board brought business personnel to Washington to serve as public officials, and "a hierarchy of primary contracts" resulted in a consolidation of business empires. The NRA gave representation to labor and the consumer, but in the WPB, "it was the business interest alone which was enthroned" (Hamilton 1957, pp. 97–98).

All of these problems were compounded by the development of the corporation; its treatment as a natural individual by a series of legal "fictions"; its internationalization; its ability to create subsidiaries and complex and intricate patterns of control; its ability to choose and change its domicile; and its ability to exist in perpetuity or dissolve itself and reappear under a new name. The "elaborate web of 'as ifs' which the courts have woven, have put corporate affairs pretty largely out of the reach of the regulations we decree" (Hamilton 1946a, p. 4). The techniques of public control encounter legal fictions "which have left fact far behind." Hamilton did not provide a program for the "domestication of the corporate ghost":

> But as a necessary antecedent to positive action we can bring our fictions up to date. The corporation is not a person; nor can it be made a person by a heroic act of "judicial contemplation." The corporation is a legal form into which a going concern is cast; the corporation is a device through which persons operating within bodies of social usage carry on. If the law cannot escape the fiction as an essential of its trade, it can at least replace its shopworn stock with fictions that bear some resemblance to reality. (Hamilton 1946b, p. 744)

CONCLUSION

Hamilton's ideas and career is revealing of the institutionalist movement in many respects. It provides an outstanding example of the way in which Veblen's analysis of pecuniary or business institutions was blended with other elements into a critical examination of existing institutions and an experimental approach to social control. Although Hamilton is interested in tracing the development of particular institutional arrangements and legal norms, he does not pursue a general theory of institutional change. The role that both technological developments and legal developments play in Hamilton's analyses is worthy of note. New technology plays an important role, but it has its impact largely by changing the structure of costs, and there are no mentions of Veblenian "machine discipline." The Veblenian element is most clearly displayed in the general idea that existing market institutions are not sufficient to control large-scale business activity in ways compatible with the public advantage. Hamilton's concern with legal institutions and the interpretations of the Supreme Court limiting institutional adjustment to new conditions is a theme that recurs frequently in the institutionalist literature. Hamilton moved from economics into a law school, a move also made by Robert Hale at Columbia. Like Commons and Hale, Hamilton had close contacts with legal scholars in the realist tradition.

Hamilton's work also highlights the place institutionalists gave to consumption and the potential role of the consumer. Institutionalism is sometimes presented in highly "producerist" terms, with the emphasis on productive efficiency, but this would be a mistake. Not only did Hamilton work to promote the consumer interest in the New Deal, but so did others, even "planners" such as Rexford Tugwell (Tugwell 1935a). There was, in fact, a huge amount of work on consumption behavior, mostly empirical, done in the 1920s and 1930s. The vast bulk of this work utilized institutionalist notions of socially defined standards of living.

Hamilton's various schemes of social control also significantly add to the picture of the policy positions taken by institutionalists in the interwar period. It has been common to divide institutionalists into those who believed in commissions (mainly the Wisconsin group) and the "planners" such as Tugwell and Ezekiel. Bringing Hamilton into this indicates a much greater complexity and diversity of opinion within institutionalism. All the members of the institutionalist group used the rhetoric of "social control," but what was meant by that by different people varied significantly. In Hamilton's case, it is clear that he was not a proponent of big government, or of commissions, or of industrial government by trade association. His work on the decisions of the Supreme Court leave no doubt that he disagreed with the interpretation of the Constitution as severely limiting to the exercise of the police power of the state. The state must have the power to govern and to regulate in the public interest. At the same time, his suggestions for the coal industry have little direct role for government in the operation of the industry, he did not favor a British-style nationalization, and was concerned about the "dead hand" of bureaucracy.

His proposals for the provision of health services also avoid direct government involvement in the delivery of medical services, the model proposed being based on that of the university. Even in the case of the NRA, he was trying to create a flexible form of control with input from industrialists, workers, and consumers, within a framework of public oversight, and not simply a scheme imposed from outside. This was Hamilton's version of industrial "self-government." His occasional use of that term led to accusations that he was suggesting a control by business interests alone, but that was never Hamilton's idea. Self-government of industry always meant, for Hamilton, the participation of all interests. This notion of "representation of interests" does provide a commonality between Hamilton and Commons, but Commons's plans for commissions tended to include only business and labor interests, with the "public interest" represented by academics and not by consumers themselves.

Hamilton's policy work brings out the "experimentalist" and instrumentalist aspects of institutionalist policy thinking very well. He was not wedded to particular instruments for policy. His ends in view always remained the same: How to provide an institutional framework that would lead business to operate in a way consistent with the public interest, and how to provide a higher standard of living and a fuller measure of life to the average citizen. This gives to Hamilton's work a consistent emphasis on improving productive efficiency on the one hand and the elimination of restrictive trade practices on the other. For Hamilton, markets had proved insufficient to properly direct the operation of business to these ends much beyond the stage of small-scale production and petty trade. The passage of the antitrust acts, although based on a faith in competition, were themselves a recognition that the market alone could not ensure the public good, and a judicial oversight of the activities of business was required. Antitrust had had limited success and did not always result in appropriate policy where technological efficiency demanded larger scale or some broader industrial coordination. The major alternative, regulation by administrative commission, had also been less than entirely successful. Commissions had been captured by the interests they were supposed to be regulating. Many supposed "controls" such as professional standards, licensing requirements, quality controls, and the like had been turned into sanctions. Patents, too, had been diverted from their proper function and become a vehicle for restriction rather than for technological advance and dissemination of knowledge. In general the "political arts" had not kept pace with the development of business and professional practice.

Hamilton must have been one of the first to explicitly discuss the issue of agency capture, and of the tendency of business to turn regulation into a barrier to entry or an aid to price fixing. This is an idea usually associated with more recent Chicago economics,[38] but Hamilton was talking about this problem in 1934, and his criticism of the commission form or organization goes back even further. On the other hand, for Hamilton, there was no going back to the market. That phase in industrial and institutional development has passed. Hayek and Mises, writing in 1944, were "voices from the grave." Each seeks a return to the separation of state and economy, but "the free market they seek to restore never was," and the currents of the time are moving in other directions. Sate and economy have become inexorably intertwined and cannot now be moved apart. There is no return to laissez-faire: "[A] great corpus of the law stands as proof of the incapacity of the industrial system to regulate itself." Mergers should not be allowed where technology does not require it and where there are dangers in the concentration of economic power. The grant of patent should be limited to "its proper office." Government procurement should not encourage concentration or restrictive practices. The problem of commissions and administrative agencies will remain until "political invention contrives an adequate substitute." Business will continue to play a strategic game with the regulator. There is no panacea; the only way forward for economic control in the public interest is that of "eternal vigilance" (Hamilton 1957, pp. 166–168).

There is one other aspect to Hamilton's career that should be mentioned. Hamilton was widely seen as a leading figure in the institutionalist movement. When he moved to Yale Law School, his attention shifted away from economics. Although his price studies appeared in 1938, he no longer occupied the same position within institutionalism as he had up until 1928. It is also the case that during the earlier part of his career Hamilton attempted to write a book titled *The Economic Order*. Several drafts of parts of this book can be found in Hamilton's papers, but the book was never completed. Clarence Ayres reports that Davenport, while visiting him in 1930, said "I used to think that Hamilton was the one who was going to tell us what institutionalism is all about; but I've about decided he isn't" (Clarence Ayres to Allan Gruchy, 11 February 1968, Clarence Ayres Papers).

---

[38] It is interesting to note that Hamilton was on good terms with Edward Levi at the Chicago Law School, who was also interested in antitrust and who brought Aaron Director into the teaching of his class. Levi had been a student at Yale Law School and also worked for Thurman Arnold on antitrust. Hamilton's work in law and economics was an inspiration to H. H. Leibhafsky who was to continue the institutionalist tradition in law and economics at Texas from 1956.

4

Morris A. Copeland

Institutionalism and Statistics

As is the case with Walton Hamilton, Morris A. Copeland's work and career has been the subject of relatively little discussion[1] and is not well known today, even among institutionalists. As noted in earlier chapters, the standard histories of institutional economics have tended to focus on a few leading figures, notably Thorstein Veblen, Wesley C. Mitchell, and John R. Commons, and have largely ignored the many others (some of whom had outstanding careers) associated with the movement. This narrow focus has given a misleading impression both of the institutionalist movement itself and also of the nature of the institutionalist contribution to economics. Along with the previous chapter on Hamilton, this examination of Copeland's career helps correct this problem. Copeland is a perfect candidate for such a case study owing to his central place within the interwar institutionalist movement, his teachers, the contacts he maintained, his work in both academic economics and in public service, and the professional standing he achieved within economics generally. Copeland's career reveals a great deal about how the ideas of the founding group were carried over into the work of their students.

STUDENT CAREER: AMHERST AND CHICAGO

Copeland's first contact with economics was as an undergraduate student at Amherst College. As noted in previous chapters, Walton Hamilton was hired to Amherst in 1915 and Walter Stewart in 1916. They created an economics curriculum with a heavy institutionalist orientation (Hamilton 1917).[2]

---

[1] Three short papers on Copeland by James Millar, John C. Dawson, and Stephen P. Taylor appear in John C. Dawson (1996).

[2] The program at Amherst is discussed at length in Chapter 6.

Copeland started with an interest in philosophy and Greek, but late in his undergraduate career he took a course in economics from Walter Stewart, followed by a seminar on social theory, also given by Stewart. This formal contact may have been brief, but Copeland and Stewart remained in touch, and Copeland was always to credit Stewart with a great influence on his thinking and with valuable advice on many occasions. With Copeland's interest turned toward economics, Walton Hamilton helped him obtain a graduate fellowship in economics at Chicago. Copeland graduated from Amherst in 1917 and went on to Chicago to write his PhD in economics under the supervision of J. M. Clark.[3] Copeland, on Stewart's advice, also studied accounting, an interest that led to an early publication "Seasonal Problems in Financial Administration" in the *Journal of Political Economy* (Copeland 1920). In addition, Copeland became familiar with the work of the psychologist J. R. Kantor. Kantor combined a stress on natural science method and a behavioristic insistence on observable phenomena with a social psychological focus on "cultural reactions and institutions" (Kantor 1922; 1924). Kantor also impressed Clarence Ayres. Indeed, Ayres was a member of Kantor's "anti-instinct cult at the University of Chicago" (Ayres 1921a).[4] The connections between Copeland and Ayres took on a more personal character when Copeland married Edith Ayres, Clarence Ayres's sister. Following her brother, she was a doctoral student in philosophy.[5] Although Copeland was later to remarry, he and Clarence Ayres maintained a regular correspondence through to the 1960s. While at Chicago, Copeland was a part of a Veblen study group, a group that also included Frank Knight (then

---

[3] As noted, Clark, Hamilton, and Moulton jointly produced *Readings in the Economics of War* (1918). In addition, Hamilton and Clark were in correspondence concerning research topics in connection with Hamilton's membership of the AEA Committee for the Co-ordination of Research, and they were both participants in the 1918 AEA session.

[4] Ayres has written that membership in this cult required the invention of an instinct. J. R. Kantor and Ayres argued that instincts, at least if regarded as general "ends" of life, were entirely arbitrary. "In this sense the most solidly based of the human instincts is Mr. Kantor's 'instinct to die'; for as he points out, death is the 'end of all activity'" (Ayres 1921, p. 564). A particularly interesting paper of Kantor's is "An Essay towards an Institutionalist Conception of Social Psychology" (Kantor 1922). Instinct theory was much debated in the early to mid 1920s. See William McDougall "Can Sociology and Social Psychology Dispense with Instincts" (McDougall 1924) and Kantor "The Institutional Foundation of a Scientific Social Psychology" (Kantor 1924). Kantor's work helps in understanding the nature of the behaviorism adopted by many institutionalists as instinct theory fell out of favor.

[5] Edith Ayres completed her PhD, "Some Ethical Factors in Logical Theory," in 1921, the same year Copeland completed his. Clarence Ayres' thesis was "On the Nature of the Relationship Between Economics and Ethics" (1917).

an instructor at Chicago), and fellow graduate students Harold Innis and Carter Goodrich (Neill 1972, p. 12).

The Meiklejohn affair at Amherst prompted the resignation of several faculty members, including Hamilton, Stewart, and Ayres. Hamilton went on to the new Brookings Graduate School in Washington; Stewart, recommended by Mitchell, was appointed Director of the Division of Analysis and Research of the Federal Reserve Board;[6] Ayres held a smattering of short-term jobs until he found regular employment in the economics department at the University of Texas in 1930; and Meiklejohn went on to head up the Experimental College at the University of Wisconsin. For the time it existed, Hamilton's Amherst program produced a stream of people of institutionalist persuasion. Copeland was one of the first of these, but other Amherst students who followed included Carter Goodrich, Willard Thorp, Winfield Riefler, and Stacy May.[7] These names all crop up later in Copeland's career.

Copeland's own PhD thesis, "Some Phases of Institutional Value Theory" (Copeland 1921), is a fascinating snapshot of a young institutionalist's intellectual concerns at the beginning of the 1920s. Copeland's thesis must have been one of the first – if not the first – to use the terms "institutionalist" and "institutionalism." Early on in his thesis, Copeland provides what must be one of the clearest statements of the institutionalist creed with respect to value theory and the nature of the "price system":

Economic [institutional] value theory investigates the social complex of habits of thought and action having to do with evaluation for purposes of exchange of property. Human behavior is the stuff the price system is made of. It is a vast, ever-changing, and evolving milieu of individual activities and social attitudes. Altho it is made up of the behavior of many individuals, or rather because it is made up of the behavior of so many individuals, it is largely independent of any one of them. It is a great, impersonal social process, a continuous flow of pecuniary values from one social organization to another, a network of prices joined by their organization into a single interdependent fabric. The study of the price system in any stage of any cultural line of development involves (a) the sub-institutions or elements of which the price system in that institutional situation is made up: (b) the functioning of these several elements among themselves: and (c) the relationship between the price system and its cultural environment. (Copeland 1921, p. A81)

The main body of the thesis discusses the price system, pecuniary valuation, and the limits and problems of pecuniary valuation. The thesis

---

[6]   Stewart was first hired at the Federal Reserve Board in 1922. Stewart's career was a fascinating one. For details see Yohe (1982, 1990) and Dorfman (1958).

[7]   The history of the Amherst program, the Brookings Graduate School, and of the remarkable group of students they produced, is discussed in detail in Chapter 6.

includes an outline of the evolution of the price system from the ancient world to "the corporate price accountancy period in the United States" (Copeland 1921, p. A82); a discussion of the elements and functioning of the price system; education and the conventional nature of exchange value; technology and division of labor; law and business property and contract; and social organization under pecuniary leadership and ideals. One interesting argument, particularly given Clark's supervision, is that increasing returns and the advantage of large scale and combination is a pecuniary phenomenon rather than a technological one; a matter of pecuniary advantage and of social organization under pecuniary leadership. The idea that increasing returns will eventually give way to decreasing returns is "merely the devout wish of the confirmed individualist" (Copeland 1921, pp. E1.6, E31.42).

Copeland also argues that "institutional economics is but a phase of a wider movement that is manifesting itself in several fields of thought," particularly behaviorism in psychology and pragmatism in philosophy (Copeland 1921 p. A11), and the thesis contains two long appendices, one entitled "Psychological Implications of Institutionalism" and the other "Philosophical Presuppositions of Institutionalist Value Theory." The first contains lengthy criticisms of instinct theory in the form given to it by Carleton Parker, Veblen, and others. Copeland defines an instinct as an initial reaction system out of which habits are formed; not a general end or goal, as in Veblen, but a specific tendency to make specific responses to specific stimuli, but also more or less capable of modification and molding by culture. Following the work of Kantor, Copeland argues that behaviorism asks how a person's ways of thinking and acting, his tastes and preconceptions, have come to be how they are. This is a matter of upbringing, education, and the individual's experience with his physical and social environment. Institutions are of interest as they "mold the development of the individual" (Copeland 1921, pp. X2.2 and X6.1-X6.72).

The second appendix contains a discussion of pragmatism focusing on the work of John Dewey. Thinking and reasoning are instruments in the solution of problematic situations and the way in which people construct and reconstruct their values. Copeland argues that pragmatism is opposed to the overly rationalistic and mechanical view of decision making implied in utility maximization (Copeland 1921, p. Y9.1). Throughout the thesis, there is an emphasis on the scientific approach, defined in objective, empirical, and instrumental terms. Copeland thought of scientific theories or hypotheses as generalized descriptions that should be capable of empirical test, and as instruments for prediction and control.

ACADEMIC CAREER TO 1933

After completing his PhD in 1921, Copeland was hired by Herbert Davenport to the Department of Economics at Cornell. Davenport also hired Sumner Slichter, another student of Clark, who had completed his PhD in 1918. Copeland and Slichter were recommended to Davenport as "our two most brilliant men" (J. M. Clark to Mrs. Sumner Slichter, 29 September 1959, J. M. Clark Papers, Box 5, Correspondence 1940–1963). Between 1927 and 1929, Copeland took leave from Cornell and served successively with the Brookings Graduate School, The National Bureau of Economic Research, The Experimental College of the University of Wisconsin, and with the Research and Statistics Division of the Federal Reserve. Copeland was appointed as a Consulting Fellow at Brookings for the 1927–1928 year. He lived at the Brookings residence, mingled with the students and staff, and participated in oral exams. Copeland overlapped not only with Walton Hamilton, but also with Isador Lubin, who by that time was on the staff of both the Institute of Economics and the Brookings Graduate School, and with John R. Commons. Commons was in Washington for the first six months of 1928 primarily to work on monetary stabilization issues, but he was also associated with the Institute of Economics and the Brookings Graduate School. This was Copeland's first meeting with Commons.

Copeland's initial involvement with the NBER overlapped with his time at Brookings. While at Brookings, he was appointed a member of the special NBER research staff assembled to produce the reports that made up *The Report of the Committee on Recent Economic Changes in the United States*, chaired by Herbert Hoover. Copeland's visit to the Experimental College of the University of Wisconsin took place during the Fall term of 1928 and was at the urging of Meiklejohn. While there, Copeland taught a course on Greek civilization and renewed his acquaintance with Commons. The appointment to the Research and Statistics Division of the Federal Reserve took up most of the 1929 year and was made by E. A. Goldenweiser, Walter Stewart's successor as director of the Division. Winfield Riefler was also on the staff at that time. In 1930, Copeland joined the Economics Department at the University of Michigan.[8] Max Handman (who had been at Texas) also joined the faculty there in 1930,

---

[8] Copeland married his second wife, Mary Phelps Enders (Polly), at about this time. She was a student of his at Cornell, so the relationship caused a stir. Clarence Ayres wrote to Copeland: "If you were going to marry ahead of your plan and without elaborate preparation, it's lucky as Hell you are going on to Michigan, and so can feel free to ignore Ithaca

and Carter Goodrich had been there since 1924. For a time, Michigan was something of a center for institutionalism. Early in 1930, Copeland and Goodrich discussed the possibility of bringing Ayres to join them, but no suitable position emerged, and Ayres went to Texas. Once in Texas, Ayres wrote to Copeland about possible research projects, and Copeland encouraged him to focus on his ideas on "the cultural incidence of machine technology" (Clarence Ayres to Morris Copeland, 2 December 1930; Morris Copeland to Clarence Ayres, 12 December 1930, Morris A. Copeland Papers, Box 1, 1927–1932 Folder). Goodrich moved to Columbia in 1931, and from 1933, Copeland was occupied in Washington and moved into another stage of his career.

Copeland's work over this period consisted of developing papers from the various parts of his thesis, research on the empirical testing of the quantity theory or "equation of exchange," and on national income accounting. The last line of research connected with his accounting background and grew into a deep concern with what Copeland came to call "social accounting," and with issues of statistical measurement more generally.

Copeland's first well-known published contribution was his chapter, "Communities of Economic Interest and the Price System," in Rexford Tugwell's *Trend of Economics* (Copeland 1924). Copeland's essay follows the major part of his thesis. He argues "that there are many wide discrepancies between the price measures that the market puts on things and the costs in human effort and suffering that have been required to make them, or their significance for consumers' welfare," and that these discrepancies should be analyzed in the hope that they may be traced to "some phase or phases of the present institutional situation, for a knowledge of causes may be of assistance in making accurately … the requisite corrections" (Copeland 1924, pp. 105–106). His discussion of these discrepancies centers on the Veblenian distinction between making goods and making money. Under existing institutions, pecuniary incentives do not always lead to "the common good of the self-seeking parties." There may be failures of coordination, differential advantages, and conflicts of interest that can lead to socially undesirable outcomes such as business depressions, competitive advertising, cut-throat competition, and the creation and use of economic power, as well as failures to provide those socially beneficial goods that do

---

for the remainder of the year; and if you are going to Michigan, it's lucky you are marrying now and getting your personal affairs straightened out so that you won't have to begin a new job and a new home both at once!" (Clarence Ayres to Morris Copeland, 12 February 1930, Morris A. Copeland Papers, Box 1, 1927–1977 Folder).

not generate adequate compensation to private producers (Copeland 1924, pp. 113–115).

These themes were followed up in a short note on advertising published in the *American Economic Review* (Copeland 1925a) and in a review of J. M. Clark's 1923 book *Studies in the Economics of Overhead Costs* (Copeland 1925b). In the former piece, Copeland argues that "the very existence of advertising evidences the absence of the conditions for a perfect market"; branding divides the market, giving each firm a degree of monopoly on its own brand, and results in prices higher than marginal cost. In the latter, he strongly emphasizes the destructive implications of Clark's analysis of overhead costs for the normal view of the benefits of competition. Later, Copeland was to call Clark's book "much the greatest institutionalist contribution" to a realistic microeconomics (Copeland 1951, p. 65). This emphasis on the pervasive nature of the failings of the system of pecuniary incentives and of market organization was a characteristic of the institutionalist literature of the period. Also characteristic was Copeland's notion that the price system might be reformed with suitable adjustments in institutions in order to bring pecuniary incentives more into line with social benefits. Here Copeland is following the lead of his teacher, J. M. Clark. As with other institutionalists of his time, including Mitchell, Copeland used Veblen's analytical categories but rejected Veblen's radical skepticism concerning the nature of the pecuniary system and its potential reform.

Copeland also developed the material contained in the appendices of his thesis. He published two early papers dealing with psychology and economics, one a critique of Frank Knight's subjective and introspective approach to issues of values (Copeland 1925c), and the other a more direct discussion of his own "natural-evolutionary" or behavioristic approach to issues of desire, choice, and purpose (Copeland 1926). Both papers show Copeland attempting to find a foundation for institutionalism in the psychology of stimulus-response, reaction-pattern, conditioning, association, and inhibition, in place of the older psychology of instinct. Such a behavioristic approach, Copeland argues, is perfectly compatible both with the idea of individuals being born with certain drives or reaction patterns, and with the idea that these drives are capable of undergoing vast development and organization into complexes of habitual behavior. This can be built into a social psychology in the following way:

> In such a view of human nature it still remains to account for the fact that in the same culture different individuals have somewhat similar desires and purposes and habits. It still remains to describe how on the one hand the child is introduced into an existing culture, how the standards of taste and common interests of the group

are inculcated in him under any given cultural situation; and on the other hand, how the set of tastes and desires common to the group came to be as it is, as a matter not of individual but of group history. ... Values, or "desirednesses" which have validity for a group of people according to such a view, are therefore to be accounted for ontogenetically in terms of social heredity or education; the individual is educated to accept the standards of his group. (Copeland 1926, p. 265)

Copeland also wrote a paper on "An Instrumental View of the Part Whole Relation" (Copeland 1927) that displays his philosophical and methodological knowledge, including Lloyd Morgan's conception of emergent properties. In this paper, Copeland argues that a whole is not just more than the sum of its parts; it is, in fact, not a sum at all, because the arrangement of the parts is an essential element of the whole. Moreover, a whole may be analyzed into parts in many different ways: "the parts are not logically given in the whole," and the analysis "is a veritable construction of the person who 'makes it'" (Copeland 1927, p. 103). Similarly, many wholes could be constructed from a given set of parts. The "notion that society ... is somehow less real than the individuals who compose it appears to derive from the metaphysical preconception that some parts or wholes are real in their own right – not mere constructs of convenience" (Copeland 1927, p. 104). The validity of any such construction is a matter of its instrumental usefulness for prediction and control.

The issues dealt with in these early papers on psychology and methodology crop up again a few years later in what are probably Copeland's best known articles: "Psychology and the Natural Science Point of View" (Copeland 1930), and "Economic Theory and the Natural Science Point of View" (Copeland 1931a), the latter being part of an AEA round table on institutional economics. In these papers, behaviorism in psychology and institutionalism in economics are associated with the natural science method:

It is a prime object of natural science to formulate hypotheses or descriptive generalizations *relevant* to the subject matter of science, which are capable of empirical test. Scientific theories should not be mere truisms, or be so abstract as to be incapable of factual disproof. They should be useful in enabling one to say *a priori* what he expects to find under certain specific conditions, within the limits of accuracy of the generalization, and they should be such as to be invalidated if he does not find *empirically* what he expected to find *a priori*. Moreover a scientific hypothesis should be so formulated as to fit existing data. (Copeland 1931a, p. 68)

Copeland also argues for the maintenance of a clear distinction between scientific observations and descriptive generalizations on the one hand and appraisals and normative judgments on the other, and further claims that the formulations of psychologists and economists should be consistent with hypotheses in other fields, particularly the natural-evolutionary hypotheses in geology and general biology. Copeland's references to natural-evolutionary hypotheses and to biology are interesting, but he does not in fact make any very detailed use of biological analogy. Most of his work was concerned with the functioning of the existing set of institutions rather than with institutional change, and his references to natural-evolutionary hypotheses are used primarily to point to the fact of social and institutional evolution and to the resulting historical limits on the validity of economic generalizations. The main burden of these papers concerns his view of proper "natural science" method. In the first of these papers, Copeland argues that behaviorism, with its objectivism and empiricism, holds out the hope of a scientific treatment of psychology, whereas the second paper argues that the key components of neo-classical economics fail to comply with the natural science approach to economics.[9] Neoclassical theories confuse positive and normative, are often untestable, fail to be relevant to current conditions, and ignore the limits on their applicability caused by technological and institutional developments. In contrast, Mitchell's theory of business cycles is seen by Copeland as "the first triumph of the empirical natural science method in the study of the behavior of prices and production" (Copeland 1931a, p.77).

Copeland's work was not confined to elaborating the themes in his thesis. He branched into other areas, but in ways very much in line with

---

[9]   Copeland's 1931 paper, "Economic Theory and the Natural Science Point of View," was prepared for an AEA roundtable on institutional economics that also contained Eveline M. Burns's paper "Does Institutional Economics Complement or Compete with 'Orthodox' Economics" (Burns 1931). There is correspondence between Copeland and Burns concerning their papers. Burns felt she was supposed to play the role of critic of institutionalism and Copeland the supporter, but was not very happy with the "for and against" approach and wished to "discuss what we have so far gotten out of institutionalism and what there is reasonable hope for expecting in the future" (Eveline Burns to Morris Copeland, 23 October 1930, Morris A. Copeland Papers, Box 1, 1927–1932 Folder). Copeland's title confused Burns, and she did not initially see the connection between a paper on economic theory and natural science and a session on institutionalism. Copeland had to explain that he regarded "Institutionalism as an attempt to apply the natural science point of view in economics" (Eveline Burns to Morris Copeland, 7 November 1930 and Morris Copeland to Eveline Burns, 14 November 1930, Morris A. Copeland Papers, Box 1, 1927–1932 Folder). There is little doubt from his correspondence that Copeland was being deliberately provocative with this paper. Frank Knight wrote to Copeland that he was "perplexed and discouraged" by Copeland's attempt to contrast neo-classical economics and natural science method (Frank Knight to Morris Copeland, 7 March 1931, Morris A. Copeland Papers, Box 1, 1927–1932 Folder). This resulted in a spirited exchange of views but with no change of opinion on either side.

his conception of science and the importance of empirical testing. While at Brookings and at the Division of Research and Statistics of the Federal Reserve Board, he conducted an empirical investigation on the equation of exchange, specifically an empirical examination of the competing hypotheses of Holbrook Working and Wesley Mitchell. Working had provided what, to Copeland, was "the most plausible empirical argument for the causal primacy of M" in the equation of exchange. Working's thesis was that changes in the volume of transactions between periods of prosperity and depression were largely accommodated by changes in the velocity of circulation, so that cyclical fluctuations in P are caused chiefly by changes in the quantity of currency in circulation in the preceding months. Mitchell's position was that the relationship between P and M was more complex. Mitchell's view, as expressed in his 1927 volume, was that "most of the time, P and T are the 'active factors' in the equation of exchange," the exception being that when "the pecuniary volume of trade [i.e., PT] has reached limits which tax MV," monetary factors "assume the 'active' role, and force a reduction in PT" (Mitchell 1927, p. 137; Copeland 1929a, p. 146; 1929c, pp. 648–651). Copeland's efforts to empirically examine these hypotheses led him to construct new estimates of the total volume of debits to individual accounts (Copeland 1928), and a series of special-purpose indexes of the various items in the equation (Copeland 1929b).[10] His test procedure consisted of an examination of the leads and lags implied in each hypothesis with the leads and lags in his data series. He concluded that Working's hypothesis was "difficult to reconcile with the facts" and that "present information about the movements of money, velocity, and the dollar volume of transactions is more nearly consonant with the second [Mitchell's] hypothesis, which attributes causal priority most of the time to the dollar volume of transactions" (Copeland 1929c, pp. 665–666). These papers were published in the *Journal of the American Statistical Association* and the *Quarterly Journal of Economics*.

Copeland's efforts along empirical lines also included a number of important papers on national income accounting. The first of these was "National Income and Its Distribution," a contribution to the volume *Recent Economic Changes in the United States* (Copeland 1929d). As mentioned earlier, this work brought Copeland into contact with the NBER. Two further papers were published as lengthy articles in the *Journal of Political Economy*, each

---

[10] Copeland had correspondence with Irving Fisher concerning issues in the estimation of velocity (Irving Fisher to Morris Copeland, 11 May 1928, and reply from Copeland 22 May 1928, Morris A. Copeland Papers, Box 1, Irving Fisher Folder).

containing close discussion and revision of national income estimates as produced by Willford King and others (Copeland 1932a; 1932b). The first of these papers, "Some Problems in the Theory of National Income" (1932a), is particularly significant for its "early and well developed" use of the "accounting approach" to national income, an approach that would later become standard (Duncan and Shelton 1978, p. 93).

In addition, Copeland was interested in the improvement of price statistics and was an active member of the American Statistical Association and a member of its Committee on Price Statistics (Copeland 1931b). This statistical work would lead Copeland's career in new directions.

WORK IN GOVERNMENT, 1933–1944

In 1933, Copeland took leave from his academic position at Michigan to serve as Executive Secretary of the newly created Central Statistical Board. There is no question that Copeland saw this appointment as an opportunity not only to contribute to government work of importance (connected with the New Deal) but also to substantially improve and upgrade the informational basis of economics and the social sciences more generally. The CSB was the outcome of a series of initiatives pursued by the American Statistical Association, the Social Science Research Council, and various Federal Departments, most notably the Department of Labor under Roosevelt's appointee as Secretary of Labor, Frances Perkins. The ASA had itself established a number of committees on statistics, including a Committee on Labor Statistics, but early in 1933, Perkins requested the formation of an Advisory Committee to the Secretary of Labor, to be associated with the Committee on Labor Statistics of the ASA. Perkins herself wrote to Copeland that she was "very anxious to have a talk with you about the statistical work in the Labor Department" (Frances Perkins to Morris Copeland, 12 May 1933, Morris A. Copeland Papers, Box 1, Frances Perkins Folder), and Copeland was asked to join this Advisory Committee. However, the growth of committees dealing with a variety of statistical issues – for example the census and tax statistics – as well as the large informational demands created by New Deal programs prompted the formation of a joint ASA/SSRC-sponsored Committee on Government Statistics and Information Services (COGSIS). This Committee began work in June 1933 with an initial membership of Edmund Day (Chairman), Stuart Rice, Meredith Givens, Bryce Stewart, Morris Copeland, Willard Thorp, and William Crum. COGSIS was created to offer "immediate assistance and advice in the reorganization and improvement of the statistical and informational services of the Federal

Government" (Rice 1933). Rice and Thorp left the Committee in September 1933, when Rice became Assistant Director of the Census and Thorp Director of the Bureau of Foreign and Domestic Commerce. However, prior to that, in July 1933, COGSIS produced a report "The Statistical Services of the Federal Government in Relation to the Recovery Program,"[11] addressed to John Dickinson, Assistant Secretary of Commerce, and Alexander Sachs, Chief of Research and Planning, Industrial Recovery Administration. The report recommended the establishment of a Central Statistical Board.

This recommendation was immediately followed, and on 27 July 1933, by executive order of President Roosevelt, a Central Statistical Board was established "to appraise and advise upon all schedules of all government agencies engaged in the primary collection of statistics required in carrying out the purposes of the National Recovery Act, to review plans for tabulation and classification of such statistics, and to promote the coordination and improvement of the statistical services involved."[12] In 1935, the Board was given a statutory basis and a broader mandate "to plan and promote the improvement, development and coordination of, and the elimination of duplication in statistical services carried on by or subject to the supervision of the Federal Government" (Copeland 1939b). The membership of the Board when first formed was Winfield Riefler, Chairman (Economic Adviser to the Executive Council), Oscar Kiessling (Chief Economist of the Mineral Statistics Division, Bureau of Mines), Mordecai Ezekiel (Economic Adviser to the Secretary of Agriculture), John Dickinson (Assistant Secretary of Commerce), Isador Lubin (Commissioner of Labor Statistics), E. A. Goldenweiser (Director of Research and Statistics, Federal Reserve Board), Alexander Sachs (Chief of Division of Economic Research and Planning, National Recovery Administration), Meredith Givens (Executive Secretary of COGSIS), E. Dana Durand (Chief Economist, Tariff Division), Corrington Gill (Director of Research and Statistics, Federal Emergency Relief Administration), Stuart Rice (Assistant Director, Bureau of the Census), W. R. Stark (Chief of Section of Financial and Economic Research of the Treasury Department), and O. C. Stine (Chief of Division of Statistical and Historical Research, Bureau of Agricultural Economics). Riefler resigned his position in February 1935 and was replaced as Chairman by

---

[11] A copy of this report is available in the Morris A. Copeland Papers, Box 3, Central Statistical Board Folder. COGSIS continued its work and made many contributions to the effort to improve statistical services in the Federal government. For assessments of the work of COGSIS, see Givens (1934) and Duncan and Shelton (1978).

[12] The executive order was reprinted in "The Central Statistical Board," *Journal of the American Statistical Association* 30 (December 1935): 714–716.

Stuart Rice. Morris Copeland was loaned by COGSIS to the Board to enable him to serve as Executive Secretary of the Board. With a small staff to assist him, he served in this capacity from 1933 until 1939.[13] In 1940, the activities of the Board were moved to the Division of Statistical Standards, Bureau of the Budget, and between 1939 and 1940, Copeland became Director of Research, Bureau of the Budget.

The CSB reviewed some 4,600 questionnaires and related forms and plans for statistical work. Questionnaires were reviewed for technique as well as the material covered, and the vast majority were revised to reduce the number of questions, reduce the number of respondents, provide conformity to practices of business or other Federal agencies, or to ensure more accurate data. The Board also reviewed the more important of the statistical releases with the purpose of improving the accuracy of the data and the information concerning sources and methods. It also acted as a statistical clearing house to help provide information on the data being collected by various agencies and to help bring together data from different sources on the same subject. It worked with various Federal agencies to produce the Standard Industrial Classification Code. It made many efforts to eliminate duplication, increase the comparability of data gathered by different agencies, provide for the filling of important gaps in the data collected, provide technical advice, and improve standards of accuracy and representativeness (Copeland 1939b; Central Statistical Board 1939). In Copeland's view, the CSB, together with the economists in government, many of whom had responsibility for the research and statistics divisions of their departments, "should be given the credit for the statistical accomplishments of the early days of the New Deal" (Letter from Morris Copeland to Joseph Duncan, 5 January 1977, Morris A. Copeland Papers, Box 2, 77, I Folder). Copeland's own efforts in the statistical area earned him a vice-presidency of the American Statistical Association in 1936. He was made a Fellow of the Association later the same year.

As one final note on this part of Copeland's career, his experiences with the CSB resulted in a concern with improving the recruitment, performance appraisal, and research opportunities for professional people in the Federal government (Copeland 1940a; 1941). This included participation in an AEA committee on Economists in the Public Service that

---

[13] The CSB went through various changes of membership, but Copeland remained Executive Secretary throughout its life. In 1939, the Committee consisted of Stuart Rice, Chair, Isador Lubin, O. C. Stine, Arthur Altmeyer, William Austin, Mordecai Ezekiel, Ernest Fisher, Corrington Gill, E. A. Goldenweiser, George Haas, Oscar Kiessling, Richard Patterson, Clyde Seavey, Frederick Stephan, and Morris Copeland.

reported in 1946. He also maintained his interest in the organization of government statistical services, arguing for the creation of a "focal agency" to oversee the statistical operation for each major aspect of society (Copeland 1948).

Despite the workload imposed by his positions with the CSB and Bureau of the Budget, Copeland did not ignore his other interests. He continued to produce papers on issues in national income accounting, publishing such work in the *JASA* (Copeland 1935), the NBER *Studies in Income and Wealth* series (Copeland 1937; Copeland and Martin 1938), and in the *JPE* (Copeland and Martin 1939) and *AER* (Copeland 1939a). These papers also display Copeland's social accounting approach to national income, and the 1935 and 1937 papers were cited by Richard Stone in his 1947 work for the United Nations, which defined the UN's Standard National Accounts system (Dawson 1991).[14] A number of these pieces also discuss Kuznets's work on national income and capital formation (Kuznets 1937). Copeland's own analysis of public investment expenditures (Copeland 1939a) examines both the quantity and composition of public investment, and notes the failure to use public investment expenditures in a countercyclical fashion – a foreshadowing of some of his slightly later discussions of economic stabilization. These papers generally end with a plea for better data or further developments in social accounting techniques – for example, capital asset accounting for the public sector.

Copeland also maintained his interest in the theoretical aspects of institutional economics. At Taussig's request, he wrote a long review of Commons's *Institutional Economics* for the *QJE* (Copeland 1936), and, following from his earlier interest in Clark's *Overhead Costs* and his note on advertising, he became deeply interested in Chamberlin's theory of monopolistic competition. Copeland was clearly familiar with Commons's *Legal Foundations* (Commons 1924a) and had considerable respect and knowledge of his legal scholarship and efforts to develop a legal/economic terminology of transactions and going concerns, but his review concentrates on issues of social value and is not uncritical in nature. The review opens with an explicit recognition of the "fundamental philosophical difference" between Commons's institutionalism and those in the "Veblenian tradition" (Copeland 1936, p. 334). Copeland notes the apparent similarity between Veblen's distinction between the technological and the pecuniary

---

[14] Copeland and Richard Stone held "lively late night discussions" in 1945 when both were working on "The Impact of the War on Civilian Consumption in the United Kingdom, the United States and Canada" (John C. Dawson to Malcolm Rutherford, 9 March 2001).

and Commons's distinction between efficiency and scarcity, but finds neither Veblen's "ethical insinuations" concerning the pecuniary system, nor Commons's desire to reconcile them in his notion of "reasonable value," to offer constructive guidance of how to synthesize these principles in any concrete case. However, Copeland's main complaint about Commons's version of institutionalism involves the nature of, and emphasis given to, the concept of "artificial selection." Copeland, in line with his naturalistic approach, wishes to draw a sharp distinction between descriptive judgments and ethical judgments, whereas Commons does not. This leads to a deeper problem, because Commons talks of artificial selection in terms of the selection of the "best" practice, and also sees ethical standards as evolving over time. As Copeland puts it:

> … it would seem that we must consider separately those ethical tastes that constitute the "artificially" selective conditions which practices survive or fail to survive, and that these selective tastes cannot be considered as evolving on a par with the practices selected. Otherwise we will have the practices acting as selective conditions for the survival of the tastes quite as much as the tastes acting as selective conditions for the survival of the practices, and the selection will cease to be "artificial." If social evolution is to be a process of "artificial" selection some tastes apparently must be held constant for a long enough period to allow the selection to be worked out. (Copeland 1936, p. 343)

Tastes may be regarded as short-term constants, but for long-run changes in tastes, we "shall need to fall back on natural selection" (Copeland 1936, p. 343). Moreover, Commons's work tends itself to be selective, emphasizing those phases of institutional and social evolution that lend themselves to interpretation in terms of artificial selection. On the other hand, Copeland does not himself provide any theory of natural selection that might apply to social evolution, and in his later work on this topic states clearly "there seems to be nothing in the socioeconomic evolutionary process that corresponds to natural selection" (Copeland 1981a, p. 2). Copeland also finds difficulty with Commons's stress on the best existing practice because it "limits the possibilities of economic planning." For Copeland, this had a restraining influence on Commons's thinking on issues such as unemployment compensation. Copeland sees a continuum of types of planning in place of Commons's dichotomy between those who would wish to remodel the competitive system and those who look to a more modest "rationing of Producing Power" (Copeland 1936, p. 345). Other criticisms include aspects of Commons's "profit margin" cycle theory, Commons's failure to discuss Mitchell's theory of business cycles, and his relative lack of emphasis on statistical investigation.

Copeland reviewed Chamberlin's book in 1934 for the *JPE* (Copeland 1934) and wrote a long paper seeking to "supplement" Chamberlin's theory, published in the *QJE* in 1940 (Copeland 1940b). In his review, Copeland points out that most economists have long recognized the existence of markets that could not be made to fit the theoretical categories of perfect competition or perfect monopoly. Chamberlin's work "opens up new vistas for what has been called pure, abstract, or deductive economics" (Copeland 1934, p. 249), but Copeland regrets that Chamberlin continues to accept the usual neoclassical oversimplifications in other areas such as the treatment of time, overhead costs, the lack of distinction between the costs of establishing and maintaining a business, and problems of variation of demand from period to period. Copeland's main paper on monopolistic competition is itself an exercise in pure theory involving what he calls an "Imaginary Economic State." Copeland utilizes a series of spatial models of increasing complexity to probe issues of entry, market structure, location, quality differentiation, advertising, and the relationships between Chamberlin's two demand curves. Copeland's models display features such as absorption of delivery charges, cross haulage, class price discrimination, national advertising, chain plants, and diversified lines of goods produced by one concern. He also argues that under the conditions of his models, perfect competition could not be maintained without regulation or planning. Copeland ends by stressing the importance of developing the theory of imperfect competition, particularly in terms of its implications for general equilibrium, and its "dynamic" aspects.

In 1940, World War II affected Copeland's career. In that year, he was appointed as Chief of the Munitions Branch of the War Production Board. He was recruited into this post by Stacy May, then Director of the Planning and Statistics Division of the War Production Board. For the next few years, much of Copeland's work concentrated on detailed issues of war production and planning (for example, Copeland 1942a), but he also investigated the impact of wartime expenditures on national income (Copeland 1942b). As the end of the war came into view, Copeland's attention turned to postwar stabilization of employment. In the papers he published on this subject, it is apparent that Copeland had absorbed aspects of Keynesian thinking, although with an awareness of what he saw as the shortcomings of Keynes's simplified model, and with something of a continued attachment to Wesley Mitchell's approach to business cycles. In a 1944 paper published in the *AER*, Copeland proposed an elaborate system of stabilizing the level of private investment expenditure by the Federal government "selling" forward agreements to private businesses in exchange for government bonuses in the form of tax credits. This would function together with improved business information and forecasting, and public expenditure programs large enough to both fully compensate for the remaining business fluctuations and achieve full employment. This system of "business stabilization by agreement" would be supplemented by credit controls to prevent "the development of unsound financial structures" during periods of business expansion, and countercyclical tax policy (Copeland 1944). Copeland would return to these ideas later in his career.

THE NBER AND THE MONEYFLOWS PROJECT, 1944–1952

In 1944, Copeland left government service and joined the research staff of the NBER to work on the "moneyflows" project, the last NBER project initiated by Wesley Mitchell before his retirement. As mentioned earlier, Copeland's contacts with the NBER went back to 1928 and the *Recent Economic Changes* project, and Copeland had been a regular participant in the NBER Conference on Income and Wealth, and had published in a variety of NBER volumes. Copeland knew Mitchell personally, was an admirer of Mitchell's approach (he had come to think of himself as something of a disciple of Mitchell's), and had consulted with Mitchell over issues in his own work during the 1930s (Millar 1980, p.121, n.7). The moneyflows project was originally conceived by Gardiner Means and Theodore Yntema and was undertaken by the NBER at the request of the Committee for Economic Development.[15] Members of the Division of Research and Statistics of the Federal Reserve Board were involved with the project planning. For the first two years, the Committee for Economic Development provided finance and the Board provided space and equipment. After mid-1947, the project was continued under the auspices of the Federal Reserve Board as a special project to construct statistical measures of the money circuit. Both Riefler and Walter Stewart (who at that point both held appointments at the Institute for Advanced Studies at Princeton) had input into the planning of the project and provided other advice. The first draft manuscript was produced in 1948. The final version appeared in 1952 as *A Study of Moneyflows in the United States* (Copeland 1952a). The dedication of the book is to Alexander

---

[15] Both Yntema and Means were involved with the Committee on Economic Development. Means was discussing a possible project dealing with "transactions flows" as early as 1941 and was closely involved with the early planning of the moneyflows project (Gardiner Means to Weldon Jones, 17 October 1941, Gardiner Means Papers, Box 6, Correspondence Folder; Gardiner Means to Morris Copeland, 3 November 1944, Gardiner Means Papers, Box 20, Correspondence C Folder).

Meiklejohn, and the acknowledgements give generous tribute to Mitchell, Riefler, and Stewart. An enthusiastic introduction was written by Riefler.

The basic conception of the moneyflows project can be found outlined in a memorandum written by Wesley Mitchell in 1944 and partially reproduced in the *Moneyflows* book (Copeland 1952a, p. 3). In this memorandum, Mitchell conceives of the economy as composed of four groups (consumers, business enterprises, governments, and philanthropic agencies). Units in each of these groups make and receive payments to other units in the same and the other groups. For each group, a double entry account is kept with payments classified by the unit and group making the payment, the purpose of the payment, and the form of currency. The accounts for all groups for a year are fitted together with each payment reported twice. All economic activities are represented except dealings of commercial banks with one another, and services rendered or received without pay. This basic accounting conception was followed by Copeland, except that the number of groups was expanded to eleven, and the classification of payments based primarily on the basis of the object of the expenditure (Copeland 1952a, p. 4). Following Commons, the basic unit of analysis is a "transaction" with two parties – a payer and recipient. Fourteen types of transaction are distinguished. Each transaction involves a money outflow for one transactor and an equal inflow for another. Each sector's inflows and outflows are shown for each of the fourteen types of transaction. These fourteen types are reduced to four principal types: final product moneyflows, nonfinal product moneyflows, transfer moneyflows, and net moneyflows through financial channels. These moneyflows together constitute the "main money circuit" that is measured.

As would be expected, the book contains a large amount of technical discussion, but also a close analysis of the relationship between moneyflow accounts and national income accounts, discussion of the "social accounting approach" as opposed to the quantity theory approach, a lengthy critique of hydraulic analogies in monetary theory, the development of an alternative analogy based on an electrical circuit (which involved an elaborate "wiring diagram for the main money circuit"), a discussion of the "scorekeeping" function of money and its historical evolution, and a discussion of the application of the findings to the analysis of economic expansions and contractions. There are a large number of interesting points in all of this that would take another chapter to deal with properly, but two worth stressing in the present context are the institutionalist preconceptions that underlie the study and the views expressed with respect to the issue of economic fluctuations.

For Copeland, the moneyflows project was very clearly a project in institutional economics:

> How does our highly specialized and highly complicated economy get along as well as it does without a general economic manager? ... Broadly our answer is, institutions serve in lieu of a general manager, and one of these institutions is money. At bottom our system of economic coordination rests on legal foundations: on the law of property, of contract and negotiable instruments, of torts, of bankruptcy, and of association, and on various legal regulations and restraints.... Erected on this legal foundation we have a pervasive practice of buying and selling goods and services for money and of producing for sale, a system of prices, a system of moneyflows, and a system of pecuniary incentives. (Copeland 1952a, p. 212)

Within the limits imposed by institutions, individual transactors make choices, but their choices are both mutually conditioning and conditioned by what has gone before. Choice is a process of readjustment: "It starts with an established scheme of personal relationships, with organizations that are going concerns, with trade practices, trade connections, etc. And, what is of more immediate concern, it starts with a set of expectations regarding business prospects, with a set of ownerships and outstanding obligations that can be summarized in balance sheets, and with an existing volume and composition of moneyflows to be modified" (Copeland 1952a, pp. 212–213). Transactors have some discretion to readjust previous sources or dispositions of money, but the system of moneyflows imposes two constraints: The moneyflow account of each transactor must always be in balance, and there must be another party to each moneyflow transaction, normally a party that willingly enters into it. In this way, the system of moneyflows "plays an important role in the pecuniary institutional coordination of economic activity" (Copeland 1952a, p. 213). It should be emphasized here that Copeland's point is not simply that money is an institution, but rather that the modern economy is governed by a set of institutions that are fundamentally pecuniary in nature. Copeland's moneyflows looks at economic activity through the flows of monetary receipts and disbursements that are part and parcel of that activity. As in Mitchell's work on cycles, the "real" and the "monetary" are intimately interconnected, and lines of causation run in both directions.

On the analysis of economic expansions and contractions, Copeland argues that transactors generally have more discretion in changing expenditures than receipts. Moreover, most transactors respond somewhat slowly and passively to changes in their receipts (a group Copeland calls "Sheep"), but some are more active, either actively dishoarding (Bulls) or actively hoarding (Bears). Banks are seen as playing the role of "discretion modifiers." Whether moneyflows increase or decrease depends largely on whether Bulls or Bears predominate. Copeland argues that within the 1936 to 1942 time period of his investigation, households did not play a very active discretionary role, that industrial corporations changed from Bulls in 1937 to Bears in 1938, and that the Federal government played a highly active discretionary role over the whole period (Copeland 1952a, pp. 258–266). Upswings are generated by the influence of Bulls, the banking system supplies the funds they demand setting off a cumulative expansion in moneyflows.

As in Copeland's earlier work, he rejects the simple quantity theory relation running from M to PT; indeed he rejects the entire equation of exchange approach, at least in its usual form, as mired in inappropriate hydraulic analogy and inadequate for a proper understanding of the system of moneyflows (Copeland 1952a, pp. 267–279). Other implications follow from his analysis. First, that the banking system has more influence on the downward than upward side: They can start or accelerate a depression, but can't do much to stop it; they can accelerate, restrain or stop an expansion, but can't start one all by themselves. That is, they can't convert Bears into Bulls. Copeland uses this asymmetry to critique Fisher's 100 percent money proposals as a means to economic stability. In Copeland's view, Federal Reserve expansion of total bank credit in a recession might prevent the downswing being accelerated by the actions of banks, but "there is no reason to believe that this would restrain bearish stinting and hoarding." Thus "the most important thing a liberal Federal bank credit policy can accomplish in such a time is to keep banks from accelerating the downswing" (Copeland 1952a, pp. 298–299). Second, that as transactors have more discretion to change expenditures than receipts, the demand side has primacy over supply and "for the most part it is correct to assign a more direct role to changes in aggregate demand as accounting for changes in total gross national product" (Copeland 1952a, p. 337). Copeland felt his work gave support to the Keynesian contention on this point.

Copeland's moneyflows were converted into what has become known as "flow of funds" accounts. These accounts are kept by the Federal Reserve for the United States, by central banks in many other countries, and by the Word Bank (Dawson 1996). The flow of funds accounts have been utilized in a large amount of empirical work, particularly in finance, and aspects of Copeland's monetary theory, for example his "thesis that banks act as financial intermediaries in the same fashion as other financial institutions," are now quite commonplace (Cohen 1972). They have not, however, had as much impact on monetary theory and policy debates as Copeland (and

Mitchell) originally hoped. It is sometimes claimed that the problem is that the accounts were structured without a clear theoretical model in mind, or that, unlike national income accounts, they have "not found their Keynes" (Cohen 1972, p. 13). It is true that Copeland worked almost alone on these accounts and had only a very small number of graduate students interested in developing or utilizing them. In any event, the language of macroeconomic and monetary debate soon became the language of Keynesians and monetarists.[16]

ACADEMIC CAREER AFTER 1949

After completing the bulk of the work on the moneyflows project, Copeland returned to university life at Cornell in 1949, becoming the Robert J. Thorne Professor of Economics in 1957. He also maintained his staff connection with the National Bureau through to 1959. He was a Fulbright Lecturer at the Delhi School of Economics in 1952, and taught in the spring term of 1954 at Columbia University. Recognition of his work in the form of the Presidency of the AEA came in 1957. After his retirement from Cornell in 1965, he took visiting positions at Missouri (1966–1967) and at the State University of New York at Albany (1967–1971). In 1971, he gave Amherst College $500,000 to fund the Copeland Colloquium, intended to bring a number of fellows from diverse backgrounds together for the promotion of cross-disciplinary discussion. In the same year, he retired to Venice, Florida, but continued to write, his last publications appearing in 1981. He died in 1989 at the age of ninety-three.

Copeland's work in this period falls outside of the main time frame considered in this book, but there are a few points from his work in the 1950s that have relevance to the discussions in Chapters 10 and 11 on the institutionalist reaction to Keynesian economics and to neoclassical developments.

In his discussions of Keynes, Copeland presents Keynes as an "expurgated version" of Mitchell's theory of business cycles (Copeland 1951, p. 59; 1952b). He sees the Keynesian model as oversimplified and as failing to deal with many of the issues included in Mitchell's work, but Copeland finds merit in the empirical nature of the Keynesian model and in its treatment of time. He rejects the *ex-ante* and *ex-post* constructions of the Stockholm

---

[16] In this, it is ironic that the monetarist position developed from the monetary component of the NBER project on business cycles that Arthur Burns asked Milton Friedman to take on in 1948 (Hammond 1996, pp. 46–48).

school and urges "the merit of the handling of time reference in Keynes's *General Theory*, and of the similar handling in Hick's *Value and Capital*" (Copeland 1952b, p. 14). He also discusses issues in general equilibrium, particularly the problem of dealing with large numbers of endogenous variables in formal mathematical models. However, if the model contains many exogenous variables, "economists must admit that model analysis instead of being the whole of economic analysis is only a part" (Copeland 1952b, p. 23). In terms of policy, Copeland continued to promote versions of his "business stabilization by agreement" scheme, but now involving the creation of a "GNP Scheduling Agency" (Copeland 1966, pp. 46–52).

The issue of "model analysis" and its limitations became one of the major themes of Copeland's later work. His "Institutional Economics and Model Analysis" (Copeland 1951) was presented at an AEA session on institutional economics also including Clarence Ayres's paper "The Co-ordinates of Institutionalism" (Ayres 1951). Copeland talks of the development from the implicit models of the neoclassicism of the 1920s, to the explicit mathematical models of Keynesian and neo-classical economists of the 1940s and 1950s (Copeland 1951). According to Copeland, model analysis and institutional economics clashed in the 1920s, and still clash. Despite this, institutionalist criticism had been quieted both because neo-classical models had become more realistic, and because the policy implications of Keynesian and imperfectly competitive models had shifted "the center of gravity" of economics to the left, which in turn generated more vocal criticism from the right (Copeland 1951, pp. 58–59). Institutionalists had gained victories in pushing the discipline toward more realistic theories and more empirical implementation, but these victories were of "very limited scope," involving "only those planks of the institutionalist platform that could most readily be translated into the language of model analysis and put up in neat geometrical or algebraic packages" (Copeland 1951, p. 59). He thought the conflict was less severe with the more empirically minded model analysts, but although he was optimistic about the possibility of improved empirical models, he still saw a problem in the many aspects of the economic world that they fail to capture. As a result, he argued that economists should turn their attention to "those phases of economic theory that lie outside the scope of present model analysis" (Copeland 1951, p. 65).

A slightly later paper, "Statistics and Objective Economics" (Copeland 1955), published in *JASA*, makes a number of related points. Copeland claims that the efforts of the group of institutionalists led by Wesley Mitchell, who "yearned to make their subject an empirical science," did have a substantial impact on the profession through the accumulation of time series data and other measurements. He talks about the impact of national income accounts and of empirical Keynesian analysis, and describes aggregate-level empirical work on the consumption function as "behavioristic quantitative analysis" (Copeland 1955, p. 83). However, he sees less progress on the microeconomic side and expresses doubt about the applicability of the newer "mathematical-statistical method" to economics. He doubts time series can be thought of as samples, especially because of the structural differences that exist between different cultures and between different time periods even within a given culture (Copeland 1955, pp. 76–78). Moreover, and in contrast to Mitchell's hopes that quantitative work would lead to a focus on institutions (Mitchell 1925), Copeland sees statistical work as having diverted attention from qualitative and institutional issues such as law and economics and technological change (Copeland 1955, p. 91).

Copeland's Presidency of the AEA in 1957 gave him more opportunities to express his institutionalist leanings. He used his Presidency to organize a centenary session on Veblen's economics at the AEA conference in 1957. Papers from this session were put together with those from a special conference organized at Cornell by Copeland's colleague, Douglas Dowd, and published as *Thorstein Veblen: A Critical Reappraisal* (Dowd 1958). The contributors included Walton Hamilton, Clarence Ayres, and Carter Goodrich, as well as Copeland himself.[17] Copeland's essay (Copeland 1958b) stresses Veblen's evolutionary conception and its implications for the historical relativity of economic truth, and the need for a sense of cultural perspective. These are aspects of Veblen's method Copeland approves of, but he finds Veblen's concept of science as genetic inquiry into cumulative change to be too narrow.

More importantly, Copeland used his Presidential Address to revisit his conception of welfare economics as the analysis of the problems of existing pecuniary institutions. Copeland's Address opens with the argument that an adequate treatment of the "free enterprise economy" requires specification of the "central management functions" that are performed without a general manager, a description of the institutions that perform these management functions, an explanation of how these institutions work, an analysis of any deficiencies in the way these institutions perform these functions, and finally, a consideration of the public policy implications of such deficiencies and possible institutional reforms. From this base, he goes on to consider

---

[17] Other contributors were Douglas Dowd, Joseph Dorfman, Joel Dirlam, Forest Hill, Paul Sweezy, Myron Watkins, Allan Gruchy, Norman Kaplan, Lawrence Nabers, Melvin Brockie, Leslie Fishman, Philip Morrison, and G. W. Zinke.

the shortcomings of model-analysis. Model-analysis ignores key institutions, plays down historical and cross-country differences, and provides an insufficiently comprehensive and systematic basis for considering the deficiencies of the existing institutional system (Copeland 1958a, pp. 2–3). In particular, Copeland points to the profit system as functioning within sets of legal rules and practices that generate many divergences between what is profitable and what is good public policy, and actual market competition as usually diverging widely from the conditions required for perfect competition. Competition, in Copeland's opinion, is an inadequate regulator, and the market requires supplementing in the form of institutional changes, government regulations, and some degree of industry planning (Copeland 1958a, pp 9–11). Simplified model-analysis has played a role in supporting the view of such regulations as "distortions" rather than as supplements to the market.

CONCLUSION

There are many aspects of Copeland's work and career that are very revealing of the institutionalist movement in the interwar period and beyond. Copeland's connections with Amherst, Chicago, the Brookings Graduate School, the NBER, and the Federal Reserve, and with people such as Stewart, Hamilton, Clark, Mitchell, Commons, Ayres, Goodrich, Riefler, Thorp, May, and Lubin place him at the very heart of interwar institutionalism. Copeland can be seen very much as a model of the institutionalism of that time. Copeland, however, ceases to be a model of institutionalism in the 1950s and drops from sight of other institutionalists. In 1964, John Gambs (a Carter Goodrich student) could write to Allan Gruchy that he knew nothing about Copeland except as a name from the 1930s, and could even question whether he should be asked to contribute to a Festschrift for Clarence Ayres (John Gambs to Allan Gruchy, 4 April 1964, Allan Gruchy Papers). This is symptomatic of the changes that occurred within the movement after World War II.

This outline of Copeland's career gives more detail and life to the picture of interwar institutionalism as a close network of people and institutions that was sketched in Chapter 2. Institutionalism involved an active professional network of contacts that had a great deal to do with hiring decisions and research opportunities provided. Institutionalism was a movement in a true sociological sense. It also reinforces the view of interwar American economics as broad and relatively open, with institutionalism as a significant movement within the American economics profession and in no sense marginalized. Copeland and many other institutionalists of his generation had extremely successful careers, often combining academic work with service in government and international agencies. It also brings into view some of the linkages between institutionalists and the Research and Statistics Division of the Federal Reserve. Copeland's involvement with the ASA and his frequent publication in *JASA* should also be understood as quite typical. In the interwar period, the ASA had a substantial membership of economists, a good proportion of whom had strong institutionalist connections, and *JASA* published a great deal on economic statistics. Mitchell, Mills, Riefler, Thorp, and Goldenweiser were all presidents of the ASA. Copeland's involvement with government during the New Deal was also typical of institutionalists, and his work for the CSB is noteworthy.

In terms of the nature of Copeland's institutionalism, several points stand out. His Veblenian emphasis on pecuniary institutions, but applied primarily to an analysis of the failings of the existing set of pecuniary institutions and incentives, is typical of interwar institutionalist work. Also typical is Copeland's reformist rather than radical policy stance. His work on social-psychological foundations is particularly interesting in indicating the influence of J. R. Kantor and the nature of the behaviorism that many institutionalists adopted as instinct theory fell out of favor. This version of behaviorism stressed the roles of social conditioning and education, retaining an institutional referent. Copeland also made frequent reference to the importance of legal institutions, and it is clear that he attempted to incorporate ideas from Clark and Commons into his research. His critiques of Commons and of Ayres are also of interest as indicating areas of internal dispute and the degree of diversity that existed within institutionalism. Copeland's work on monetary issues was a part of what might be constructed as an institutionalist research program on money, one that involved the NBER, the Federal Reserve, and individuals such as Mitchell, Stewart, and Riefler, as well as Copeland.[18] This program was generally anti-quantity theory in approach, but it did not survive the development of the Keynesian/monetarist controversy.

[18] Perry Mehrling (1997) discusses Allyn Young, Alvin Hansen, and Edward Shaw as an "institutionalist" monetary tradition. None of these people were centrally located within the institutionalist movement but there were important links between the monetary work of Mitchell, Stewart, Riefler, and Copeland and that discussed by Mehrling. In particular, Young and Mitchell knew each other well, and Mitchell was interested in Young's monetary work. Young was very much a supporter of the Federal Reserve view as it emerged in the mid 1920s, and Young's student, James Angell, was a colleague of Mitchell's at Columbia and was at one point the person assigned to do the monetary component of Mitchell's

Most of all, Copeland's career indicates that the linkage between institutionalism and quantitative statistical work was by no means limited to Mitchell, but included Stewart, Copeland, Thorp, Lubin, Ezekiel, Riefler, and many others. For Copeland, the desire to make economics more scientific, more realistic, and more relevant meant expressing theories in terms that were empirically testable and working to improve economic data and measurements; a creed he practiced as well as preached.

The success of the work that Copeland and others did to improve government statistical services resulted in the kind of data gathering and measurement work that so occupied them becoming a function of government agencies. Although some people are familiar with the institutionalist underpinnings of Mitchell's business cycle project and of the work done by the NBER on national income, very few people recognize that the "accounting" approach to national income was not there from the beginning, and that Copeland was an important pioneer of that approach. Even fewer people recognize the institutionalist foundations of Copeland's moneyflows project and the flow of funds accounting that emerged from it. Moreover, the central role of institutionalists such as Copeland in creating the kind of statistical operation now commonly undertaken by government is rarely appreciated. Perhaps one of the greatest, but least recognized, legacies of interwar institutionalism to the conduct of economics as a whole is to be found in the informational foundation it provided for the subsequent development of empirical economics. With the arrival of econometrics, this ideal was taken over by the profession at large, but in the interwar, it was a view much more commonly found among institutionalists than neoclassical economists (Rutherford 1999).

Like other institutionalists, Copeland was skeptical about standard economic model building, but he was by no means antitheoretical. His interest in Chamberlin and Keynes and his attempts to combine their insights with those of Clark and Mitchell was a not uncommon institutionalist response. Copeland's observations concerning the role of these theoretical developments and the related shifts in the policy implications of economic theory in decreasing the visibility of institutionalism in the post–World War II period are perceptive and undoubtedly correct, but other factors may also have played a role.

The development of econometric methods linked to more mainstream neoclassical or Keynesian models diminished the appeal of the

business cycles project. Cohen (1972) makes a few remarks concerning Copeland's moneyflows and later work by Gurley and Shaw.

institutionalist style of empiricism. Not all Institutionalists were antieconometrics (notably Ezekiel), but neither can it be said that they were generally very enthusiastic. Copeland was clearly a skeptic, arguing as late as 1966 that the "mathematical manipulation of figures" was not a "satisfactory substitute for a genuine empirical approach" (Morris Copeland to Joseph Willits, 28 Nov 1966, Arthur F. Burns Papers, Box 133, Joseph H. Willits Folder). As will be seen further, similar attitudes prevailed at the NBER.[19] Econometric techniques might have been married to an institutionalist research agenda, but instead they provided an empirical component for more mainstream economics, and by doing so also provided a counter to the institutionalist claim to represent empirical science in economics. The irony here is that the institutionalist success in improving economic data did much to prepare the way for the spread of the econometric techniques.

---

[19] This culminated in the Ford Foundation deciding to "take no action" on the NBER's request for funding in 1966 (Marshall Robinson to Arthur F. Burns, 24 June 1966, Arthur F. Burns Papers, Box 127, Ford Foundation Folder). The "official" NBER position on econometrics can be found stated in a document prepared by Geoffrey Moore ("Memorandum on Position of National Bureau of Economic Research Re Econometric Studies," 13 June 1966, Arthur F. Burns Papers, Box 139, Econometric Studies Folder). Letters between Geoffrey Moore and Arthur F. Burns, Joseph Willits and Arthur F. Burns and minutes of Special NBER Board Meetings indicate much discussion of this issue in 1966 and 1967 (Arthur F. Burns Papers, Boxes 133 and 134, Joseph H. Willits Folders). See Chapters 9 and 11 in this book for more detail.

PART THREE

CENTERS OF INSTITUTIONAL ECONOMICS

5

Institutionalism at Chicago and Beyond

For most economists, the terms "Chicago economics" and "institution-alism" denote clearly antithetical approaches to the discipline. Members of the modern Chicago School such as George Stigler have often made highly dismissive remarks concerning American institutionalism. Stigler in par-ticular devoted himself to fierce attacks on the work of Gardiner Means, John Kenneth Galbraith, Richard Lester, and anyone else who ventured to question either the virtues of the free market or the empirical superiority of competitive price theory. Some of these attitudes have their roots in the interwar period, most obviously in Frank Knight's views on the centrality of price theory to any properly "scientific" economics (Knight 1924), and in his bitingly critical attacks on the policy positions of institutionalist and other advocates of regulatory intervention and of the "social control" of business (Knight 1932). Nevertheless, what this chapter seeks to reveal is the central place of the University of Chicago in the formation and early history of the institutionalist movement. In the period up to 1918, the Economics Department at Chicago contained, at various times, virtually all of those individuals most closely associated with the founding of the institutional-ist movement: Veblen, Hoxie, Mitchell, Hamilton, Moulton, and Clark. In addition, the department of philosophy contained John Dewey and George Herbert Mead. Chicago has a strong claim to be seen both as the birthplace of what became known as institutional economics and a place from which institutionalism spread to other institutions. Although a significant institu-tionalist element continued to exist at Chicago through most of the 1920s, it declined sharply in the late 1920s and 1930s.

Table 5.1. *Selected Chicago faculty, 1892–1930*

Laurence Laughlin (1892–1916)	John M. Clark (1915–1926)
Adolf C. Miller (1892–1902)	Harry A. Millis (1916–1938)
Thorstein Veblen (1892–1906)	Jacob Viner (1916–1946)
John Dewey (Philosophy) (1894–1904)	Clarence Ayres (Philosophy) (1917–1920)
George H. Mead (Philosophy) (1894–1931)	J. R. Kantor (Psychology) (1917–1920)
Herbert J. Davenport (1902–1908)	Willard E. Atkins (1919–1923)
Charles E. Merriam (Poli Sci) (1902–1940)	Paul Douglas (1920–1949)
Robert F. Hoxie (1906–1916)	Frank Knight (1917–1919 and 1927–1952)
Chester W. Wright (1907–1944)	Hazel Kyrk (Econ/Home Ec) (1925–1952)
James A. Field (1908–1927)	Henry Schultz (1926–1938)
L. C. Marshall (1908–1928)	Henry C. Simons (1927–1946)
Walton H. Hamilton (1914–1915)	William Ogburn (Sociology) (1927–1951)
Harold Moulton (1914–1922)	John U. Nef (1929–1964)

CHICAGO AND THE FORMATION OF INSTITUTIONAL ECONOMICS

The Chicago Department of Political Economy was begun in 1892 with Laurence Laughlin as its head. Lists of selected faculty members and graduate students from 1892 through to 1930 are provided in Tables 5.1 and 5.2. This is not a complete listing of either faculty or graduate students but indicates those who in various ways had the most to do with the history of institutional economics.

Laughlin was extremely conservative in his economic and political views, and very much at odds with the historicist or "new" school influence in American economics. On the other hand, he was anti quantity theory in his monetary views, and he built a department that was both diverse in its interests and had significant representation of those broadly critical of "orthodox" economics (Nef 1934). Most obviously, Laughlin brought Thorstein Veblen with him from Cornell and shortly thereafter placed him in charge of editing the *Journal of Political Economy*. As Hodgson has argued (Hodgson 2004, p. 143), Veblen's years at Chicago (from 1892 to 1906) were remarkably creative ones. Veblen's thinking underwent some significant changes

Table 5.2. *Selected Chicago graduate students, 1892–1930 (Date of PhD)*

Herbert J. Davenport (1898)	J. R. Kantor 1917 (Philosophy)
Harry A. Millis (1899)	Willard E. Atkins (JD 1918)
Wesley C. Mitchell (1899)	Sumner Slichter (1918)
Katherine B. Davis (1900)	Edward Mittleman (1920)
Henry W. Stuart (1900 Philosophy)	Harold Innis (1920)
Sophonisba Breckinridge (1901 Poli Sci)	Hazel Kyrk (1920)
Edith Abbot (1905)	Morris Copeland (1921)
Robert F. Hoxie (1905)	Carter Goodrich (1921)
E. H. Downey (PhD student 1909)	Leverett Lyon (1921)
Harold Moulton (1914)	Edith Ayres (1921 Philosophy)
Edwin Nourse (1915)	Helen Wright (1922)
Clarence Ayres (1917 Philosophy)	Margaret Reid (1931 Home Economics)
Max Handman (1917 Sociology)	Ruth Allen (1933)

around 1896, when he appears to have developed his particular evolutionary stance (Hodgson 2004, p. 135; Camic forthcoming).[1] Soon afterward, he published a number of his key methodological essays, including "Why Is Economics Not an Evolutionary Science" (1898) and "The Preconceptions of Economic Science" (1899–1900), as well others. These essays laid out his critique of standard classical and neoclassical economics, his dismissal of utility maximization as a basis for understanding economic behavior, and outlined his program for an evolutionary economics based on the concepts of cumulative causation and "selective adaptation" of habits of thought and institutions.

His first major book, *The Theory of the Leisure Class*, appeared in 1899. It contained his analysis of the wasteful "conspicuous consumption" of the pecuniary elite, but also a more general theory of consumption behavior based on the notion of socially defined "standards of living." His most important book, *The Theory of Business Enterprise* (1904), made extensive use of the testimony given to the U.S. Industrial Commission on matters of corporate finance and control. Here Veblen developed his ideas concerning

[1]   Hodgson attributes this change to the visit to Chicago of Conway Lloyd Morgan (Hodgson 2004, pp. 134–139). Camic argues that the main influence might have come from Veblen's translation of Gustav Cohn (Camic forthcoming).

the growth of a division between making goods and making money, related both to technological and financial developments. With larger scales of business and the development of corporate finance, making money could often be achieved in ways inimical to productive and technological efficiency (via monopoly, restriction of output, financial misrepresentation and manipulation, insider dealing, and many other kinds of activity related to business strategy in imperfect markets). Veblen saw effective control of corporations passing into a few hands, with the bulk of smaller owners, and preferred stock and bond holders, effectively disenfranchised. He also developed a theory of business cycles related to the ability of firms to borrow or issue bonds on the basis of expected earnings and becoming highly leveraged. This both fueled upswings and made firms highly susceptible to any downturn in earnings. Veblen combined this with a notion of technological advance tending to outpace the growth in consumption expenditure, leading to a chronic tendency to low profitability. Veblen makes some significant references to John A. Hobson's underconsumptionism at this point. According to Veblen, the business solution was to attempt to restrict output through cartels, but he raised the possibility of the growth of a more socialistic ideology among the working and engineering classes, stemming from the ways of thinking engendered by contact with the "machine process," and potentially leading to a substantial shift in institutions (Veblen 1904).

Veblen's teaching at Chicago included courses on Scope and Method of Political Economy, History of Political Economy, Socialism, and Economic Factors in Civilization. This last course became quite famous and was the one in which Veblen developed his ideas on economic and institutional change – ideas that would later find expression in *The Instinct of Workmanship* (1914). Although Veblen left Chicago for Stanford in 1906,[2] and would later move to Missouri and then the New School, his influence did not disappear. His presence on the faculty had a substantial impact on a number of graduate students, particularly Herbert Davenport, Wesley Mitchell, and Robert Hoxie. Henry W. Stuart in philosophy also absorbed ideas from Veblen and Dewey. Davenport became an important American representative of a somewhat Austrian and subjectivist version of price theory, with a heavy emphasis on the role of the entrepreneur, but he included a Veblenian concern with predation and exploitation in his work, and maintained both an interest in institutional economics and a lasting friendship with Veblen. Davenport taught for a few years at Chicago from about 1902,

---

[2] The various marital problems Veblen had and the reasons for him leaving Chicago are discussed in Jorgensen and Jorgensen (1999).

but moved to become head of the Economics Department at Missouri (in 1908)[3] and then at Cornell (in 1916).

Mitchell's 1899 doctoral dissertation, the "History of the United States Notes," was prepared under Laughlin's supervision, but Mitchell was deeply impressed with Veblen's criticism of hedonism, and his analysis of pecuniary or "business" institutions and their failings (including business cycles). In Mitchell's case, however, these Veblenian ideas were combined with a strongly empirical bent and John Dewey's instrumentalist philosophy (Dewey was a member of the Philosophy Department at Chicago from 1894 to 1904). Mitchell spent a year at the Bureau of the Census and then taught at Chicago as an instructor in 1901 and 1902. Despite Laughlin's efforts to retain him, he left for Berkeley in 1903.[4] After leaving Chicago, Veblen moved to Stanford and he and Mitchell resumed close contact. The later development of Mitchell's work will be discussed further in this chapter.

Robert Hoxie completed his doctorate in 1905, and his earlier work in particular is full of Veblenian terminology. Hoxie's essay, "The Empirical Method of Economic Instruction" (Hoxie 1901), contains the argument that economics must become a study of "the life process and genesis of economic organization, essentially cognate with the biological sciences" and with the aim of providing a "systematic account in causal terms of groups of facts whose relationships are subject to cumulative change" (Hoxie 1901, p. 486). In 1906, Hoxie turned his attention to the particular issues of labor and trade unionism, but this interest was directly prompted by Veblen's ideas on the impact of the machine process on the habits of thought of industrial workers (Fishman 1958, pp. 223–227; McNulty 1973, p. 464). Hoxie himself stated the thesis as follows:

The laborer, like the rest of us, is a product of heredity and environment. … Now, it is well known, that the environment of the laborer under the modern capitalistic system has tended to become predominantly one of physical force. He has been cut off from all knowledge of market and managerial activities. The ideals, motives, and cares of property ownership are becoming foreign to him. … Even outside the strictly mechanical occupations the machine and the machine process are coming to dominate the worker and the growth in size of the industrial unit renders his economic relationship ever more impersonal. (Hoxie 1907, p. 348)

---

[3] Davenport moved at least in part because Veblen had left earlier.

[4] Mitchell went to Berkeley at the urging of Adolf C. Miller who had been one of his teachers at Chicago. Miller left Chicago in 1902 to head the Department of Economics at Berkeley. Miller married Mary Sprague; Mitchell married her sister, Lucy. Lucy Sprague became Dean of Women at Berkeley.

The result of this for Hoxie, as for Veblen, was a "distinctive trade union point of view" or a distinctive "spiritual basis" for unionism. This generated an ideological gulf separating workers from employers and rendering them "incapable of mutual understanding" (Hoxie 1907, pp. 359–361). Hoxie's work on trade unions, then, was motivated by this Veblenian idea and, according to Fishman, with the problem of just exactly how the prevailing pecuniary institutions are to be "disestablished" and institutions more in line with industrial habits of thought established in their place (Fishman 1958, pp. 222, 226), an issue on which Veblen was uncomfortably vague. What Hoxie found, and published in a series of works beginning in 1908, was not consistent with the Veblenian point of view. Hoxie's investigations led him to the view that there were many different types of union, each with different motivations and programs and emerging out of different sets of environmental and temperamental conditions (Hoxie 1917, pp. 31–52). Moreover, Hoxie argued that the "dominant motive of the average wage-worker must ever be to secure the greatest possible pecuniary results from his toil" (Hoxie 1908, pp. 693–694), and that the dominant form of union-ism was what he called "business unionism," unions organized to do busi-ness with employers and to "bargain for the sale of the product which it controls" (Hoxie 1917, p. 336). These unions profess belief in natural rights and accept "as inevitable, if not as just, the existing capitalistic organization and the wage system, as well as existing property rights and the binding force of contract" (Hoxie 1917, p. 45).

These findings resulted in Hoxie turning away from the Veblenian model. In his last book, published posthumously in 1917, Hoxie characterizes Veblen's theory as seeing society as made up of two warring classes that are the result of modern machine industry creating separate material environ-ments and mental disciplines for each. He goes on:

What is wrong with this theory? … Existing facts in this connection as to class solidarity confute it. … [I]t places too much stress on the economic environment as a formative force. Man is the outcome of his total social environment. The indi-vidual, according to Veblen, cannot react on this environment: he is not a center of force. But cannot we do something to change this environment by education, shop arrangements, etc.? Again, there are no such rigid economic environments and disciplines. There is much more social interaction than supposed. (Hoxie 1917, pp. 366–367)

It is worth noting that Veblen ultimately accepted part of Hoxie's analy-sis and came to present major unions such as the A. F. of L. as business unions concerned only with pecuniary gain. Partly for that reason, Veblen turned his attention to the engineers as a possible force for institutional reconstruction (Veblen 1921). He did not, however, feel the need to abandon his more basic idea that institutional change would come about only through a process of habituation to machine technology.

Hoxie was clearly more empirical and pragmatic in his approach than Veblen. Hoxie taught at Chicago from 1906 until his suicide in 1916, and his teaching method was empirical, problem-centered, and focused on the actual functioning of institutions. It inspired many students. E. H. Downey was a student of Hoxie's and was also much influenced by Veblen. Downey describes Hoxie as using the "problem method" in his classes, focused on the current problems of the labor movement. Hoxie's method was pragmatic and related to the issue of social control. His graduate classes especially had the character of a "joint enterprise in the discovery of truth" (Hoxie 1917, pp. xxx–xxii). Downey was to move on to the Universities of Missouri and then Wisconsin and become a leading expert in workers' compensation. It should be remembered that Hoxie also knew John R. Commons and the Wisconsin group of labor economists well, and worked on a book on scientific management for the U.S. Commission on Industrial Relations (Hoxie 1915).[5]

As mentioned earlier, Hamilton claimed it was Hoxie who first used the term "institutional economist" to describe himself (Hamilton 1916a), and Hoxie's focus on institutions, his pragmatism, his problem-centered approach, and his concern with social control were all elements that fed into the notion of institutional economics put forward by Hamilton (Hamilton 1919a). While at Chicago, Hamilton wrote a lengthy review of J. A. Hobson's *Work and Wealth* (Hamilton 1915), critiquing Hobson's continued attachment to utilitarian principles, but approving of his "attack upon the ethical character of competitive society" and of his attempt to provide a theoretical basis for the "social reform movement" (Hamilton 1915, pp. 563, 583). Hamilton's time at Chicago was also a period in which he became seriously interested in the problem of teaching economics. Some of Hamilton's interest was likely prompted by Hoxie's approach, but there was quite a widespread interest in teaching issues at Chicago at the time that also involved L. C. Marshall, James A. Field, and Chester Wright. Wright, an economic historian, arrived at Chicago in 1907; Field and Marshall, a year later. Field concentrated initially on population, Marshall on commerce and law. In the years from 1913 to

---

[5]   Hoxie was deeply unhappy with his scientific management book. Commons persuaded him to publish it. For a discussion of some possible causes of Hoxie's suicide, see McNulty (1973), Nyland (1996), and Hodgson (2001).

1919, all three were involved in an attempt to move economics instruction away from the "rigorous drill in orthodox theory" or the "straight-jacket of conventionalized theory" to a method of instruction emphasizing the development of economic institutions, inquiry into current problems and issues, and the fostering of creativity and originality (Field 1917). To this end, they produced a book of readings to supplement the usual texts (Marshall, Wright, and Field 1913) and Marshall produced a book, *Readings in Industrial Society* (Marshall 1918), with a heavy emphasis on the institutional development of industrial society, the money economy and financial organization, machine industry, the wage system and the worker, industrial concentration, competition, private property, and social control. This book contained a significant number of readings taken from Veblen, Mitchell, Hamilton, Moulton, Hoxie, J. M. Clark, Edwin Cannan, and J. A. Hobson. Hamilton held both Field and Marshall in high regard, and Ayres regarded Marshall's book as a contribution to the institutional type of economics then developing (Ayres 1918).

In addition to Hoxie and Hamilton, J. M. Clark was hired to Chicago from Amherst by Laughlin in 1915. Clark's doctoral dissertation had been on railway regulation and Laughlin wanted a "railway man" (J. Laurence Laughlin to H. C. Adams, 7 April 1915, H. C. Adams Papers, Box 10, Folder April 1915). At this point in his career, however, Clark was turning his interest to issues such as social value, economics and psychology, institutional reform, and "social control." A number of these aspects of Clark's work have already been mentioned. Clark and Hamilton also collaborated with Harold Moulton. Moulton completed his PhD at Chicago in 1914 and became an assistant professor at Chicago in the same year. He developed interests in monetary and financial economics with an institutional orientation, and his work contained a clear underconsumptionist position. He was promoted rapidly and stayed at Chicago until 1922 when he moved to head up the new Institute of Economics.

Outside of economics, Charles Merriam joined the faculty of political science in 1902. His approach to his subject was an empirical one, and he was to become, along with Mitchell and Ogburn, a major figure in the founding and operation of the Social Science Research Council. In addition, John Dewey was in the Department of Philosophy until 1904.

In the period of the mid- to late 1910s, then, there was a significant group of faculty and graduate students who would become associated with institutionalism. Indeed, if the references to Veblen in economics journals in the period up to 1918 are examined, it will be seen that almost all of them come from people associated with Chicago, in particular

Hoxie, Mitchell, Hamilton, and Clark. Interest in Veblen, and in institutionalism, however, was not confined to the individuals mentioned so far but also included Harry Millis (PhD 1899), Edwin Nourse (PhD 1915), Sumner Slichter (PhD 1918), Clarence Ayres (PhD 1917), Max Handman (PhD 1917), and Willard Atkins (JD 1918). Millis was a labor economist and had been Commons's first graduate student at Indiana. Commons always thought of Millis as one of "his boys." After completing his doctorate, he worked at Stanford (1903–1912), overlapping with Veblen. Millis returned to Chicago in 1916 and became the mainstay of the teaching in labor economics. Slichter was also a Commons student from Wisconsin and continued his work in labor economics, particularly on labor unions and wage bargaining. His dissertation on labor turnover was supervised by Millis. He was later hired to Cornell by Davenport, to be joined by Morris Copeland. Nourse was an agricultural economist with a particular interest in cooperatives. He would later be hired by Moulton to the Institute of Economics. Outside of economics, there were Clarence Ayres in Philosophy and Max Handman in Sociology. As mentioned previously, Ayres came to Chicago after a year with Walton Hamilton at Amherst. Ayres would adopt a pragmatic philosophy based on John Dewey. Although Ayres's time at Chicago did not overlap with Dewey's, pragmatic philosophy continued to be represented at Chicago by George H. Mead. Ayres also had significant contact with J. R. Kantor, a critic of instinct theory. Ayres completed his PhD on ethical issues in economics in 1917 and remained teaching at Chicago until 1920. Handman's 1917 thesis dealt with Marx. He had previously been a colleague of Veblen's at Missouri, and after receiving his PhD moved to the University of Texas teaching sociology and economic history. Willard Atkins completed a JD degree in 1918 and taught economics at Chicago for several years before moving to New York and heading the heavily institutionalist department at Washington Square College.

It is also worth mentioning that Laughlin and his successor as head, L. C. Marshall, encouraged women students and that the Department of Political Economy had close connections with the then-independent Chicago School of Civics and Philanthropy. Although not usually spoken of as a part of the institutionalist canon, much of the work done by these women was statistical and institutional in character. The first female PhD in economics (in 1900) was Katherine Bement Davis who came under the influence of Veblen and wrote her thesis on "Causes Affecting the Standard of Living and Wages." Sophonisba Breckinridge obtained her PhD in 1901 in political science, but she also studied economics and her thesis was written under Laughlin on the topic of monetary history. She taught a course on "The State in Relation to Labor" in the Department of Political Economy in 1902 (Hammond 2000b). She studied in Chicago's Law School, graduating in 1904, and then taught in Chicago's Department of Household Administration. In 1907, she began teaching in the Department of Social Investigation in the School of Civics and Philanthropy. She became the director of that Department in 1908, and Dean of the School in 1909. The second female PhD in economics was Edith Abbott, a student of Laughlin, Veblen, Mitchell, and Breckinridge (from whom she took courses in the Department of Household Administration). Her thesis was "A Statistical Study of the Wages of Unskilled Labor in the United States" (1905). In 1908 she was hired by Breckinridge to teach statistics in the School of Civics and Philanthropy. She also taught in the Department of Political Economy in 1909–1910 (Hammond 2000a).

Breckinridge and Abbott had a major impact on the School of Civics and Philanthropy. They encouraged their students to take graduate degrees in economics or political science and also worked to restructure the curriculum of the School itself, "emphasizing statistics, empirical research and the scientific method, and making it increasingly like the graduate training in economics, political science and law that they themselves had received" (Hammond 2000b, p. 84). They produced a remarkable stream of empirical research and worked to make the School a part of the University, which they succeeded in doing in 1920 with the establishment of the Graduate School of Social Service Administration.

VEBLEN AND MITCHELL BEYOND CHICAGO

Many of the key players in the formation of institutionalism spent time at Chicago prior to 1918 and Hamilton's manifesto, but a number of those who were a central part of creating institutionalist ideas at Chicago left well before the movement coalesced. In particular, Veblen moved to Stanford and Missouri and then the New School, Mitchell to Berkeley and then Columbia, and Hamilton to Amherst and then Brookings. Hamilton's programs at Amherst and Brookings and the institutionalist group at Columbia are the subject of later chapters. This section will deal with Mitchell and Veblen, and some of their colleagues and students, from the time they left Chicago through to their respective moves to New York.

In 1903, Mitchell moved to Berkeley, where he stayed until 1913. His colleagues at Berkeley included Adolf Miller, Jessica Peixotto, and, for a short time, Carleton Parker.[6] Harry Millis was at Stanford from the same year, to be joined in 1906 by Veblen and Allyn Young. Henry W. Stuart was a member of the Philosophy Department at Stanford.[7] Mitchell already knew Young from his year at the Bureau of the Census, and Mitchell had a significant amount of contact with his Stanford colleagues.

Mitchell's work up to the end of 1906 consisted of his study of the Greenbacks, a continuation of his Chicago dissertation work, but even before he completed this he was expressing the desire to engage in a larger and "more penetrating" study (L. S. Mitchell 1953, p. 165). The study Mitchell embarked on he called "the money economy": an investigation of "the highly organized group of pecuniary institutions," including "how they evolved a quasi-independence and in turn affected not only the activities but the minds of their makers" (L. S. Mitchell 1953, p. 167). The Veblenian nature of this proposal is strikingly clear.

Mitchell's money economy project contained many components, including a study of the interrelation of price movements and business cycles, but it also came to involve a historical dimension: a study of the development of the money economy in Europe (and particularly in England from the eleventh to the sixteenth centuries). Mitchell visited Harvard during the 1908–1909 academic year, where he came into contact with Edwin Gay and conducted much of his historical research. The only component of the historical research published by Mitchell himself can be found in the form of a brief historical background to the phenomenon of business cycles (Mitchell 1927, pp. 66–74), but he did present his work on the topic in more detail in an address given at Stanford in May 1910 (Mitchell 1910c).

In Veblen's discussion of the evolution of pecuniary institutions, the analysis runs almost exclusively in terms of the development of the technology of handicraft industry and its associated habits of thought. Mitchell's discussion refers to a broader range of explanatory variables. The introduction and spread of money transactions and markets Mitchell links first to the commutation of dues in kind and in labor in the manorial system, and the gradual rise of estate management for profit rather than for direct subsistence. These developments are linked to the substantial savings in

---

[6] Parker had previously spent time in England at the LSE. At Harvard, he was taught by Ripley and Gay. In Germany, he studied at Berlin and Heidelberg. See Cornelia Parker (1919).

[7] Henry Waldgrave Stuart wrote his thesis on "Valuation as a Logical Process" and wrote a number of other papers on issues of valuation relevant to economics. He was part of a Stanford/Berkeley group that included Mitchell, Veblen, and Young, who formed a club to read and discuss each other's papers. He remained at Stanford.

transactions costs provided by the system of money rents, the greater incentives to efficiency, and the scarcity of labor resulting from the Black Death. Second, Mitchell discusses the substitution of money payment for knight service. This occurs as a result of the Crown's need for money to finance foreign military campaigns, the greater efficiency of mercenaries, and the obvious benefits to tenants of avoiding direct military service. Finally Mitchell refers to the growth of commerce in towns and the gradual freeing of market prices from regulation. The interest of the nobility in promoting freer trade is mentioned as a factor in this process, as is the difficulty of regulating prices in the face of exogenous shocks such as fluctuating harvests, the Black Death, war, and currency debasement. Technological change and the growth in capital requirements as the scale of manufacturing increased are mentioned by Mitchell but given no special priority as a causal factor (Mitchell 1910c). Indeed, Mitchell's argument is predominantly one that at a certain point in history, and under the particular conditions that then existed, money transactions became more efficient than the older system of payments in kind and in labor. The use of money and market transactions gradually spread and displaced nonmonetary forms of organization and exchange. In Mitchell's own words:

Why men have extended so widely this practice of putting their dealings with each other upon a pecuniary basis is a problem of details. Sometimes both parties probably foresaw an advantage from the change.... Sometimes one party forced the arrangement on the other, as villeins wrung commutation from reluctant landlords after the Black Death. Sometimes a clear appreciation of the benefits of novel uses of money lagged behind the practice.... But soon or late, men have come to understand at least the clearest effects of money economy. (Mitchell 1910c, p. 354)

In Mitchell's treatment, then, the initial spread of money transactions and market exchange is explained in terms of economic advantage rather than in terms of technological change specifically. Where Mitchell reverts to a more Veblenian style of argument is in the analysis of the longer-term and unintended effect of the growing use of money on habits of thought. Money transactions were introduced within a system of feudal preconceptions. The growth of the use of money and markets had a corrosive influence on those preconceptions, resulting instead in the development of a pecuniary habit of mind. Mitchell takes this to the point of arguing that what we would now think of as economic rationality is itself an institutional product of long habituation to a way of life based upon monetary calculation and attention to pecuniary advantage (Mitchell 1910a; 1910b; 1910c). He has no difficulty with the Veblenian characterization of modern western civilization as a business or pecuniary culture built on the principles of pecuniary gain. However, nowhere in Mitchell does one find a discussion of the type supplied by Veblen on the cultural impact of machine technology.

Mitchell's experience with the money economy project was not incidental to the development of his views on Veblen or to the subsequent direction of his own work. Later in 1910, Mitchell abandoned the project and turned his attention to the problem of business cycles that was both more specific and more amenable to quantitative analysis. As he put it in a later piece on Veblen:

Problems of cumulative change in "life history" are extremely difficult to treat by any method of measurement. Each change is by hypothesis a unique event, begotten by an indefinite number of causes. To disentangle the tangled skein is impossible. Without the aid of elaborate technique it is hard to do more with such problems than what Darwin and Veblen have done – that is, to study the evidence and select for particular attention what seem to be the salient factors. ... It is only when he comes to recent changes that an investigator has tolerably accurate data. These materials Veblen did not reject; but he made no great effort to exploit them. In this respect, at least, his practice resembled that of most orthodox economists. (Mitchell 1936a, p. 298)

Mitchell came to the view Veblen's work as too speculative, and in place of such speculation, Mitchell proposed a program of studying a particular problem open to empirical examination with the institutional component made explicit but taken as a given. In this manner, Mitchell turned his attention to the statistical examination of the problem of business cycles conceived of as an undesired and unintended consequence of the existing pecuniary habits of mind and institutions: the profit-seeking nature of business enterprise, the functioning of other pecuniary institutions such as banks, and the operation, interrelations, and leads and lags in the movements of prices in various markets. What he produced was a close empirical "analytical description" of the business cycle consisting of four phases – prosperity, crisis, depression, and revival – with each phase creating the conditions for the next (Mitchell 1913). Business cycles, then, were a microcosm of the kind of cumulative causation discussed by Veblen. Mitchell also explicitly linked institutions with his work on business cycles via his argument that it is institutions that create the patterns of aggregate behavior that result in cycles (Rutherford 1987).

Mitchell's project on business cycles took most of his effort through until 1913, but his time at Berkeley was a period during which he also produced a number of essays that would play an important part in defining the institutional approach. Of particular significance in this respect was his two-part article, "The Rationality of Economic Activity" (Mitchell 1910a; 1910b), and his article on the consumption behavior of households, "The Backward Art of Spending Money" (Mitchell 1912). Mitchell's articles on rationality refer to Veblen, William James, and William McDougall, and their ideas concerning the formation of habits. For Mitchell, this work undermined confidence in the conception of "conduct as guided by calculation" (Mitchell 1910a; 1910b; 1944, p. 214). Mitchell is not arguing that rationality is absent, but that traditional economics overstates the rational element. For Mitchell, rationality is not a given attribute of human conduct, but itself an institutional product, an outcome of the growth of pecuniary institutions and conduct. The widespread use of money and monetary calculation creates economic rationality. However, because economic rationality is itself an acquired attribute, it is "not a solid foundation upon which elaborate theoretical constructions may be erected without more ado" (Mitchell 1910b, p. 201). In particular, rationality does not involve thinking things out anew on every occasion, but rather the development of habits and routines that are reasonably successful (Mitchell 1910b, p. 199). Also, those areas of life less permeated by pecuniary norms tend to remain less rational and more subject to other social norms. This idea forms the basis of Mitchell's discussion of household expenditure patterns (Mitchell 1912).

Work by Veblen and Mitchell also impacted on some of Mitchell's Berkeley colleagues. Jessica Peixotto was a Berkeley PhD with an interest in socialism, poverty, standards of living, and social economics generally. She and Mitchell discussed their mutual interests (Cookingham 1987, p. 51), and Mitchell described her and her students' work as dealing "in a forthright manner with the world in which men sweat, make mistakes, and indulge their passions, not with a world in which dream creatures, making nice calculations on a rational basis, maintain a wavering equilibrium" (Mitchell 1935, p. 3). Peixotto was later to conduct work on professional standards of living (Peixotto 1927) and make budget and cost-of-living studies for a wide variety of economic groups. All her work made use of the idea of socially defined standards of living that members of a social group attempted to achieve.

Carleton Parker completed his undergraduate work at Berkeley but went to Harvard and then Germany for graduate work before returning to Berkeley in 1913. His work focused on labor economics, labor unrest, and especially the casual laborer and the IWW in California. In 1916, he moved to the University of Washington to head the Department of Economics and the new School of Commerce. William Ogburn and Rexford Tugwell were both colleagues of Parker at Washington. While still at Berkeley, Parker's students included F. C. Mills and Paul Brissenden. Both had also been taught by Mitchell and both later moved on to do doctorates at Columbia. In the fall of 1913, Parker took a position with the California Immigration and Housing Commission and in 1914 hired Mills and Brissenden as special investigators for the Commission (and also for the U.S. Commission on Industrial Relations). Under an assumed name, Mills worked in labor camps, attended IWW meetings, and kept extensive field notes that fed into Parker's and the Commission's research (Parker 1920; Woirol 1984).[8] Brissenden also worked on the IWW.

In the summer of 1915, William Ogburn taught summer school at Berkeley and introduced Parker to a range of psychological literature that was to deeply influence his thinking. Parker's courses on labor problems included books by Veblen, Hoxie, McDougall, Wallas, Thorndike, Lippmann, and Freud, and his research turned to the psychological bases of labor unrest (in terms of the repression of instincts). This thesis was expressed in two articles, "Towards Understanding Labor Unrest" and "Motives in Economic Life" (Parker 1920). Parker's excitement with this line of research took him East for discussions with Veblen in Missouri, Commons and others in Wisconsin, Mitchell, Boas, Walter Lippmann, Herbert Croly, Edward Thorndike, and John Dewey in New York, Irving Fisher at Yale, Edwin Gay, Harold Laski, Felix Frankfurter, and Taussig at Harvard, and John Watson in Washington (Cornelia Parker 1919, pp. 102–111). Very sadly, Parker died of pneumonia in 1918.[9]

The Department at Berkeley did, nevertheless, retain an institutionalist component. Jessica Peixotto was joined by labor economists Ira Cross and Paul Taylor, both of whom had Wisconsin backgrounds. Cross completed his MA under Commons and his PhD, on the history of the labor movement in California, at Stanford under Millis in 1909. At Stanford, Cross overlapped with Veblen and Young, and was a teaching assistant to Veblen. He moved to Berkeley in 1914, where he stayed. Paul Taylor completed his

---

[8] Mills was given the nickname "Turk." Mark Perlman recalls Paul Brissenden saying that this was because when Mills did field research for the U.S. Commission on Industrial Relations, "he would report in secretly and then disappear 'over the hills like a Turk'" (Mark Perlman to Malcolm Rutherford, 8 January 2001).

[9] Cornelia Stratton Parker wrote a very loving biography of her husband (Cornelia Parker 1919). She taught briefly at Berkeley (in social economics) and then moved to New York where she studied at the New School, taking courses from Veblen, Laski, Beard, and Robinson. Perhaps inspired by the undercover work done by Mills for her husband, she took jobs in a variety of employments and wrote up her experiences. See Cornelia Parker (1922; 1934). Mark Pittenger (1997) discusses Mills, Cornelia Parker, and a number of other efforts to document working-class life. For more information on Mills's undercover work, see Woirol (1984; 1992).

PhD at Berkeley in 1922 on the Sailors' Union. He then worked as lead investigator on a SSRC project on Mexican migration, a project headed by Edith Abbott. This work in turn involved him with research on the migration of labor to California during the dust bowl years. His second wife was Dorothea Lange whose photographs of migrant labor became iconic (Lange and Taylor 1939).[10] In addition, Berkeley was to gain several Columbia graduates of institutionalist persuasion: Charles Gulick in 1926, Leo Rogin in 1927, and Robert Brady in 1929. Gulick was also a labor economist; his thesis on the labor policy of U.S. Steel was supervised by Henry Seager and Wesley Mitchell. He would also write on trust and corporation issues with Seager (Seager and Gulick 1929). Rogin worked with Mitchell at Columbia and developed his famous history of economic thought course at Berkeley (Dimand and Koehn 2008). Brady had been strongly influenced by Veblen and Mitchell; J. K. Galbriath was to call him "Berkeley's Veblenian" (Galbraith 1981, p. 31).[11]

As mentioned previously, Veblen left Chicago in 1906 and went to Stanford, but only stayed until the end of 1909.[12] Veblen taught courses on the History of Political Economy and Economic Factors in Civilization. He published a number of important articles while at Stanford, notably the second of his essays on Marx, and articles on J. B. Clark's economics, the nature of capital, and on the limitations of marginal utility (Veblen 1907; 1908a; 1908b; 1909), but Stanford never formed a group of economists who would associate closely with Veblen or with institutionalism. Things were different at Missouri where Davenport found him a position in 1911. While at Missouri, Veblen not only continued to teach his Economic Factors course, but also courses in Corporation Finance and Trusts and Corporations. He published a number of books, including *The Instinct of Workmanship* (1914) – as close as he came to a general statement of his evolutionary system – his penetrating assessment of German imperial ambition (Veblen 1915), his analysis of the requirements for peace in Europe (Veblen 1917), and his *Higher Learning in America*, a scathing attack on

---

[10] Lange worked for a time for the photographic division of the Resettlement Administration, headed by Roy E. Stryker, a Columbia and New Deal colleague of Rexford Tugwell (see Chapter 8). Photographs by people such as Dorothea Lange and Lewis Hine played an important role in the efforts for labor and agricultural reform.

[11] Berkeley continued to have a significant social economics group consisting of Peixotto, Emily Huntington (who also worked on consumption and budget studies), Barbara Armstrong (who worked on social insurance), and others (Cookingham 1987). For more detail on Brady, see Dowd (1994).

[12] Veblen left Stanford because of problems created by his wife. See Dorfman (1934) and Jorgensen and Jorgensen (1999).

the conduct of universities by businessmen, written with the University of Chicago clearly in mind (Veblen 1918). Just one year later, the collection of Veblen's essays, *The Place of Science in Modern Civilization* (Veblen 1919b), appeared. All of this caused a considerable revival of interest in Veblen's work. Veblen also gathered a group of like-minded faculty and graduate students around him at Missouri. Max Handman studied and taught sociology there, Walter Stewart came to Missouri to study with Veblen, as did E. H. Downey. Isador Lubin was a student of both Veblen's and Handman's, and William Camp and Leon Ardzooni followed Veblen from Stanford to continue their studies.[13] Myron Watkins was also a student at Missouri and took courses from Veblen. Camp later taught in agricultural economics at North Carolina State College and Berkeley. Downey left Missouri and completed his graduate work at Wisconsin, but not before publishing a highly Veblenian critique of marginal utility theory, "The Futility of Marginal Utility" (Downey 1910). Downey argues, with references to Veblen and Dewey, that marginal utility theory is a type of scholasticism and that it "has not contributed, and it cannot contribute, to the elucidation of any practical problem" (Downey 1910, p. 268). Lubin would become extremely close to Veblen. In 1918, Lubin and Veblen worked briefly with the World War I Food Administration, where Veblen's recommendations for working with the IWW to bring in the harvest were met with silence.[14] Lubin later moved to Michigan and then to the Brookings Graduate School where he completed his PhD, and worked for the Institute of Economics and the Brookings Institution. Watkins was to go on to become an expert on cartels, antitrust, and regulation at New York University and at Brookings.[15] Veblen worked for the *Dial* magazine before obtaining a position at the New School for Social Research.

Mitchell's move from Berkeley in 1913 was at least partly prompted by the fact that both Veblen and Young had left Stanford. Similarly, Veblen began to want to leave Missouri as colleagues such as Handman had moved on. Berkeley retained some institutionalist component, and Berkeley students such as Mills and Brissenden followed Mitchell to Columbia. William Ogburn also first enters the picture at Berkeley with his connections to

---

[13] Other graduate students of Veblen's at Missouri included DR Scott, Claud Clayton, and Fred Yoder. See Dorfman (1934) and Vaughn (1999; 2001a; 2001b).

[14] Veblen followed Lubin to the Food Administration. Veblen wrote two early essays on the price of wheat in 1892 and 1893 (see Dorfman 1973). A number Veblen's Food Administration memoranda are reproduced in *Essays in Our Changing Order* (Veblen 1934).

[15] Watkins completed his PhD at Cornell in 1917 on the subject of Say's Law.

Parker. Ogburn would become closely associated with Mitchell at Columbia, an association he would retain on his move to Chicago in 1927. Neither Stanford nor Missouri maintained an institutionalist presence after Veblen left, but a number of Veblen's Missouri colleagues and students, notably Lubin, Stewart, Downey, and Handman, became members of the institutionalist movement and played significant roles in it.

CHICAGO AND INSTITUTIONALISM IN THE 1920S

At Chicago, the loss of Veblen, Mitchell, Hamilton, and Hoxie weakened the institutionalist presence, but it most certainly did not disappear. The interwar period is sometimes seen as a period in which the "first Chicago School" was formed, but this did not begin to occur until the very late 1920s and 1930s. Indeed, throughout much of the 1920s, the Department continued to have a significant institutionalist element. The primary representative of neoclassical economics was Jacob Viner who was hired in 1916. Even though he brought with him a strong commitment to neoclassicism and rigorous teaching of graduate theory, he was a scholar of considerable breadth and by no means doggedly free market in orientation. He became close friends with J. M. Clark. Clark remained on the Chicago faculty until 1926 when he was hired away by Columbia (Viner was the other candidate seriously considered). At that point, Clark had already published his important work on the behavior of firms with high levels of overhead costs (Clark 1923) and had just completed his book, *The Social Control of Business* (Clark 1926), which detailed numerous types of market failures and the need for regulation of business. The Department also still contained Leon C. Marshall in commerce, Chester Wright in economic history, Harry Millis in labor economics, and James Field in population economics, who were all as much institutionalist as anything else.

Paul Douglas was hired in 1920, and Douglas combined neoclassical and institutional elements. His work included important empirical applications of neoclassical theory, a broad interest in labor issues, and a reform sensibility more in line with the institutionalists (Reder 1982, p. 3). Douglas also championed underconsumptionist ideas and led the effort to have Veblen nominated for the Presidency of the American Economic Association. Moreover, the PhD-level exams given in economics in the late 1920s often contained questions on Veblen, Parker, Hamilton, or on institutional economics more generally (A. G. Hart Papers, Box 60). This indicates that such material was being taught regularly in the core economics courses at Chicago.

Graduates from the early 1920s included several individuals who took to institutionalist ideas and approaches. Harold Innis (PhD 1920) wrote under Wright's supervision but was much influenced by Veblen. He went on to have a major impact on economics and economic history in Canada. According to Innis, there was an informal group, including Innis, Morris Copeland, Carter Goodrich, and Frank Knight, who met to discuss the work of Veblen, so it is clear that interest in Veblen's work at Chicago survived his departure by many years (Neill 1972, p. 12).[16] As noted in the previous chapter, Morris Copeland graduated in 1921 with a thesis titled "Some Phases of Institutional Value Theory," prepared under J. M. Clark's supervision, and was hired to Cornell by Davenport. Another Amherst student, Carter Goodrich, was awarded his doctorate from Chicago in 1921 and became closely associated with the institutionalist movement. Goodrich's thesis dealt with "The Frontier of Control: A Study of British Workshop Politics" (Goodrich 1920). This was prepared on the basis of work with Henry Clay in England, an opportunity arranged by Walton Hamilton. Goodrich later specialized in labor economics and American economic history and taught at Michigan and Columbia.

Other graduates with institutionalist credentials included Hazel Kyrk (PhD 1920), Edward Mittleman (PhD 1920), Leverett Lyon (PhD 1921), Edith Ayres (1921), and Helen R. Wright (PhD 1922). Marshall and Field acted as mentors to Hazel Kyrk who began her graduate work at Chicago in 1910. Kyrk specialized in the economics of consumption, a topic that Field was to develop into a well-known course on the standard of living. Kyrk wrote on "The Consumer's Guidance of Economic Activity" under Field. This work won the prestigious Hart, Schaeffner, and Marx prize and was published as *A Theory of Consumption* (Kyrk 1923). In 1925, she was appointed to the Department of Home Economics at Chicago, and later held a joint appointment with the Department of Economics. She continued to work in the fields of consumption and household economics, publishing her *The Economic Problems of the Family* in 1929. Kyrk was highly critical of marginal utility theory as a basis for a theory of consumption and emphasized the social nature of the formation of consumption values. She echoed Mitchell's view, expressed in his essay "The Backward Art of Spending Money" (Mitchell 1912), that the "business man's calculation of

---

[16] Part of Knight's contribution to this group can be found in his review of Veblen's *Place of Science* (Knight 1920). Innis' interest in Veblen can be seen in Innis (1929). This interest in Veblen may have been prompted by the several books Veblen authored between 1914 and 1919.

profit and loss cannot be transferred to a field not controlled by pecuniary standards" (Kyrk 1923, p. 144). Thus, the key idea is that consumption patterns relate to conventionally defined "standards of living." Kyrk undertook to measure and critically analyze existing standards of living, and to create policy to help achieve higher standards of living. In her later work, Kyrk discussed the household in both its producing and consuming roles, the division of labor between the sexes, employment and earnings of women, adequacy of family incomes, and issues of risks of disability, unemployment, provision for the future, social security, and the protection and education of the consumer (Dorfman 1959, pp. 570–578; Hirschfield 1998; Beller and Kiss 2001, 2003).

Mittleman was a Commons student from Wisconsin and continued to work on the history of labor unions. Edith Ayres (Clarence Ayres's sister) completed her doctorate in philosophy in 1921 and maintained an interest in consumption economics and in the philosophy of economics (Edith Ayres 1938). She later became a member of the institutionalist group at Washington Square College, contributing three of the chapters on consumption for the institutionalist text *Economic Behavior* (Atkins et al. 1931), a book to which Clarence Ayres also contributed a chapter.[17] Helen Wright was encouraged to pursue her PhD in economics after studying with Breckinridge and Abbott in the School of Civics and Philanthropy. Her dissertation was on "The Political Labour Movement in Great Britain, 1820–1914." She, along with Edwin Nourse, was then hired to the Institute of Economics by Harold Moulton. She also taught in the Brookings Graduate School and coauthored two books on the American bituminous coal industry with Hamilton (Hamilton and Wright 1925, 1928). Leverett Lyon (PhD 1921) would go on to Washington University and then to the Brookings Graduate School, teaching alongside Hamilton and Helen Wright. When the School disappeared in the merger that formed the Brookings Institution in 1928, Wright was invited to join the Graduate School of Social Service Administration by Abbott, and in 1941 she succeeded Abbott as Dean of the School. Lyon continued to work for the Brookings Institution.

In the later 1920s, however, the character of the Chicago Department began to change noticeably. Clark left for Columbia in 1926, Field retired in 1927, Marshall left in 1928 to become professor of law and Director of the Institute of Law (a center for legal realism) at Johns Hopkins. The new

---

[17] The contributions of Edith and Clarence Ayres are not indicated in the author list but are mentioned in the preface (Atkins et al. 1931, p. xii). Clarence Ayres wrote the last chapter, "Whither Bound?"

additions to the Chicago faculty in economics were of a much more neoclassical persuasion. Henry Schultz, a student of Henry Moore's at Columbia, came in 1926. Lloyd Mints took over the teaching of the money and banking courses in 1927. Frank Knight and his student, Henry Simons, arrived in 1927. Knight's close but critical relationship with the institutionalists is discussed in more detail later in this chapter. Aaron Director initially joined the Department to work with Paul Douglas but soon became a leading member of the group that gathered around Frank Knight. On the other hand, Chicago also hired John Nef in 1929.[18] Nef had completed a major work on the history of the British coal mining industry, had worked with Richard Tawney in England, and was a graduate of the Brookings Graduate School to which Hamilton had recruited him. Hamilton and Moulton helped him obtain the position at Chicago (Nef 1973). Influenced by his Brookings experience, Nef was never happy with disciplinary divisions and (along with Knight, Robert Hutchins, and others) was instrumental in founding the interdisciplinary Committee on Social Thought in 1941.[19]

Despite Nef's hiring, there is no question that the institutionalist element at Chicago declined quite precipitously after the late 1920s. Of Chicago PhDs after 1930, only two can really be associated with institutionalism. Hazel Kirk passed on her antineoclassical views and her interest in household economics to her student Margaret Reid who graduated in 1931 from the Department of Home Economics, and in 1933, Ruth Allen graduated with a thesis of "The Labor of Women in the Production of Cotton," supervised by Millis and with a committee that included Paul Douglas, Frank Knight, and Lloyd Mints. Allen went on to become an important member of the institutionalist group at the University of Texas (Bernasek and Kinnear 1995). Allen, however, seems to have been the last Chicago PhD who developed close ties with the institutionalist movement.

CHICAGO, KNIGHT, AND THE CRITICISM OF INSTITUTIONAL ECONOMICS

Some criticisms of institutionalism did begin to emerge from Chicago from about the late 1920s onward, but these lines of attack did not come from a consistent point of view. In 1928, Henry Schultz complained that "some economists, among whom are to be included not a few members

---

[18] Nef was orphaned and brought up in the George H. Mead household. See Nef (1973).
[19] See Emmett (forthcoming) for more on the Committee on Social Thought and its evolving concept of interdisciplinary work.

of the institutional school, have, unfortunately, gotten the impression that any attempt to derive a law of demand must needs be based on no better psychology than that of James Mill. A few of them go so far as to deny the existence of the law of demand" (Schultz 1928, p. 95). Schultz was later to continue his critique of the institutionalists approach to empirical work in a sharp rebuke to the work of the Wisconsin Tariff Research Committee, a Committee that included J. R. Commons and Walter Morton (Schultz 1935), and in a public lecture given in 1937 that was explicitly critical of Mitchell's quantitative methods (Schultz 1937). In a 1928 AEA roundtable on quantitative methods, Viner (1928) defended qualitative neoclassical theory and expressed concerns about the applicability of natural science methods to economics. This contribution is clearly a response to Mitchell's view that quantitative work would lead to a very different kind of economics focused on quantitative measurement and empirically testable propositions (Mitchell 1925). Knight pursued a more radical line of attack, being altogether critical of the scientism of those who espoused quantitative and empirical methods. Knight also attacked the behaviorism of institutionalists such as Copeland, and the policy interventionism of those such as Sumner Slichter (Knight 1924; 1932). Knight's criticisms were not limited to institutionalists, however, and he was hostile to both Schultz and Douglas (Reder 1982, p. 6).[20]

Knight's particular relationship with the institutionalist group is worth close examination. In a recent article, Geoff Hodgson argues that Knight should be classified as an institutional economist, although a "maverick" institutionalist (Hodgson 2004, pp. 322–344; but see Emmett 1999, 2009). Hodgson's argument is based largely on Knight's views on the limits to price theory, his deep interest in issues of institutional change and what he called "historical sociology," his teaching of a course on "Economics from an Institutional Standpoint," and his admiration for the work of Max Weber. Indeed, Knight arrived in Chicago in 1927 with the expectation of teaching in institutional economics and not in economic theory (Emmett 2009, pp. 111–123). From his earlier stay at Chicago, he knew the work of institutionalists such as Veblen, Commons, Mitchell, Copeland, and Ayres

---

[20] It is worth noting here that in 1935, the hostility between Knight and Douglas spilled over into the issue of the continued appointment of Simons and Director. Both had extremely poor publication records, and the Department, with the sole exception of Knight, was opposed to reappointing them. Nevertheless, Knight accused Douglas of conducting a personal vendetta against him and of being motivated by a "thirst for blood" (Frank Knight to Paul Douglas, 5 January 1935, and Paul Douglas to Frank Knight, 5 January 1935, Frank Knight Papers, Box 59, Folder 16).

extremely well. He also had a close personal friendship with Clarence Ayres and corresponded frequently both with him and other institutionalists such as Morris Copeland and Max Handman on issues including valuation, behaviorism, economic history, and the treatment of consumption. Knight's thesis had been supervised at Cornell primarily by Allyn Young, and J. M. Clark helped Knight with the revision of his thesis before it was published as *Risk, Uncertainty and Profit* (Knight 1921; Emmett 2009, p. 190, n 3.1).[21] Knight contributed as the conservative critic to Tugwell's *Trend of Economics* (Tugwell 1924b), and his concern with valuation and consumption issues also led him to read and critique Hazel Kyrk's instrumental theory of valuation contained in her *Theory of Consumption* (Frank Knight Papers, Box 36, Folder 22). In addition, Knight greatly encouraged Abram Harris's work on the interpretation of Veblen, Marx, and institutional economics (Harris 1932; 1934). Nevertheless, Knight subjected the ideas of the institutionalists to sustained criticism, attacked all varieties of "scientism," held a deeply distrustful view of political processes (and of those who sought political position or influence), and consistently maintained the central importance of standard price theory in any economic analysis, whether theoretical or historical in nature. Knight was especially hostile to the combination of Dewey's pragmatism and the program of "social control" that lay at the heart of so much institutionalist thinking (Hands 2006; Fiorito 2009). These aspects of his thinking clearly separate him from the members of the institutionalist movement in vital respects.

For Knight, economic theory deals with the problem of rational choice, of using given means to achieve given ends, or the sphere of "economizing" behavior. Economic theory of this type is highly abstract and general: "There are no laws regarding the *content* of economic behavior, but there are laws universally valid as to its *form*. There is an abstract rationale of all conduct which is rational at all, and a rationale of all social relations arising through the organization of rational activity" (Knight 1924, p. 135). These general laws, in Knight's view, are not institutional or historically relative. Institutions "supply much of their content and furnish the machinery by which they work themselves out, more or less quickly and completely, in different actual situations," but the "general laws of choice among competing motives or goods are not institutional" (Knight 1924, p. 137). For Knight, specific content came from the application of economic theory to

---

[21] Knight was a graduate student at Cornell where he was supervised initially by Alvin Johnson and then by Allyn Young. Johnson left to help start *The New Republic*. (Emmett 2009, p. 190, n. 31).

particular historical situations where resources, technology, institutions, social values, and norms could be taken as given but the theory itself was to be understood as an ideal type, both abstract and general.

The broader task of understanding the changing institutions, social values, and norms was the subject matter of institutional economics or of historical sociology. These issues, and particularly the question of the development of capitalism and of its particular values, much concerned Knight. Knight made it clear that he did "not take the American institutional economics very seriously," but he did "take economics from an institutional standpoint very seriously" (Earl Hamilton, Economics 305 notes, Summer 1935, Frank Knight Papers, Box 38, Folder 8). What Knight wanted to do was to take up the institutionalist "challenge" and "make some real contribution toward an understanding of institutional development" (Frank Knight to Clarence Ayres, 16 February 1937, Clarence Ayres Papers, Box 3F290, Frank Knight Folder). However, even in this context he argued that a proper understanding of the principles of the price theory was absolutely central. In his review of Sombart's *Modern Capitalism*, Knight complained that its "most striking feature … is the author's failure to understand the elementary mechanics of the competitive economic organization" (Knight 1928, p. 90), a complaint he extended to most historians and institutional economists. Of the American institutionalists, his most generous comments concerned Commons's work, which he regarded as hopelessly unsystematic but highly "suggestive and valuable" (Knight 1935). Kenneth Parsons's article "John R. Commons' Point of View" (Parsons 1942) originated as a paper for Knight's course, Knight being interested in the issue of whether Commons had "a system" (Parsons 1976). Knight admired Weber on the grounds that "he is the only one who really deals with the problem of causes or approaches the material from that angle that can alone yield an answer to such questions, that is, the angle of comparative history in the broad sense" (Knight 1928, pp. 101–102).

In Knight's view, both legal developments and the religious element stressed by Weber were major factors in the development of capitalism. In particular, he pointed to the "change in the content of the property concept, its differentiation into numerous forms, and the liberation of both men and things from the prescription of authority and tradition," the development of rationality, science, and of deliberative action, and the constructive rather than purely acquisitive nature that the "spirit of enterprise" gained under capitalism (Knight 1928). All the same, from the various outlines and course notes available, it appears that although Knight provided an extremely informed discussion of many episodes in economic history, and presented and critiqued a wide variety of treatments of institutions and institutional change, he did not succeed in providing a complete or well-articulated treatment of his own views on institutional change.

Knight taught his course on "Economics from an Institutional Standpoint" from the early 1930s through to at least 1942, but the course was not always offered. There is also mention of his teaching a seminar on Max Weber, a seminar attended by both Friedman and Stigler (Leeson 2000, p. 57). However, what most students took from Knight seems not to have been his concerns with issues of long-term institutional change, but his views of the central importance of price theory and of competitive markets. Knight's own work included both the "as if" approach to the theory of rational choice and the claim that the problem of monopoly and monopolistic competition was much overstated. Related to this was his generally positive appraisal of the competitive price system, at least as compared with any alternative political processes, and his classical liberal philosophy and set of values. These ideas became an important part of the later "Chicago View" and were communicated to students through Knight's introductory course material, later published as *The Economic Organization* (Knight 1951), as well as through his courses on theory and on the history of economic thought, the latter concentrating on Adam Smith. Among his students, Knight's concerns about the limits to price theory, and the problems created by changing social values, seem to have been largely ignored or dismissed (Stigler and Becker 1977; Emmett 2009).

The mid-1930s, however, did see the development of a small group of Knight's students who were beginning to function "in a loosely coordinated fashion to advance their common ideas" (Reder 1982, p. 7). This group included Henry Simons, Aaron and Rose Director, George Stigler, and Milton Friedman. Henry Simons produced his *Positive Program for Laissez Faire* in 1934, which at the time was seen as a highly free-market tract. It does propose strong enforcement of antitrust laws, a monetary rule to stabilize the price level, and a 100 percent reserve policy. All the same, Simons's monetary views were not unique to Chicago and were shared by some institutionalists, such as John R. Commons. Simons's further proposal that the regulation of natural monopolies should be replaced by public ownership was endorsed by institutionalists concerned with regulation issues, such as Columbia's James Bonbright.

In the immediate post–World War II period, the dominant position of Keynesian, imperfect competition and institutionalist ideas in the profession led Simons to make proposals to preserve "at least one place where some political economists of the future may be thoroughly and competently

trained along traditional-liberal lines" (Coase 1993). Simons was pessimis-
tic about the prospects, but his hopes were to come to pass. Simons, who
had been teaching part-time in Chicago's Law School, died (possibly a suicide) in 1946, and Aaron Director was appointed to the Law School the
same year. Milton Friedman was hired to the Economics Department and
Allen Wallis to the Business School in 1946. Stigler was considered for the
position filled by Friedman (he failed to impress the administration) but
was eventually appointed in 1958 (in the School of Business with a joint
appointment in Economics). F. A. Hayek was also at Chicago from 1950,
although his appointment was with Nef's Committee on Social Thought
and he was never appointed to the Economics Department. It has been
argued that the "the key to the development and eventual dominance of
the 'Chicago View'" in the post–World War II period was the uniting of
Friedman, Stigler, and Wallis on the Chicago faculty (Reder 1982, p. 10), but
recent work has also highlighted the role of Hayek, particularly in developing the funding sources for the Free Market Project that was instrumental
in the creation of Chicago neoliberalism (Van Horne and Mirowski 2009).
Some of this later history of Chicago economics and its role in turning economics away from institutionalist methods and policies will be discussed
in Chapter 11.

CONCLUSION

A number of points come out of this discussion. First, it was the University
of Chicago that was the home of Veblen, Mitchell, Hoxie, Hamilton, and
Clark during the years the outlines of the "institutional approach" emerged.
Veblen was important in this, but institutionalism was by no means Veblen's
invention. Hoxie's experience in attempting to apply the Veblenian hypothesis concerning the habits of thought of industrial unionized workers, and
Mitchell's not dissimilar experience in his Money Economy project shifted
attention away from Veblen's general evolutionary system and toward the
critical appraisal of existing institutions and the need for new forms of
social control. Those following Veblen also adopted a much more empirical
approach and a reformist attitude based of John Dewey's pragmatic philosophy. This orientation is apparent in the work of Hoxie, Hamilton, and
J. M. Clark in the periods they were at Chicago, and in Mitchell's move to
the study of business cycles.

A second point is that the "institutional approach" was something that
was seen as applying to the method of instruction as well as research. The
problem-centered approach is clearly found in Hoxie's teaching and in the

teaching materials produced by Field and Marshall. As will be seen, this was an approach carried on and very much developed by Hamilton at Amherst and Brookings.

It is also clear that institutionalism persisted at Chicago much later than usually thought – well into the 1920s. Not only was J. M. Clark still at Chicago, but so were Millis, Field, and Marshall, and the number of graduate students from the early 1920s who adopted institutionalist ideas is quite striking. Chicago only declined as a center for institutionalism in the late 1920s, but as it did, other centers emerged, and many of these were seeded from Chicago, Berkeley, or Missouri. The obvious examples are Columbia University with Mitchell, J. M. Clark, F. C. Mills, and Paul Brissenden; Amherst College with Hamilton and Stewart; Michigan, for a time, with Goodrich and Copeland; The Brookings Graduate School and the Institute of Economics with Moulton heading the Institute and Hamilton the Graduate School and with Nourse, Lubin, Helen Wright, and Leverett Lyon; the Washington Square College of New York University headed by Willard Atkins and with Edith Ayres; and the University of Texas with Handman, followed by Clarence Ayres and Ruth Allen. Subsequent chapters will discuss many of these centers.

In the 1930s, Chicago did begin to become a place associated with a critical attitude toward institutionalism. Frank Knight in particular pursued his own attempt to develop the "institutional standpoint" to deal with those factors taken as a given by standard price theory. This attempt was explicitly in reaction to, and critical of, the work by those associated with American institutionalism. Knight's primary objections were to the "scientism" of the institutionalists and their notions of social control. These methodological and political objections remained at the heart of Chicago critiques of institutionalism, although some of Knight's students later transformed this into a caricature of institutionalism as entirely "descriptive," and embarked on a wide-ranging defense of the market without Knight's concerns with the limits to economic theory and the need for the explicit discussion of values.

6

Amherst and the Brookings Graduate School

We have already examined Walton Hamilton's contribution to the definition of the institutional approach and his own extensive writings, but Hamilton also had a significant impact on institutionalism through the educational programs he pioneered and students he trained. After his own graduate education at Michigan, and a short stay as a faculty member at the University of Chicago, Hamilton was centrally involved in two fascinating educational experiments, the first at Amherst College (1916–1923) and the second at the Robert Brookings Graduate School of Economics and Government (1923–1928).

The list of graduates Hamilton and his colleagues produced is quite outstanding in terms of their future careers in academics and in government. A surprisingly large number of the cohort of institutionalists trained in the interwar period got their start with Hamilton and his colleagues at one or the other of these places. These include Clarence Ayres, Morris Copeland, Mordecai Ezekiel, Anton Friedrich, Carter Goodrich, Isador Lubin, Stacy May, Robert Montgomery, Paul and Carl Raushenbush, Louis Reed, Winfield Riefler, and Willard Thorp. A number of his students were associated with the Research and Statistics Division of the Federal Reserve, and many became centrally involved in the New Deal administration. Other students, while less obviously institutionalist, nevertheless absorbed much from Hamilton's programs, whereas others still became among the best known critics of institutionalism.

Hamilton and his students formed many connections with other academic centers of institutionalism, including the NBER and the Economics Departments at Columbia, Wisconsin, Michigan, Texas, and elsewhere. There were also close links between Hamilton and British liberal and Fabian economists and academics. Hamilton's interests in the coal industry, in unemployment insurance, in regulation, in new forms of social control, and in the policy ideas of the British Labour Party led him and a number of his students to develop personal connections with people such as William Beveridge, Henry Clay, J. A. Hobson, R. H. Tawney, and Graham Wallas (Rutherford 2007).

Beyond the influence of Hamilton's students, his educational experiments are of considerable interest in themselves. Hamilton rejected the idea of education as "ritual" and attempted to design programs that would treat education as an "adventure," a genuine intellectual inquiry in which the student could participate (Hamilton 1923). Hamilton's educational approach was problem-centered, his aim was to "teach the art of handling problems" and to produce people who could make "contributions to an intelligent direction of social change" (Hamilton 1926). He would start with an issue or a problem, search for the information and tools to approach that problem with little regard to conventional disciplinary boundaries, and be open and creative in the search for solutions. These ideas of being investigative, of being actively involved in the development of new methods of social control, and of being "on the frontier" of economic and social research, were a central part of what many young economists in the 1920s found so exciting and attractive about Hamilton and his programs.

THE AMHERST PROGRAM

The program at Amherst College was taught primarily by Hamilton and Walter Stewart. Both had been graduate students at Michigan, and at that time Michigan was something of a hothouse for young economists seeking a broader institutional or sociological orientation.[1] This was undoubtedly due to the presence of H. C. Adams and C. H. Cooley on faculty. Hamilton's fellow graduate students included David Friday and Walter Stewart, and all three were listed as instructors in economics for the 1911–1912 academic year. Indicative of the ideals of this group, Friday, writing to Stewart in 1912, stated his conviction that "the day of the sociological economist is a hand" and that "presently the older generation will give up their seats of power and we will come into our own" (David Friday to Walter Stewart, 21 September 1912, H. C. Adams Papers, Box 13, David Friday Folder). Both Friday and Stewart played important roles in the institutionalist movement in the

---

[1] Others associated with institutionalism, who spent time at Michigan were Leo Wolman in the 1916–1917 year and Isador Lubin between 1919 and 1922. Carter Goodrich was hired to Michigan in 1924 and Morris Copeland in 1930. A number of Brookings students came from Michigan.

1920s,[2] but Stewart had much greater significance in terms of Hamilton's later career.

Prior to his arrival at Michigan, Stewart had worked as an assistant in economics at the University of Missouri and had overlapped with Thorstein Veblen for one semester. Stewart left Michigan after a year to study with John Dewey at Columbia over the summer, and then returned to Missouri to study with Veblen.[3] Beginning as an instructor, Stewart rose in rank and remained at the University of Missouri until 1916. He developed interests in money and banking, but never completed his doctorate.

Hamilton completed his PhD at Michigan in 1913 and then taught there and at Chicago. One outcome of his teaching experience at Michigan and Chicago was his book of readings *Current Economic Problems*, which first came out in 1915 (Hamilton 1919a). The collection clearly indicates Hamilton's developing "institutional" point of view, with its emphasis on modern industrialism and "the pecuniary basis of economic organization," and also the problem-centered approach to economics that was to become the hallmark of his teaching.

In 1915, Hamilton was recruited to Amherst College by its new president, Alexander Meiklejohn. An enthusiastic educator with liberal ideals, Meiklejohn attempted to bring about innovations in the curriculum and in teaching methods, and hired a number of young faculty. Clarence Ayres was hired as an instructor for the 1915–1916 academic year and assisted Hamilton in his introductory course.[4] Walter Stewart joined the Economics Department at Amherst in 1916. John M. Gaus, an Amherst graduate himself, and later to become one of the founders of public administration, taught political science first as an instructor and then as an associate professor. As mentioned previously, Amherst was also something of a home away from home for Veblen, who visited now and again, usually staying at

[2] Friday was appointed a professor of economics at Michigan in 1913. Details of Friday's later career, which included stints in private consulting, being Chair of the Department of Economics at New York University, President of Michigan Agricultural College, and later a professor at the New School for Social Research, can be found in Dorfman (1959, pp. 403–405). His best-known work was *Profits, Wages, and Prices* (Friday 1920), a book commonly cited in the institutionalist literature in the 1920s. Friday also served on the Board of the NBER.

[3] Stewart had been an undergraduate at Missouri, graduating in 1909. Shortly after he returned to the University to teach as an assistant and remained there for a year and a half before moving to Michigan. Veblen began teaching at the University of Missouri in February 1911.

[4] Ayres had majored in philosophy (with a minor in economics) at Brown. His work as an assistant for Hamilton course "An Introduction to Social and Economic Problems" was his own introduction to institutional economics.

the Stewarts' house, next door to Hamilton's. As noted previously, Veblen gave a series of lectures at Amherst in May 1918, based on the material later published as *The Vested Interests* (Veblen 1919a), and there were occasional larger gatherings including others with an interest in Veblen's ideas, such as Leo Wolman and Isador Lubin.

The Economics program at Amherst was designed by Meiklejohn, Hamilton, and Stewart, with advice from Wesley Mitchell (Hamilton 1917). The program itself consisted of a general freshman course, "An Introduction to Social and Economic Problems" (later called "An Introduction to Social and Economic Institutions"), to be taken by all students as an entry point into the more advanced courses in economics, history, philosophy, and political science. As the title of the course suggests, it consisted of "an analysis of the more important social problems of contemporary interest," and was explicitly designed to interest and challenge the student, create discussion, and give the student "a more active relation to intellectual matters than do the traditional subjects." The course discussed general problems of social organization and of the welfare of society, and sought to provide not final answers, but "a revelation of the disciplines in which the facts and principles necessary to their fuller appreciation are to be found" (Hamilton 1917, pp. 3–4, 12). The teaching materials produced for this course by Hamilton and Ayres are quite remarkable; they consist entirely of pages and pages of questions with which Hamilton and his quiz masters would try to prod, provoke, irritate, and stimulate his students. One student, Dexter Keezer, has described Hamilton beginning a course by talking about the law of contributory negligence, citing cases of how somebody had lost an arm but was awarded no damages because he had been standing two feet from the position he should have been in. Keezer thought he must be making the cases up and so went to the library to check (Keezer 1972, Taped Interview by Robert Coleberd, Brookings Institution Archives, A86–011). This kind of attempt to stir students up was Hamilton's primary technique in a great deal of his teaching, and it probably had no greater success than at Amherst.

In contrast, Stewart was a much quieter individual and did not use Hamilton's specific teaching methods, but he was fully committed to the problem-centered approach. In 1918, Stewart described his attitude to "Economic theory" to H. C. Adams by telling about his and Hamilton's teaching experience at Amherst:

We began with the belief that Economic theory in order to be relevant and useful should grow out of a consideration of current economic problems. This made economic theory mean more, of course, than merely value theory. This approach had its teaching difficulties, especially the danger that the student instead of getting an understanding and a breadth of view will get only a confused vagueness. Confronted by this difficulty we were forced to carry into an advanced course our own problems, such as, what are the fundamentals underlying our approach; how can we formulate the question definitely without narrowing it to where it becomes irrelevant; how can the viewpoint and method of economic theory be kept in harmony with the work now being done in other social sciences. Out of the experience in this course I have come to certain conclusions with myself, and I cannot be content with a "general economics" which gets its generalization by ignoring the difficulties which we confronted. (Walter Stewart to H. C. Adams, 8 June 1918, H. C. Adams Papers, Box 11, Folder 1918 June 1–15)

The program in economics proper was originally intended to consist of two full-year introductory courses, followed by a number of advanced courses. Of the introductory courses, the first was titled "The Pecuniary Order" and the second "Wealth and Welfare." Sections of these courses were offered by both Hamilton and Stewart in 1916–1917. The outline for "The Pecuniary Order" states its content as "a survey of the organization of society in its pecuniary aspects," including money, banking, accounting, the mechanism of the market, including investment and speculation, and "a study of the rise of the pecuniary calculus, its varying domain, its potency as an organizing force in society, the institutions and values which are beyond its pale, and its adequacy as a guide in programs of social reform" (Hamilton 1917, p. 12). The Hamilton papers contain collections of what might be materials for this course, including a "fragment" of an outline called "The Pecuniary Order," written by Walter Stewart. This begins with a "General Statement" that reads:

The Pecuniary Order is an organized and continuous process; it is the economic aspect of our experience. Economic activity which proceeds upon an institutional basis has been directed so largely by considerations of price that the economic organization of today may be viewed as a price system. Through its long history this system has proved its capacity for growth, having been constantly including and discarding elements and reorganizing itself to meet new situations. In its current phase it is going through the painful process of digesting the machine industry. The disintegration of the old order incidental to this change in technology has been accompanied by new integrations and specializations of function into the present order. The development of institutions and new activities are mutually conditioning, never taking place separately but always affecting one another accumulatively. By studying in turn the growth of these various agencies, treated as aspects of the developing system, the influences organizing the order may be understood. Such a survey of the pecuniary order from different points of view indicates its organic character, the interdependence of the functionally related parts, and gives some hint as to the direction in which the whole system is moving. (Stewart n.d., Walton Hamilton Papers, Box J13, Folder 5)

The course outline that follows contains sections titled "Institutional Basis of Pecuniary Order," "Pecuniary Calculation," "Pecuniary Competition," "The Markets," "Contract and Property," "Corporation a Unit of Business Organization," "Accounting and Corporate Policies," "The Wage Earning Class," "The Investment Organization," "Speculation," "Insurance," and "Special Control by Government." An edited version of this outline also appears in a collection of material that seems likely to have been assembled for Hamilton's version of the course – material that included selections from Veblen, Cooley, Mitchell, Sidney Webb, as well as from Hamilton's own *Current Economic Problems*.

The course "Wealth and Welfare" discussed the welfare of society as a whole, the division of society into pecuniary groups, distribution as affected by market prices and by social arrangements, the distribution of opportunity, and programs such as cooperation, welfare work, scientific management, trade unionism, and socialism. The course title suggests Hamilton's interest in J. A. Hobson's welfare economics.

Amherst College Calendars indicate that in the 1917–1918 academic year, the first course was renamed "The Economic Order," a title that Hamilton also used on a number of draft book manuscripts, and the second course was first moved to the advanced level and then broken up into courses on "Labor in Industrial Society" (usually taught by Hamilton) and "Problems of Labor and Management" (usually taught by a Professor Crook). Its place at the introductory level was taken over by a slightly more orthodox course in "Economics" or "Principles of Economics" described as "a study of current problems in their relation to economic principles" and taught by Professor Crook. Hamilton's course on labor issues reflected his research interests of that time and his soon-to-be-published book on wages written with his student Stacy May (Hamilton and May 1923).

Other advanced courses included various (and varying) offerings of electives in topic areas such as public finance (taught by Crook), business cycles (Stewart), and money and banking (Stewart). Stewart's views of business cycles were based on Mitchell's work, whereas his institutionalist view of money emphasized "the socially organized character of banking activity" and the importance of understanding monetary and banking institutions and their "cumulative relations in time" (Stewart 1917). Also offered regularly at the advanced level was "The Theory of Modern Industrialism," described as a genetic study of institutions and problems of contemporary society and taught by Hamilton and Stewart. This is presumably the advanced course spoken of by Stewart in his letter to Adams.

In 1918, both Hamilton and Stewart were involved in work relating to the war, and the Amherst teaching program became thinner than normal. Stewart worked with Mitchell's Prices Section of the War Industries Board (as did Isador Lubin and Leo Wolman), whereas Hamilton worked with the War Labor Policies Board as an economic expert dealing mainly with reconstruction issues. Harold Moulton was also employed there, and it was at this time that Hamilton, Moulton, and J. M. Clark were discussing directions for economic research, and, with Mitchell, Stewart, and others, planning the conference session in which Hamilton presented his paper, "The Institutional Approach to Economic Theory" (Hamilton 1919a).

In the 1919–1920 academic year, the Amherst economics program returned to its previous configuration. Interestingly, R. H. Tawney was a visitor at Amherst that year and cotaught a senior course in "The Control of Social Development" with Hamilton and Stewart. Tawney's *The Acquisitive Society* was published in 1921, and selections soon appeared in Hamilton's course material. In 1920, Ayres returned to Amherst as a member of the Philosophy Department. At least one of his courses, "The Moral Order," was more a course in social theory than philosophy, with readings from William Graham Sumner's *Folkways*, Charles Horton Cooley, Emile Durkheim, John Dewey and Veblen. In 1921, Henry Clay was a visitor. There is no record of Clay doing any teaching, but he came to know both Hamilton and Stewart well. Hamilton was to maintain correspondence with both Tawney and Clay, and he also knew other British economists such as the Webbs, John A. Hobson, and William Beveridge. His relationship with Clay was particularly close (the Hamiltons visited Clay in England in the summer of 1922) and they corresponded frequently. Hamilton admired Clay's *Economics: An Introduction for the General Reader* (Clay 1916), and Clay often expressed admiration for the work he had seen being done by Hamilton, Stewart, and others such as Leo Wolman (Henry Clay to Wesley Mitchell, 11 November 1921, Wesley Mitchell Papers, Series C, Box 8, Henry Clay Folder).

As mentioned earlier, the Amherst experiment came to an end in 1923 with the enforced resignation of Alexander Meiklejohn. The reasons for this action were most likely a combination of Meiklejohn's liberalism and his hiring of many young faculty, which upset others. The official reasons related to his somewhat extravagant lifestyle and personal financial difficulties. There were many protests over his firing, and Hamilton, Stewart, Ayres, and others all resigned their positions. Stewart, on leave from Amherst as Director of the Division of Research and Statistics at the Federal Reserve Board, was offered the Presidency but declined (Yohe 1982; 1990).[5] Hamilton's address to the graduating class of 1923 praised the merits of "education by adventure" and intellectual freedom as opposed to the "slavery" of education by ritual and of merely accepting opinions on authority (Hamilton 1923). Students also protested (Parsons and Cutler 1923), but all protests were in vain. Meiklejohn moved on to Wisconsin where he established the Experimental College. A few years later, he was joined by John Gaus.[6]

THE AMHERST STUDENTS

During the time that Hamilton, Stewart, and Ayres were at Amherst, there can be no doubt at all that the economics students were very explicitly exposed to a substantial amount of the "institutional approach" to economics. The students "got the point of view that the economic and social order was a matter of human arrangement, not one of inevitable natural laws, and hence that it was subject to human control" (Parsons and Cutler 1923, p. 290).

A list of the Amherst graduates of most relevance here is provided in Table 6.1. All of those listed went on to careers in economics or related areas. Copeland's subsequent career has already been discussed. Like Copeland, Goodrich also went on to Chicago for doctoral work. Edward Morehouse and Paul Raushenbush moved on to Wisconsin, and Thorp and Reed went to Columbia. Several, including Addison Cutler, Dexter Keezer, Stacy May, Winfield Riefler, and Carl Raushenbush, followed Hamilton to the Robert Brookings Graduate School. One final Amherst student very worthy of mention is Talcott Parsons.

Goodrich started in English and was a student of Robert Frost. His shift into economics inspired Frost's poem "The Runaway."[7] Goodrich was

---

[5]   Stewart wrote relatively little but commanded great respect. From the Federal Reserve, where he made major contributions, he went into private business with Case & Pomeroy. Between 1928 and 1930, he was a special adviser to the Bank of England where he set up a research and statistics division similar to the one at the Federal Reserve. He was on the Board of Trustees of the Rockefeller Foundation from 1931 to 1950, becoming Chairman of the Board in 1940. He held an appointment at the Institute of Advanced Studies at Princeton from 1938, acted as adviser to successive Secretaries of the Treasury, and was a member of the Council of Economic Advisers between 1953 and 1955. He maintained close connections with the NBER, serving on the Board and advising on monetary projects. See Yohe (1982 and 1990) and Rutherford (2007).

[6]   Meiklejohn headed the Experimental College for the five years of its existence (1927–1932). Gaus spent the years between 1923 and 1927 at the University of Minnesota.

[7]   This was the recollection of Casey Shulberg, Goodrich's grandson, at Goodrich's memorial service: "Grandfather was a student of Robert Frost and worked with him on a literary

Table 6.1. *Selected Amherst students, 1917–1924 (Date of Graduation)*

Morris Copeland (1917)	Paul Raushenbush (1920)
Carter Goodrich (1918)	Willard Thorp (1920)
Dexter Keezer (1918)	Carl Raushenbush (1922)
Edward Morehouse (1918)	Addison Cutler (1924)
Winfield Riefler (1919)	Talcott Parsons (1924)
Stacy May (1919)	Louis Reed (1924)

interested in labor problems and American economic history. After his graduation in 1918, Hamilton arranged for Goodrich to visit Britain to work with Henry Clay, then with the Ministry of Labour. The material from this research became his University of Chicago doctoral thesis, published as *The Frontier of Control: A Study of British Workshop Politics* (Goodrich 1920). R. H. Tawney wrote the foreword for this book. Goodrich returned to Amherst as a faculty member in 1921 and taught with Hamilton. In 1924, he moved to Michigan, and in 1931 was recruited to Columbia by Wesley Mitchell. Goodrich was later assistant to the Ambassador to Great Britain in 1941, and became very much involved with the International Labour Organization, chairing the governing body of the ILO from 1939 to 1945. He was a consultant to the United Nations from 1948 to 1951.

Willard Thorp began in mathematics, but Hamilton persuaded him to move to economics by showing him "that mathematics could be used through statistics as a tool in economics" (Thorp 1947). He graduated in 1920, taught at Amherst in the 1921–1922 academic year, then went to Columbia and, in 1923, also joined the research staff of the National Bureau of Economic Research. He completed his PhD dissertation on "The Integration of Industrial Operation" in 1925 and, along with Mitchell, produced the volume *Business Annals* for the NBER (Thorp and Mitchell 1926). Thorp would later return to Amherst as professor of Economics and write an institutionalist textbook, *Economic Institutions* (Thorp 1928), but he remained on the staff of the NBER until 1933, and would later serve on the Board. He became Director of the Bureau of Foreign and Domestic

---

magazine, *The Amherst Monthly*, when the poet wrote 'The Runaway.' When Grandfather changed his major interest to economics from literature, Frost said he had lost a poet to economics. Grandfather met Frost again at a reading of his poems some thirty years later, and learned for the first time that Frost was thinking of him when he wrote 'The Runaway'" (Perlman 1971).

Commerce in 1933 and was a member of the Industrial Committee of the National Resources Committee, a group that also included Lauchlin Currie, Corwin Edwards, Mordecai Ezekiel, Isador Lubin, and Gardiner Means. Thorp joined the State Department in 1945, became Assistant Secretary of State for Economic Affairs in 1947, and also served as an American representative to UNESCO. He became President of the American Statistical Association in 1947.

Louis Reed graduated in 1924 and also went on to complete his PhD at Columbia University. He and Carl Raushenbush (who later attended Brookings) both became part of the institutionalist group that formed at the Washington Square College of New York University. Reed was, for a time, a member of the research staff for the Committee on the Costs of Medical Care. He then moved to the Social Security Board and the Public Health Service, contributing many papers and a number of books on health economics and health insurance.

Edward W. Morehouse graduated in 1918 and went to Wisconsin to do his doctoral work. He studied under J. R. Commons and completed his doctorate in 1920. Morehouse married R. T. Ely's daughter and moved with Ely to Northwestern University where he became editor of the *Journal of Land and Public Utility Economics* (later *Land Economics*). Paul Raushenbush graduated from Amherst in 1920 and also went to Wisconsin for graduate work, but did not obtain a doctorate. For several years, he was an assistant professor of economics at Wisconsin and worked at the Experimental College with Meiklejohn. He, along with his wife, Elizabeth Brandeis, was closely involved in the drafting of the Wisconsin unemployment compensation law in 1932. His wife, the daughter of Justice Louis Brandeis, also taught economics at Wisconsin and was active in many labor and social issues and in the League of Women Voters. The careers of Morehouse and Paul Raushenbush will be picked up again in Chapter 7.

Another, and very famous, Amherst student, Talcott Parsons, became a critic of institutionalism. Parsons took Ayres's philosophy course, "The Moral Order," as well as a course from Walton Hamilton (Parsons 1976, p.175). According to Parsons, he received enormous stimulus from Hamilton and Ayres: "without their influence I would probably never have become a social scientist at all" (Parsons 1976, p. 179), "so institutional economics was really my jumping off place" (Parsons 1959, p. 4). After Amherst, Parsons went to study at the London School of Economics (with introductions provided by Hamilton) and was exposed to the work of Leonard Hobhouse, Harold Laski, Bronislaw Malinowski, and R. H. Tawney – influences not out of line with those he had absorbed at Amherst. Parsons then moved to Heidelberg where he developed an interest in the work of Max Weber, and obtained his doctorate from there in 1927. Parsons's earlier work shows some definite institutionalist and historicist influences (Parsons 1928/1929), but later, after moving to Harvard, Parsons became increasingly critical of historicism and institutionalism (Parsons 1934; 1935), and shifted toward a concept of economics as an analytically abstract discipline, and of sociology as a search for uniform general laws (Camic 1991; Hodgson 2001).[8]

THE BROOKINGS GRADUATE SCHOOL

The Brookings Graduate School was one of three organizations developed by Robert S. Brookings in Washington DC. In 1916 he established the Institute for Government Research (IGR) to promote work in the area of public administration, specifically concerning the efficiency of governmental administration and budgeting. In 1922, inspired by his wartime experience as chair of the Price Fixing Commission of the War Industries Board, he established the Institute of Economics, with help from a substantial grant from the Carnegie Corporation, for a term to expire at the end of 1931. Brookings hired Harold Moulton as the Institute's first director, and Moulton recruited a research staff including Helen Wright and Edwin Nourse. Moulton and Nourse had overlapped as students at Chicago, whereas Wright was a new Chicago PhD. Thomas Page (of the U.S. Tariff Commission) was also recruited, as was Isador Lubin.[9] At the time of his move to the Institute of Economics, Lubin was an instructor engaged in graduate work at the University of Michigan. The primary research areas that the Institute set itself were areas of key contemporary policy importance, such as postwar international finance (Moulton), labor issues and the coal industry (Wright, Lubin), tariffs (Page), and agriculture (Nourse).[10]

---

[8] Parsons sent a copy of his "Some Reflections on 'The Nature and Significance of Economics'" (Parsons 1934) to Hamilton with the inscription "Another blast from the semi-enemy's camp for your delectation" (Walton Hamilton Papers Box J53, Folder 3). Later, Karl Polanyi described Parsons in a letter to Carter Goodrich as "our friend and opponent" (Karl Polanyi to Carter Goodrich, n.d., Carter Goodrich Papers, Box 3, Polanyi Folder).

[9] Others hired in the early days were Charles Chase, Horace Drury (Columbia PhD), Leo Pasvolsky (who had been working toward a PhD at Columbia and later obtained his doctorate from the Brookings Institution), Arthur Suffern (Columbia PhD), and Henry Schultz (Columbia PhD). Schultz left for Chicago after a year, very dissatisfied with his time at Brookings.

[10] This policy orientation is what differentiated the Institute of Economics from the National Bureau, but even though the Institute did not see itself as primarily involved

Brookings's vision, however, had always included an educational as well as a research component. Brookings felt that existing graduate programs did a poor job of training people for policy research or for senior public service positions, and he wished to establish a school to provide a type of training more directed to policy analysis and governmental careers than the usual graduate training with its orientation toward teaching. In 1923, the Robert S. Brookings Institute of Economics and Government was established as a graduate school at Washington University of St. Louis (with which Brookings had been much involved). A key feature of this program was the establishment of a "Residence Foundation" in Washington, DC (funded by gifts from Mr. and Mrs. Brookings), where advanced students could live, profiting both from close association with each other and with the Institute for Governmental Research and the Institute of Economics. The intent was to have students work on thesis topics "falling within the general range of problems" with which the two other Institutes were concerned (Moulton 1928, p. 3). The Residence Foundation was also willing to provide its facilities to advanced graduate students taking their degrees from other universities. For a variety of reasons – academic, financial, and legal – this arrangement underwent a series of rapid changes, with the residential period in Washington, DC being extended from one to two years in April of 1924,[11] and the formal connection with Washington University being severed altogether in November 1924. At that point, the Robert Brookings Graduate School of Economics and Government was incorporated in Washington, DC as an independent entity.[12]

in data collection, it nevertheless attempted to stress the "scientific" nature of the work and the importance of its nonpartisan stance. A reputation for "objectivity and scientific competency" was seen as vital for the Institution to be able to make a contribution to a better informed public debate of the merits of "policies already established or under consideration" ("A Proposed Educational Division," Brookings Archives, Item 17, Box 1, Memoranda on the Early History of the Brookings Institution File). The objective and scientific character of the Institute of Economics was hotly disputed by Abraham Flexner, of the Rockefeller General Education Board, who regarded Brookings as wishing to use the Institute of Economics to engage in political propaganda. Beardsley Ruml, however, thought that Moulton was interested in a more objective approach (A. F. [Abraham Flexner], "Institute of Economic Research," 22 December 1923, Laura Spelman Rockefeller Memorial Archives, Series 3.6, Box 49, Folder 517).

[11] This had been much discussed between Brookings and Hamilton in the fall of 1923. See Robert Brookings to Wickliffe Rose, November 13, 1923, and attached memos from Walton Hamilton to Robert Brookings, n.d., Laura Spelman Rockefeller Memorial Archives, Series 3.6, Box 49, Folder 517.

[12] The first change was made on academic grounds. The final separation of the RBGS from Washington University, made formal in November 1924, was a result of both

In May 1923, Hamilton was appointed to head the Washington, DC program on the recommendation of his friend Moulton. As the School gained independence, its philosophy took on a noticeably Hamiltonian slant. The School would be distinctive in that it would give its attention to "problems rather than disciplines, to relevant inquiries rather than to academic categories." It is "to teach the art of handling problems rather than to impart accumulated knowledge; and its end is to turn out craftsmen who can make contributions to the intelligent direction of social change." The School "is, and was meant to be, experimental," and "invites a more intimate, a more incisive, and a more individual method of instruction." Moreover, the School is to provide residence for its students to expose the students to "personal contact with many men of note," and to provide an informal means of education (Hamilton 1926a). In this way, Hamilton brought his educational philosophy as developed at Amherst to the graduate level.

For the 1924–1925 academic year, the first for which the RBGS existed as a separate entity, there were three primary faculty members: Hamilton; Walter Shepard, a political scientist who had been appointed at Washington University about the same time as Hamilton;[13] and the English economist J. A. Hobson, for whom Hamilton had arranged to visit Washington. In the 1925–1926 year, there were four "resident" members of staff: Hamilton, Shepard, Leverett Lyon (who had been Dean of Commerce and Head of the Department of Economics at Washington University), and Helen Wright who was "loaned" on a year-by-year basis from the Institute of Economics. This complement of four was as large as the core faculty of the School ever became, but the teaching and supervision of students in the School was supplemented by the staff of the Institute of Economics, particularly Lubin, Moulton, and Nourse, by various other "associate members" of staff who were employed in one or other of the Institutes or were otherwise available to be called on to direct student reading or teach in specialized areas (these included David Friday), and later by visiting "consulting fellows" who stayed in residence and participated in the instruction and supervision of students (these included Morris Copeland). The School also used its location to attract a large number of visiting speakers

---

financial concerns relating to the taxation of Brookings' estate and a belated recognition that the University of Washington had no authority to operate a School outside of the St. Louis area.

[13] Shepard had been at Missouri at the same time as Veblen, but the two had little contact with each other (Dorfman 1934).

who gave either single informal talks or seminars, short series of talks, or short courses.

The students were expected to have completed at least one year of graduate education before coming to the School, and many held MA degrees from other institutions. The School offered fellowships of up to $1,000, and had no shortage of applicants. A system of selection gradually evolved in which prospective students were invited to the School for a "conference." The students were selected on the basis of their potential to benefit from the particular nature and atmosphere of the school with its emphasis on self-motivation, wide-ranging intellectual curiosity, and on the analysis and creative solution of social problems.

The School attracted and produced some remarkable students. In the first 1923–1924 academic year, the School had seventeen students, including Isador Lubin and Helen Everett who were members of the Institute of Economics staff (working on a study of the British coal industry), as well as students at the School. The next year, the total number of students rose to thirty-two and reached a peak of forty students in 1926–1927. A total of 114 students are listed as having attended the School between 1923 and 1928 (RBGS General Catalogue 1923–1928). Some attended only for a year or two, but many of these completed PhDs elsewhere. In addition, the School played host to a number of Laura Spelman Rockefeller Memorial Fellows from Europe, including Eveline Burns. Between 1925 and 1930, the RBGS itself awarded sixty-six PhD degrees, a rate of production that placed it among the leading graduate schools in economics and political science.[14] Many of these graduates went on to distinguished careers in government and/or in academics, and many played key roles within the New Deal Administration. Isador Lubin, Mordecai Ezekiel, and Winfield Riefler are examples of Brookings graduates who went on to important positions in public service. Their careers, and the careers of many other graduates, are outlined below.

The residential nature of the RBGS also deserves special emphasis. This created a close community of students, many of whom developed a strong loyalty to the School and to Walton Hamilton. There were a significant

---

[14] The first year PhDs were awarded was in 1925. Students who had been enrolled in the RBGS obtained their degrees with that designation through to 1930. Although the School had ceased to exist in its previous form as of the end of the 1928 academic year, a program for second-year students was offered in 1928–1929. A complete list of PhDs awarded and of students who attended the School by year can be found in the Brookings Institution Archives, Item 41, Office Files of Elizabeth H. Wilson, 1922–1961, Box 3, Folder: Historical Notes, 1953.

number of women students – 10 in each of the 1926–1927 and 1927–1928 years – and the students became a close group. There were sing-alongs, dancing after dinner, and weddings.[15] Mordecai Ezekiel recalled that the residents used to "roll up the rugs" and have dances after supper a few times a week. There was a Brookings song book, an example from which is as follows:

> On the economic frontier,
> Far from Smith and Mill,
> Stands dear old R.B.G.S.E.G.,
> Would it had a hill!
> Hail to Brookings, Alma Mater,
> Alma Pater too,
> World's salvation in the balance,
> Gosh! What shall we do?
> (Brookings Songs Folder,
> Brookings Institution
> Archives, Item A86–011,
> Box 1)

Thanks to Hamilton's law and economic interests, occasional suppers were given for Brookings students by Justice Brandeis. Not surprisingly, the students were enthusiastic about the School, as were visitors such as Bronislaw Malinowski. He wrote:

---

[15] The material collected by Robert Coleberd and now in the Brookings Institution Archive contains a RBGS song book. A pencil note on it from Harvey Young reads "We would assemble in the lounge after dinner and have a sing-song" (Brookings Institution Archives, Item A86–011, Box 1, Brookings Songs Folder). The social aspect of the School are remarked on in a letter written back to John R. Commons by three of his "Friday Nighters":

My good fortune brought me to that centre of iconoclastic social science known as the Brookings School. … When I arrived there on a September evening … I found about two dozen happy young people sitting in a spacious dining-room under a Venetian candelabrum. I was rather confused because of the great number of girls who seemed to dominate the conversation completely. Their names – Ida and Esther, Jean and Winifred, Margaret and Anita, Elizabeth and Marguerite – were being called all over the place. I felt considerably relieved when the crowd adjourned to a large drawing-room where a pleasant hour was spent in dancing to the tunes of an enormous victrola (orthophonic). This was my first impression; since then I have become acquainted with all of them and find that they are very interesting and hard working people, though some of them might profitably spend a semester or two in the University of Wisconsin. (Dorothy Whipple, Heinrich Pollak, and Ewan Clague to John R. Commons, 9 November 1926, John R. Commons Papers, Box 3, Folder 6)

Among the marriages between students at the School were Anita Marberg and Max Lerner, Jean Flexner and Paul Lewinson, Idella Gwatkin and Carl Swisher, Rose Stahl and Ralph Fletcher, Margaret Keister and John White, Elizabeth Webb and Roy Veach. Ruth Ayres married Meredith Givens, a Wisconsin PhD who was in Washington for a time, and Helen Everett married Alexander Meiklejohn (his second marriage).

Put up at Robert Brookings School, finding there at once a number of old acquaintances and of new interests. The more I saw of this school, of its staff and students, the better I liked it. Its size, system and personal quality make it one of the best sociological workshops I know of – if not *the* best. (Extract from Letter from B. Malinowski to Outhwaite, 1 June 1926, Laura Spelman Rockefeller Memorial Archives, Series 3.6, Box 49, Folder 518)

All of this created great intellectual excitement. There was a great deal of talking (and singing) about "being on the frontier." Walter Morton has recalled that many of the students at Brookings were "talking about the new frontiers of economics," and that "some of us called them the 'new frontiersmen'" (Walter Morton to Robert Coleberd, 4 March 1973, Brookings Institution Archives, Item A86–001, RSB Graduate School 50th Anniversary, Box 1, Letters in Reply Folder).

Despite the enthusiasm of students and visitors, and the undoubted successes of the graduates of the program, the School disappeared in the amalgamation that formed the Brookings Institution at the end of 1927. The discontinuance of the School created considerable student protest, including an article in *The Survey* (Peck and Galloway 1928) and the resulting correspondence concerning questions raised by Charles Beard (Moulton 1928). The School continued for the 1928–1929 year, but Hamilton and Wright both left.[16] Wright went to the School of Social Service Administration at the University of Chicago, where, in 1941, she succeeded Edith Abbot as Dean, and Hamilton accepted an offer from Yale Law School he had been considering. The place of the School was taken by the "Training Division" of the Brookings Institution, which was designed as a vehicle through which more advanced doctoral students could be involved in the work of the Brookings research staff. The last RBGS doctoral degrees were awarded in 1930, and the Charter of the School was surrendered in 1931. The Brookings Institution itself awarded a small number of PhD degrees via its Training Division through to 1936.

---

[16] During the 1928–1929 academic year, a course was offered partly by visitors, including Wesley Mitchell, J. M. Clark, Sumner Slichter, and Frank Knight, and partly by Institute of Economics staff. The students themselves ran a seminar on the novel in which each student gave a presentation on one of the great novelists (George Marshall to Robert Coleberd, 25 September 1974, Brookings Institution Archive, A86–001, Box 2, Folder Reunion October 16 II). Hamilton was greatly missed. Hamilton and Wright returned for the oral exams of students, but even this became an issue when Wright discovered that there would not be at least two members of the examining committees from the former School staff (Helen Wright to Fred Powell, 13 May 1929, Brookings Institution Archive, Item 136, Correspondence of the Training Division, 1928–1941, Box 2, Folder W).

Why was the School terminated? There seem to have been two inter-connected reasons: the financial difficulties facing various of the Brookings enterprises, and a divergence between Robert Brookings and Hamilton on the nature of the School and the type of graduates being produced. It must also be said that Hamilton had not maintained good relations with the major personalities involved in the IGR, and had little or no support from that quarter.[17]

The major financial problem was the imminent ending of the Carnegie grant that had been funding the Institute of Economics. Although this grant was given with no assurance of any further funding, Brookings and Moulton had hoped to persuade Carnegie to provide a permanent endowment for the Institute. In this they failed.[18] To many of the students, it seemed that the School, which was relatively well endowed, had been sacrificed to save the Institute of Economics, but the story is a little more complex. Other than Carnegie, the most promising source of funding was the Laura Spelman Rockefeller Memorial Foundation, which had provided funding for the

---

[17] In his 1926 report to the Board of Trustees, Hamilton complained that the School had tried to build links with the IGR but had failed due to the interests of the IGR being much too narrowly focused on issues of administrative "economy and efficiency" to furnish "a proper research complement to the School's work in politics" (Hamilton 1926a, p. 16). This drew an angry response from W. F. Willoughby of the IGR, who blamed the lack of interaction between the IGR and the School entirely on Hamilton (W. F. Willoughby to Robert S. Brookings, 24 May 1926, Brookings Archive, Item 17, Box 1, Appendix 4 to Moulton 1928). Another cause of friction concerned the use of the Rockefeller funding, which, although given to the School, was intended to be used as a "research fund" to support the IGR (the Institute of Economics being already provided for by funding from Carnegie). In order to do this, the Trustees of the School assigned the funds to the IGR and assumed control over the IGR by becoming members of the IGR's Board. IGR Board members who were not also Trustees of the School had to resign. The School staff argued that they should also have some access to these funds to support their own research, but were not successful. Finally, Hamilton and Wright's second book on the bituminous coal industry, which suggested a consolidation of the coal industry under the control of work-ers and consumers, "provoked sharp dissent in its conclusions by two staff members" (42 Year Report, Brookings Archive, Item 18, Box 1). Dorothy Ross claims that "Pressures from the coal companies and the conservative political scientists of the IGR conspired to bring Hamilton down and to eliminate the graduate school altogether" (Ross 1991, p. 417). However, Hamilton and Wright's second book did not appear in print until 1928, whereas the amalgamation plan was finalized and agreed to by the end of 1927. As noted in Chapter 3, Hamilton and Wright's proposals were modeled on those proposed in 1919 by Henry Clay for the British coal industry (Dorfman 1974, p. 14).

[18] The reasons for Carnegie's refusal involved changes in policy with respect to the granting of permanent endowments, financial retrenchment, and the irritation of one member of the Carnegie Board with Moulton's work on the financial condition of France (Moulton 1928; Robert Brookings to Harold Moulton, 1 June 1926, Brookings Archive, Item 30, Box 1, Robert S. Brookings [1925–1926] Folder).

research activity of the IGR. Those at Rockefeller were insistent, however, that an amalgamation of Brookings's various organizations should be undertaken before anything further could be considered (Beardsley Ruml, memorandum "Institute for Government Research, Institute of Economics, Washington Graduate School of Economics," 24 January 1924, Laura Spelman Rockefeller Memorial Archives, Series 3.6, Box 49, Folder 517). Once the new Brookings Institution was formed, Brookings and Moulton set about the task of increasing the Institution's endowment funding. As part of that effort, they were awarded more than $2 million by Rockefeller in 1928 (well before the Carnegie grant expired).

Of course, such an amalgamation need not have involved the demise of the School in something like its existing form, and several versions of amalgamation plans were produced in which the School and the Institutes were maintained as a separate "Divisions" within a larger Brookings Institution. What to do about the School was an issue much considered by Brookings, Moulton, and the Executive Committee. Brookings also asked Abraham Flexner, of the General Education Board, to examine this issue and report back to him. Flexner did make an extended visit to the School, spoke with the staff, and requested written statements concerning the future of the School from Hamilton and Lyon. These were prepared. Flexner did not complete a written report, but he was heard to remark that a faculty consisting of "three men and a girl" was hopelessly weak (Moulton 1928, p. 21). Hamilton's own suggestions involved not only maintaining the School in as independent a form as possible, but also significantly enlarging its resident faculty.[19] However, Brookings's own thinking was moving along very different lines, with his main concern being the integrating of the training function with the research activity of the Institutes. Brookings was clearly concerned that the School was operating largely independently and was following its own path in its "experiment" in graduate education. The School was being guided more by Hamilton's educational philosophy than by Brookings's original intentions. The students were not closely involved with the research work of the Institutes, the School had developed particularly few connections with the IGR, and from the lists of graduates produced in 1927, it seemed that a high proportion were moving into university or college careers and not into the kind of nonacademic positions that Brookings had intended. In fact, in 1927, the number of public service or research

---

[19]   Hamilton indicated that given his wishes, he would like, over a two-year period, to try to hire Carl Becker in history, Joseph Redlich in politics, Walter Stewart in economics, and Arthur Macmahon, John Dickinson, or John Gaus in administration (Hamilton 1927).

positions of the type that Brookings had originally had in mind was not large. With the New Deal, many such positions did materialize – particularly in economics – and numerous RBGS graduates did move into government positions, but from the perspective available in 1927, it could be argued that the School was not meeting its original mandate and was simply duplicating the role of university graduate programs.[20] In any event, the School disappeared in the amalgamation, Hamilton and Moulton's friendship came to an end, and many students remained embittered.

THE BROOKINGS PROGRAM

The program of study was *extremely* informal. Students were expected to "present" two languages and complete an individualized program of study, write a thesis, and pass an oral exam. Traditional lecture courses were "under a ban," and there "was never a requirement of attendance upon courses, an accumulation of credits, or a system of majors and minors" (Hamilton 1926a, p. 6). This made it possible for students with government jobs to complete PhDs at the School, attending such courses, seminars, and talks as they could. For example, many of the young economists that Walter Stewart recruited to his Research and Statistics Division of the Federal Reserve Board (including William J. Carson, Winfield Riefler, and Woodlief Thomas) completed their doctorates at the School.

The student's program did not specify credits or courses, but rather a series of areas and topics to be mastered. These areas were not confined to economics or political science. For example, the program outlined for Mordecai Ezekiel contained six major divisions: (i) "Economic Foundations" including preclassical, classical, neoclassical, historical, and institutional economics, with the emphasis clearly on the last; (ii) "Description of the Modern Economic Organization," including "the pecuniary mechanism and institutions" and a series of more specific elements related to Ezekiel's interest in agriculture; (iii) "Technical Equipment for Economic Research," including quantitative analysis and "the scientific method in research and analysis"; (iv) "The Art of Economic Invention," dealing with issues of institutional design and "the invention of mechanisms for check, control, or direction of industries or of the economic organization as a whole"; (v) "Frontier Studies in Related Fields," including social psychology, political science, history, and philosophy; and (vi) "General Reading," including

---

[20] It may also have been the case that other universities were not keen on the School because it tended to "poach" some of their better graduate students.

modern English and American literature, and selected essays in philosophy (including Descartes, Locke, Montesquieu, and Voltaire). Also noted was Ezekiel's choice of French and German languages (Tentative program of work to be offered by Mordecai Ezekiel, 15 May 1925, Mordecai Ezekiel Papers, Box 14, Student Notes and Papers Folder). Progress was checked by periodic "conferences" between the student and the staff, and lack of satisfactory progress could result in a student being asked to leave.

Courses were offered, but these were of various lengths, changed from year to year to accommodate the interests of students, and generally incorporated much discussion, reading, and student presentations. Some of the "major" courses offered by the regular faculty were Hamilton's "Modern Economic Organization," Lyon's "The Nature of Industry," Shepard's "Comparative Political Institutions," and Wright's "The Neo-Classical System of Economics." Wright also taught "The Uses of Statistics," Moulton gave a series of lectures on "The Credit System," and Lubin taught on "Systems of Economics." Hamilton also gave courses titled "The Control of Industry" or "Control of Industrial Development," courses with a heavy emphasis on social control, forms of regulation, and discussions of the Sherman and Clayton acts, the coal industry, and radio (Hamilton Papers, Box J6, Folder 1).

Information on course content is in most cases sketchy, but notes from Hamilton's course from 1925 (Mordecai Ezekiel Papers, Box 14, Student Notes and Papers Folder) add considerably to the information on course content available from the program outlines. The notes from Hamilton's course on "Economic Organization" display his style of throwing out questions, problems, different points of view, possible points of study, and assignments to students. He asks questions such as: "Why start with a study of the price system?" or "Is demand antecedent to and independent of an actual market situation?" or "What meaning do various authors have when they use the term competition?" As he proceeds, he suggests many readings from Cannan, Commons, Cooley, Marshall, Mitchell, Pigou, Smith, Tawney, and Veblen, as well as from works in history, philosophy, and biography.

The course has a clear focus on the institutional organization of economic activity and expresses a critical view of classical and neoclassical theory. It begins with a general and historical discussion of the "Pecuniary Organization of Society," the price system and its direction of the industrial system, and with references to the classical, neoclassical, and institutionalist "explanations" of the price system. This is followed by a more in-depth discussion of the competitive system and its development, which includes discussions of property, the "separation between those who own and those who direct" in the case of the "modern corporation," and a very lengthy discussion of contract, including such questions as "Does the contract include all the features of the relations, or are some of them fixed by law (or custom) and only a few left for contract?" Hamilton then proceeds to the issue of whether profit making ensures that social ends are properly served, defining the "liberal" view as "Profit [is] a device for getting things done, but in no sense a sacrosanct thing, and subject to modification in particular cases where it fails to work properly." In the next section on "Competition," he notes the confusions in meaning (particularly between competition and laissez-faire) and insists that competition is "complementary to a great number of other institutions, and its nature is modified by the way these institutions impinge upon it" (Mordecai Ezekiel Papers, Box 14, Student Notes and Papers Folder).

Hamilton moves on to discuss production, including issues of advance in technique, the functioning of the patent system, and measurement through indexes of production. He then discusses capital, investment, and savings (which includes discussion of both personal and corporate savings), and the possibility that the "maladjustment of saving and production of durable goods" might provide an explanation of business cycles. He then talks of various forms of organization of industry, including competitive, monopolized, nationalized, and various forms of control, including rate regulation and the possibility of new forms of control by bodies of producers and consumers.

The final sections of the course deal with the "Classification of Economists" and "The Clash Between Institutional and Neo-Classical Economics." This is of considerable interest, considering that neither Commons nor Mitchell (in his Types of Economic Theory course) presented the relationship between neoclassical and institutional economics in quite such antagonistic terms (Rutherford 2004). In Hamilton's view, institutionalists "recognize that the whole system is in process of change, and is subject to direction and control, and may best be directed by knowledge of specific problems and the facts of the case." In this, Hamilton makes much of the work of Veblen and Cooley, of John Dewey's instrumentalism, and Mitchell's statistical approach. He argues that Mitchell accepted Veblen's "general point of view," but became interested in working it out on a specific problem. In contrast, neoclassicals are "system-builders, leaving practical questions out of the system"; thus they tend to "come to a defense of the system rather than to a practical program" (Mordecai Ezekiel Papers, Box 14, Student Notes and Papers Folder). Hamilton's course, then, is very explicitly institutionalist and antineoclassical in orientation.

Ezekiel's notes from Lyon's course, "Nature of Industry," also exist. The course is heavily institutionalist too. It begins with a discussion of the problem of psychology and economics, including references to Veblen and J. M. Clark, then deals with the history of the organization and control of industrial activity, stressing the role of custom, religion, laws and court decisions, trade practices, as well as individual enterprise, public enterprise, and the issue of culture lag. The course also has sections on capital creation and a great deal on ways of organizing industries, the roles of government and private enterprise, and government administration. A significant amount of the rest of the course is made up of student presentations on topics relating to their particular areas of interest, such as "Frontier Problems in Transportation," "Measuring Production," "Elements in Business Forecasting," and "Aspects of Mineral Production."

From about 1925, Hamilton began to develop further his interest in law and economics. He wrote to Commons, indicating that several of his students were studying the *Legal Foundations of Capitalism*.[21] In the 1926–1927 academic year, the School formally introduced "group inquiries" in which a group of more senior students with interests in a single field were put together with a member of staff in collecting "points of view, ideas, and materials." This inquiry would be made the only occupation of the students involved, and would last some fifteen weeks. Each student would be expected to produce an "essay of some consequence." In that year, group inquires were led by Shepard on "The State and the Individual," Hamilton on "The Place of the Supreme Court in the Economic Order,"[22] Hamilton and Wright on "Types of Industrial Control," Graham Wallas (formerly of the LSE, visiting Brookings for a semester) on "The Ends and Means of Social Control," Moulton and Lubin on "The Economic Position of Great Britain," and by Lyon and Charles Hardy on "The Market Economy."[23] The School also experimented with six- or seven-week reading courses designed to open up a subject area to students and to provide a basis for later group

---

[21] Walton Hamilton to John R. Commons, 8 June 1925, John R. Commons Papers, Box 13, Folder 1. Despite this interest in Commons's work, Hamilton did not think that highly of Commons's legal scholarship (Lubin, 1974, Taped Interview with Robert Coleberd, Brookings Institution Archives, Item A86–011).

[22] This course was soon retitled "The Judicial Control of Industry." Outlines are available in the Hamilton Papers (Box J4, Folder 1), but these consist entirely of lists of court cases organized under headings such as "The Institutional Basis of Industry," "The Competitive System," "The System of Regulation," "The State in Industry," and "Law and Order."

[23] Graham Wallas had been a leading member of the Fabian group and a professor of politics at the LSE until 1923. He was on the staff of the School for part of the 1926–1927 academic year. Hardy was a Member of Council of the Institute of Economics.

inquiries and special investigations by students. These were offered primarily by regular staff and associate members, but some were offered by visitors. For example, in 1926–1927, reading courses were given by Helen Wright in "The Coming of Industrialism," George Sabine, a philosopher from Ohio State, on "Political Classics," Walter W. Cook, a prominent legal realist from Johns Hopkins, on "The Logic of Inquiry," Lewis Lorwin, a staff member of The Institute of Economics, on "Proposals for Economic Reorganization," and by Leverett Lyon on "Financial Institutions." To some extent, these reading courses and group inquires replaced the "more extended courses of reading and discussion" (Lyon 1927, pp. 6–7).

In addition to these types of courses, it was a policy of the School to attract visiting speakers. One of Hamilton's concerns was to provide enough breadth for the students, particularly given the small size of the core faculty. In this he was spectacularly successful, and in a very short time, the School accumulated a vast list of speakers, some of whom gave "short courses" running between two and ten sessions, some a short series of informal talks, and some only a single talk. For the 1926–1927 academic year alone, the School listed fourteen short courses, including Walter W. Cook on "The Logic of the Law," David Friday on "Economic and Financial Stabilization in Europe," A. A. Goldenweiser on "Race and Culture," John Mecklin on "Individual and Social Psychology," Max Otto on "What Is Truth, What Is Right, What Is Man," Joseph Redlich on "Recent Developments of Democracy in Central Europe," and Gaetano Salvemini, a leading antifascist and formerly a professor of history at the University of Florence, on "What Is Fascismo" and "Dante and His Times" (Lyon 1927). Others who, at various times, gave short courses or series of talks included economists (Clarence Ayres, John R. Commons, Herbert Davenport, William Foster, Carter Goodrich, Alvin Johnson, Laurence Laughlin, Willard Thorp), historians (Charles Beard, Carl Becker, William Dodd), philosophers (Morris Cohen, Alexander Meiklejohn), legal scholars (Felix Frankfurter, Roscoe Pound, Thomas Powell), political scientists (Harold Laski), anthropologists (Bronislaw Malinowski, Clark Wissler), writers (Lewis Mumford), journalists, directors of research foundations, government officials, and members of international organizations. Single talks were given by economists such as Eveline Burns, Gustav Cassel, J. M. Clark, Edwin Gay, Sumner Slichter, Walter Stewart, Rexford Tugwell, and Leo Wolman, legal scholars such as Robert Hutchins and Herman Oliphant, historians such as Paul Mantoux, political scientists such as Charles Merriam, and numerous others running from the President of the International Seaman's Union, to the Director of Maternity Work, Kentucky Mountains, to professors of English literature and zoology (RBGS General Catalogue 1923–1928). Again, many of these short-term visitors would stay in residence and interact with the students. Veblen also stayed at the residence for a period of weeks but did not give any talks, despite being invited (Dorfman 1972, Taped Interview by Robert Coleberd, Brookings Institution Archives, A86–011).

Another of Hamilton's concerns was with the development of good writing skills among his students. He argued that the usual doctoral thesis was far too large a project to be completed by a relative novice in a period of two years. With a few notable exceptions, theses "are inchoate speculations or mere descriptions; the run of them exhibits few qualities of workmanship above clerical heroics" (Hamilton 1926a, p. 11). Hamilton argued for developing the "art of inquiry and the art of writing" together, beginning with "simple and unpretentious bits of work" and gradually moving on to more ambitious projects. To this end, Hamilton encouraged his students to begin by writing reviews of the latest books in their areas of interest. He and John White (a student) put together a compilation called *A Book of Book Reviews* (Hamilton and White 1926), a work that was much more than just a sample of reviews, but a real pedagogical tool and guide to review writing. The group inquiry courses also encouraged writing and were designed to get students to produce work of publishable or near-publishable quality. Another innovation of the School was to substitute a requirement of a series of essays of publishable quality (or actually published) in place of the usual "monumental tome."[24] Mordecai Ezekiel wrote in his diary for 13 March 1926:

Much to my surprise the Robt. Brookings felt I had about all the work I needed, accepted my various magazine articles in lieu of a thesis, and gave me my preliminary and final oral exams, the latter yesterday. They accepted mathematics as one of my languages. As a result as soon as I do a paper on Hobson ... I can get my degree. Probably in June. (Mordecai Ezekiel Papers, Box 5, Diaries 1922–29 Folder)

In another case, a piece of work carried out jointly by Dexter Keezer and Stacy May was accepted as meeting the thesis requirements of both students. Oral exams could also be very informal. In the case of Max Lerner, he was invited to a Saturday morning discussion over tea or coffee with Hamilton. Over time, other staff members arrived and joined in the discussion. After a couple of hours of discussion, Hamilton announced Lerner had just successfully completed his oral examination. The questioning was less to find out what Lerner knew than to discover "how he would handle problems"

---

[24] This is the first "essay" approach to thesis writing in economics that I know of.

(Isador Lubin 1974, Taped Interview by Robert Coleberd, Brookings Institution Archives, Item A86–011).

Hamilton's students received virtually no formal training in neoclassical theory at all. Some Brookings students would have received previous graduate training in neoclassical economics, but not those who came from Amherst or from many other places. At Michigan, Chicago, and Harvard, students certainly *were* drilled through neoclassical theory, and this type of "drill sergeant" approach to teaching, still common in economics, can itself be seen as related to the nature of neoclassical theory and the desire to impart a thorough understanding of an established and complex theoretical framework. In Hamilton's own programs, in contrast, no one was drilled through Marshall or neoclassical theory as Hamilton himself had been drilled by Taylor. Moreover, this almost complete lack of training in standard theory (except for material covered in the students' own reading) did not seem to have been a barrier to governmental employment in the 1920s and 1930s. Even within the academic world, Amherst and Brookings graduates found employment in all but the few most theoretically inclined economics departments.

For Hamilton, the institutional approach to economics required not just exposure to institutionalist ideas, but a very particular type of training, explicitly designed to develop an investigative approach to economic and social problems, an interest in methods of social control, and a willingness to disregard conventional disciplinary boundaries. Hamilton clearly spent much more time and effort thinking about and implementing educational strategies than did other institutionalists. His programs provided a remarkable combination of problem-centeredness and intellectual breadth. Hamilton's methods of instruction would now be thought of as a paradigm of "active learning" and of interdisciplinarity. As Stacy May explained, Hamilton was the type who could take students and get them genuinely excited about finding something out, and in the kind of work that had to be done in order to find something out. The former students who recalled the School at its Fiftieth Anniversary Reunion spoke repeatedly of the informality and the interdisciplinarity of the program (Brookings Banquet, 17 October 1973, Taped by Robert Coleberd, Brookings Institution Archives, A86–011). Hamilton was able to impart great intellectual excitement, to have his student see themselves and the work they were doing as "on the frontier." As I have argued elsewhere, this idea of institutionalism as breaking new ground, of moving past the sterile "value theory" of orthodox economics, of being in line with recent developments in law and the other social sciences, and of being both scientific and relevant to the solution of social problems, is what explains the great appeal that institutionalism possessed in the 1920s. This is nowhere better seen than in Hamilton's programs. Even those who did not become associated with institutionalism clearly took away a great deal from the nature of Hamilton's educational philosophy.

THE BROOKINGS STUDENTS

Brookings produced a large number of students, many of whom had significance in terms of the future of the institutionalist movement. Table 6.2 lists selected students with the dates they attended the School. Those who received their PhD from the school are denoted with an asterisk. The later careers of these students are clearly indicative of the School's orientation.

The Brookings graduates with perhaps the most notable governmental careers in economics were Winfield Riefler, Isador Lubin, and Mordecai Ezekiel.[25] Riefler had a significant career with the Federal Reserve Board, and his book, *Money Rates and Money Markets* (1930), was the product of his Brookings thesis research. He became Economic Adviser to the Executive Council during the New Deal, Chairman of the Central Statistical Board, and later (along with Walter Stewart) held an appointment at the Institute of Advanced Study at Princeton. Riefler also played a major role in various NBER monetary projects and became heavily involved with the League of Nations. He was President of the American Statistical Association in 1941. Another Brookings graduate, Woodlief Thomas, also had a substantial career with the Research and Statistics Division of the Federal Reserve Board.

Lubin stayed with the Institute of Economics for some time, working first on miner's wages and the cost of coal (Lubin 1924) and then on the British

---

[25] Many others not listed in the table also had successful government careers. These include Oscar Kiessling, with the Bureau of Mines; Henry Chalmers, as Chief of the Division of Tariffs, Department of Commerce; Leon Truesdell, as Chief of Population Division, Bureau of the Census; Norman Myers with the Department of Interior, Petroleum Division; William Young with the Department of Agriculture; and Harry Cassidy as Director of Social Welfare in British Columbia, Canada. Paul Lewinson, who wrote *Race, Class, and Party: A History of Negro Suffrage and White Politics in the South* (1932), became Director of the Industrial Records Office of the National Archives and led the research staff that produced the *Guide to Documents in the National Archives for Negro Studies* (1947). After a year at Brookings, Robinson Newcomb planned to write his dissertation at the University of North Carolina on the topic of black businessmen in the Raleigh/Durham area, but objections from white business people resulted in the University ordering the destruction of his work. He moved back to Brookings to complete his PhD. His later career was in government, dealing with housing issues (see Hall and Badgett 2009).

Table 6.2. *Selected Brookings Graduate School students, 1923–1930 (Dates of Attendance; * indicates PhD awarded from Brookings Graduate School)*

Helen Everett (1923–1925)*	Carl Raushenbush (1924–1925)	Woodlief Thomas (1925–1928)*
Ralph Fuchs (1923–1925)*	Winfield Riefler (1924–1927)*	Addison Cutler (1926–1927)*
George Galloway (1923–1926)*	Frank Tannenbaum (1924–1925 and 1926–1927)*	Breck McAllister (1926–1928)*
Isador Lubin (1923–1925)*	William Carson (1925–1928)*	John U. Nef (1926–1927)*
Stacy May (1923–1925)*	Anton Friedrich (1925–1926)	Gustav Peck (1926–1927)*
C. Panunzio (1923–1924)*	Paul Homan (1925–1926)*	George Terborgh (1926–1928)*
Theresa Wolfson (1923–1924)*	Thor Hultgren (1925–1927)	Lazar Volin (1926–1928)
Mordecai Ezekiel (1924–1926)*	Max Lerner (1925–1927)*	Paul Webbink (1926–1928)
Elsie Gluck (1924–1926)	Robert Montgomery (1925–1926)*	John Aikin (1927–1929)*
Lewis Jones (1924–1926)*	Walter Sandelius (1925–1926)*	Frieda Baird (1927–1929)*
Dexter Keezer (1924–1925)*		Eleanor Bontecou (1927–1928)*
Harry H. Moore (1924–1926)*		Carl Swisher (1927–1930)*
Walter Morton (1924–1925)		

Source: Brooking Institution Archives

coal industry with Helen Everett (Lubin and Everett 1927).[26] These books complemented those by Hamilton and Helen Wright on the American bituminous coal industry (1925; 1928).[27] At this time, the coal industry on both sides of the Atlantic was mired in excess capacity, old equipment, low

[26] Lubin, it should be noted, was close friends with Leo Wolman and also provided a great deal of help to Joseph Dorfman in the latter's work on his Veblen book.

[27] Hamilton and Lubin were keen on having their books on coal jointly reviewed because they felt that their investigations were not primarily descriptive, but rather investigations into economic theory (Isador Lubin to Max Handman, 5 December 1927, Isador Lubin Papers Box 1, Correspondence 1927 Folder).

wages, and poor working conditions, and was regarded by both Lubin and Hamilton as indicating the failure of private competitive industry. Lubin's work on the British coal industry brought him into contact with Tawney, Beveridge, and others in England, and the book was reviewed both by Tawney and by J. A. Hobson. Lubin was then put in charge of the Institute of Economics' study of unemployment. He became very much engaged with issues of the measurement of unemployment and closely involved with those members of Senate pushing to improve government statistics, introduce federal unemployment exchanges, and provide unemployment insurance. In 1933, he was appointed Commissioner of Labor Statistics, a position he kept until 1946, doing much to improve the statistical work of the Bureau. He was a member of the Central Statistical Board and of the Industrial Committee of the National Resources Committee. Later, during World War II, he became a special adviser to President Roosevelt. After the war, he helped negotiate Allied policy on German reparations and represented the United States in the Economic and Social Council of the United Nations (UNESCO), and in the General Assembly of the International Labour Organization. Lubin's coauthor on his coal book, Helen Everett, wrote the entry on "Social Control" in the *Encyclopaedia of the Social Sciences* (Everett 1931), and married Alexander Meiklejohn, moving with him to Wisconsin. She also wrote the chapter on the women's dress industry for Hamilton's *Price and Price Policies* (Hamilton and Associates 1938).

Mordecai Ezekiel was employed as an economist in the Department of Agriculture while attending Brookings. He had a particular interest in statistical methods and published *Methods of Correlation Analysis* in 1930 and for many years taught both statistics and economics courses at the USDA Graduate School.[28] Ezekiel did much to formulate the details of what would become the Agriculture Adjustment Administration, and helped draft the Agricultural Adjustment Act. Along with Rexford Tugwell, Ezekiel was a strong supporter of extending the concept of planned production to industry in general (Ezekiel 1936; 1939a). Later in his career, Ezekiel worked with the Food and Agriculture Organization of the United Nations, becoming Special Assistant to the Director General, and then moved on to serve

---

[28] The Graduate School of the Department of Agriculture is another fascinating educational institution. Ezekiel learned his statistics there before going to Brookings, and later taught both economics and statistics there. The statistics instruction was very advanced and, particularly during the New Deal years, the economic instruction was heavily institutionalist in orientation. For a discussion of the USDA Graduate School, see Rutherford (forthcoming).

as Chief of the United Nations Division of the United States Agency for International Development.

Among other well-known graduates can be counted Dexter Keezer, Max Lerner, Stacy May, and Theresa Wolfson. Keezer taught as an instructor at Cornell while Copeland was there, but later moved to Brookings. His thesis, coauthored with Stacy May, dealt with the legal issues of "affectation with a public interest" and was later published as *The Public Control of Business* (Keezer and May 1930). For this work, they spent most of their time at the Supreme Court Library and received much advice from Felix Frankfurter. After Brookings, Keezer went into journalism and publishing but continued to write on economic affairs and was asked to join the Consumers' Advisory Board of the National Recovery Administration. Between 1934 and 1942, he was President of Reed College and served on the National War Labor Board during World War II. Stacy May did his undergraduate work at Amherst and Columbia, where he took courses in law. He knew Hamilton very well from Amherst where he had not only been an undergraduate, but had also taught worker's education classes organized through local trade unions (May 1972, Taped Interview by Robert Coleberd, Brookings Institution Archives, A86–011). Prior to his thesis work with Keezer, May had coauthored *The Control of Wages* with Walton Hamilton (Hamilton and May 1923). May's career after Brookings included brief teaching stints at Dartmouth College and Cornell. He became Assistant Director of the Social Sciences Division of the Rockefeller Foundation between 1932 and 1942, served as Director of the Planning and Statistics Division of the War Production Board during World War II, and went on to work on with Nelson Rockefeller on his overseas economic development program. Lerner began as an assistant editor of the *Encyclopaedia of the Social Sciences* and later held a number of college positions. He contributed several papers on law and economics for the *Yale Law Review*, including a lengthy appreciation of the pragmatic and experimental approach to the "living law" to be found in the opinions of Justice Brandeis (Lerner 1931), but for the most part, he directed his career to more popular commentaries on economic and political affairs from his liberal point of view. In this he was highly successful. He edited *The Nation* between 1936 and 1938. Lerner also wrote on Veblen (Lerner 1935) and produced an edited collection of Veblen's writings (Lerner 1948). Theresa Wolfson had a long career at Brooklyn College. She worked on women-in-the-trade-union movement, coauthored a book on freethinker and reformer Frances Wright (Perkins and Wolfson 1939), was active in labor mediation and arbitration, and lectured widely on labor problems.

Riefler, Lubin, Ezekiel, and, to a lesser extent, Keezer and May were certainly active in the network of individuals that made up the institutionalist movement in the interwar period. There were other Brookings students who had connections of various types to institutionalism. Robert Montgomery was with the economics faculty at the University of Texas, and returned after graduating from Brookings to become a part of the institutionalist group that formed there.[29] William J. Carson, hired in to the Research and Statistics Division of the Federal Reserve by Walter Stewart, became a professor of finance at Wharton. He later served for many years as the Executive Director of the NBER. Thor Hultgren stayed for two years at Brookings and later worked for the NBER, specializing in transportation. Carl Raushenbush only stayed a year at Brookings, but then joined the institutionalist group at Washington Square College of New York University. Another of the Washington Square group, Anton Friedrich, also spent one year at Brookings, and Frieda Baird spent the 1930–1931 academic year at Washington Square as well. Walter Morton spent a year at Brookings in 1924–1925, before returning to Wisconsin. Another Wisconsin student, Elsie Gluck, spent two years at the School, and Commons student Ewan Clauge stayed at the Residence when first in Washington, although he never attended the School. Gustav Peck worked with Leo Wolman on "Labor Groups in the Social Structure" for the report of the President's Committee on Social Trends (Wolman and Peck 1933). Harry Hascall Moore became Director of Study for the Committee on the Costs of Medical Care and wrote the pioneering *American Medicine and the Peoples' Health* (1927). Lewis Jones went to the London School of Economics for further study and later also worked for the Committee on the Costs of Medical Care. He became President of the University of Arkansas, and later President of Rutgers. George Galloway cofounded the National Planning Association and wrote extensively on planning and on the federal budget. Paul Webbink became Vice President of the Social Science Research Council, and in that capacity a close colleague of Mitchell and Ogburn. Lazar Volin had a long career at the USDA, becoming a leading expect on Soviet agriculture. George Terborgh became an economist for the Machinery and Allied Products Institute, but continued to write for the Brookings Institution, contributing to the critical analysis of the NRA codes.

---

[29] Clarence Ayres obtained his first regular academic job since his time at Amherst in 1930 in the Economics Department at the University of Texas, replacing Max Handman who had gone to Michigan to replace Carter Goodrich, who had gone to Columbia!

Less obviously an institutionalist, but still a person with a strongly inter-disciplinary perspective, was John Nef. Nef wrote on the early history of the British coal industry for his Brookings thesis. He had begun on this subject in 1922 while at Harvard, but it had attracted the attention of both Hamilton, then still at Amherst, and R. H. Tawney in England. His spent several years in London and Paris, returning in 1926, whereupon he was invited to Brookings by Hamilton. Moulton and Hamilton actively helped him obtain a position in the Economics Department at Chicago (Nef 1973, pp. 106–107, 191). Nef's interests were broad, covering the rise of industrial civilization, its cultural foundations and impacts. His dissatisfaction with specialized graduate education expressed itself in his work in founding the interdisciplinary "Committee on Social Thought" at Chicago and later the Center for Human Understanding (Nef 1973).

Paul Homan had a slightly different reaction to exposure to the Brookings experience. Homan's thesis consisted of a number of the essays, later pub-lished as *Contemporary Economic Thought* (1928), including essays on Veblen, Mitchell, and J. A. Hobson. As a result, Alvin Johnson asked Homan to write the entry on the "Institutional School" for the *Encyclopaedia of the Social Sciences*. In this piece and in his "An Appraisal of Institutional Economics" (1932), Homan attacked the idea that there was a "distin-guishable body of economic knowledge or theory" that could be prop-erly called institutional. Whereas Homan's work clearly shows his intimate knowledge of the institutionalists he is discussing, his arguments helped create a growing skepticism concerning the ability of institutionalism to live up to its earlier promises, and a tendency to see institutionalists as bound together only by their rejection of standard theory.[30] Homan also wrote on the New Deal and on antitrust issues, and was editor of the *American Economic Review* between 1941 and 1951.

Addison Cutler also became a critic of institutionalism, but from a very different perspective. He was a graduate of Amherst and obtained his Brookings PhD in 1930, having been enrolled from 1926. He then became an assistant professor of economics at the University of North Carolina.

---

[30] Interestingly, the charge Homan was given by Alvin Johnson was to "attempt to systematise and establish relations between the work of Veblen, Mitchell, Commons, and the younger men in America and the *sozial politische* orientation in Germany (Sombart, Weber, the group of the *Archiv fur Sozial wissenschaft*.)" (Paul Homan to Rexford Tugwell, December 18, 1930, Rexford G. Tugwell Papers, Box 11, Paul Homan Folder). Homan wrote to Mitchell, Dorfman, Tugwell, and others to ask for their opinions, and received a wide variety of responses, including the claim, from Mitchell and Dorfman, that Veblen alone should be classified under the category of institutional economics. J. M. Clark defended a broad view of institutionalism against Homan (Clark 1932).

With Keezer and Frank Garfield (both colleagues from Amherst), he coedited a book of readings, *Problem Economics* (1928). Keezer regarded Cutler as brilliant. Ayres later described him as an "Amherst bred, Hamilton trained 'institutionalist' who later went Marxist" (Clarence Ayres to I. Leo Sharfman, 9 July 1945, I. Leo Sharfman papers, Box 1, Ayres Folder). This Marxist point of view is evident in his 1938 paper critical of institutionalism, "The Ebb of Institutional Economics" (Cutler 1938). As with the critique by Homan, this paper shows very close familiarity with Hamilton's work and with his institutionalism. Cutler's later career was with the Federal Reserve Bank in Cleveland and the University of Cincinnati.[31]

Outside of economics, RBGS graduates became lawyers and professors of law, political science, and sociology. Ralph Fuchs became a professor of law at Indiana, was involved in the drafting of the Administrative Procedure Act, served as Special Assistant to the U.S. Attorney General and to the Solicitor General, became an expert on administrative law, and was an active civil libertarian and involved with the American Association of University Professors and the National Association for the Advancement of Colored People. Eleanor Bontecou became a dean at Bryn Mawr, a professor in the Graduate School of Social Service Administration, University of Chicago, and an attorney in the Civil Rights and Research Sections, Criminal Division, Department of Justice. Breck McAllister became Special Assistant to the U.S. Attorney General in 1929. He then joined the New York Bar but continued to contribute frequently to law journals.[32] While at Brookings, Frank Tannenbaum used to visit remote areas of Mexico on a mule. He became an adviser to the Mexican government in the 1930s, was involved with the Farm Security Bill during the New Deal, and became a very well-known professor specializing in Latin American history at Columbia University (1929; 1933; 1946). Carl B. Swisher became a professor of political science at Johns Hopkins and a well-known scholar of the Supreme Court and American constitutional development (1930; 1943). Walter Sandelius became a professor of political science at the University of Kansas, and John Aikin the same at the University of California at Berkeley. Constantine Panunzio became a professor of sociology at the University of California at Los Angeles and well known for his books on immigrant

---

[31] Among many other students who followed career paths in economics were Montgomery Anderson, Orval Bennett, and Fred Berquist.

[32] The 1931–1932 issue of the *Yale Law Journal* has articles by Hamilton, Fuchs, Lerner, and McAllister. Very much related to the theme pursued by Keezer and May, McAllister wrote on the early history of the doctrine of "affectation with a public interest" (McAllister 1930). This was also one of Hamilton's themes (Hamilton 1930).

experience. Portions of his book *Immigration Crossroads* (1927) were submitted as his Brookings thesis.

CONCLUSION

Institutionalism in the interwar period was a great deal more than Commons and Mitchell and their programs at Wisconsin and Columbia. Hamilton's version of institutionalism probably captures the essentials of what institutionalism meant better than the work of any other single member of the institutionalist group. American institutionalism in the period immediately after World War I was a combination of the Veblenian view of the significance of "pecuniary institutions" and their failings, with an emphasis on legal institutions and their evolution, an emphasis on empirical work broadly defined, and a highly reformist attitude gained both from the earlier progressive movement in America and from John Dewey's instrumentalist philosophy. Hamilton has all this, with his heavy emphasis on the importance of understanding the institutional nature of the "economic order," on the analysis of the economic problems within that order, on the importance of the relationship between law and economics, and on the need for new methods of "social control." In his educational experiments at Amherst and Brookings, Hamilton expounded this institutionalist view to a generation of students. As we have seen, the unique pedagogical features of his approach go far to explain its appeal to his students. Hamilton's institutionalism was an investigative approach to specific problems within only a very broad conceptual framework concerning the institutional character of the economic order. His general direction and stress was on applied issues of economic policy, an emphasis that was only strengthened by the specific purposes of the Brookings Graduate School.

Of course, the other side of this emphasis was that the idea of developing systematic theory in the sense of a body of theoretical principles was not an important part of Hamilton's program. The lack of systematic theory within institutionalism was the point that critics such as Homan and Parsons began to emphasize in the 1930s. Although it may be ironic that these critics should themselves have been products of the institutionalist orientation of Hamilton and his programs, it was perhaps their intimate knowledge of Hamilton and his institutionalism that allowed them to be effective critics.

Furthermore, and despite Brookings' view of the number of students going into academic careers, many of the most able students in economics from Brookings did in fact go into public service and made their contributions there rather than in academic economics. It is very noticeable that the students who did pursue academic careers in economics, such as Morris Copeland and Carter Goodrich, did not do their doctoral work at Brookings, but went from Amherst to other schools such as Chicago. Riefler, in a particularly telling comment on the legacy left by Brookings students in the area of economics, observed:

It did not leave a lot of books written, it did not leave a lot of text books, and it did not leave a lot of academic writing. … I think that for the caliber of the group they deposited less of that kind, so an economist coming on thirty or forty years later wouldn't get the flavor of that whole movement at all. … Jack Viner would say "if you're going to be an economist you've got to write something," and I would say "you've got to *be* somebody." (Riefler 1972, Taped Interview by Robert Coleberd, Brookings Institution Archive, Item A86–011, Robert S. Brookings Graduate School 50th Anniversary)

It has sometimes been claimed that Wisconsin institutionalism did not reproduce itself because many graduates pursued governmental as opposed to academic careers (Biddle 1998a). This issue will be addressed in Chapter 7, but in the case of the Brookings Graduate School there can be no doubt that the most able of the economics graduates did not go into academic careers and did not themselves produce very much academic output or have numbers of graduate students. On top of this, the ending of the School and Hamilton's resulting move to Yale Law School instead of to an economics program was itself a major loss to the vitality and visibility of the institutionalist movement in economics. As we have already seen, Hamilton did retain involvement in economics, particularly during the New Deal when he was a member of the National Recovery Administration. He also served several terms as the Yale University representative on the board of the NBER, but he was no longer in a position to promote institutionalism in economics in the way he had at both Amherst and at Brookings.

7

Wisconsin Institutionalism

During the period between the World Wars, the University of Wisconsin ranked in the top four universities in terms of the numbers of PhD students, well behind Columbia, but close to Chicago and Harvard (Froman 1942; Biddle 1998a).[1] In terms of the production of graduate students of an institutionalist orientation over the whole interwar period, Columbia and Wisconsin dominate the picture. There is no shortage of literature on John R. Commons's career and writings, but there is relatively little written about the nature of Wisconsin economics more generally, or on the careers pursued by the graduate students produced by Commons at Wisconsin (for a partial exception, see Chasse 2004). Commons produced an extremely large number of graduate students, and what became of these students, and the economics they produced in turn, are important questions in understanding the history of institutionalism as a whole. It has been suggested that Wisconsin institutionalism failed to reproduce itself because graduates tended to have careers in government or in non-PhD-granting institutions, and thus had lower "fertility" than graduates from other schools (Biddle 1998a). In the case of Wisconsin, Jeff Biddle's investigation for students graduating between 1920 and 1946 found mixed evidence, but the information contained in Lampman (1993) allows for a more specific approach. Lampman's book identifies those PhD students supervised by Commons and others of institutional persuasion, and also contains some information on the later employment of graduates. This, combined with material from numerous other published and archival sources, can provide a quite detailed picture of Wisconsin institutionalism in terms of the development of the

---

[1] The rankings vary a bit as between numbers of PhD candidates, numbers of PhDs awarded, and on the definition of an economics PhD. It is hard to rank Brookings because it only existed between 1923 and 1928 and produced PhDs both in economics and political science.

Department of Economics, the faculty, the instructional program offered, the graduates produced, and their later careers.

THE EVOLUTION OF A DEPARTMENT

The history of the teaching of economics at the University of Wisconsin is usually traced back to the hiring of Richard T. Ely as the first full-time professor of economics in 1892. Ely's appointment placed him at the head of a new School of Economics, Political Science and History, a disciplinary combination very much in line with the German model within which he had received his own graduate education. Some commerce courses were offered within the school, also a common arrangement at that time. At Wisconsin, Ely joined his former student, Frederick Jackson Turner, in history. From Johns Hopkins, Ely brought with him an assistant professor in economics and finance, William A. Scott, and two graduate students, David Kinley and Charles Bullock. Although Scott had been an Ely student, his economics was of a more Austrian and marginalist type.

Ely's original School only lasted until 1900, at which point political science formed a separate department, but still within the School of Economics and Political Science, while history formed a separate school altogether. A further reorganization in 1903 resulted in separate departments of Political Economy, Political Science, and History, all within a College of Letters and Science. The Department of Political Economy developed significantly in the early 1900s with the appointment of T. S. Adams and H. C. Taylor in 1902, John R. Commons in 1904, and E. A. Ross in 1906. Adams provided strong instruction in statistics, Taylor – himself a Wisconsin PhD – much developed the field of agricultural economics, Commons took on major research efforts in the history of labor, and Ross provided stature to the instruction of sociology. Ross had introduced the term "social control" in his 1901 book of that name, and he also brought to Wisconsin an admiration for the work of Thorstein Veblen, particularly his *Theory of the Leisure class* (Dorfman 1973, p. 65). Ross's admiration for Veblen was not shared by Ely (Ely 1932). Agricultural economics became a separate department within the College of Agriculture in 1909, but students continued to be able to take courses in both departments. Commerce remained within Political Economy until 1927, and sociology until 1929. In history, Turner left Wisconsin for Harvard in 1910 (Lampman 1993).

Until the end of the first decade of the century, Ely undoubtedly was the dominant personality in Wisconsin economics. The core courses in general economics and economic theory were taught largely by Ely and Scott, whereas Commons's teaching was confined to labor economics (Lampman 1993, pp. 36–37). Although Ely had been significantly influenced by his exposure to German historical economics, by his Social Christianity, and by the English work on labor history undertaken by the Webbs, his teaching became highly eclectic, drawing on a variety of not always consistent sources. His course on the distribution of wealth, for example, utilized texts by John A. Hobson and J. B. Clark. Ely's attitude was that students could work through both and then reach their own conclusions.[2] Similarly, the second (1908) and later editions of Ely's widely used textbook *Outlines of Economics* (with Allyn Young, T. S. Adams, and Max Lorenz as coauthors) included a treatment of both marginal utility and marginal productivity theory. Thus, although Ely was known for his empirical work, notably his admonition to "look and see" and for his earlier reformist attitudes, he was by no means antagonistic to marginalist theory, and it is generally agreed that he became increasingly conservative in his opinions, particularly after surviving the accusation that he was teaching anarchism to students – made by a regent of the University in 1894 (Rader 1966, pp. 130–158). The fact that Ely and his Department were well within the mainstream in terms of the American economics of the time can also be seen in the PhD students produced around the turn of the century – among them David Kinley (1893), Charles Bullock (1895), Balthasar Meyer (1897), B. H. Hibbard (1902), Henry Taylor (1902), Allyn Young (1902), Lewis H. Haney (1906), and Max Lorenz (1906).[3] Students such as these certainly absorbed some of Ely's empiricism and interest in specific policy issues, but none of the students produced from Wisconsin at this point would play roles in the institutionalist movement as it developed around 1918.

This is not to diminish Ely's contributions to the circumstances that created Wisconsin institutionalism. Ely, after all, pioneered the study of American labor and labor movements, taught both Commons and Ross,

[2] Ely to Ross, 16 December 1902, Ely Papers Box 23, Folder 4. John A. Hobson visited the United States in 1902–1903 and taught at Wisconsin between January and April 1903.

[3] Kinley became President of the University of Illinois; Bullock a long-time professor in economics at Harvard; Meyer a member of the Economics Department at Wisconsin until 1910, and then a member of the Interstate Commerce Commission; Taylor a professor of agricultural economics and the first Chair of that department at Wisconsin, then moving to the U.S. Department of Agriculture where he established the U.S. Bureau of Agricultural Economics; Hibbard a professor of agricultural economics at Wisconsin between 1914 and 1940, and Chair of the Department of Agricultural Economics; Young a professor of economics at (among other places) Stanford, Cornell, Harvard, and the LSE; Haney a well-known historian of economics and business organization at University of Texas and later at New York University; Lorenz a statistician for the Interstate Commerce Commission and the inventor of the Lorenz curve.

and brought them to Wisconsin. He also developed (along with Taylor and Hibbard) the field of agricultural economics and contributed significantly to the study of public utilities, regulation, and to the study of the relation between law and economics. This last is worthy of some emphasis because it is basic to Wisconsin institutionalism. Ely's interest in law and economics went back to his student days at Heidelberg, and connected with his interests in labor legislation, public utility regulation, agriculture, and land tenure. Ely had hoped to establish a School of Jurisprudence at Wisconsin to closely connect the study of economics and law (on the German model), but these plans did not bear fruit. Nevertheless, a "Legal Philosophical Society" did emerge at Wisconsin, a society that included Wisconsin's Chief Justice, two members of the Supreme Court, and faculty members from economics (including Ely), philosophy, and the Law School.[4] Ely became an admirer of Roscoe Pound's "sociological jurisprudence" and produced his own book, *Property and Contract*, in 1914. He wrote to Pound in 1916 to say that he hoped to make his "new line of work," as begun in *Property and Contract*, my "crowning life work" (Ely to Roscoe Pound, 3 April 1916, Ely Papers, Box 53, Folder 6). Interestingly, Pound had developed his sociological approach to law while a colleague of E. A. Ross's at the University of Nebraska. Pound also pointed Ely to the work of W. N. Hohfeld at Yale. Both Pound and Hohfeld can be seen as precursors to the realist movement in legal scholarship that developed close links to institutional economics, but it would be Commons who would later take up and use Hohfeld's legal terminology.[5]

Another feature of Wisconsin very much related to the nature of the institutionalism that developed there was the extremely close relationship between the university and the Wisconsin legislature, summed up in the "Wisconsin Idea" (McCarthy 1912). This involved a combination of the progressive political ideals of politicians such as Robert M. La Follett, Sr., with the close involvement of the university and its faculty in providing expertise

---

[4] Ely to Roscoe Pound, 9 June 1915, Ely Papers, Box 51, Folder 4. A Department of Law was established at Wisconsin in 1848. This became the College of Law in 1889 and the Law School in 1909. Wisconsin became known for its "law in action" approach to legal education. Walter W. Cook, who would later become a well know legal realist at Columbia and Johns Hopkins, was at Wisconsin Law School from 1906 to 1910. Another of the realist group, William Underhill Moore was also at Wisconsin for a brief time, before moving to Chicago.

[5] There were close connections between the realist movement in law and institutional economics, which involved not only Commons and Wisconsin, but Walton Hamilton, who moved to Yale Law School in 1928, and Robert Hale at Columbia, who also moved from economics to law. More of this connection is discussed in Chapter 8.

and advice to the legislature, and direct service to the state through out-reach, extension, and work on state boards and commissions – a practical application of social control. An important aspect of this was the Wisconsin Legislative Reference Library established in 1901 and headed by Charles McCarthy. McCarthy also taught in the Political Science Department pro-viding instruction in courses on the "Theory and Practice of Legislation" and "Practical Bill Drafting" (McCarthy 1912, p. 254). McCarthy was an admirer of Ely's earlier and more reformist economics, but Ely's involve-ment in Wisconsin's progressive legislative program was never large and was quickly overtaken by that of Commons (Rader 1966, p. 175).

Commons's career prior to Ely bringing him to Wisconsin was hardly a stellar one. He studied with Ely at Johns Hopkins but never received his doctorate degree. He held a series of teaching appointments in economics and sociology between 1890 and 1899, but then lost his job at Syracuse due to his supposed radicalism. Commons's work up to that time included some early expressions of Social Christianity, interest in distributional issues, pro-motion of proportional representation, and a concern with raising the eth-ical level of competition. In a long, multipart essay, "The Sociological View of Sovereignty" (Commons 1899–1900), Commons first expressed his view of the state as a "series of compromises between social classes," each seeking control over the coercive apparatus of the state. Strangely, references to this essay are virtually nonexistent in the later institutionalist literature.

After losing his job at Syracuse, Commons worked on a series of price indexes, on a report on immigration for the U.S. Industrial Commission, and on taxation, labor relations, and conciliation for the National Civic Federation (NCF). It was in this last job that Commons became impressed with the processes of collective bargaining he witnessed as a "new way of settling labor disputes" (Commons 1901). It was on the basis of this expe-rience with the NCF that Ely called Commons to Wisconsin, initially to work on a history of labor in the United States. What transpired, however, was that Ely's position and influence within the Department of Economics began to be eclipsed by Commons in only a few years after the latter's arrival, and it was Commons and his students, rather than Ely, who really made Wisconsin's institutionalism.[6]

The history of labor project was a large undertaking, one that was oper-ated through the American Bureau of Industrial Research that Ely had founded and that was funded through private donations. The project,

---

[6] This was despite Commons's bouts with illness and some severe family problems. Commons's autobiography deals with some of this but glosses over other issues (Commons 1934b).

however, became the center of a bitter dispute between Ely and Commons over the involvement of the Carnegie Institution (Commons Papers, Box 1; Folders 5 and 6). Carnegie had been funding a study of the history of labor conducted by Carroll D. Wright, but Wright died in 1909. Carnegie wanted Commons to take over the project, and the issue became one of the relative roles, contributions, and credit to be given to Ely's Bureau and the Carnegie Institution. The first part of the project, the eleven-volume *A Documentary History of American Industrial Society*, appeared in 1910–1911, the title page reading "Prepared under the auspices of the American Bureau of Industrial Research, with the co-operation of the Carnegie Institution of Washington." The second part of the project, the *History of Labor in the United States*, ultimately appeared in 1918 (volumes I and II) and 1935 (volumes III and IV). The work of the first two volumes was financed by Carnegie, the last two by gifts from Henry W. Farnam[7] and funds from the University of Wisconsin. In this way, Commons asserted his independence from Ely's oversight.[8] Commons also involved many of his students in these projects. The *Documentary History* involved John B. Andrews, William Leiserson, and Helen Sumner. The first two volumes of the *History of Labor* involved John B. Andrews, Henry Hoagland, Edward Mittleman, Selig Perlman, David Saposs, and Helen Sumner, whereas the last two involved Elizabeth Brandeis, Don Lescohier, Selig Perlman, and Philip Taft. A selected list of Wisconsin graduate students, many of them Commons's, is provided in Table 7.2.[9]

In addition, Commons and two of his students, John A. Fitch and William Leiserson, were involved in the conduct of the Pittsburgh Survey (1907–1908). The survey was headed by Paul Kellogg, who became the editor of *The Survey* magazine, and funded by the Russell Sage Foundation. John Fitch, through direct observation in steel plants and a multitude of interviews, produced his famous book, *The Steel Workers* (1910). This book

[7] Henry Farnam of Yale had been the lead figure in the Carnegie Institution's Department of Economics and Sociology. This department was discontinued in 1916, but the balance of its appropriations was transferred to those involved, at first simply named the "group of collaborators." An "additional gift" was made to this group at some point prior to the publication of the first volume of the *History*, and the group was renamed the Board of Research Associates in American Economic History.

[8] According to Mark Perlman, both Ross and Commons came to strongly dislike Ely (Perlman to Rutherford, 23 March 2005). My own reading suggests to me that Ely was a person who was always extremely concerned with his prestige and standing, and in the habit of coopting others into revising his books.

[9] The table does not include many well-known graduates in agricultural economics, including O. C. Stein, L. C. Gray, John D. Black, and Holbrook Working.

contained photographs of steel plants and workers taken by Lewis Hine, later to become famous for his photographs of child labor undertaken for the National Child Labor Committee.

This level of external research funding was extremely unusual in economics before the 1920s, and although it was Ely who had pioneered the development of external funding sources, it was Commons who ultimately benefitted the most. The significant amounts of money given to these projects allowed Commons to involve large numbers of graduate students in his work – to an extent that appears to have been unique in the American economics of the time.

In addition, Commons's connections to the progressive politics of Wisconsin were much closer than Ely's. These predated his arrival at Wisconsin; Commons had been providing advice to Robert M. La Follett since 1902. Once in Wisconsin, Commons became involved in drafting the Civil Service Law of 1906 and the Public Utility Act of 1907. He was also very closely involved in the production of legislation dealing with workmen's compensation and setting up the Wisconsin Industrial Commission, and with proposed legislation dealing with unemployment compensation (the Huber bill of 1921; see Commons 1921). Commons himself served on the Wisconsin Industrial Commission, which administered the workmen's compensation system. Commons did not work alone on draft legislation, but with Charles McCarthy and his staff, with other university faculty from the law school, with the American Association for Labor Legislation (founded by Ely and Commons, among others, in 1906), and, again, with students.[10]

Commons and McCarthy were also key players in the work of the U.S. Commission on Industrial Relations between 1913 and 1915. Commons was one of the commissioners, whereas McCarthy was appointed as research director in 1914 and oversaw the work of a large staff of labor economists and their students. William Leiserson acted as McCarthy's assistant, and others involved in the investigations included Paul Brissenden, Robert Hoxie, F. C. Mills, Carleton Parker, and Leo Wolman, and present or past Wisconsin students Francis Bird, Ira Cross, Frederick Deibler, E. H. Downey, William Duffus, Henry Hoagland, Selig Perlman, David Saposs, Sumner

---

[10] For a nice discussion of the legal issues surrounding Ely and Commons's efforts at labor legislation, see Gonce (2006). Paul Raushenbush reports that although Commons had ideas of key importance concerning legislation, he was not a particularly good legislative draftsman (Raushenbush and Raushenbush 1979, p. 69). People such as Commons, Edwin Witte, Harold Groves, Paul Raushenbush, Elizabeth Brandeis Raushenbush, John Andrews, and others were very much involved with the actual drafting of legislation.

Slichter, Peter Speek, and Edwin Witte, among many others.[11] Commons's close involvement of his students in what they later called "action research" (Raushenbush and Raushenbush 1979, p. 9) was an extremely appealing aspect of what Wisconsin offered to students. In contrast, Ely was seen by many of Commons's students as having become conservative and a bit of an "old fogey" (Saposs Papers, Box 1, Folder 1).

Not surprisingly, Commons quickly became the center for graduate student research in economics at Wisconsin. Commons established himself as one of the leading American labor economists, recognition coming with his election as president of the American Economic Association in 1917. It was Commons and his legion of students who transformed the Department of Economics. By 1918, Ely had moved out of teaching the core theory courses, although he was replaced in part by William Kiekhofer, one of Ely's students but a person of essentially orthodox persuasion. Ely's teaching and research interest focused increasingly on land economics, and in 1920, he founded the Institute for Research in Land and Public Utility Economics. In 1925, at the age of 71, and as a result of financial issues and disputes, he moved himself and his Institute to Northwestern. On the other hand, Commons had moved into teaching in the core theory sequence in the form of his course, "Value and Valuation." This was a full-year graduate-level course and came to contain large parts of Commons's work on law and economics and on reasonable value.

Up to this point, Commons's research and the research he supervised was almost entirely to do with trade union histories, issues in labor economics and labor legislation, and public utilities. Not all of this work was descriptive. In his article on the Shoemakers (Commons 1909), Commons developed an interpretation of trade union history as a series of responses to new competitive challenges. Commons's scope expanded in the 1920s with his work on the Pittsburgh Plus case, on monetary economics and stabilization of the business cycle, and the broader development of his interest in law and economics. Commons worked on the Pittsburgh Plus case with Frank Fetter and William Z. Ripley (Commons 1924b). His work on price stabilization and the Federal Reserve was conducted mainly in the mid- to

---

[11] In addition, McCarthy also employed E. A. Goldenweiser, Arthur Suffern, Edgar Sydenstricker, and many others. Lists of investigators and research work can be found in the Charles McCarthy Papers Box 8, Folder 6, and Box 24, Folder 13. McCarthy and Frank Walsh, who chaired the Commission, had a serious falling-out over issues of budget and Walsh wishing to focus on hearings involving John D. Rockefeller and other employers rather than research. Walsh dismissed McCarthy, and Leiserson resigned. Commons and Commissioner Mrs. B. J. Harriman wrote a dissenting report (Harter 1962, pp. 131–159).

late 1920s (Commons 1925a; 1927), although his interest in unemployment and unemployment insurance – conceived of as designed to help prevent unemployment – predated that (Commons 1921; 1925b). Commons supervised several students with dissertations dealing with business cycles, among them Alvin Hansen, and he visited Brookings while working on banking issues. In 1924, Commons began publishing on law and economics with his *Legal Foundations of Capitalism* (Commons 1924a). It was this book that made Commons more than a labor economist and brought him fully into the institutionalist movement. The book made extensive use of Hohfeld's taxonomy of rights, duties, privileges, and exposures and introduced Commons's analysis of transactions (Fiorito 2010b). The book was soon being cited by J. M. Clark and Wesley Mitchell, and, as noted previously, discussed by Hamilton and his students at Brookings. The original manuscript of *Legal Foundations* had included a long chapter on the subject of reasonable value. On Mitchell's advice, Commons took this chapter out of the book and in 1925, circulated a revised version called "Reasonable Value" (Commons 1925c; Rutherford, Samuels, and Whalen 2008). This was used in his teaching and was later to form the framework for *Institutional Economics* (Commons 1934a). In the interim, Commons published a number of articles refining his treatment of transactions and much developing his ideas on working rules, court decisions, legislative decision making, and reasonable value (Commons 1925d; 1931; 1932). The culmination of all of this work was Commons's *Institutional Economics*, but the book only appeared the year after Commons's retirement from Wisconsin.

Only a few years after Commons had begun to produce graduate students, it became very noticeable that Wisconsin began to hire its own PhDs to the faculty. The economics faculty listed in Table 7.1 and hired between 1912 and the late 1920s were all Wisconsin products, and the vast majority were students of Commons. Commons's student Selig Perlman began teaching in the Department as an instructor in 1917 and was quickly followed by Martin Glaeser, Don Lescohier, and Edwin Witte (as a lecturer from 1922 until 1933, when he replaced Commons). In 1926 and 1927 they were joined by Elizabeth Brandeis, Harold Groves, Walter Morton, and Paul Raushenbush. All of these individuals were graduate students of Commons. Raushenbush never completed his doctoral work, and Glaeser went to Harvard for his doctorate before returning, but all the others were supervised or cosupervised by Commons. The economics faculty thus became preponderantly Wisconsin trained – with a very high proportion being students of Commons.

Table 7.1. *Selected Wisconsin faculty, 1890–1940*

Frederick J. Turner (History) (1890–1910)	Harry Jerome (1915–1938)
Richard T. Ely (1892–1925)	Selig Perlman (1917–1959)
William A. Scott (1892–1931)	Don D. Lescohier (1918–1953)
T. S. Adams (1902–1915)	Edwin E. Witte (1922–1957, 1959)
Henry C. Taylor (Econ & Ag Econ) (1902–1919)	Arthur J. Altmeyer (1925–1933, 1958–1959)
John R. Commons (1904–1933)	Edward W. Morehouse (1923–1925)
Edward A. Ross (Sociology) (1906–1929)	Alexander Meiklejohn (Ex College) (1923–1938)
Max Otto (Philosophy) (1910–1947)	Harold M. Groves (1926–1968)
Willford I. King (1912–1917)	Walter A. Morton (1926–1969)
Henry R. Trumbower (1912–1918, 1927–1952)	Paul A. Raushenbush (1927–1933)
William Kiekhofer (1913–1952)	Elizabeth Brandeis (Raushenbush) (1927–1966)
E. H. Downey (1914–1915)	John Gaus (Political Science) (1927–1947)
Benjamin Hibbard (Econ & Ag Econ) (1914–1940)	Milton Friedman (1940–1941)

Source: Lampman (1993)

Some other aspects of the University of Wisconsin relevant to the development of institutionalism should also be mentioned here. At Commons's urging, the university involved itself with workers' education and operated a School for Workers through the University Extension Division. Commons served as an adviser, and Selig Perlman and a number of other Commons students would become associated with workers' education in Wisconsin and elsewhere. The university also hosted the Experimental College between 1927 and 1932. It must be said that the Experimental College was always a highly controversial institution within the University, providing a two-year program involving an intensive study of Greek civilization in the first year and of American civilization in the second. Former Amherst students Paul Raushenbush and Edward Morehouse moved to Wisconsin to pursue doctoral-level work. John Gaus also moved to Wisconsin, becoming a very well-known faculty member in political science and public administration. Paul Raushenbush taught both at the College and in the Economics

Department. Clarence Ayres and Morris Copeland taught at the College during 1928 and 1929, and Hamilton visited in 1930.[12]

As mentioned previously, Wisconsin also had ties with Brookings and the National Bureau of Economic Research. Commons himself visited the Institute of Economics and taught at the Brookings Graduate School when in Washington for the first six months of 1928, and Wisconsin students such as Walter Morton, Elsie Gluck, and Paul Raushenbush all spent at least a year at the school. Brookings also hosted Wisconsin philosopher Max Otto for a part of the 1926–1927 academic year. Otto was himself a Wisconsin philosophy PhD (1911) and taught there until 1947. He was an important representative of American pragmatism, a student of the work of William James, a humanist, and a close friend of John Dewey. Otto provided many Wisconsin students with their exposure to Dewey's instrumentalism.[13] As president of the AEA, Commons had been involved in some of the early discussions concerning the founding of the NBER, and he later served on the Board as the representative from Wisconsin. Wisconsin graduates such as Willford King and Harry Jerome[14] served on the research staff of the Bureau.

Connections with Texas were much fewer. E. E. Hale completed his MA at Wisconsin in 1923. He never completed his doctorate due to disagreements with his committee, but became a long-standing faculty member at Texas. Much later on, Louis Junker completed a PhD on Clarence Ayres's social and economic thinking (1962) but he too reported less than sympathetic faculty (Louis Junker to Clarence Ayres, 6 April 1972, Clarence Ayres Papers, Box 3F289). Junker taught for many years at Western Michigan and remained an advocate for Ayres's system of thought.

THE WISCONSIN PROGRAM IN ECONOMICS

Fairly detailed lists of courses offered in economics and related areas for 1918–1919 and 1928–1929 are available in Lampman (1993, pp. 38–42). A much more detailed listing with course descriptions and prerequisites

---

[12] Copeland did have contact with Commons both at Brookings and Wisconsin.

[13] In 1912, attempts were made to have Otto dismissed from Wisconsin as an "enemy of religion." Otto was a Unitarian and concerned to provide a nontheistic basis for moral action. Otto was supported by university President Van Hise. Later attacks on Otto were mounted in 1932. Parsons makes a number of interesting comments that indicate the extent to which Dewey's philosophy was taught by Otto and others at Wisconsin (Parsons's interview 1976).

[14] The Lampman book does not provide information on King's thesis supervisor. Jerome was supervised by Ely. His thesis was "The Relation of Custom to Price."

is available for the 1927–1928 academic year in the Martin Glaeser papers (Box 2, Folder 22). Because the institutionalist complement of faculty – including Commons, Perlman, Raushenbush, Glaeser, Groves, Morton, Witte, Brandeis, Lescohier, and Jerome, as well as Ross in sociology – were all teaching in the 1927–1928 or 1928–1929 years, what follows will focus on the program as it existed in the late 1920s.

The Department of Economics description of courses for the 1927–1928 and 1928–1929 academic years lists courses under eleven headings: economic theory, agricultural economics, accounting, business administration, finance, insurance, labor, land economics, public utilities, sociology, and statistics (Department of Economics, Description of Courses, Martin Glaeser papers, Box 2, Folder 22). Within the Department of Economics, undergraduates could major in either economics or sociology. Graduate programs in sociology as well as economics were also available.

Introductory economics at the undergraduate level was taught by Kiekhofer. Other undergraduate courses of note listed under economic theory included the Economics of Consumption (taught by Margaret Pryor, a 1927 Wisconsin PhD), which focused on income distribution, selling methods, the conflict of interests between consumer and producer, the actual functioning of the consumption process, standards of living, the role of government, and the consumer cooperative movement. Commons offered a course on Public Value (also open to graduate students) based "mainly on a study of reported legal cases, involving a correlation of law, economics and psychology." In the 1928–1929 year, Paul Raushenbush taught an undergraduate course, Economic Institutions – a course that likely would have reflected his instruction from Walton Hamilton at Amherst and Brookings. Raushenbush himself described this course as dealing with the "social control of business" (Raushenbush and Raushenbush 1979, p. 4). Specifically graduate-level courses included a history of economics course offered by Scott, and the very substantial course, Value and Valuation, offered by Commons and described as an advanced research course "in the correlation of law and economics, taking up different subjects and authors in different years, and covering in general the development of economic and legal theory as related to the modern phases of collective action." As mentioned earlier, it was in this course that Commons developed and taught his theories of law and economics, culminating in his theory of reasonable value. In addition, Martin Glaeser taught a course called Economic Institutions (sometimes referred to by students as "institutional economics") and described as a "consideration of the institutional approach to economics as contrasted with other types of approach," together with the study of economic institutions "such as property and contract, with emphasis on their legal basis," and specific works illustrating the "institutional method in treating economic problems." By the 1930s, this course was including the study of Commons's Institutional Economics (1934a) and Berle and Means's The Modern Corporation and Private Property (1932). The graduate Seminary (seminar) in Economic Theory was taught by Kiekhofer and described in orthodox terms.

The section on agricultural economics included courses on rural life, farm accounting, agricultural marketing, farmer movements, and a graduate seminar in rural social organization. Hibbard taught advanced agricultural economics. The section on land economics included two courses also taught by Hibbard: Outlines of Land Economics and a graduate-level course Land Problems (taught with George Wehrwein, a 1922 Wisconsin PhD). The section on finance courses included courses on taxation and public finance taught by Harold Groves, whereas Walter Morton offered Risk and Risk Bearing (the outline includes the business cycle as a factor of uncertainty and a "critique of the price system") and The Credit System (a course on money and banking). Groves taught the graduate seminar in public finance.[15]

The section on labor is remarkable for the number of courses listed: a total of ten courses taught by Brandeis, Commons, Lescohier, Perlman, and Witte. The course descriptions also give an excellent feel for the Wisconsin style of labor economics. The Evolution of Industrial Society (Perlman) dealt with "the principal theories of the evolution of industrial society" from the manorial system to "welfare capitalism." Labor Problems (Perlman) is described as dealing with the "psychologies of unionism and of capitalism," scientific management and union job control, unions and employers' associations, and types of "industrial government." Labor Legislation (Witte and Brandeis) focused on "government action in relation to labor," protective legislation and its constitutionality, collective bargaining and its legal status, and Wisconsin legislation and the work of the Wisconsin Industrial Commission. Brandeis used to get her students to attend hearings and legislative sessions and to follow the progress of bills dealing with labor issues (Raushenbush and Raushenbush 1979, p. 15). Wages and Prices (Lescohier) provided an analysis and interpretation of the trends of wages in America since 1840, theories of wages, wage differentials, minimum-wage legislation,

---

[15] Scott also taught courses on money and on financial history. Other courses under finance included courses in business finance offered by Charles Jamison. There were many other courses in accounting and business that are not discussed here, most being basic and unremarkable.

the "family wage plan," technology and wages, and a critical examination of wage statistics and their sources. Capitalism and Socialism (Commons) gave a historical and interpretative view of the development of economic and political philosophies and of organized movements, including capitalistic, socialistic, communistic, anarchistic, and trade union thought and practice. Perlman's other two courses reflected the content of his *Theory of the Labor Movement* (1928). American Labor History contained discussion of the strength of private property, the lack of class consciousness, the "inadequacy" of the political instrument, intellectuals, antimonopoly and job-conscious unionism, welfare capitalism, and "left wing" unionism; Foreign Labor Movements covered British, German, and Russian labor movements. Similarly, Lescohier taught two other courses based on his book, *The Labor Market* (1919). Labor Management dealt with "pathological" conditions in modern industry, such as excessive labor turnover, restriction of output, strikes, industrial accident, industrial disease, and low wages, and possible remedies for these conditions, whereas his course entitled The Labor Market discussed employment fluctuations, the facts and possible causes of unemployment, the methods of mitigating unemployment, the organization of the labor market, and unemployment insurance plans. The graduate Seminary in Labor (Commons, Perlman, and Lescohier) was designed for students working on their dissertations and was focused on American labor history from 1896 to date. It is difficult to imagine that any other university offered so much by way of instruction in labor economics.

The section on public utilities lists a number of courses given by Henry Trumbower on transportation and railway issues. The principal courses on public utility economics and utility regulation more generally were given by Glaeser. These courses covered basic public utility economics, the legal bases for utility regulation, regulation by special franchises, municipalities, state commissions, federal regulation of railroads, valuation issues, taxation, and public ownership. A lot of this material is contained in Glaeser's *Outlines of Public Utility Economics* (1927). The graduate seminar was cotaught by Trumbower and Glaeser.

Sociology offered a vast number of courses, some twenty five in the 1927–1928 course listing, indicating its imminent move to separate departmental status. The main instructors were Ross, Helen Clarke, John Lewis Gillin, and Kimball Young.[16] Clarke taught the courses on social work and social

---

[16] John Gillin received his PhD from Columbia in 1906 and was recruited to Wisconsin by Ross who had been one of his teachers. Best known for his work on criminology, he became President of the American Sociological Society in 1926. Kimball Young received his PhD in 1921 from Stanford and became a well-known figure in social psychology.

administration. The course listings covered general sociology (based on Ross's *Principles of Sociology*, 1920), social problems, social origins (historical ethnology), social pathology (using Gillin's *Poverty and Dependency*, 1921), methods of case work, criminology and penology (using Gillin's *Criminology and Penology*, 1926), principles of social service, immigration and race problems (taught by Lescohier), history of social thought (taught by Young with an emphasis on Bagehot, Compte, Cooley, Ellwood, Giddings, Gumplowicz, Ratzenhofer, Simmel, Spencer, Tarde, and Ward), social agencies and legislation, the individual and social adjustment, cultural anthropology (including the family, clan, society, the institutions of property, and systems of jurisprudence and social control), and a large number of graduate seminars on social psychology, social institutions (containing a discussion of "the theory of social evolution," followed by a detailed examination of a specific social institution), correctional policies, degeneracy and society, poor-law policy, cities, social mobility, the American family, and a research seminar.[17]

Finally, the section on statistics lists nine courses and also points to an additional three courses offered in mathematics and dealing with mathematical statistics. As mentioned earlier, Wisconsin maintained considerable strength in statistics until Jerome's death in 1938, and this is obvious in the course offerings and descriptions. The courses included an introductory course in economic statistics covering the statistical data available and the techniques of analysis (averages, dispersion, sampling, probability, index numbers, trends, seasonal variation, business cycles, business forecasting, and correlation); similar introductory courses were available for commerce and sociology students. Lescohier's course on wages and prices listed under labor was also listed here (it had a prerequisite of an introductory statistics course). There were a substantial number of courses designed for graduate students. These included Jerome's courses in Statistical Methods, Statistical Analysis of the Business Cycle, Advanced Statistical Technique, and the

He left Wisconsin in 1940 and became President of the American Sociological Society in 1943. Helen Clarke earned a BA from Smith and an MA from Chicago, the latter in 1926.

[17] As might be expected from the course titles, there is a certain amount of material dealing with "social biology," eugenics, degeneracy as related to biological factors, and problems of race and racial assimilation. This type of material was very clearly a standard part of sociology at the time. Ross's work contained such material, and Ross and Commons both favored the immigration restriction acts of the early 1920s, which were directed against Southern and Eastern European immigration. Ross and Commons's work on immigration is full of racial and ethnic stereotyping (Commons 1908). Kimball Young is said to have been "prejudiced against virtually all social categories and virtually no individual human beings" (http://www.asanet.org/governance/youngk.html).

Seminar in Statistical Research, as well as a course titled Technique of Field Investigation, taught by Lescohier. Jerome's course on business cycles used Mitchell's *Business Cycles: The Problem and Its Setting* (1927) as the primary reference, and it is quite clear that Jerome's students would have been exposed to current NBER research on business cycles. Jerome's advanced course paid particular attention to index numbers, sampling, probability, the analysis of time series, and partial and multiple regression. The seminar was devoted to those wishing to work on a specific set of problems (in 1927–1928, the primary issue involved changes in productivity and economic welfare), or those working on an applied thesis involving extensive quantitative work. Lescohier's course on field research (open to graduates and senior-level undergraduates) is described as taking "two or three field investigations actually contemplated" and working out "the detailed plans and methods for such investigations."

What these course listings show is the real extent of the institutionalist point of view in Wisconsin's Economics Department. Not everyone on faculty or every course had an institutionalist orientation, but the overwhelming majority of the faculty and the courses they offered were clearly institutionalist. Even compared to Columbia, where there was a very substantial group of those of institutionalist persuasion (see Chapter 8), Wisconsin economics seems much more uniformly institutionalist in character. A good part of this, of course, came from the hiring of their own (and particularly Commons's) students. Commons's course on Value and Valuation, the courses on "economic institutions" and "the institutional approach," the many references to legal institutions, and the course offerings on labor problems and policy issues, public utilities and regulation, and business cycles and quantitative methods, as well as the close connection with progressive social reform, all tie Wisconsin economics closely to the institutional type of economics as it was defined at the time: as empirical, focused on institutions, and concerned with social control (Hamilton 1919a). The Wisconsin style of institutionalism, however, did have its particular characteristics. The heavy emphasis on labor economics and issues stands out, as do the presence of courses on field research and the influence of Commons's type of legal/economic analysis. For example, Glaeser's text on public utility economics made significant use of Commons's work on law and economics, valuation issues, and his terminology of going concerns, transactions, and price and wage bargains, and Groves always presented his work on public finance within an institutionalist framework. Moreover, students not uncommonly complemented the instruction available in the Department of Economics with courses in history (especially during the

Table 7.2. *Selected Wisconsin graduate students 1893–1942 (Date of PhD, if obtained)*

David Kinley (1893)	Selig Perlman (1915)	Maurice Leven (1927)
Charles J. Bullock (1895)	Martin Glaeser (MA 1916)	Edward W. Morehouse (1927)
Balthasar H. Meyer (1897)	Peter Speek (1916)	Walter A. Morton (1927)
B. H. Hibbard (1902)	Francis Bird (1917)	Edwin E. Witte (1927)
Henry C. Taylor (1902)	Paul Taylor (BA 1917)	Elizabeth Brandeis (Raushenbush) (1928)
Allyn A. Young (1902)	Alvin Hansen (1918)	Ewan Clague (1929)
Lewis H. Haney (1906)	Harry Jerome (1918)	Meredith B. Givens (1929)
Max O. Lorenz (1906)	William M. Duffus (1920)	Elsie Gluck (1929)
Ira B. Cross (MA 1906)	Henry Hoagland	Theodore W. Schultz (Ag Econ) (1930)
John A. Fitch	Edward Mittleman	Arthur J. Altmeyer (1931)
John B. Andrews (1908)	Don D. Lescohier (1920)	Wilber Cohen (PhB 1932)
Helen L. Sumner (Woodbury) (1908)	Paul Raushenbush	Philip Taft (1935)
William M. Leiserson (BA 1908)	Harlan L. McCracken (1923)	Himy B. Kirshen (1937)
Frederick Deibler (1909)	E. E. Hale (MA 1923)	James Earley (1939)
Theresa McMahon (1909)	Henry Trumbower (1924)	Henry W. Spiegel (1939)
David Saposs (BA 1911)	Calvin B. Hoover (1925)	Kenneth Parsons (1940)
Willford I. King (1912)	William E. Zeuch (1926)	Walter Heller (1941)
Ezekiel H. Downey (1913)	Anna Mae Campbell (Davis) (1927)	Joseph Pechman (1942)
Sumner Slichter (MA 1914)	Harold Groves (1927)	

Source: Lampman (1993)

time Turner was at Wisconsin), law, political science, and philosophy (particularly from Otto). In contrast, relatively little by the way of neoclassical theory was taught (except by Kiekhofer), and this not at a particularly rigorous level.[18] Nothing at Wisconsin compared to the courses on theory given at Chicago by Knight or Viner, or the kind of instruction given at Harvard by Frank Taussig, Allyn Young, or later by Joseph Schumpeter. In this lack of strong instruction in neoclassical theory, Wisconsin was not dissimilar from Columbia. Commons and his students did not dismiss standard theory, but many had little interest in it, and those that did felt that what insights it offered were seriously incomplete and had to be reinterpreted and reworked in order to be placed within the broader institutional frame of reference (as Commons himself did in *Institutional Economics*).

WISCONSIN STUDENTS

A basic listing of selected Wisconsin graduate students is given in Table 7.2. A very large number of these students were Commons's. Of course, many more students than this took Commons's courses and became one of his "Friday nighters." Commons supervised or cosupervised to completion forty-six PhD students during his Wisconsin career – more than 40 percent of the total PhD cohort over that period. Of these, thirty-one completed in 1926 or later. No one else on the faculty had anything close to Commons's numbers of PhD students. Ely had fourteen listed PhDs over the same period, Glaeser, Kiekhofer, and Scott had six each, and Perlman, Ross, and Trumbower had four each (Lampman 1993, p. 43).

Commons's PhD students can be divided roughly into three groups. The first group consists of those graduate students who worked with Commons and either graduated with a PhD or went on elsewhere in the period prior to 1918. The vast majority of these students were involved in Commons's work on *The Documentary History*, the first two volumes of *The History of Labor in the United States*, or worked for McCarthy and the U.S. Commission on Industrial Relations, and virtually all of them worked on issues in labor economics. Commons graduated nine PhD students in the period from 1908 to 1917, but one of the interesting points about this group was the number of them who did not complete their doctorates at Wisconsin but went on to other universities. The second group are those who completed doctorates from 1918 to about 1925. This is a relatively small group of six students, and those involved worked on issues of labor economics, business cycles, and, in one case, on economic history. The last

---

[18] Kiekhofer apparently believed that graduate theory instruction should involve going back over an introductory textbook, such as his own, with more attention to the footnotes (see Martin Bronfenbrenner in Lampman 1993, pp. 134–135).

group involves the very substantial number of students who completed from 1926 to Commons's retirement in 1933, a total of thirty-one students. These students worked on a much greater variety of topics, including labor economics, law and economics, productivity changes, and issues relating to tariffs.

A list of Commons's graduate students should probably also include Harry Millis. Millis went on to complete a PhD at Chicago and was a faculty member at Stanford between 1903 and 1912, and in 1916 moved to back to the University of Chicago. Millis became a very well-known figure in labor and industrial relations working both as an academic and as a mediator. Between 1934 and 1935 and again between 1940 and 1945, Millis was a member of the National Labor Relations Board, the latter period as its chairman. Leiserson was also a member of the NLRB between 1939 and 1943. Commons wrote to him in 1940, on the news of Millis's appointment, that it was "just grand... two of my best boys" (Commons to Leiserson, 15 November 1940, Leiserson Papers, Box 9).

Among the first group of Commons's Wisconsin graduate students are all of those who made the most substantial contributions to the *Documentary History* or to the first two volumes of *History of Labor in the United States*: John B. Andrews, H. E. Hoagland, William Leiserson, E. B. Mittleman, Selig Perlman, David Saposs, and Helen L. Sumner (Woodbury). There were other students who either contributed to this research or who were involved with the U.S. Commission on Industrial Relations, such as Francis Bird, Frank Carlton, Ira Cross, Frederick Deibler, E. H. Downey, John Fitch, Sumner Slichter, and Peter Speek (some students who graduated after 1917 were also involved, such as Don Lescohier and E. E. Witte, but they are discussed later). Among the better known of Commons's Wisconsin students from this period, only Theresa McMahon appears to have been uninvolved with these projects, and she specialized in sociology.

One remarkable fact, however, is that of the primary contributors to the *Documentary History* or to the first two volumes of *History of Labor in the United States*, only Sumner, Andrews, and Perlman actually completed PhDs at Wisconsin. Leiserson moved to Columbia, Mittleman to Chicago, and Hoagland to Columbia. Ira Cross left Wisconsin after his MA and went to Stanford, and Slichter went to Chicago after completing his MA. Saposs stayed on at Wisconsin, working as Commons's closest assistant for a number of years before he was "fired" in 1917.[19] He later took some graduate

---

[19] Saposs claims he was fired as a result of pressure from Ely and university President Van Hise, who objected to his antifraternity and prostudent self-government activities (Saposs Papers, Box 1, Folder 1). For a brief biography of Saposs, see Howlett (2003).

work at Columbia but did not complete a doctorate. This rather remarkable diaspora of the first generation of Commons's students begs some explanation. According to David Saposs, who worked closely with Commons from 1913 until 1917, and who knew many of the other students well, Ely had become very jealous of Commons and blocked some of Commons's students from graduating (Saposs interview, Saposs papers, Box 1, Folder1). In this respect, Saposs makes special mention of Edward Mittleman and Sumner Slichter, but it is unclear how many students left Wisconsin for this reason, or for this reason alone. Slichter's father became Dean of Graduate Studies at Wisconsin, which may also have played a role in his son's move to Chicago. Leiserson moved to Columbia on the basis of financial offers and opportunities Wisconsin could not match, despite Commons and T. S. Adams's desire to retain him (Eisner 1967, pp. 11–12). All the same, there may well be something to what Saposs claims. Ely left Wisconsin in 1925, and the number of students Commons graduated from then on took a dramatic upward jump. There seems to have been no similar later movement of key Commons's students to other institutions. Martin Glaeser did choose to complete his PhD at Harvard rather than Wisconsin, but this seems to have been due to a temporary disaffection caused by disputes over attitudes to America's involvement in World War I, and his departure was short-lived.[20]

The later careers and contributions of a number of these students are worth mentioning briefly. Commons's first Wisconsin PhDs graduated in 1908: John B. Andrews and Helen Sumner Woodbury. Andrews became the central figure in the American Association for Labor Legislation, the most significant organization lobbying for labor legislation reform between 1910 and World War I (Chasse 1991; 1994). The AALL worked to promote improved working conditions, workplace health and safety legislation, unemployment compensation, national health insurance, and social security. Almost all reform-minded labor economists were members of the AALL. Helen Sumner Woodbury coauthored *Labor Problems* (1905) with T. S. Adams, which became a widely used textbook, and went on to write important works on women's suffrage, the history of women in industry,

[20] Martin Glaeser completed his Wisconsin MA in 1916 and was appointed as a part-time lecturer in public finance in 1917. His decision to take his PhD at Harvard appears to have been as a result of his sympathy with Senator La Follette's stand on America's involvement in World War I. Glaeser refused to sign a petition protesting La Follette's position and was then not reappointed to his position as a lecturer, although he was back teaching at Wisconsin from 1919 onward (Glaeser Papers Box 2, Folder 28). Ely was a major supporter of the prowar platform. Glaeser did not complete until 1925 and will be discussed as a part of the second group of students.

and on industrial courts in Europe. In 1913, she joined the Children's Bureau, becoming assistant chief, and then chief, investigator. There she wrote extensively on child labor and child labor legislation (Lobdell 2000).

Others who completed their PhDs in this first period include Frederick Deibler, E. H. Downey, Theresa McMahon, and Selig Perlman. Deibler, McMahon, and Perlman all had academic careers at Northwestern, Washington, and Wisconsin, respectively. Deibler chaired the Department of Economics at Northwestern from 1916 to 1942 and worked in labor economics and mediation. Theresa McMahon's PhD was in sociology, and she worked with Ross as well as Commons, absorbing some of Ross's admiration for Veblen. Her thesis was published as *Women and Economic Evolution* (1912), and she went on to a long career at the University of Washington, working primarily on consumption and standards of living (McMahon 1925). On a more practical level, she championed minimum wage legislation and the eight-hour workday for women (Dimand 2000). One of her best students, Ewan Clague, she helped go to Wisconsin for his doctoral work.[21] After her retirement in 1937, Witte recruited her to the Advisory Board for Social Security, where she was a staunch supporter of Witte's positions. She also had a great deal of contact with Commons after his retirement, visiting him in Florida and spending considerable effort helping him with his manuscripts (Witte Papers, Boxes 4, 5, and 6). Perlman, of course, stayed at Wisconsin, becoming a leading labor economist and an authority on both American and European labor movements. His classic work, *A Theory of the Labor Movement*, appeared in 1928. Perlman was also closely involved with Wisconsin's School for Workers, but not, like most of his colleagues, with New Deal legislation (Witte 1960). Downey's career took him into state government. He had been significantly influenced by Thorstein Veblen and Robert Hoxie, but his career concentrated on workplace accident and compensation issues, primarily for the Insurance Commission of Pennsylvania, and he became one of the leading experts in this field until his early death in 1922 (Downey 1924).

The most notable of those who moved away from Wisconsin include Ira Cross, William Leiserson, David Saposs, and Sumner Slichter. Cross went to Stanford for his doctorate and coincided with Thorstein Veblen, Harry Millis, and Allyn Young. He was not happy at Stanford and accepted a call to Berkeley in 1914, becoming a full professor and Chair of the Department

---

[21] Other students of McMahon included Alice Hanson, George Stigler, Aryness Joy, N. H. Engle, and John Wolfard. Carleton Parker, Paul Douglas, William Ogburn, and Rexford Tugwell were all her colleagues at the University of Washington for short periods of time (Theresa McMahon Papers, Box 1, Folders 2, 3, and 7).

in 1919. His *History of the Labor Movement of California* appeared in 1935, and he wrote widely on labor issues and was closely involved in employment management, labor relations, and labor education. He was a remarkable teacher, and his own students included labor economists such as Paul Taylor (a Wisconsin BA) and Clark Kerr (Cross, taped interview).[22] Leiserson moved to Columbia for his doctorate but remained in very close contact with Commons and a large number of the other Wisconsin students of his time (see Leiserson Papers). He worked briefly for Wisconsin's Industrial Commission, as assistant director for research under McCarthy for the U.S. Commission on Industrial Relations, and held faculty positions first at the University of Toledo and then at Antioch College (1926–1933). While at Antioch, he chaired the Ohio Commission on Unemployment Insurance and developed the "Ohio Plan" for unemployment compensation that, ironically, became the major competitor to the "Wisconsin Plan." Leiserson's plan was based on insurance-against-risk principles, whereas the Wisconsin approach emphasized the prevention of unemployment through individual employer accounts and rating. His major contributions came through his work in labor mediation, as Chairman of the Labor Adjustment Board for the Rochester clothing industry (1919–1926), the National Labor Board (1933–1934), National Mediation Board (1934–1939 and 1943–1944), and the National Labor Relations Board (1939–1943). Leiserson was instrumental in Millis's appointment to the NLRB in 1940 (Eisner 1967). After leaving Commons's employ, David Saposs spent several years working on a number of investigations, including the controversial investigation of the 1919 steel strike funded by the Inter-Church World Movement.[23] He taught at Brookwood Labor College[24] from 1922 until 1933

---

[22] Cross was called to Berkeley by Carleton Parker, but Parker left for the University of Washington shortly thereafter. The University of Washington president was at that time of a more "liberal" view than Berkeley's. As noted in Chapter 5, the Berkeley Economics Department contained a significant group of social economists. Solomon Blum was a faculty member at Berkeley and supervised Paul Taylor's PhD. The "liberal network" in the Bay Area came to include the Meiklejohns, who moved there from Wisconsin after the closure of the Experimental College.

[23] The main investigators were the Bureau of Industrial Research in New York (Herbert Croly, Orway Tead, Sargent Florence, and others) and the Labor Bureau (George Soule and David Saposs). The Report of the Commission of Inquiry, *Report on the Steel Strike of 1919*, appeared in 1920.

[24] Walton Hamilton and Stacy May were also involved with the Brookwood experiment. Hamilton served on its educational committee, as did William Ogburn, Joseph Willits, and Leo Wolman (see Hamilton 1924). Hamilton's student, Stacy May taught at the college during 1922–1923. Brookwood's support of industrial unionism caused a split with the AFL in 1928. Serious divisions within the faculty arose in 1933.

and took graduate courses in economics and labor history at Columbia between 1924 and 1926. His research focused on radical labor movements and the labor movement in France (Saposs 1926; 1931). Between 1935 and 1940, he served as chief economist and head of the research division of the NLRB. He was accused of being a communist and his bureau was abolished in 1940. He then worked in a variety of positions including Senior Research Associate, Twentieth Century Fund; consultant to the U.S. Co-ordinator of Inter-American Affairs (Nelson A. Rockefeller); and two stints as Special Assistant to the Commissioner of Labor Statistics. Slichter completed his PhD at Chicago in 1918 and went on to a successful academic career in labor economics and industrial relations at Cornell (where he was a colleague of Morris Copeland) and Harvard (where Alvin Hansen would join him in 1937). Slichter was a contributor to the Tugwell volume *The Trend of Economics* (1924) and initially a strong supporter of increased "social control" and intervention in the economy, specifically in the form of some type of "industrial government" that could give representation to workers, property owners, and consumers (Slichter 1931). Slichter was also concerned with the phenomenon of technological change and unemployment issues, being one of the first to use the term "technological unemployment" (Slichter 1928; Woirol 2006). Later he became concerned at the growth of union power and the possibilities for cost-push inflation (Leeson 1997).[25] He was also an early (pre-Keynesian) advocate of deficit spending by government during recessions, but never an adherent of Hansen's stagnation thesis. Throughout his career, Slichter maintained close contacts with Wisconsin, particularly with Witte.

The best known among the second group of students are Harlan McCracken, Alvin Hansen, Calvin Hoover, and Don Lescohier. Martin Glaeser might also be included here as although his PhD was from Harvard he was present in Wisconsin both before and after his graduation in 1925. All of these individuals had academic careers, Hansen at Minnesota and then Harvard, Lescohier and Glaser at Wisconsin, and Hoover at Duke. Hansen, Lescohier, and Glaeser all had close contact with Ely as well as with Commons. During this period, Commons was working on monetary economics and stabilization issues and had students working on cycles. The best known of these, of course, was Alvin Hansen, his thesis dealing with "Cycles of Prosperity and Depression, 1902–1908." His further research on unemployment and cycle theories resulted in his moving away from his

---

[25] As Leeson (1997) points out, Slichter's concern about maintaining price stability with full employment declined after 1947. Leeson argues this was due to Cold War considerations.

teachers' opinions, resulting in his widely respected book *Business Cycle Theory* (1927). Hansen's later development of his stagnationist position and his adoption of Keynesian ideas have been too well documented to repeat here (Barber 1987; Leeson 1997; Mehrling 1997), but what is worth emphasizing is Hansen's role in spreading the Keynesian message through his fiscal policy seminar, and that his version of Keynesian economics was always closely joined to a Wisconsin style of social reform program. For Hansen, Keynesian deficit financing of government expenditure and a "full employment program" went hand in hand with a "comprehensive system of social security," adequate public education including adult education and research, adequate public health facilities and services, adequate provision of housing including public housing, urban redevelopment and renewal, river valley development along the lines of the TVA, conservation of agricultural and forest resources, and transportation facilities ("A Full Employment Program," Hansen Papers, Research Notes, Box 2). Hansen was also closely involved in the discussions surrounding unemployment compensation schemes and the social security system (Hansen and Murray 1933),[26] as well as with the development of the Employment Act of 1946. Hansen's deep respect for Commons can be seen in the remarks he prepared for Commons's seventieth birthday in 1932, which detailed Commons's contributions to American economics (Hansen 1932).

Hansen placed Commons's work in three areas: labor economics, working rules and institutions, and business cycles. In the area of labor economics, Hansen located Commons's contributions in his empirical work on industrial and labor history and in his interpretation of that history in terms of changing market and bargaining positions and the impact of major price swings on economic life. In the area of working rules and institutions, Hansen pointed to Commons's practical work in the development of new rules and institutions designed to resolve conflicts, and also to his theoretical work as found in *The Legal Foundations of Capitalism* and "Reasonable Value," most importantly Commons's view of the current era of economics as being the "era of stabilization" with the development of new working rules and institutions designed to resolve class conflict and achieve the "Reasonable Stabilization of Capitalism." Finally, Hansen claims that Commons's work on business cycles, price stability, and the Federal Reserve was a major contribution. Hansen argues that Commons's work in this area did not go far enough to deal with the problem in its more

---

[26] Merrill G. Murray was a 1936 Wisconsin PhD supervised by Witte. His thesis dealt with unemployment compensation within the social security program.

recent and international manifestations, but that Commons's work played "an important part in this first gigantic laboratory experiment in stabilization, and despite temporary defeat and reverses the lessons of this experiment will not be lost."

Another student of business cycles, Harlan McCracken,[27] is also worth mentioning here. McCracken's thesis dealt with the classification of business cycle theory and specifically with the differences between Ricardo and Malthus on the issue of a general overproduction. In an article coauthored with Commons and William Zeuch (1922), and in his book, *Value Theory and Business Cycles* (1933), he also discusses Malthus and Ricardo, arguing that "Malthus serves as the logical starting point for the consideration of business cycles" due to his emphasis on the short run and on the demand side (Kates 2008, p. 5; McCracken 1933, pp. v-vi). It is in this book that Say's Law is first described using the phrase "supply creates its own demand" (Kates 2008, p. 7).

What is particularly interesting about this is that Keynes was familiar not only with Commons's work on price stabilization, but also with his "Reasonable Value" manuscript, and with McCracken's 1933 book on cycles (Kates 2008; Whalen 2008). In a 1925 address, Keynes utilized Commons's idea of the arrival of a new era in economics – the era of stabilization (Commons 1925e; Whalen 2008, p. 226), and Keynes, in *The General Theory*, takes a view of Malthus similar to McCracken's and describes Say's Law as "supply creates its own demand" (Kates 2008). As Robert Skidelsky has argued, Commons was an important, if still largely unacknowledged, influence on Keynes (Skidelsky 1992, p. 229).

Lescohier taught labor economics at Wisconsin for many years, his best-known work being *The Labor Market* (1919), a book that in many ways was the American equivalent of William Beveridge's *Unemployment: A Problem of Industry* (1909), with its emphasis on types and causes of unemployment and idleness, labor turnover, inefficiencies in the labor market, and employment exchanges. As noted earlier, Lescohier also taught a course on field research methods. Hoover's PhD thesis was on a topic in institutional economic history, "Capital and Contract in Genoa in the Twelfth Century." Hoover spent his career at Duke University undertaking a great deal of research on the economies of Europe and Soviet Russia. In 1933, he became an Adviser to the Department of Agriculture, and after World War

---

[27]　Both Hansen and McCracken were at the University of Minnesota in the early 1930s. See Kates (2008) for a much fuller discussion of McCracken and Keynes. McCracken's work came to my attention only because of Kates's paper.

II, he was involved in the implementation of the Marshall Plan. Glaeser focused on public utility economics, and was therefore a little apart from the group of Commons's students involved in the work on labor history. He recalls being welcomed at Harvard and that Wisconsin was held in high regard there. He worked most closely with William Z. Ripley (Ripley and Commons had worked together on the Pittsburgh plus-pricing case), but also took Roscoe Pound's graduate course on jurisprudence and a course in the history of political thought from Harold Laski (Glaeser "Richard T. Ely Centennial–1854–1954," Glaeser Papers, Box 2, Folder 28). Glaeser also took Commons's course on Value and Valuation on more than one occasion. He was very familiar with Commons's legal/economic categories and concepts and imported them freely into his own work on public utility economics (Glaeser 1927). Glaeser was much involved with the work of the TVA during the New Deal.

As mentioned previously, the number of students Commons graduated after 1925 took a sharp upward leap. Between 1926 and 1933, Commons graduated thirty one PhD students – far too many to discuss in detail, but some further comment is warranted on a subset: Arthur Altmeyer, Elizabeth Brandeis, Anna Mae Campbell Davis, Ewan Clague, Harold Groves, Edward Morehouse, Meredith Givens, Paul Raushenbush, and E. E. Witte.

Harold Groves, Elizabeth Brandeis, and Paul Raushenbush were together the prime movers in the drafting and ultimate passage of the Wisconsin unemployment compensation law of 1932 (the Groves Act). Groves and Brandeis completed their doctorates in 1927 and 1928 respectively, and both wrote on topics in labor economics. Raushenbush had a thesis under preparation but never completed it. Groves and Brandeis had academic careers at the University of Wisconsin, whereas Raushenbush moved into the administration of Wisconsin's unemployment compensation system in 1934. Groves taught public finance with an explicitly institutionalist approach (see Groves 1964), and Brandeis taught labor legislation and American economic history.[28] Groves was elected member of the Wisconsin legislature in 1930 and, with the encouragement of Philip La Follette, introduced a preliminary unemployment compensation bill in 1931, drafted with the help of Edwin Witte. A revised version drafted by Groves, Brandies, and Raushenbush (with

[28] Brandeis taught part time and remained at the rank of lecturer until 1962. Her first exposure to economic history was as an undergraduate at Radcliffe, where she took a course from Edwin Gay. Prior to becoming a graduate student at Wisconsin, she worked for the District of Columbia minimum wage board, but the DC minimum wage law was declared unconstitutional in 1923. Initially she went to Wisconsin to study law, and met her future husband, Paul Raushenbush, in a law course.

help from Arthur Altmeyer on the administrative sections) was presented in 1932. The main features of the bill were the establishment of individual employer reserves (a change from the earlier Huber bill, and Groves's own innovation), contributed to by employers only, and experience rating. Each firm (plant) was to be responsible for its own unemployed. With a vast amount of work, the bill passed, becoming the first unemployment compensation law in the United States. Paul Raushenbush was appointed head of the Unemployment Division of the Wisconsin Industrial Commission to administer the law, taking over from E. E. Witte (who had temporarily occupied the position) in 1934. Raushenbush was also closely involved in the drafting of the 1934 Wagner-Lewis bill designed to encourage the passage of state unemployment compensation laws, and which contained a tax offset provision suggested by Justice Brandeis (Raushenbush and Raushenbush 1979, pp. 173–185). Action on this bill was suspended in 1934 in favor of work on a broader social security bill. Here again Raushenbush was called on by Altmeyer to help draft alternative model unemployment compensation bills for the states (Raushenbush and Raushenbush 1979, p. 41), but it was Witte who, in 1934, was placed in charge of the overall effort (likely suggested by Altmeyer) as executive director and secretary of the Committee on Economic Security.[29]

Witte was a Wisconsin undergraduate and graduate student at the same time as David Saposs and knew virtually all of those involved in Commons's early work on labor history very well. As an undergraduate, Witte had majored in history, earning his BA in 1909, but was then attracted to Commons's teaching in labor economics. He spent some years as a graduate student of Commons before working for the Wisconsin Industrial Commission as a statistician, as a staffer for U.S. Congressman John M. Nelson, a researcher for the U.S. Commission on Industrial Relations, again for the Industrial Commission as secretary, and then, from 1922, as Chief of the Wisconsin Legislative Reference Library, succeeding Charles McCarthy. Witte's work for the Industrial Commission involved him with industrial accident compensation issues, and his work for the Reference Library with many issues surrounding proposed legislation concerning such things as minimum wages, pensions, and unemployment insurance. His own primary research interest over this time concerned the use of court injunctions

---

[29] It should be mentioned here that although health insurance was ultimately not included in the social security act, due to the degree of opposition, many Wisconsin faculty and students were involved in supporting it. This included Commons, Andrews, and Witte, among others (Chasse 1994). Walton Hamilton was also much involved, as was Harry Millis.

in labor disputes, the topic of his PhD thesis that he eventually completed in 1927.[30] Only shortly thereafter, Witte became part of a group with Felix Frankfurter and Herman Oliphant (of Harvard and Columbia Law Schools respectively), drafting a bill to limit the use of "yellow dog" contracts and court injunctions, a bill that was passed in 1932 as the Norris-LaGuardia Act. Witte was also a lecturer at Wisconsin, in economics, political science, sociology, and law, but only became a regular faculty member in the Department of Economics in 1933, replacing Commons on his retirement. His most significant contribution to the Wisconsin teaching program was his course on The Role of Government in the Economy (Witte 1957; Samuels 1967; 2004).

As mentioned earlier, Witte had been involved in the initial drafting of the Groves bill and maintained a substantial interest in unemployment insurance issues. On the passing of the Groves Act, he had been appointed to administer the law (working with Paul Raushenbush). The Groves Act approach to unemployment compensation was by no means universally accepted. Even within the circle of Wisconsin graduates, there were proponents of different approaches; both William Leiserson (the "Ohio Plan") and John B. Andrews and the AALL (the "American Plan") had different model bills.[31] At Wisconsin itself, differences over this issue led to a permanent falling out between Walter Morton on the one side and Harold Groves and Elizabeth Brandeis on the other (Walter Morton Interview 1978). Outside of Wisconsin, people such as Paul Douglas and Eveline Burns proposed schemes more along European lines, with contributions from employers, employees, and the state, and with pooled reserves. Even Witte, who had studied the British system in detail during a visit in 1931, had his doubts about the Wisconsin scheme (Schlabach 1969, pp. 87–92).

Witte is often seen as the father of the Social Security Act passed in 1935 (Cohen 1960), and there is no doubt that his tenacity, amazing work capacity, close concern with the politically possible, and ability to keep those with differing views focused on the main task were vital to the ultimate success of the act (Witte 1937; Schlabach 1969). Other Wisconsin graduates were also very much involved in the formulation and passage (and later

[30] A significantly revised version of his thesis was published in 1932 as *The Government in Labor Disputes*.

[31] The Ohio Plan was closest to the European model of pooled reserves but still involved no state contributions. Andrews' American Plan was closest to Commons's design in the Huber bill, but could also be seen as a compromise position between the Ohio and Wisconsin (Groves) plans by having a pooling of reserves by industry. For details of the debate and references, see Schlabach (2001).

administration) of the Social Security Act, notably Arthur Altmeyer and Witte's own student, Wilbur Cohen. Altmeyer obtained his PhD in 1931, his thesis being a case study of the Wisconsin Industrial Commission. Between 1922 and 1933, he was secretary of the Wisconsin Industrial Commission, but in 1933 became Chief of the compliance division of the NRA, then Second Assistant Secretary of Labor, and then Chairman of the Technical Board of the Committee on Economic Security. After the passage of the Social Security Act, he worked for many years as a member and then Chairman of the Social Security Board (Altmeyer 1966). Other Commons students who worked on Social Security included Ewan Clague. Clague's thesis was on the issue of the productivity of labor (supervised by Commons and Jerome), he then taught at Wisconsin for a few years before moving to the Department of Labor to work on labor productivity measures.[32] He was then involved in work on unemployment issues, and in 1936, he took over the operation of the Bureau of Research and Statistics of the Social Security Board, replacing Walton Hamilton. He continued to work in various positions for the Social Security Board, and between 1936 and 1939 also taught "social economy" on a part-time basis in the Washington area. In 1946, he was appointed Commissioner of Labor Statistics. Although not directly involved in the Social Security Act, another student that should be mentioned is Meredith Givens. Givens was also a Commons/Jerome student, with a strong background in statistics. He worked with the Unemployment Compensation Division for New York State, did important work on the New York unemployment compensation law, was involved with the American Statistical Associations efforts to improve government statistics as executive secretary to the Committee on Government Statistics and Information Services (see Chapter 4), and was a key player in the Social Science Research Council, dealing with research proposals on topics in labor economics and unemployment, and with close contacts with the Department of Labor.

Outside of the area of unemployment insurance and social security, and more centrally concerned with the analytical aspects of Commons's work on law and economics, two of Commons's students stand out: Edward Morehouse and Anna Mae Campbell Davis. As things transpired, neither of these students went on to long-term academic careers. Morehouse wrote a thesis dealing with the rule making in the Rochester clothing industry during the time that Leiserson served as Chairman of the Labor Adjustment

---

[32] For the importance of this work on labor productivity and its link to the debate over technological unemployment, which involved people such as Jerome, Willford King, Paul Douglas, E. E. Day, Woodlief Thomas, Rexford Tugwell, as well as Slichter and Hansen, see Woirol (2006).

Board. Commons and Morehouse published a part of this research in 1927 in the *Yale Law Journal,* an article that added a great deal of meat to Commons's idea of the rule-making function of quasi-judicial bodies and of the manner in which rules and customs established within an industry are taken over and approved:

> Flexibility was the outstanding characteristic of the system of "industrial jurisprudence" worked out in the Rochester clothing market.... Nevertheless, flexibility of "substantive rights" or remedies would not accomplish the underlying purpose of stabilizing labor relations in the market if the common rules established by mutual agreement or by decision of the arbitrator were not rooted in the customs and usages of the parties themselves.... Both employers and workers acted according to these customs and usages. When they clashed, as they often did, it was the arbitrator's task, if mutual adjustment failed, to explore the technological, political, business, and other factors in the dispute. Bearing in mind the desirability, from the standpoint of efficiency, of keeping the bargaining process going, he might approve the customs of the employer or of the workers, or might find a middle ground which would prove acceptable to both sides. (Commons and Morehouse 1927, p. 428)

Leiserson himself doubted that he was quite the rule maker portrayed by Morehouse (see also Morehouse 1923), but this was met with skepticism by Commons and Morehouse. Morehouse, Commons, and Karl Llewellyn at Yale Law School also carried on a significant correspondence concerning Commons's legal economic framework as found in *Legal Foundations* and Commons's drafts of his manuscript, "Reasonable Value."[33] A lot of this discussion concerned Commons's terminology and his concept of custom. Morehouse married Richard T. Ely's daughter and moved with Ely to Northwestern in 1925, where he worked as a research associate in Ely's Institute for Research in Land Economics and Public Utilities, became an associate professor at Northwestern, and editor of *Journal of Land and Public Utility Economics.* His research focused increasingly on public utility economics, and he had much contact with Glaeser and James Bonbright of Columbia, but he also taught a course called Economic Institutions using Commons's *Legal Foundations* and "Reasonable Value." In addition, in about 1927, he and Anna Mae Campbell Davis produced numerous outlines for a book of case materials for the teaching of "volitional economics," and the two then collected and "briefed" all of the cases mentioned in *Legal Foundations* and "Reasonable Value," as well as additional material. This

---

[33] Commons Papers, Box 3, Folder 5; Morehouse Papers, Box 1, Folder 2. Llewellyn was a leading member of the legal realist group. Commons was invited to teach at Yale Law School for a summer term in 1926 (Commons to Llewellyn, 15 November 1925, Commons Papers, Box 13, Folder1). Walton Hamilton was hired to Yale Law School in 1928.

case book, as far as I can discover, was never finally produced or published. The outlines show lists of cases organized in chapters headed: Changes in the Meaning of Words, with sections on property, liberty, and physical, economic, and moral power; Going Concerns; The Transaction; The Rent Bargain; The Price Bargain; The Credit Bargain; The Wage Bargain, including sections on statutory rules, administrative rules, and extrajudicial rules of wage bargains; The Tax Bargain; and Stabilization, including sections on public purpose, fair and unfair competition, discrimination and extortion, and reasonable value (Morehouse Papers, "Materials for the Study and Teaching of Volitional Economics, December 1927, Box 1, Folder 2). In 1931, Ely left the Institute and a year later moved to New York. The Institute ceased operation in 1932. In 1931, there were discussions about Morehouse accepting a position in Commerce at the University of Wisconsin, but there was opposition. Morehouse eventually removed his name from the competition, instead accepting the position of Chief Economist and Director of the rates and research department of the Public Service Commission of Wisconsin, and moving permanently out of the academic world. Between 1934 and 1946, he also worked as a consultant for the TVA, again with much contact with Glaeser.

Anna Mae Campbell Davis also completed her PhD in 1927 on the subject of "Law and Economics in the Commodity Transaction," dealing with marketing practices and judicial decisions. She and Morehouse tried to have their dissertations published but without success. Before completing her dissertation, she taught at Goucher College in Maryland and was able to attend the jurisprudence seminar given by noted legal realist, W. W. Cook, at Johns Hopkins (Campbell to Commons, 31 October 1926, Commons Papers, Box 3, Folder 6). In 1931, she passed her Wisconsin bar exams and in 1932 she received a post-doctoral award from the SSRC for a year of study in England working on the common law courts and the history of capitalism in England prior to 1700. Commons wrote her a letter of introduction to William Beveridge at the LSE (Commons Papers, Box4, Folder 6). She did not continue in an academic career, however, and from 1933 onward, she practiced law in Madison, concentrating on labor law and civil liberties cases.

Apart from Commons, other Wisconsin faculty produced some notable students. Lescohier supervised William Duffus (1920), who as a student at Stanford had become friendly with Veblen, and continued to work in the area of labor economics. Harry Jerome supervised Maurice Leven who was to work for the Brookings Institution as a statistician. Selig Perlman supervised Philip Taft (1935), who worked in labor economics and became a well-known labor economist at Brown, as well as Robert Lampman (1950) and Edwin Young (1950), who both remained at Wisconsin. Morton supervised James Earley (1939), who taught at Wisconsin from 1937 to 1968, and Francis C. Genovese (1953). Ed Witte supervised Himy Kirshen (1937), who became Dean of the School of Business Administration at University of Massachusetts at Amherst and wrote on law and economics very much in the Commons style (Kirshen 1932). Many years later Witte supervised Warren J. Samuels (1957). Groves supervised Walter Heller (1941) and Joe Pechman (1942). Glaeser supervised Harry Trebing (1958). Other later Wisconsin graduates include Henry Spiegel (1939), Kenneth Parsons (1940), Raymond Penn (1941), and A. Allan Schmid (1959).

WHAT HAPPENED TO WISCONSIN INSTITUTIONALISM?

This chapter began with the issue of the decline in the position of institutionalism and the hypothesis of a relative lack of "fecundity" among Wisconsin graduates, resulting in a failure to reproduce that kind of economics. It is certainly true that Wisconsin graduates contributed to matters of policy to a remarkable extent, and it is also true that Commons encouraged his students to obtain practical experience, but as far as the period through to Commons's retirement in 1933 is concerned, the information in Lampman (1993) demonstrates both that Commons had a large number of graduate students and that many of his students *did* go on to academic careers. Many did supervise PhD students themselves and some on the same order of magnitude as Commons. Lampman (1993) lists Witte with fifty-four PhD students completed through 1960, Groves with forty-eight, Perlman with forty-six, Glaeser with twenty-seven, Morton with twenty-six, and Lescohier with seven. The careers of Commons's students (and the list includes not only those at Wisconsin but also Cross, Hansen, Hoover, Millis, and Slichter, among others) are, in that respect, quite different from those of the economics graduates from the Robert Brookings Graduate School, and probably compare with the graduates from the other major PhD institutions. On the other hand, it is clear that among the major PhD institutions, Wisconsin graduates were hired heavily by Wisconsin itself (and, to a lesser extent, by Harvard and Northwestern). This pattern of hiring one's own was not so uncommon in the interwar period, but it may indicate that Wisconsin graduates were not so well regarded in the East, except perhaps at Harvard where the links with Wisconsin went back to Charles Bullock and Allyn Young. Wisconsin's habit of hiring its own did fall out of favor in later years, and university administrators fought against it from about the mid-1930s onward.

In thinking about employment histories, it is also important to remember that after about 1933, the effect of the Great Depression on university finances was such as to make academic positions increasingly difficult to find for the graduates of any university, and university hiring in general declined and did not really boom again until after the end of World War II. At the same time, the New Deal and the growth of governmental programs opened up alternative job opportunities for economics graduates, but again quite generally. Given the nature of the Wisconsin training, it is unsurprising that Wisconsin graduates had a very major presence in the Department of Labor and in the Social Security Administration. The extent of this involvement was very substantial, but it included those with academic jobs as well as those without. A letter to Commons from Ewan Clague in Washington, DC in 1934 talks of a get-together of Commons's "Friday nighters" in Washington. The letter has thirty-seven signatures, ranging from Witte and Hansen, to Leiserson, Altmeyer, and Clague, to then-current graduate students. The presence of Wisconsin students in government during the New Deal was large, and the effect of the depression on the availability of academic positions could have been a factor in individuals such as Morehouse, Davis, Clague, and Givens not becoming or remaining academics. There is no real evidence, however, that Wisconsin graduates were, in this respect, particularly unusual in their career patterns, at least up to this point in time. The real issue, it appears, is not so much what happened to Commons's students, but what happened to the students of his students, who graduated into an academic world in which Wisconsin's academic ranking had fallen significantly (Biddle 1998a, p. 120), and economics departments in general were less amenable to institutionalism. It is much harder to trace the careers of these students, but scanning the list proved in Lampman, one suspects that relatively few of them were as clearly institutionalist in orientation as those of the previous generation, or produced graduate students in a manner similar to Commons, Witte, Perlman, Groves, or Glaeser. This then points to the ultimate lack of "fecundity" of Wisconsin-style institutional economics as itself a result of other causal factors, most obviously the shifts taking place both at Wisconsin and within the profession at large.

Institutionalism at Wisconsin was very much a matter of the presence on the faculty of John R. Commons and a good number of his former students. Commons provided not merely instruction in labor economics, but taught his central ideas concerning law and economics in the theory sequence in the form of his course on Value and Valuation, and also provided a focus for student identity in his Friday nights. These were important elements, and once Commons retired, there was nothing of quite the same nature to replace them. Witte did teach his courses on Government and Business and the Role of Government in the Economy (at the graduate level), which to some extent substituted, but it was offered as a course in the area of "Economic History and Institutions" and not as a part of the theory sequence of courses. The Friday night tradition also ended with Commons. Institutionalism at Wisconsin thus lost its central personality, much of its theoretical core, and its social center. Witte's definition of institutional economics in 1954 as little more than a "practical problems approach" did not help the status of Wisconsin's institutional economics in the profession (Witte 1954, p. 133).

Wisconsin also did very little hiring after Witte in 1933 until after the end of World War II. The Great Depression, as mentioned earlier, had a strongly negative effect on the availability of academic positions quite generally, but Wisconsin's financial position was especially difficult. Wisconsin salaries became quite uncompetitive, and Wisconsin emerged from the war years with a much reduced ranking in the academic world. Harry Jerome was not replaced on his death in 1938, and the teaching of statistics passed to faculty in the School of Commerce. There were efforts to overcome this problem made by Harold Groves, which resulted in the Friedman affair in 1941.[34] James Earley (a Walter Morton student) was hired in 1937 and Paul Ellsworth (from Harvard) in 1943, but it was not until 1947 that a major renewal of faculty took place with the influx of Theodore Morgan (Harvard), Eugene Rotwein (Chicago), Edwin Young (Wisconsin, supervised by Perlman), and Martin Bronfenbrenner (Chicago).[35] The majority

[34] Bringing Friedman to Wisconsin was the idea of Harold Groves who wanted him to work on an NBER project at Wisconsin. Friedman was seen at that time as someone with strong empirical skills, and trained in good part at the National Bureau. Groves had the idea that Friedman should review the statistics offerings at Wisconsin. This, of course, put Friedman, as a very junior (and visiting) member of the faculty, in a very unenviable position. Friedman wrote his report, a critical one, as one might expect. Groves wanted Friedman appointed as an assistant professor, despite his not having his PhD. The vote on that was 5 to 4 against. Groves, Lescohier, and Perlman voted in favor. The matter then became heavily embroiled in university politics. There may have been some anti-Semitism involved; Selig Perlman certainly thought so, and his relationships with those opposed cooled substantially. It is, however, clear that major issues involving university politics and the relationship between the Departments of Economics and Commerce were also key factors.

[35] It is interesting to note that the two major centers for institutionalism, Wisconsin and Columbia, had relatively little to do with each other in terms of hiring of each other's graduate students. There were contacts with the NBER and with Columbia labor economists such as Leo Wolman, but neither Wisconsin hire from Columbia nor Columbia from Wisconsin. The tendency in both places was to hire their own – a tendency that may have resulted in a degree of intellectual stagnation in both places.

of these hires were from outside Wisconsin and these and later hires began the shift of the Department away from its previous institutionalist focus. Both Earley and Morgan were of Keynesian orientation, and one can see in the lists of course offerings, provided by Lampman (1993), for 1938 and 1948 the more explicitly institutionalist elements tending to become confined to specific field areas, particularly labor and public utilities, whereas more standard microeconomics and more Keynesian macroeconomics come to make up the theory sequence.

In terms of other universities that absorbed something of a Wisconsin influence, one can point to Northwestern (Deibler and Morehouse), Berkeley (Cross and Taylor), and Harvard (Hansen and Slichter). Even Chicago had some links to Commons and Wisconsin, primarily through Harry Millis, but also later through Theodore Schultz. It would not be correct to label Schultz an institutionalist, but he held Commons in high regard, had a broad view of economics, and was instrumental in hiring Margaret Reid to Chicago (who clearly was institutionalist in approach). Frank Knight too had an interest in Commons's work, although a critical one.[36] But none of these places became centers for institutionalism in the sense that Wisconsin was.

Institutionalist work on public utilities survived both at Wisconsin and in government, notably at the hands of Martin Glaeser, Ray Penn, and their students. Even here, however, there was a gradual loss of the Commons type of legal/economic terminology used by Glaeser. Further work in the Commons tradition in law and economics was undermined both by the loss of Morehouse and Davis to the academic world, and by the more general decline of the legal realist movement in law. Moreover, Commons did not communicate his system of thinking very clearly, and interest in the more analytical aspects of Commons's work was only maintained by a few.

A different type of factor at work relates to the particular type of economics taught at Wisconsin. As is obvious from the course materials discussed earlier, Wisconsin economics had an extremely heavy emphasis on labor law, arbitration and mediation, and on issues of industrial accident insurance and unemployment compensation. This focus, in terms of teaching, research, and involvement in matters of public policy and administration, however, began to migrate from economics departments into

---

[36] Of the American institutionalists, Knight's most generous comments concerned Commons's work, which he regarded as hopelessly unsystematic but highly "suggestive and valuable" (Knight 1935). Kenneth Parsons's article, "John R. Commons' Point of View" (Parsons 1942) originated as a paper for Knight's course, "Economics from an Institutional Standpoint," Knight being interested in the issue of whether Commons had "a system" (Parsons Interview 1976).

newly established schools of public administration and industrial relations (Kaufman 1993; 2003). Harvard's Littauer School of Public Administration was founded in 1936, and the first school of industrial relations at Cornell in 1945. In 1946 and 1947, Witte himself became involved in the organization of the Industrial Relations Research Association, and became its first president (Schlabach 1969, p. 218).[37]

Despite these developments, a Wisconsin tradition in institutional economics has survived into the present in the persons of Warren Samuels, Allan Schmid (who was supervised by Penn), and Harry Trebing, all at Michigan State (Schmid 2004). In addition, Dan Bromley, currently in Agricultural Economics, has done much to maintain the tradition of Commons at Wisconsin. Bromley, however, was not exposed to institutionalism before arriving at Wisconsin as a faculty member.

CONCLUSION

In the history of economics at Wisconsin we can clearly see the pattern of the growth of institutionalism through the 1930s, followed by a relative decline. In Wisconsin's case, the early period in which Ely dominated is characterized by a combination of historical and neoclassical influences, but also by the production of graduates who did not particularly associate with institutionalism. Institutionalism at Wisconsin seems to have been largely the result of the arrival on faculty of John R. Commons and E. A. Ross. Initially, Commons's connections with the group developing the institutional approach lay in the area of labor economics and in such issues as the reform of labor law, workmen's compensation, and unemployment compensation. With the publication of *The Legal Foundations*, however, Commons's more general contributions in law and economics were widely referred to as an important contribution to institutional economics. There can be no doubt that by the mid- to late 1920s, Commons and his students were thinking of themselves as institutionalists, and this is evident in the course titles and descriptions found, in Commons's own use of the term to describe his own work, and in the interactions between Commons's students and other members of the institutionalist group.

Wisconsin institutionalism did have a particular emphasis on labor issues and on law and economics, but this is not so different from the work of others in the movement, such as Walton Hamilton and Leo Wolman.

---

[37] In 1947, Wisconsin established its own Industrial Relations Center. This was an interdisciplinary research center involving faculty from law and economics.

It must also be recognized that there cannot have been very many, if any, other professors of economics in the United States over the period Commons was at Wisconsin, who produced as many graduate students, or whose students had such a marked impact on government legislation and policy. In this sense, Commons and his students were extremely successful. The system of modern industrial relations, certain aspects of public utility regulation, workmen's compensation, unemployment insurance, and social security can all be seen as developments to which Commons and his students made substantial contributions.

Despite this undoubted success, institutional economics could not maintain its position after World War II, even at Wisconsin. The new hires at that point became predominantly Keynesian or more neoclassical in orientation. This development seems less to do with the failure of Wisconsin institutionalists to reproduce themselves as suggested by Biddle, than with the larger shifts taking place in the economics profession at large.

8

Institutional Economics at Columbia University

Apart from Wisconsin, the leading center for institutional economics between the wars was Columbia University. In general intellectual terms, Columbia at least equaled Chicago and Harvard, and New York was the preeminent center of American intellectual life. Moreover, in terms of the numbers of doctoral students in economics, Columbia was *the* leader, and by quite a margin (Froman 1942). Between 1913 and the early 1930s, Columbia became the academic home of a particularly large concentration of economists of institutionalist leaning. These included Wesley Mitchell, J. M. Clark, F. C. Mills, Paul Brissenden, James Bonbright, Robert Hale, Joseph Dorfman, Carter Goodrich, Rexford Tugwell, Gardiner Means, Leo Wolman, Horace Taylor, A. F. Burns, and, later on, Karl Polanyi.[1] A. R. Burns and Eveline Burns should also be included as being, at the least, sympathetic to institutionalist ideas. Furthermore, over the period in question, the Department of Economics was a graduate department offering degrees within the Faculty of Political Science. The Faculty also contained the graduate departments of Sociology, History, and Public Law. The Law School contained a large contingent of members of the realist school, including, at various times, W. W. Cook, Karl Llewellyn, Underhill Moore, and Herman Oliphant. A. A. Berle was also a member of the Department of Public Law and the Law School. Robert Hale moved from Economics to the Law

---

[1] It has been remarked to me that Wolman was not a liberal and was quite skeptical about unions. Wolman certainly had doubts concerning certain aspects of the Wagner act and its administration, but he supported social security, unemployment insurance, workmen's compensation, minimum wage laws, and many aspects of the New Deal. Moreover, Wolman was very much a part of the institutionalist group. He was also "largely the architect" of the voluntary joint contributory scheme of unemployment insurance first established in the Chicago garment industry, and that had J. R. Commons as its administrator (Dorfman 1959, p. 521).

School, and Gardiner Means was a member of the economic research staff of the Law School between 1927 and 1933, and was an associate in law from 1933 to 1935. From 1919 to 1927, the Sociology Department included William Ogburn. Until 1917, History had Charles Beard, and James Harvey Robinson until 1919. Outside of the Faculty of Political Science, the Philosophy Department contained John Dewey, whose instrumentalist philosophy was widely influential and closely connected to institutional economics. There were also close relations between the School of Business, established in 1916, and the Department of Economics. James Bonbright and Paul Brissenden, as well as other economists, were appointed in the School of Business, and F. C. Mills held a joint appointment. In addition, there was Mitchell's National Bureau of Economic Research, which had close connections with several Columbia faculty and employed many Columbia students and graduates.

There has been substantial material produced on the work and careers of Wesley Mitchell (Biddle 1998b), J. M. Clark (Shute 1997), and Rexford Tugwell (Sternsher 1964), but virtually nothing on issues that relate to the place of Columbia within the institutionalist movement or American economics. Questions arise concerning how Columbia became to be such a center for institutionalism, the relationships between the various people of institutional orientation who were there, the overall character and content of Columbia institutional economics, the graduates who identified themselves with institutionalism, the point at which one can begin to see signs of the weakening of institutionalism at Columbia, and how the more general decline of institutionalism was reflected in the history of the Columbia Department.

To aid the discussion, Table 8.1 provides a listing of those Columbia faculty members in economics and other departments who form the central points of discussion in the paper. This is not a complete listing, but it does list those associated with institutionalism, the more important representatives of the neoclassical approach, and significant faculty in other departments. Table 8.2 provides a selective listing, by date of PhD, of graduate students, focusing on those most associated with institutionalism, but also listing some others who feature in the story to follow.

BACKGROUND: COLUMBIA ECONOMICS, 1900–1913

Columbia's position as a center for social science research in the early years of the century was a very major one. Columbia had developed itself in a way that conformed to the model of the German research university "while

Table 8.1. *Selected Columbia faculty, 1877–1947*

Richmond Mayo-Smith (1877–1901)	James Angell (1924–1966)
E. R. A. Seligman (1885–1930)	Karl Lewellyn (Law) (1925–1951)
F. H. Giddings (Sociology) (1894–1928)	J. M. Clark (1926–1957)
James Harvey Robinson (History) (1895–1919)	Adolf A. Berle (Law) (1927–1964)
J. B. Clark (1895–1923)	Gardiner Means(Law) (1927–1935)
Henry L Moore (1902–1929)	A.R. Burns (1928–1963)
Henry Seager (1902–1930)	Eveline Burns (1928–1942), (Social Work) (1946–1967)
Charles Beard (History) (1904–1917)	Carter Goodrich (1931–1963)
Vladimir Simkhovitch 1904–1942	Leo Wolman (1931–1958)
John Dewey (Philosophy) (1905–1929)	Joseph Dorfman (1931–1971)
Wesley Mitchell (1913–1919, 1922–1944)	Harold Hotelling (1931–1946)
Robert Hale (Econ/Law) (1915–1949)	Robert Lynd (Sociology) (1931–1961)
Underhill Moore (Law) (1916–1929)	Abraham Wald (1939–1950)
F. C. Mills (1919–1959)	A. F. Burns (1941–1958)
William Ogburn (Sociology) (1919–1927)	Abram Bergson (1945–1956)
W. W. Cook (Law) (1919–1922)	Ragnar Nurkse (1945–1946, 1947–1959)
James Bonbright (1920–1961)	A. G. Hart (1946–1978)
Rexford Tugwell (1920–1937)	William Vickery (1946–1959)
Paul Brissenden (1921–1954)	Karl Polanyi (1947–1953)
Herman Oliphant (Law) (1922–1929)	George Stigler (1947–1958)

distinguishing itself from other reforming American universities" by the extent to which quantitative and statistical methods were adopted (Camic and Xie 1994, pp. 781–782). In psychology, sociology, anthropology, as well as economics, Columbia had developed a particular reputation for being at the forefront in the use of statistical and quantitative methods. The individuals most involved in the development of this orientation were James Cattell in psychology, Franklin F. Giddings in sociology, Franz Boas in anthropology, and Richmond Mayo-Smith and Henry Moore in economics (Camic and Xie 1994).

In examining the Columbia Economics Department of the early 1900s, this combination of German influence and statistical methods is very

Table 8.2. *Selected Columbia graduate students, 1893–1959 (Year of PhD)*

W. Z. Ripley (1893)	P. Sargant Florence (1918)	Ralph Souter (1933)
Alvin Johnson (1905)	Paul Douglas (1921)	A.F. Burns (1934)
J. M. Clark (1910)	James Bonbright (1921)	Joseph Dorfman (1935)
B. M. Anderson Jr. (1911)	Frederick Macaulay (1924)	Eli Ginzberg (1935)
William Leiserson (1911)	Charles Gulick (1924)	Moses Abramovitz (1939)
Lawrence K. Frank (BA 1912)	Stuart Rice (1924)	Solomon Fabricant (1939)
William Ogburn (1912)	Willard Thorp (1925)	Milton Friedman (1946)
Oswald Knauth (1914)	George Stocking (1925)	William Vickrey (1947)
N. I. Stone (1915)	Henry Schultz (1925)	Mark Perlman (1950)
Arthur Suffern (1916)	Simon Kuznets (1926)	Forest Hill (1950)
Henry Hoagland (1917)	Horace Taylor (1928)	Kenneth Arrow (1951)
F. C. Mills (1917)	Robert Brady (1929)	Daniel Fusfeld (1953)
Paul Brissenden (1917)	Louis Reed (1930)	Harvey Segal (1956)
Robert Hale (1918)	Leo Rogin (1931)	Julius Rubin (1959)
	John Gambs (1932)	

evident. The Department contained some notable people, including E. R. A. Seligman, Henry R. Seager, Henry L. Moore, and, of course, J. B. Clark. Giddings was also a member of the Department of Economics until a semi-autonomous Department of Sociology was formed in 1904. Seligman and J. B. Clark had both studied in Germany and absorbed a large amount of historical school literature. Seligman studied in Heidelberg and Berlin, and on returning obtained both an LLB and a PhD at Columbia. J. B. Clark had also studied under Karl Knies at Heidelberg. Seligman taught graduate courses in history of political economy, railroad problems and regulation, and did a great deal to establish the field of public finance. Clark's work on marginal productivity theory had established him as America's leading economic theorist. Clark was also concerned with the problem of combinations and trusts, and taught the course on socialism. Clark's interests, however, moved increasingly into the area of international relations, and he retired in 1923.

Henry R. Seager and Henry L. Moore were appointed in 1902. Henry L. Moore had done his graduate work at Johns Hopkins under J. B. Clark and became a pioneer in mathematical statistics and mathematical economics (Mirowski 1990). Moore brought sophisticated statistical tools to the task of providing an "inductive complement" to the neoclassical theory he had learned from Clark (Moore 1908). However, Moore did not enjoy teaching the more elementary statistics courses, and instruction in statistics was supplemented by the appointment of Robert Chaddock in 1911. As the Chair of the Department, it was Seligman's desire to put Columbia "as far in the lead in practical statistics, as she is already in the lead in economics and sociology" (quoted by Dorfman 1955, p. 188).

In contrast, Seager had been a student of Simon Patten's at Pennsylvania. He shared an interest in the problem of trusts with J. B. Clark and taught the course on Trusts and Corporations. He was also known as a labor economist of progressive outlook and as an early and effective advocate of social insurance (Seager 1910). He knew J. R. Commons well, and students of Commons, such as William Leiserson and Henry E. Hoagland, went on to complete their doctorates at Columbia under Seager. He remained an important and respected figure within the Columbia Department until his death in 1930, and he produced many students in labor economics.

One other appointment that might be mentioned was that of Vladimir Simkhovitch in 1905 to teach economic history. He had been trained at Halle where he had met Wesley Mitchell. In 1908, he took over J. B. Clark's course on socialism.

At this point, particularly with J. B. Clark and Moore, the Department probably possessed more strength in neoclassical theory than any other leading department in America, as well as strengths in the analysis of the major issues of the time, including railroad regulation, labor problems, public finance, and corporations and trusts. Some notable graduates from the program in the period before Mitchell's arrival were William Z. Ripley (PhD 1893), Alvin Johnson (PhD 1905), J. M. Clark (PhD 1910), B. M. Anderson Jr. (PhD 1911), and William Leiserson (PhD 1911). Paul Douglas was also a student at Columbia in 1913 and 1914, although he did not graduate until 1921. He took courses from J. B. Clark, Seligman, Chaddock, and Seager, as well as from Charles Beard in History. He also read Dewey's work (Douglas 1971, pp. 28–29).[2]

In Alvin Johnson, J. M. Clark, and B. M. Anderson Jr., Columbia had produced a crop of exceptionally able young theorists. Nevertheless, it cannot

---

[2] Paul Douglas's autobiography (Douglas 1971) does not mention Mitchell, although he was at Columbia in about 1914. It took him many years, until after he was employed at Chicago, to finally submit his dissertation.

be said that the Department as a whole, or the students they produced, were in any sense narrowly neoclassical in nature. Both Anderson and J. M Clark were interested in theoretical issues of social value, and there was a general concern with issues of economic and social reform. As Paul Douglas's autobiography makes clear, New York was an intellectual ferment and a hotbed of reform movements (Douglas 1971, pp. 31–32), and the atmosphere in the city was reflected at Columbia. Training in economics also drew on the broader resources of the Faculty of Political Science. Until 1917, every doctoral student had to offer a major area and two minor areas.[3] For economics students, one minor area had to be sociology, the other minor area could be drawn from other departments in the Faculty of Political Science, such as History or Public Law. From Giddings, the Sociology Department had developed a stress on quantitative methods, and both the sociology and economics students were taught by Chaddock, who was later aided by Frank A. Ross of the Department of Sociology. One notable graduate was William Ogburn (PhD 1912), who returned to Columbia as a member of the Sociology Department in 1919 and became a major figure in the promotion of statistical methods in sociology. The relationship between the Departments of Economics and Public Law was also noteworthy. For example, William Ripley took administrative law as his second minor area, whereas J. M. Clark split his between American history and constitutional law (Shute 1997, p. 10). Seligman's own background in law contributed to the close interweaving of economics and law – a feature that was to continue to be characteristic of Columbia.

MITCHELL AT COLUMBIA: 1913–1918

Mitchell thought of himself as somewhat "unconventional" in his economics, but this appears to have been no barrier to his career.[4] Mitchell had taken a great deal from his exposure to Veblen and John Dewey during his

---

[3]   After 1917, the final examination for the doctoral degree was restricted to economics alone. Seven subjects had to be taken, of these three subjects were required of all candidates (the history and theory of economics, statistics, and economic history) and three of the four others were to be selected from a list of eight (public finance, money and banking, the labor problem, trade and transportation, corporations and trusts, business economics, insurance, and agriculture).

[4]   After spending a year at Harvard in 1908–1909, Mitchell was made an offer of a permanent job there. Mitchell turned it down partly because of the emphasis on teaching at Harvard, but he also wrote to Taussig that he was concerned he was too unconventional in his economics. Taussig replied: "One reason we wanted you was to get a man who was *not* conventional" (F. A. Taussig to Wesley Mitchell, 16 February 1910, Wesley Mitchell Papers, Box 13). Irving Fisher also tried hard to get Mitchell to accept a position at Yale.

graduate student years at Chicago. Veblen's emphasis on the role of institutions in molding behavior, his criticism of the psychology of hedonism, and his critique of business or "pecuniary" institutions all greatly impacted on him. Mitchell disapproved of Veblen's failure to check his conclusions against facts, but elements of Veblen's thinking remained clearly evident in his work, notably in his insistence on seeing business cycles as a phenomenon of the institutions of a developed money economy (Mitchell 1927).

Despite this "unconventionality," he was warmly received at Columbia in 1913. Simkhovitch, having known Mitchell from Halle, was particularly keen to have him as a colleague, but Mitchell was extremely well regarded by the rest of the Department and by the profession at large. He had a wide interest in theory, including recent European and American contributions, and in 1913 he had just finished *Business Cycles* (Mitchell 1913), a book that cemented his reputation as a scholar of the first rank. He was seen at Columbia as a "man interested in theory and equipped to attack theoretical problems in a truly scientific spirit, and with the aid of the broadest training here and abroad" (Dorfman 1955, p. 191), and Mitchell's quantitative approach matched well with the Columbia orientation.

The Columbia reaction to his *Business Cycles* was enthusiastic. Seager wrote to Mitchell: "It is a splendid achievement … I had no idea that you had so nearly finished or that it was to be such an exhaustive study. Its publication sets a new standard for American economic scholarship" (Henry Seager to Wesley Mitchell, 5 November 1913, Wesley Mitchell Papers, Box 13). Slightly later, Henry Moore wrote:

Since I first read Prof Clark's Theory of Distribution, no work by an American economist has given me such great satisfaction. Your grasp of the whole complex of facts, your cautious step by step progress and your sagacity in tracing the relation of economic changes must give keen pleasure to all of your readers. You have difficulty in concealing your contempt for pretentious, speculative treatments of economic questions, and your enthusiasm for inductive research makes your statistical tables glow. I am glad with all my heart that we are so closely associated in the same university. (Henry Moore to Wesley Mitchell, 13 September 1914, Wesley Mitchell Papers, Box 11)[5]

---

[5] Although Moore had been a student of J. B. Clark and placed more emphasis on theory than Mitchell, Mirowski has pointed out that Moore's work utilized pragmatic and empirical notions of science, and that his methodological position, which gave priority to empirical findings, was not that far from Mitchell's or F. C. Mills's. The relationship between Mitchell and Moore deteriorated later, as Mitchell "spurned Moore's weather theory and rejected the use of periodograms in economic analysis" (Mirowski 1990, pp. 603–604; see Mitchell 1927, pp. 259–260). Joseph Schumpeter also taught at Columbia for the 1913–1914 year and came to know Mitchell. He wrote to Mitchell on his appointment

On Mitchell's side, the move to New York was prompted partly by Lucy Sprague Mitchell's desire to be in New York to pursue her interest in educational reform, but Mitchell was also interested in New York as a place compatible with his research interests. Since Veblen and Allyn Young had left Stanford, Mitchell felt he lacked colleagues in California who understood and were interested in his work. To pursue his research on the nature and functioning of the "Money Economy" (of which *Business Cycles* was a part), he felt he "needed the chance to come into contact at first hand with the workings of pecuniary institutions and to observe how the minds of the men who control the powerful business enterprises are formed by their daily tasks" (L. S. Mitchell 1953, p. 231). Mitchell had resigned from Berkeley without a job in New York, but made an arrangement with Columbia to teach one course related to his current research for the nominal salary of $700. The following year, he was elected Professor of Economics.

At the time of his appointment, Mitchell was primarily interested in working on his Types of Economic Theory, relating the history of economic thought to the development of the institutions of the money economy. In some years, he taught a full-year course on Types of Economic Theory, in other years he taught a one-semester course on Types of Economic Theory and a semester course on Business Cycles. The former course dealt with current economic theory, including Jevons and Marshall's neoclassical economics; a large amount of material on American contributors such as J. B. Clark, Frank Fetter, Joseph Davenport, B. M. Anderson Jr.; European contributors such as Walras, Schumpeter, Schmoller, and the German Historical School; J. A. Hobson's welfare economics; and finished with a lengthy section on Thorstein Veblen (Dorfman 1967). Over the next few years, Mitchell developed his material on the Classical economists and became interested in Wieser. He began a book manuscript on Types of Economic Theory, but it was never completed.[6]

Mitchell's Types of Economic Theory course was to become the standard graduate theory course at Columbia. In this manner, Mitchell brought his broad perspective, his admiration of Veblen, and his ideas on the impact of pecuniary institutions on habits of thought explicitly into the teaching of

---

to Columbia: "I rejoice in the thought that you will as a matter of course rise to a position of leadership in our science and, let us hope, have it in a state different than it is now" (Joseph Schumpeter to Wesley Mitchell, no date, Wesley Mitchell Papers, Box 12).

6   Some of this material appeared as articles, including "Wieser's Theory of Social Economics" (Mitchell 1915), "The Role of Money in Economic Theory" (Mitchell 1916), and "Bentham's Felicific Calculus" (Mitchell 1918).

economic theory. Some of the notable Columbia economics graduates from this period who would have been exposed to Mitchell's teaching include Oswald Knauth (PhD 1914), N. I. Stone (PhD 1915), Arthur Suffern (PhD 1916), Paul Brissenden (PhD 1917), Robert Hale (PhD 1918), and P. Sargant Florence (PhD 1918). Most of these graduates were to maintain some connection to Columbia or to the NBER, but Suffern was to move to the Institute of Economics to work on labor issues in the coal industry (Suffern 1926), complementing the work by Lubin and Hamilton previously mentioned, and Florence was to join the heavily institutionalist Bureau of Industrial Research in New York, and then move to the University of Birmingham in England where he worked on empirical studies of industrial structure, becoming a professor in 1929.[7]

WAR, THE NBER, AND THE NEW SCHOOL: 1918–1922

Mitchell's presence at Columbia was interrupted by World War I and by a short period at the New School for Social Research. During the war, Mitchell headed the Prices Section of the War Industries Board and worked on a study of prices during the war, work that also involved Leo Wolman, Walter Stewart, and Isador Lubin. Mitchell's concern with statistical and factual knowledge, and the need for improved research in the social sciences, was given new urgency by his experience of the wartime administration. In 1918, Mitchell became President of the American Statistical Association. His Presidential Address, "Statistics and Government" (Mitchell 1919) specifically related his war experience to the need for more work on "social statistics." The idea of a research bureau to undertake objective and factual investigation in economics was first broached in 1917 in discussions between N. I. Stone and Malcolm Rorty. They involved Edwin Gay and Wesley Mitchell, and also enlisted the support of others such as T. S. Adams, John R. Commons, and Allyn Young. The NBER was established in 1920, with Mitchell as Director of Research. The original research staff included Oswald Knauth and Frederick Macaulay, both Columbia PhDs, and Willford King, from Wisconsin. The history of the NBER is dealt with in detail in Chapter 9.

It was late in 1918 when Walton Hamilton introduced the term "institutional economics." Soon after Hamilton's introduction of the term, Mitchell changed from describing Veblen's approach as "evolutionary" or "genetic" to "institutional" (Mitchell 1967/1969, p. 610, n. 3), so that the

---

[7]   For Mitchell's other connections to economics in England, see Rutherford (2007).

final section of his Types of Economic Theory course became "Thorstein Veblen's Institutional Approach." Mitchell himself became to be seen as the leading exponent of the quantitative branch of the institutionalist movement, and it was largely Mitchell's work, and the recognized quality of his quantitative approach, that gave such strength to the institutionalist claim to be following empirical scientific methods (Rutherford 1999).

After the war, in 1919, Mitchell resigned from Columbia and was closely involved with the establishment of the New School for Social Research, along with Alvin Johnson, Charles Beard, James Harvey Robinson, and other "liberals," notably Herbert Croly and Walter Weyl.[8] Veblen was also employed at the New School for a few years until he retired, and Leo Wolman was a faculty member there from 1919 to 1928. Harold Laski taught at the New School until his move to England, and A. A. Goldenweiser, brother of A. E. Goldenweiser, taught anthropology. Graham Wallas also lectured at the New School during its first term of operation.

According to letters from Herbert Croly to Graham Wallas, those involved with the New School were very interested in the LSE as a model (Rutherford 2007). Croly wrote that "this school of ours … is an attempt to do something, in a more elaborate way, similar to what you started to do in England many years ago when you started the Fabian Society, and which is now being carried on, in a somewhat different way, by the London School of Economics." The New School's object is "to work out a technique of social progress and to turn out people who are capable of carrying on a work of that kind in a scientific spirit and from a psychological point of view" (Herbert Croly to Graham Wallas, 29 March 1919, Graham Wallas Papers, 1/62). Croly also hoped to draw directly on Wallas's experience:

> I may add that I was particularly pleased by the generous way in which you propose to give the school the benefit of your own experience at the London School of Economics. I think the administrators of the school particularly need assistance of this kind. At one time we were hoping to send somebody to London in order to study the curriculum and method of instruction employed in that school. This, I hope, we can still do but your assistance will be even better. (Herbert Croly to Graham Wallas, 16 May 1919, Graham Wallas Papers 1/62)

Veblen's critique of universities in his *Higher Learning in America* (Veblen 1918) may also have been an influence in that the school was established

---

[8] The impetus for the formation of the New School (originally thought of as the "Free School") was the question of freedom of speech that erupted in 1917 in a dispute between Charles Beard and the University President Nicholas Murray Butler over American intervention in World War I. Beard resigned, and other faculty protested in various ways. James Harvey Robinson was the prime mover in establishing the New School.

without a large endowment from business sources. The New School generated a great deal of interest and excitement initially, but because it could not offer degrees and was dependent on a largely adult education audience, it failed to attract serious research students,[9] and Mitchell returned to Columbia, at a much improved salary, in 1922.

THE DEVELOPMENT OF INSTITUTIONALISM AT COLUMBIA: 1920–1932

As indicated by Paul Homan, institutionalism not only derived from Veblen and Dewey, but also stood in a "close spiritual relation" to the work of the legal realists in jurisprudence, of Charles Beard and J. H. Robinson in history and government, and of W. F. Ogburn in sociology (Homan 1937, p. 388). As can be seen from Table 8.1, there was a significant constellation of talent at Columbia in the years up to 1920 that provided the intellectual atmosphere within which the institutionalist point of view could grow. This atmosphere was one of a desire to move away from old orthodoxies, a desire to be more truly scientific, and a progressivist desire to bring social scientific knowledge to bear on the pressing social and economic issues of the day. Mitchell brought with him to Columbia both his Veblenian notions of the importance of institutions in shaping economic behavior and his quantitative and statistical approach, but it was not Mitchell alone who was responsible for the development of institutionalism at Columbia. As well as Mitchell, there was Seager in economics, John Dewey in philosophy, Robinson and Beard pursuing their progressive agenda of the "New History," and in the Law School, a number of representatives of legal realism including Walter Cook, Underhill Moore, and Herman Oliphant. The realist approach to law was a demand for law to become like the other empirical social sciences (Schlegel 1995). The study of the law should be "fact based," with notions of precepts and principles of law being replaced by a focus on actual practices and behavior. Also important was the appointment of William Ogburn to the Sociology Department in 1919. Ogburn knew many of the institutionalist economists well. In 1915, he had known Carleton Parker at Berkeley and taught at the University of Washington in 1917–1918, where his colleagues included Carleton Parker and Rexford Tugwell, before moving back to Columbia. Ogburn's statistical approach also blended well with Mitchell's.

---

9   Under New York law, the School required an endowment of $500,000 before it could offer degrees. The School turned to adult education. It was only with the coming of World War II that Alvin Johnson was able to establish the "University in Exile" at the New School.

With all of these elements gathered together at Columbia, it is no surprise that institutionalism emerged within the corps of graduate students produced in the period around 1920. In the first half of the 1920s, the growth of the institutionalist presence at Columbia was produced primarily by the hiring of Columbia graduates F. C. Mills, Paul Brissenden, Robert Hale, and James Bonbright. Some were hired into the School of Business, and a number of business courses "became a regular part of the Department's offering under the Faculty of Political Science" (Dorfman 1955, p. 196).

As noted earlier, both Mills and Brissenden had been at Berkeley and had worked with Mitchell and Parker. At Columbia, Mills studied with Mitchell, Henry Moore, and with John Dewey. He completed his PhD in 1917 on the topic of "Contemporary Theories of Unemployment and Unemployment Relief," was appointed Assistant Professor of Business Organization in 1920, and was soon to be made Associate Professor of Business Statistics. He wrote a widely used statistics textbook (Mills 1924b) and worked for many years as a member of staff at the National Bureau of Economic Research. Brissenden focused on labor economics, and his dissertation, *The IWW: A Study of American Syndicalism* (Brissenden 1919), became the standard work on the history of the IWW. He was appointed to the School of Business and became much involved with labor mediation and arbitration, and later with the study of the use of court injunctions in labor disputes, also E. E. Witte's main topic of interest.

Robert Hale had a background in law (LLB from Harvard) and began teaching economics at Columbia in 1915. He attended John Dewey's lectures in philosophy in 1915–1916 and completed his doctoral dissertation, "Valuation and Rate Making: The Conflicting Theories of the Wisconsin Railroad Commission," in 1918. Mitchell was a member of his dissertation committee (Fried 1998, p 10). He was appointed a lecturer in Legal Economics in 1922, by which time he was already well embarked on his critique of the court's treatment of "fair value" in rate regulation cases. Hale knew Commons's work on law and economics well, and he worked with Walton Hamilton on public utility regulation. James Bonbright began as an instructor in economics in 1919 and completed his Columbia PhD dissertation on "Railroad Capitalization: A Study of the Principles of Regulation of Railroad Securities" in 1921. He and Hale had a common interest in the basis for rate regulation and became close friends. Bonbright became a member of the School of Business where he developed courses on Corporation Finance and the Regulation of Public Utilities. In the 1920s, he wrote many articles dealing with corporate finance issues (including problems with no-par stock, the rights of security holders in corporate reorganizations, and railroad capitalization), and public utility rate regulation (including valuation and depreciation issues).

In addition to Columbia's own graduates, Rexford Tugwell was appointed as an instructor in 1920 and became assistant professor in 1922. Like Seager, Tugwell had been a student of Simon Patten, and he also knew Ogburn from his time at the University of Washington. He was placed in charge of the development of the Contemporary Civilization course taught to undergraduates, out of which came the text book *American Economic Life and the Means of Its Improvement* (Tugwell, Munroe, and Stryker 1925). He published his paper, "The Economic Basis for Business Regulation," in 1921 (Tugwell 1921), which was a condensed version of his University of Pennsylvania doctoral dissertation *The Economic Basis of Public Interest* (Tugwell 1922a). As the titles suggest, these pieces are a defense of the regulation of business in the light of increasing returns, consolidations, monopoly power, and the resulting damage to the interests of consumers. Large-scale businesses are "affected with a public interest," which can justify regulation. Tugwell was also working on following up his interest in psychology and economics that he had absorbed from Carleton Parker and William Ogburn, and published a discussion of this topic, "Human Nature in Economic Theory," in 1922 (Tugwell 1922b). Once at Columbia, Tugwell attended lectures given by John Dewey, out of which he developed his idea of "experimental" or instrumental economics (Tugwell 1924a; 1982, p. 157), and took Mitchell's course on Types of Economic Theory on more than one occasion (Tugwell 1982). Tugwell, however, was passed over for promotion to the graduate faculty.[10]

Of course, not all of Columbia's hires in the 1920s were of people with an institutionalist viewpoint. For example, in 1924, James W. Angell was hired

---

[10]   Tugwell indicates that the nature of his book, *Industry's Coming of Age*, might have "caused my superiors to decide, Mitchell dissenting, that I might stay on at Columbia, perhaps, because I seemed to be administering the teaching of economics in the college successfully, but that I was not likely to develop into a real economist" (Tugwell 1982, pp. 184–185). Mitchell had written to Tugwell expressing concern over his lack of scientific research standards (Horace Taylor to Rexford Tugwell, 11 March 1929, Rexford Tugwell to Horace Taylor 12 March 1929, and Wesley Mitchell to Rexford Tugwell, 23 May 1929, Rexford Tugwell Papers, Boxes 15 and 25). Ginzberg recollects that Simkhovitch also was opposed to Tugwell, and goes on, "there was no small amount of surprise and chagrin among members of the graduate department when their little esteemed colleague, Tugwell, together with Raymond Moley and Adolph Berle – turned out to be charter members of FDR's Brain Trust" (Ginzberg1990, p. 17). Tugwell and Dorfman were close while they were both at Columbia and later collaborated on several history-of-thought projects. In 1937, Tugwell wrote a generous review of Mitchell's work (Tugwell 1937), and Mitchell responded with a letter of thanks that also expressed his "high appreciation of the courage

to cover monetary economics. Angell was a student of Allyn Young from Harvard and was significantly closer to neoclassical economics than many at Columbia. Nevertheless, he had good relations with Mitchell, and, in the mid- to late 1930s, had many discussions with Mitchell concerning his proposals for studies on money for the NBER (Mitchell Papers, Box 46).

This hiring in the early 1920s created a significant group of young institutional economists at Columbia, but the institutionalist complement at Columbia received a major boost from the appointment in 1926 of J. M. Clark to a new chair as Research Professor in Economics. The other candidate seriously considered was Jacob Viner, but although Viner was regarded as the better teacher,[11] Clark was seen as having the greater research potential. Undoubtedly, sentiment for Clark's father, and Columbia's "ambivalent attitude towards Jews," played a role (Ginzberg 1990, p. 15), but Clark also fit in well with the institutionalist research agenda that had been established at Columbia. Clark himself described his main research interest as "social-institutional-dynamic theory" (Dorfman 1955 p. 194).

Clark had played an active role in the formation of institutionalism. Although never a student of Veblen's, Clark had taken Veblen's critique of his father's neoclassical economics seriously. What resulted from this combination of diverse intellectual parents was an interest in the development of a "dynamic social or institutional economics, or 'realistic economics'" (J. M. Clark to Roche-Agussol, 14 September 1918, Joseph Dorfman Papers), and a concern with the "social control of business." Clark knew Mitchell's work on business cycles well, developing his concept of the accelerator from his study of Mitchell (Clark 1917), was familiar with the work of Carleton Parker and Wesley Mitchell on psychology and economics, had produced a sophisticated criticism of utility maximization (Clark 1918), and had directly critiqued orthodox theory (Clark 1921). Clark was at one with Walton Hamilton in calling for an economics "relevant to the issues of its time" and based on a more properly "scientific" method (Clark 1919).[12]

When he arrived at Columbia, Clark had just published his *Social Control of Business* (Clark 1926), a work very much in line with the proregulatory

and good temper you showed when you were exposed to so much unfair criticism while in public office" (Wesley Mitchell to Rexford Tugwell, 4 January 1938, Rexford Tugwell Papers, Box 15).

[11] Viner and Clark were warm friends at Chicago, and remained so afterward. Clark was a shy individual but a very careful thinker. In conversation and in seminars, he was prone to silences of epic length. His Research Chair obliged him to do only as much teaching as he wished, and he usually spent only two days a week in the Department.

[12] Clark did not share Mitchell's methodological views, but he was interested enough to ask Mitchell to write a piece concerning the development of his methodological position,

perspective expressed by Tugwell and Hale, and which explicitly referred to their work as well as to Veblen, Hamilton, and Commons. Clark argued that industry was quite generally affected with a public interest, and that "individualism" did not afford sufficient safeguards. His book discussed a vast number of market problem and failures that, in various ways, called for additional measures of social control. Clark was very familiar with Mitchell's work on business cycles, a topic to which Clark was to make many contributions in the 1930s (Clark 1934; 1935b).

Further, in 1928, Eveline Burns was appointed as a lecturer, and her husband, A. R. Burns, was appointed at Barnard College. Between 1926 and 1928, the Burnses were on Rockefeller Fellowships. Eveline Burns had been in the Department of Economics at the London School of Economics, specializing in wage theories and regulation. In the United States, she studied labor economics at The New School, Columbia, the Brookings Graduate School, Harvard, Chicago, and Stanford. Her supervisors included Wolman at the New School, Seager, Mitchell, and Brissenden at Columbia, Hamilton at Brookings, Paul Douglas, Jacob Viner, and Henry Schultz at Chicago, and F. A. Taussig and Allyn Young at Harvard. She taught labor economics and later moved into the area of social security.[13] A. R. Burns developed a research interest in industrial organization.

On top of all of this, on Mitchell's return to Columbia in 1922, he launched into a major project to update his 1913 work on business cycles with the aid of the NBER. This project was originally conceived of as consisting of two main volumes, *The Problem and Its Setting* and *The Rhythm of Business Activity*, along with accompanying volumes of statistical data. In the 1920s, members of the NBER research staff included Leo Wolman and Columbia graduates such as Simon Kuznets, Frederick Macaulay, F. C. Mills, and Willard Thorp.

---

and to persuade him to let him publish the letter as a part of his "Wesley C. Mitchell's Contribution to the Theory of Business Cycles" contained in the collection, *Methods in Social Science* (Clark 1931).

[13] Eveline Burns was hired as a lecturer by Seligman, with a promise that she would be given a regular position as soon as obstacles in the form of funding and certain objections to the hiring of a woman were overcome. This regularization of her position did not occur, and she complained about her lack of status in 1937 (Eveline Burns to Wesley Mitchell, 8 December 1937, Wesley Mitchell Papers, Box 46). Mitchell attempted to come up with a solution (V. G. Simkhovitch to Wesley Mitchell, 20 January 1939, Wesley Mitchell Papers, Box 46), but she left Columbia in 1942, never having been more than a lecturer. She returned as Professor of Social Work to the New York School of Social Work, which had become part of Columbia University, in 1946.

There was a significantly institutionalist character to this research staff. Thorp had done his undergraduate work at Amherst. He completed his Columbia PhD dissertation in 1925 and, along with Mitchell, produced the volume *Business Annals* for the NBER (Thorp and Mitchell 1926). Thorp would return to Amherst as a Professor of Economics and write an institutionalist textbook, *Economic Institutions* (Thorp 1928), but he remained on the staff of the NBER until 1933. Kuznets came to Mitchell's attention as a result of his MA essay dealing with Schumpeter and critiquing Schumpeter's scientific methodology. Mitchell was impressed enough with this essay to offer Kuznets a position at the National Bureau in order to teach him how to do empirical economics (Perlman 2001). Kuznets completed his doctoral dissertation on "Cyclical Fluctuations, Retail and Wholesale Trade, United States, 1919–1925" in 1926. He became a full member of the NBER research staff the following year, working both on seasonal fluctuations and national income accounting. Kuznets's own empirical work shares Mitchell's sensitivity to institutional context and the effect of variation in institutions on empirical relationships (Kuznets 1963; Street 1988). Wolman's principal NBER work was his empirical study of union membership, *The Growth of American Trade Unions, 1880–1923* (Wolman 1924). Mills wrote *The Behavior of Prices* (1927), and in the late 1920s and early 1930s developed a concern for the effects of technological change combined with price inflexibilities as a cause of depression (Mills 1932; 1936; Woirol 1999). All of this work was closely related to Mitchell's overall project on business cycles. The first of the projected volumes, *Business Cycles: The Problem and Its Setting*, appeared in 1927.

The years between 1929 and 1932 saw a number of changes and the last major influx of institutional economists into the Department. In 1929, John Dewey retired, although he continued writing for many years more. Within Economics, Moore retired in 1929, Seager died in 1930, and Seligman retired in 1931. On Seager's death, Mitchell was appointed Acting Chief Executive Officer of the Department, a post he held for only about a year before asking to be relieved. Seligman's Chair passed to Robert Haig, a former student and Professor in the School of Business, Seager's course on trusts and corporations was taken over by A. R. Burns, who was elected to Faculty of Political Science in 1935, while Eveline Burns developed the speciality of social insurance. A number of new appointments were made also, and several of these indicate Mitchell's preferences. Carter Goodrich was hired from Michigan in 1930 to develop the area of American economic history. Goodrich had been a student at Amherst with Hamilton and Stewart, and at the time of his appointment to Columbia he was a colleague of Morris Copeland at Michigan. His interests also included labor economics; his best-known work was *The Miner's Freedom: A Study of Working Life in a Changing Industry* (Goodrich 1925). In 1931, Leo Wolman was hired to take over the area of labor economics. Wolman had a long history of contact with Mitchell and at the time of his appointment to Columbia he was on the staff of the NBER. Wolman was also on the research staff of The Amalgamated Clothing Workers of America, and, as remarked by Ginzberg, "no major economics department had, up to that point, picked a professor from the ranks of the trade union movement, even if from its research staff" (Ginzberg 1990, p. 17). Mitchell clearly had much to do with this appointment, although Wolman also had support from the Chair of the Department of Public Law and others. In addition, a junior appointment was found for Joseph Dorfman, Mitchell's student then working on his biography of Veblen. Dorfman completed his study in 1934. The only clearly noninstitutionalist hire was Harold Hotelling, who was hired from Stanford in 1931 to take over Moore's courses in mathematical statistics and mathematical economics.

Thus, the effect of the hiring done by the Department through the years from 1920 to 1932 was to transform its character from one that had a substantial neoclassical element to one in which the institutionalist presence was dominant, and strong neoclassical representation was reduced to a minority consisting of Moore (later Hotelling) and Angell. As might be expected, a number of the Columbia graduates produced at this time became associated with institutionalism or displayed institutionalist ideas. Those who were hired by the University (Bonbright, Brissenden, Hale, and Mills) or by the NBER (Kuznets, Macaulay, and Thorp) have already been mentioned, but there were many others.

An interesting student for whom both Wesley Mitchell and his wife were important mentors, studied with Mitchell and Dewey, and who also attended classes in the Law School, was Lawrence K. Frank. Frank completed a BA at Columbia in 1912, but did not receive a higher degree. He became a business manager at the New School between 1920 and 1922, and then spent several years as assistant to Beardsley Ruml at the Laura Spelman Rockefeller Memorial. In the early 1920s, he wrote a number of articles on economics and law from an institutional point of view. He developed a theory of business cycles (Frank 1923b) that drew very explicitly on Veblen and Mitchell. Business cycles result from the "habits and customs (institutions) of men which make up the money economy, with its money and credit, prices, private property, buying and selling, and so on, all loaded, so to speak, on the industrial process" (Frank 1923b, p. 639).

Frank looked forward to the "emancipation" of economics from speculative theorizing and the development of a properly scientific method based on "studies of the several specific varieties of habitual behavior and their aggregate group occurrence" (Frank 1924, p. 32). Frank also was in favor of "industrial integration," arguing along Veblenian lines (Veblen 1904, p. 46) that the cost savings from integration would be significant, mentioning explicitly the savings from the vast reduction in the quantity of "pecuniary transactions" between independent business units required (Frank 1925, p. 192). Frank also discussed the "ceremonial" aspects of existing institutions and the barriers they created for scientific and technological advance (1925, pp. 184–185).[14] Frank went on to a significant career in human development and is considered the originator of the child development movement in the United States.

Other students of note were Charles Gulick (PhD 1924), who coauthored *Trust and Corporation Problems* with Seager (1929) and moved to Berkeley; George Stocking (PhD 1925), who wrote *The Oil Industry and the Competitive System: A Study in Waste* (Stocking 1925), went on to the University of Texas, and coauthored important works on cartels, monopoly, and antitrust with Myron Watkins (1946; 1948); Horace Taylor (PhD 1928), who wrote *Making Goods and Making Money* (Taylor 1928, a title used by Mitchell in 1922 for a paper to a joint session of the American Society of Mechanical Engineers and the American Economic Association (Mitchell 1923a), and who later took over Tugwell's responsibilities for the undergraduate economics program at Columbia; Robert Brady (PhD 1929), who worked closely with J. M. Clark, wrote on "Industrial Standardization," and went to Berkeley where he maintained a strong institutionalist presence for many years (Dowd 1994); Louis Reed (PhD 1930), who was for a while a member of the institutionalist group at the Washington Square College of New York University in the early 1930s; Leo Rogin, who also went to Berkeley, and John Gambs (PhD 1932), a Carter Goodrich student who became one of the founders of The Association for Evolutionary Economics. Ralph Souter might also be mentioned here. Souter was a lecturer in economics at Columbia between 1930 and 1935. He came to Columbia from New Zealand on a Rockefeller Foundation traveling fellowship and wrote a dissertation entitled "Prolegomena to Relativity Economics" (1933), which, according to Geoffrey Hodgson, attempted a synthesis of a type

---

[14]   Asso and Fiorito (2004b) point out that Frank's view of technology and institutions, which stressed the "ceremonial" character of the latter, anticipated aspects of Ayres's later treatment. They could not find evidence that Frank's work directly influenced Ayres.

of Marshallian evolutionary economics and the best of institutionalism. Souter also argued for the integration of the social sciences and was critical of Talcott Parson's attempts to create an autonomous discipline of sociology. He returned to New Zealand in 1935 and held a Chair at the University of Otago (Hodgson 2001). There were also several prominent labor economists produced, some showing elements of institutionalism in their thinking. Among these might be placed Paul Douglas (PhD 1921), who spearheaded the attempt to have Veblen nominated for the Presidency of the AEA in 1925.

Not everyone was happy about this dominance of the institutionalists. Henry Schultz, a student of Moore, completed his dissertation on "The Statistical Law of Demand" in 1925 and spent an unsatisfactory year working for Harold Moulton at the Institute for Economics before being appointed to Chicago. Some of his later complaints about institutionalism were mentioned in Chapter 5.

THE CONTENT OF INSTITUTIONAL ECONOMICS AT COLUMBIA

An examination of the major publications of the Columbia faculty that have a clear institutionalist orientation reveals a number of areas of concentration: (i) business cycles and unemployment; (ii) public utility economics, particularly as related to issues of valuation and rate making; (iii) issues of monopoly, imperfect competition, and market failures of various kinds; (iv) corporation finance; (v) labor unions; (vi) regulation and planning; and (vii) law and economics. A good part of this literature was discussed in Chapter 2, and material on institutionalist research on business cycles and depressions will be dealt with in more detail in the next two chapters. I will not repeat myself here, but there are some special features that deserve mention. The first of these is the very large amount of quantitative research carried out by Mitchell, Mills, Wolman, and others at Columbia. The second is the amount of work done in valuation, rate making, and regulation, and the very close interrelationship that existed at Columbia between research in economics and law. The third is the more general interdisciplinary interest that was a feature of Columbia social science.

In terms of the quantitative empirical character of so much of Columbia institutionalism, it is important to stress that Columbia and the NBER really was *the* center for this aspect of the institutionalist movement. Even for institutionalists of quantitative orientation outside of Columbia, such as Morris Copeland, the NBER played an important role in providing support for their work. Mitchell and the NBER's quantitative emphasis was also shared by many others in the social sciences at Columbia, particularly William Ogburn. Ogburn was a leader in the area of quantitative sociology and edited the *Journal of the American Statistical Association* (JASA) from 1920 until he left Columbia for Chicago in 1927. He was succeeded in that role by Frank A. Ross, also of the Sociology Department. Throughout the interwar period, *JASA* published extensively in the areas of economic and social statistics, with the work of many of the more quantitatively orientated institutionalists well represented. Ogburn's own work combined his quantitative approach with an interest in the somewhat Veblenian issue of the impact of technological change in creating "maladjustments" within the social organization (Ogburn 1922). He also worked on the measurement of social trends and, after he left Columbia, along with Mitchell was involved with the Committee on Recent Social Trends. Mitchell chaired this committee and Ogburn was director of research from 1930 to 1933. Out of this came *Recent Social Trends in the United States* (1933). This work contained essays by Sophonisba Breckinridge, Edwin Gay, Lawrence Frank, Meredith Givens, Harry Haskell Moore, Robert Lynd, Charles Merriam, William Ogburn, Stuart Rice, and Leo Wolman.

On the interrelations between law and economics, it has already been mentioned that both Tugwell and Clark utilized the legal concept of "affectation with public interest" in their discussion of the possible reach of regulatory authority; indeed, Tugwell's 1922 thesis was almost entirely a discussion of the evolution of this concept through various court cases. In addition, Bonbright was concerned with issues in corporation law, and both Bonbright and Hale were interested in court decisions concerning the valuation of concerns for rate-making purposes, but the contacts between law and economics at Columbia went well beyond that and linked to the realist approach to law, which had considerable importance in the 1920s and 1930s. Realism was represented at Columbia by Robert Hale, Karl Llewellyn, Underhill Moore, Herman Oliphant, and Walter Wheeler Cook.[15] Hale moved from Economics to the Law School, a move in which Underhill Moore and Walter Cook were instrumental. Llewellyn moved from Yale to Columbia in 1924, and at that point he was already very familiar with the work of Hale, Walton Hamilton, and John R. Commons (see Llewellyn 1925). For the legal realists, "real rights" were defined as a prediction of "what the courts will do in a given case, and nothing more pretentious"

---

[15] However, Cook left for Yale, and by 1926 had moved on to Johns Hopkins, where he formed the Institute of Law. Oliphant also left Columbia to join Cook at Johns Hopkins.

(Llewellyn 1930, p. 448). The answers that courts were "called upon to give could not be deduced mechanically from an abstract jurisprudence of rights, but emerged instead from the unexamined and unarticulated cultural and political assumptions of the judges themselves" (Fried 1998, p. 12).

There was also a considerable interest in the role of the law in shaping economic behavior and outcomes, and in issues of regulation and corporate law. For both institutionalists and legal realists, the law was seen as a key instrument of social control. Hale's work developed the Veblenian view of the obsolescence of the traditional legal doctrines of natural liberty and free contract in an age where concentrations of economic and market power were common (Duxbury 1995, p. 108). Hale attacked the notion that government regulation represented "coercion" while markets were noncoercive. He wrote a scathing review of T. N. Carver's *Principles of National Economy* (Hale 1923), pointing out the coercive elements in all market transactions. As Hale put it, when the government protects a property right, it is not only abstaining from interference with the owner when he deals with the thing owned, but also "forcing the non-owner to desist from handling it, unless the owner agrees" (Hale 1923, p. 471). In consequence, Hale opposed the traditional distinction between the private and public domains, and viewed the doctrine of "affectation with public interest" as being no more limiting to regulation than argument based on what best serves the "public welfare" (Fried 1998, p. 106). Hale also developed Veblen's insights on the value of business property in the context of the courts' view that regulation should permit a "fair return" on capital. For Hale, the value of a property as a going concern is based on the expected return, hence the notion of "a fair return on the actual value" simply turns out to be "the earnings that the company is already expecting" (Hale 1921; 1922). Thus, the value of a concern cannot be established independently of its expected revenues, and any regulation of price had, of necessity, to affect the value of the concern.

In 1930, Llewellyn produced his realist manifesto, "A Realistic Jurisprudence – The Next Step" (1930), quickly followed by his study of contract "What Price Contract? – An Essay in Perspective" (1931). Llewellyn' insight here was to ask why the legal machinery of contract was required at all. If promise, performance, and adjustment did not "normally occur without the law's intervention, no regime of future dealings would be possible" (1931, p. 718). In a complex and mobile society, however, legal means of enforcement of promises become necessary, but "a contract is no substitute for performance; rights are a poor substitute for goods," and the contact itself will not fully define the relationship between the parties while it is still ongoing. A legal contract provides a framework for group organizations and relationships between individuals or groups, but a "framework which almost never accurately indicates real working relations, but which affords a rough indication around which such relations may vary, an occasional guide in cases of doubt, and a norm of ultimate appeal when the relations cease in fact to work" (1931, pp. 736–737).[16]

There was also much interest in other areas touching on economics and business law. Underhill Moore had a particular interest in banking law, especially in the way the courts upheld banking practices that seemed to depart from existing legal rules, provided the rules in use were common in the area concerned. Moore was to write "An Institutional Approach to the Law of Commercial Banking" (Moore and Hope 1929). Oliphant's course on Trade Regulation included material on antitrust law as well as trademarks and the common law of unfair competition (Waller 2000). It is also interesting that in 1926, John Dewey wrote a path-breaking paper on the "Historic Background of Corporate Legal Personality" (Dewey 1926) that swept away earlier debates over corporate personality and focused on "whatever specific consequences flow from the right-and-duty bearing units" (Dewey 1926, p. 661). This interest in corporations and corporate law was strengthened further with the arrival of Adolf A. Berle in 1927. Berle, who had been a Lecturer on Finance at Harvard Business School, had received funding from the SSRC for "A Study of the Trends of Recent Corporate Development." The proposed use of a joint law and economics approach to the analysis of the corporation was much approved of (Lee and Samuels 1992, p. xx). Berle required an academic home for this project and approached Columbia Law School, where he was appointed a Lecturer, later Professor, of Law. Berle required someone to assist him on the economic side of the project and recruited Gardiner Means to that position. Means had been a graduate student in economics at Harvard and had taken courses from W. Z. Ripley, who was soon to produce his *Main Street and Wall Street* (1927), and also a course on Valuation from James Bonbright, who commuted to Harvard to lecture. Means was not impressed with the orthodox theory he learned

---

[16] The nature of the realist enterprise and its connection to economics can be seen in outline in a recent collection of realist work (Fisher, Horowitz, and Reed 1993). This collection is divided into several parts including "Law and the Market," which contains work on offer and acceptance and on contract, including Llewellyn's article on contract mentioned earlier; "The critique of the Public/Private Distinction," including Hale's paper on "Coercion and Distribution in a Supposedly Non-Coercive State"; and "Law and Organizational Society," including John Dewey on the "Historic Background of the Corporate Legal Personality," and a selection from Berle and Means's *The Modern Corporation and Private Property.* The inclusion of Berle as a legal realist is, however, not universal (see Bratton 2001).

from Taussig, feeling that it applied only to a preindustrial economy (Lee and Samuels 1992, p. xix). Both Ripley and Berle were familiar with Veblen's critical views on corporate finance.

In 1932, Berle and Means published the results of their collaboration in *The Modern Corporation and Private Property* (1932), a work that pointed to the concentration of decision-making power in very few hands. Means's contribution to this work consisted both of statistical work on the importance of the large corporation and the distribution of stock ownership, and the economic arguments concerning the implications of the separation of ownership from control for traditional theory (Lee and Samuels 1992, p. xxi). Means also collaborated with Bonbright in the production of *The Holding Company* (1932), a project that began as an effort to investigate the use of holding companies in railways but soon expanded to public utilities and holding companies in general (Lee and Samuels 1992, p. xxi). It was out of this work with Berle and Bonbright that Means later developed his concept of administered pricing.[17]

These connections between law and economics also appeared in the form of seminars. Hale cotaught a seminar in Economics, Law, and Politics with Llewellyn, J. M. Clark, and others, and in 1924–1925 and 1926–1927, a seminar on the law of business organization was cotaught by Oliphant and Bonbright with participation from Hale, Underhill Moore, and Llewellyn (Fried 1998, pp. 222–223). In 1927, Bonbright wrote to Leo Sharfman that "several of us are working jointly on a study of the whole field of judicial valuation" (James Bonbright to Leo Sharfman, 18 May 1927, Leo Sharfman Papers, Box 1).

In terms of the more general interdisciplinary interest, Mitchell and Ogburn, along with Charles Merriam from Chicago, were key figures in the founding of the Social Science Research Council (SSRC). The SSRC was funded by the Rockefeller Foundation and had the encouragement of interdisciplinary work and the coordination of the contributions of the various social sciences to the science of human behavior among its most central aims (Fisher 1993). Indeed, "the organization was premised on the assumption that social science is a collective enterprise requiring the intersection

---

[17] Means published a number of articles out of this work with Berle and Bonbright. He was invited by Harvard to combine these articles with an additional section interpreting their significance and submit the resulting manuscript as his doctoral dissertation. He did so but his committee (E. S. Mason, E. H. Chamberlin, and A. E. Munroe) found the theoretical section not well developed. The committee did eventually accept the first part of his dissertation, which contained the more factual material, and in 1933, Means received his degree (see Lee and Samuels 1992, pp. xxii).

of multiple perspectives" (Worcester 2001, pp. 31–32). Merriam, Mitchell, and Ogburn all shared the same commitment to empirical social science, and the key idea that each of the social sciences studied a particular aspect of human behavior, and should be capable of being pulled together into a more complete understanding. The SSRC created committees to oversee and fund research in a vast number of areas including scientific methods in the social sciences, corporate relation, human migration, interracial relations, crime, agriculture, industrial relations, social statistics (COGSIS), consumption and leisure, public administration, social security, the family, unemployment, national planning and social research, and social aspects of the depression (Fisher 1993). More specifically, the SSRC supported work by Kuznets, by Berle and Means, and the Committee on Social Trends. In addition, Seligman was general editor of the *Encyclopaedia of the Social Sciences*, a work that was intended as a general resource for all social scientists. The associated editor was Alvin Johnson, and Max Lerner worked as an assistant editor. The interdisciplinary interests of Columbia social scientists also show up clearly in various collections concerned with social science methods published in the 1920s and early 1930s. Ogburn coedited (with anthropologist A. A. Goldenweiser) a book of essays on the *Social Sciences and Their Interrelations* (1927) that included Dewey on Anthropology and Ethics, Boas on Anthropology and Statistics, J. A. Hobson on Economics and Ethics, Hale on Law and Economics, Seligman on History and Economics, A. B. Wolfe on Sociology and Economics, and Ogburn on Sociology and Statistics. In addition to the Ogburn and Goldenweiser collection, J. M. Clark contributed essays to *Recent Developments in the Social Sciences*, edited by sociologist Edward C. Hayes (1927), and the SSRC-commissioned volume, *Methods in Social Science: A Case Book* (1931), edited by Stuart Rice (a Columbia Sociology PhD of 1924). The latter book contained J. M. Clark's essay on Mitchell's method. A later compilation produced by the Training Division of the Brookings Institution in1931, *Essays on Research in the Social Sciences* (Brookings 1931), also contained essays by W. W. Cook, Charles Beard, J. M. Clark, Karl Llewellyn, and William Ogburn.

INSTITUTIONALISM AT COLUMBIA, 1932–1950

Considering the major work produced by institutionalists through the latter half of the 1930s, including such contributions as Clark's *Strategic Factors in Business Cycles* (1934), A. R. Burns's *The Decline of Competition* (1936), Mills's *Prices in Recession and Recovery* (1936), and Bonbright's *Valuation of Property* (1937), it would seem that institutionalism at Columbia continued in robust good health until at least the end of the 1930s. In fact, things were beginning to change even before that. By 1930, Dewey had retired, Ogburn had left to go to Chicago, and disputes over the leadership of the Law School had reduced the realist presence to Llewellyn and Hale. Also, Tugwell and Means left Columbia to join the New Deal Administration. In the early 1930s, Tugwell was producing some of his most provocative work. In his "The Theory of Occupational Obsolescence" (1931), he related unemployment to rapid technological change, combined with the failure of firms with high overheads to pass on cost savings in the form of lower prices. Instead, firms attempted to maintain prices and build up reserves. His "The Principle of Planning and the Institution of Laissez-Faire" (1932b) went much further, arguing for a radical reconstruction of institutions to permit a planned economy. This was followed up with his book, *The Industrial Discipline and the Governmental Arts*, in 1933. Tugwell, along with Berle and Raymond Moley (a 1918 Columbia PhD), formed the original Roosevelt "Brains Trust," and Tugwell joined the New Deal administration in 1933. Once established in Washington, Tugwell hired Gardiner Means, and both were lost to Columbia.

Tugwell also hired Roy E. Stryker from Columbia. The Tugwell, Munroe, and Stryker textbook, *American Economic Life*, was remarkable for its photographs and other visual material, which were collected by Stryker. Tugwell brought him to head up the Historical Section of the Farm Security Administration, which became renowned for its use of photographic documentation of rural America to arouse public opinion (Hurley 1972). Tugwell was granted three leaves of absence from Columbia, but after that it was made clear that he had to choose, and he resigned in 1937.

Things were also changing at the NBER. The NBER hired Columbia graduate students A. F. Burns and Solomon Fabricant in 1930, Milton Friedman in 1937, and Moses Abramovitz in 1938. A. F. Burns soon became Mitchell's principal collaborator. A. F. Burns was a student of Mitchell and completed his dissertation in 1934. Abramovitz was a J. M. Clark student, his 1939 dissertation dealing with the Clarkian theme of "An Approach to a Price Theory for a Changing Economy." Fabricant also completed in 1939. Friedman had been a student of A. F. Burns at Rutgers, and of Henry Schultz at Chicago. At Columbia, he attended Mitchell's course on Business Cycles but became much more a student of Hotelling. Friedman's work at the NBER was initially concerned with the estimation of the incomes of independent professionals, a project he had taken over from Simon Kuznets. It formed the basis of his 1945 Columbia PhD dissertation. Abramovitz and Fabricant seemed to absorb some of Mitchell's emphasis on institutions and the importance of institutional context, but they did not explicitly associate themselves with institutionalism. Burns, although much more Marshallian, and much more conservative than Mitchell, did share Mitchell's awareness of the limitations of relatively simple theories and the need for careful empirical investigation.

Serious problems, however, were emerging with Mitchell's research program on business cycles. The project became larger and was eventually broken up, with different parts allocated to different researchers, but the final goal seemed always to recede into the future. Reading the Mitchell papers, one can easily sense Mitchell's growing frustration and his increasing desperation to finish the measurement part of the project.

Problems were also emerging with graduate-level instruction, particularly in theory. The requirements for entry into the doctoral degree and for completion of the degree were still very loose. Neoclassical theory was little regarded, the only required theory course being Mitchell's Types of Economic Theory. Over the years, Mitchell had expanded this course to include the Classical period and to incorporate his interest in Wieser. Later, the course also gained a chapter on Gustav Cassel's mathematical approach and a final section dealing with J. R. Commons. This gave the last quarter of the course a highly institutionalist cast, with sections dealing with John A. Hobson, Gustav von Schmoller, Thorstein Veblen, and John R. Commons. Although Mitchell included material discussing Commons's *Institutional Economics* published in 1934, he did not ever include discussion of the developments in neoclassical theory of the early 1930s, or of Keynesian economics. On the other hand, in his course on Business Cycles (according to Milton Friedman, who attended the course in 1933–1934), Mitchell presented the latest research and "displayed enthusiasm and engagement – and hence had a real impact on students" (Friedman and Friedman 1998, p. 45). Hotelling did provide strong courses in mathematical economics and statistics, but relatively few Columbia students possessed the background to manage these courses.

In this context, it is not surprising that students made efforts to obtain more up-to-date and improved instruction in theory. In 1932, a group of students persuaded Mitchell, Clark, and James Angell to start a Seminar on Economic Theory (Ginzberg 1990, p. 16). Mitchell had the students study Marshall as well as Commons on law and economics, but most of the course was spent on topics such as banking, taxation, labor, public utilities, and industrial organization (Lowell Harriss to Malcolm Rutherford, 23 February 2001). A little later, Eli Ginzberg persuaded Mitchell to undertake, with his help, a Seminar on Economic Changes and Economic Theory.

A tentative outline from Ginzberg, dated 1938, suggests the seminar might include a discussion of (1) the problem of value, including Bonbright's *Valuation of Property*, Commons's *Legal Foundations*, and Keynes's *General Theory*; (2) competition and monopoly, including Chamberlin's *Monopolistic Competition* and A. R. Burns's *The Decline of Competition*; (3) the labor market, including Beveridge, Hicks's *Theory of Wages*, and Selig Perlman's *Theory of the Labor Movement*; and (4) the money market, including Hansen, Myrdal, and Keynes's *General Theory*.[18] In the late 1930s, Ginzberg persuaded Roswell McCrea (then both Dean of Business and Chair of Economics) to offer a course in neoclassical economics. Because the Economics Department did not wish to add to its existing offering, the course was offered through extension, and, interestingly, taught by Milton Friedman and Moses Abramovitz (Hammond 2001).

In addition, more skeptical opinions were being expressed concerning Mitchell's views on scientific objectivity and of his quantitative methodology. Eli Ginzberg while still a student of Mitchell and Clark, wrote – but did not publish – a paper critical of Mitchell's concept of scientific objectivity in 1931 (Ginzberg 1997), and Robert Lynd, then in the Sociology Department at Columbia, also criticized Mitchell and the NBER's notions of objectivity in his *Knowledge for What* (1939). Mitchell defended his position in a public discussion arranged by the economics student society (Biddle 1998a; L. S. Mitchell 1953, pp. 553–568). Criticism of Mitchell's idea of quantitative methods supplanting standard theory came once again from Henry Schultz, this time in the form of a lecture entitled "The Quantitative Method With Special Reference to Economic Inquiry," given in 1937 (Schultz 1937). This paper can be seen as an attack on Mitchell's opinion, expressed in his Presidential Address, that utility theory would tend to "drop out of sight in the work of the quantitative analyst." Schultz sent Mitchell a copy, who replied that he thought Schultz had been "a bit rough" on him and responded to the charge that he had "overlooked" various matters (Wesley Mitchell to Henry Schultz, 9 February 1937, Wesley Mitchell Papers, Box 12). In a subsequent letter, Mitchell concluded that they had "different degrees of faith in the explanatory power of "pure theory" as applied to the phenomena presented by experience" (Wesley Mitchell to Henry Schultz, 19 February 1937, Wesley Mitchell Papers, Box 12).

---

[18] Eli Ginzberg to Wesley Mitchell, 20 September 1938, Wesley Mitchell Papers, Box 9. The various snippets of outlines for this seminar contained in Dorfman's edition of Mitchell's *Types of Economic Theory* (Mitchell 1969) indicate that even as late as 1943, the seminar contained material on Veblen and Commons.

Moreover, the whole idea of an identifiable "institutional economics" had begun to come under attack, notably by Paul Homan in a 1932 AEA roundtable and in his entry on "The Institutional School" in the *Encyclopaedia of the Social Sciences* (Homan 1932; 1937). Although Clark responded to Homan and defended a broad view of institutional economics (Clark 1932), the growing variety of "institutionalist" work, perhaps typified by Commons's *Institutional Economics* (1934), left even some who thought of themselves as institutionalist bemused. James Bonbright's reaction to Commons's work on reasonable value was to express his failure to understand the point of view "despite the fact that I would suppose myself to be writing from the standpoint of an institutional economist." Bonbright wondered if the name "institutional economics" had "not become a name for several entirely different points of view" (James Bonbright to Wesley Mitchell, 25 March 1937, Wesley Mitchell Papers, Box 7). This was combined with the impact of the many new developments in theory that occurred throughout the 1930s. As Ginzberg's suggested seminar outline indicates, students were interested in Hicks, Chamberlin, and Keynes, as well as in the institutionalist work of Bonbright, Commons, Perlman, and A. R. Burns.

Whereas it is clear that the large majority of Columbia economists had little use for abstract neoclassical economics, stressing instead the need for empirical work and more "realistic" theorizing, people who attended Columbia in the mid-1930s recollect only occasional explicit references to "institutional economics" in the classroom. Although in the 1920s, both Mitchell and Clark had often referred to the "institutional approach to economics" and had classified each other, as well as several others, as institutionalists, there seems to have been a tendency to become more cautious in promoting the idea of a distinctive institutional approach than had been the case in the 1920s. Certainly, Mitchell never repeated the claims made in his 1924 Presidential Address, and, according to Lowell Harriss, there was "no hint of any Methodenstreit" at Columbia. Rather, Mitchell was "generous and enquiring, not inclined to evaluate neoclassical theory or compare its value (by what standards?) relative to institutionalism" (Lowell Harriss to Malcolm Rutherford, 23 February 2001). Mitchell's shift in attitude can be seen by comparing some of his concluding remarks in his Types of Economic Theory course given in 1918 with those he made in 1935. In his 1918 lectures, Mitchell concludes that:

The fundamental difficulty with these various types of orthodox theory is that they have not realized really what they are doing. They attribute to man a highly logical method of control which as a matter of fact men in modern money using societies have imperfectly learned. The other types of economic theory discussed are superior to the orthodox types in that they have a clearer realization of what the problem of accounting for economic behavior is. They do not make the mistake of imputing to mankind at large complete obedience to the logic of any given institution. They are themselves studies of certain institutions or of certain aspects of institutions in social life. (Mitchell 1967/1969, p. 785)

In 1935, he makes no such references to orthodox "mistakes" or to "superior" types of theory. Instead he argues:

But I do not see how any of us can hold that nothing can be learned from any one of the types of economic theory which we have so far considered. That is, I do not see that we are in a position to say that any of the problems which are emphasized by the writers whom we have dealt with lack significance. To me at least it appears that each and every one of these problems has some relevance for a person who wants to understand economic processes as they go on in the world about us. I should say that as emphatically regarding the highly abstract mathematical theory of general equilibrium as I should say it about Veblen's institutional theory or John Hobson's welfare economics or the neoclassicism of Alfred Marshall. (Mitchell 1949, II, p. 295)

In this atmosphere, it is not surprising that few students after the early 1930s closely identified with the institutionalist label, although Mitchell's breadth and some of the institutionalist attitude rubbed off on many graduates. For example, Eli Ginzberg (PhD 1935) and Moses Abramovitz were both Clark's students. Both thought very highly of Clark and coedited the collection of his papers, *Preface to Social Economics* (Clark 1936), but it seems neither thought of themselves as an institutionalist. The only exception to this seems to have been Joseph Dorfman (PhD 1935).

Nevertheless, even in the 1940s, the Columbia Economics program still retained an institutionalist character. Kenneth Arrow has talked about the Veblenian influence being very apparent at Columbia in the early 1940s, when it was still the case that the only required graduate "theory" course was Mitchell's course on Types of Economic Theory (Arrow 1975). However, in 1944, Wesley Mitchell retired. Clark took over teaching the history of economic thought and A. F. Burns took over Mitchell's course on business cycles. A. F. Burns also succeeded Mitchell as Director of Research at the NBER. The Burns and Mitchell's volume, *Measuring Business Cycles*, appeared finally in 1946. This work displayed what Mitchell had come to call "the NBER method" of using the concepts of specific and reference cycles as a way of approaching the cyclical behavior of many different economic processes. Welding this together into a theory of cycles was to be the next (third) stage of the project (Wesley Mitchell to Ragnar Frisch, 13 November 1936, Wesley Mitchell Papers). The Mitchell and Burns volume was immediately attacked by Tjalling Koopmans of Cowles as "Measurement without Theory" (Koopmans 1947), an attack that came as a jolt to those involved at the NBER (Interview with Anna Schwartz, 13 March 2000; see also Chapter 9 in this book).

The growing importance of mathematical statistics was also being felt within Columbia. Hotelling had found a place for Abraham Wald in 1939, and in 1942, he and Hotelling developed a separate doctoral program in mathematical statistics. At much the same time, the wartime Statistical Research Group, under the Office of Scientific Research and Development, was started at Columbia. The SRG's greatest development was sequential analysis, and the group involved not only Hotelling and Wald, but also Milton Friedman, James Savage, and George Stigler. In 1946, Hotelling left Columbia for the Institute of Statistics at North Carolina, threatening to take Wald with him. In order to retain Wald, a new Department of Mathematical Statistics was established in 1946 (Anderson 1955; Wallis 1980).

In 1945, Columbia hired Abram Bergson and Ragnar Nurkse to provide instruction in international economics. In 1947, Columbia addressed the problem caused by the loss of Hotelling and the Department's evident weaknesses in theory by hiring Albert Hart, George Stigler, and (in a junior position) William Vickrey. The 1946 Appointments Committee consisted of Clark, Goodrich, Mills, A. F. Burns, and Angell, so it cannot be said that institutionalists were not well represented. The Committee recommended Hart for the existing vacancy, Stigler for a new position, and listed Friedman, Vickrey, and H. Greg Lewis as future possibilities. The Committee expressed a preference for people who could combine theory with courses in other fields, as opposed to "theory specialists" (Report of the Committee on Appointment in Economic Theory, 16 November 1946, J. M. Clark Papers). All of the new appointees had applied interests, and Stigler had been working for the NBER since 1943. Although Vickrey was much more theoretical and neoclassical than the older faculty, he was himself a Columbia PhD and had very broad interests, including the regulation of public utilities. He and Bonbright often discussed regulation issues, and Vickrey even used to attend the meetings of the Association for Evolutionary Economics. Stigler, on the other hand, was quite out of sympathy with the institutionalists' anti-market biases and quickly developed a reputation for giving J. M. Clark's students a difficult time. To some extent, this was reciprocated.[19]

---

[19] These remarks are based on an interview with Mark Perlman (1 July 2000) and a conversation with Mark Blaug, confirmed in correspondence (Mark Blaug to Malcolm Rutherford, 12 January 1999).

At the same time, the institutionalist element at Columbia was given a stimulus by the hiring of Karl Polanyi. Polanyi was hired on a visiting basis to cover courses in European economic history left uncovered as a result of the retirement of Simkhovitch in 1944 and Shepard Clough's return to the Department of History in 1947. Carter Goodrich was primarily responsible for bringing Polanyi to Columbia. Polanyi had originally written to Walter Stewart asking about the possibility of visiting a U.S. university to help with his research, and Stewart had recommended Polanyi to Goodrich in a letter indicating that Polanyi's research interest was "to apply the institutional method to the study of the history of political and social thought in England since Hobbes" (Walter Stewart to Carter Goodrich, November 15, 1946, Carter Goodrich Papers, Box 3). Polanyi spoke on "The Controversy of Institutionalism in Economic History" to the Economics Club, and a University Seminar on Polanyi's work continued through to about 1953–1954. Columbia economics faculty who attended Polanyi's seminar included Goodrich, A. R. Burns, and Vickrey. The visiting arrangement with Economics ended in 1953, but Polanyi continued to hold a regular seminar with the group that produced *Trade and Market in the Early Empires* (Polanyi et al. 1957).[20]

Pushing a little beyond the 1947 time frame, Mark Blaug(1999, pp. 257–258) recollects his teachers at Columbia in the early 1950s being "divided between pre-war institutionalists like J. M. Clark, Arthur F. Burns, Joseph Dorfman, and Karl Polanyi, and post-war neoclassical economists like George Stigler, Abraham Bergson, Albert Hart, and William Vickrey." Similarly, Daniel Fusfeld recollects being taught microtheory by Vickery and Stigler, macrotheory by Hart and Angell, economic history by Goodrich and Polanyi, history of thought by Dorfman, statistics by Mills, business cycles by A. F. Burns, and the Soviet economy by Bergson (Daniel Fusfeld to Malcolm Rutherford, 7 October 1999).

At this point, the links between the Law School and Economics seem to have declined in importance; few former students from this period speak of taking courses in Law. Hale retired in 1949 and Llewellyn moved to Chicago in 1951. Other retirements also had effect. J. M. Clark retired in 1953, never having produced the major general statement of his views that he had embarked on in 1946 (J. M. Clark to Carter Goodrich, 13 December

---

[20] One of Polanyi's students who participated in both seminars was Walter Neale. Neale attended Columbia as a graduate student in 1947–1948 and 1950–1951, but then went to the London School of Economics, where he received his PhD in 1953. On his return, he was hired by Yale and rejoined the Polanyi group.

1946, J. M. Clark Papers). In 1953, A. F. Burns left to become chief economic adviser to President Eisenhower, Wolman retired in 1958, Mills in 1959, Bonbright in 1960, A. R. Burns in 1962, and Goodrich left Columbia in 1963, the year after an internal committee (Angell was the Chair, other members were Harold Barger, A. F. Burns, Carl Shoup, and Gary Becker) recommended abandoning European economic history as a field in favor of economic growth and development and econometrics (Report of the Committee on the Future Shape of the Department, 4 April 1962, Carter Goodrich Papers).

Doctoral students of obvious institutionalist persuasion become very hard to find after the early 1950s. Forest Hill was a Goodrich student who graduated in 1950. Hill went to the University of Texas and was the first editor of the *Journal of Economic Issues*. Daniel Fusfeld was J. M. Clark's last student and graduated in 1953 with a dissertation on the roots of the New Deal. One interesting point, however, relates to a somewhat different line of influence. Goodrich's research in the late 1950s and early 1960s dealt with the issue of canals and American economic development. Students who received their doctorates working on this general subject under Goodrich included Harvey Segal (PhD 1956), who became the second editor of the *JEI*, and Julius Rubin (PhD 1959). Goodrich also taught Robert Fogel. Given Fogel's research interests, Goodrich suggested he transfer to Johns Hopkins to work with Kuznets. Rubin was appointed at Columbia but was later denied tenure and moved to Pittsburgh, soon to be followed by Goodrich himself.[21]

CONCLUSION

Paul Homan's discussion of the institutional school in *The Encyclopaedia of the Social Sciences* talks of institutionalism deriving from the work of Veblen, Dewey, and Charles Horton Cooley. He indicates the close relationship between institutional economics and the work of Robert Hale in jurisprudence and William Ogburn in sociology, and his discussion of the major contributors to institutional economics (apart from Veblen) focuses on Mitchell, Clark, Hamilton, Berle and Means, Goodrich, and "the statistical and other writings" of Leo Wolman and others in the field of labor

---

[21] Mark Perlman was also Goodrich's student, graduating in 1950 with a thesis on the arbitration court in Australia. Perlman also worked with Paul Brissenden. Goodrich left Columbia for the University of Pittsburgh in 1963. Perlman was appointed there the same year.

economics. Commons's *Legal Foundations* is also mentioned as a contribution but more briefly (Homan 1937). Homan was highly informed as to the nature of institutional economics. That he identified so much of institutionalism with the Columbia contingent demonstrates clearly how central Columbia was in the institutionalist movement in the 1920s and 1930s.

The overall pattern of the history of institutionalism at Columbia has much in common with the Wisconsin story told in the previous chapter, although there are some differences too. Much of Columbia's institutionalism was developed internally, through the hiring of Columbia's own graduates. Mitchell's arrival at Columbia was a vitally important ingredient, but Mitchell's presence was combined with an array of other elements that were already in place at Columbia to produce the rapid growth of institutionalism in the early 1920s. Mitchell also brought with him a network of professional and personal contacts that helped bring other faculty and students to Columbia. He clearly played a vital role in the hiring in the early 1930s, which brought Goodrich, Wolman, and Dorfman into the Department.

The work of Mitchell, Clark, Tugwell, Bonbright, Hale, together with the work of Berle and Means, A. R. Burns, and the research by Mitchell, Mills, and Wolman at the NBER represent a very major body of creative endeavor over a considerable range of subjects, a broader range than found at Wisconsin. The most outstanding features of Columbia institutionalism were the empirical work on business cycles, price movements, unemployment, trade unions, labor migration; the work relating to public utility rate setting, judicial valuation, and regulation issues more generally; and the work on corporations, corporate finance, and holding companies. The latter two features involved close connections between law and economics, and between the Legal Realist movement and institutionalism, but the interdisciplinary element at Columbia was broader than that. Another difference was that by all reports, Columbia was impersonal and not very collegial in character. Faculty and students did not socialize much. One does not get the feeling of a faculty highly involved with their students, or that creating a band of faithful followers was ever a part of the Columbia ideal. This contrasts with Hamilton and the Brookings Graduate School, and with Commons and his "Friday Nighters."

The first signs of weakening of the institutionalism at Columbia can be traced back to the mid 1930s. By that time, the peak complement of institutionalist faculty were in place, but fewer students were associating themselves with institutionalism. The 1930s also saw Mitchell's research program run into difficulty, the more Marshallian A. F. Burns becoming Mitchell's principle collaborator, and, most revealing of all, saw the students themselves begin to demand more up-to-date instruction in theory. Interesting work was being produced by institutionalists such as Clark, Bonbright, and A. R. Burns through the later 1930s, but there was also Chamberlin and Keynes and the development of theories of imperfect competition and unemployment, as well as new empirical techniques such as econometrics. On top of this, the links between institutionalism and philosophy and law, which had been particularly strong at Columbia, all suffered from the later developments in these disciplines that moved them away from connections with economics. In Yonay's terminology (Yonay 1998), institutionalism at Columbia lost many of its "allies."

As with Wisconsin, we see a serious lack of hiring in the years of the Great Depression to be followed in the immediate postwar period by a renewed spate of hiring, but hiring intended to bring individuals with stronger theoretical credentials into the Department, people of more neoclassical or Keynesian persuasion. In Columbia's case, this was the hiring of Stigler, Hart, and Vickery, a group Forest Hill was to call "the economic analysis battery" (Forest Hill to Clarence Ayres, 31 October 1947, Clarence Ayres Papers).

9

The NBER and the Foundations

The type of empirical research that was a part of the institutionalist program often required significant financial support for data gathering, research assistants, and other costs – costs not involved in "armchair" theorizing. In the period before World War I, there were few sources of such funding because universities themselves did not usually provide significant funding for social science research. As mentioned in Chapter 7, the Pittsburgh Survey was funded by the Russell Sage Foundation, and Commons's early work on the history of trade unionism was funded in part by the Carnegie Institution, but this was quite unusual.

In the period immediately following the end of World War I, there was a massive upsurge of optimism concerning the possibilities and social benefits that could flow from a properly "scientific" approach to the social sciences. A great deal of this optimism came from the experience of wartime planning, including the development of data sources, data analysis, policy appraisal, and the exercise of a degree of economic control. Some of the more overt expressions of this were the founding of The National Bureau of Economic Research (1920), The Institute of Economics (1922), and the Social Science Research Council (1923). All of these organizations were dominated by institutional economists or other social scientists of similar viewpoint. These developments were made possible only by a matching willingness of a number of foundations to fund social science research.[1] By far the largest sources of funding in this period were the Carnegie Corporation (CC), the Laura Spelman Rockefeller Memorial (LSRM), and the Rockefeller Foundation (RF). After World War II, the Ford Foundation took over a great deal of the funding of social science.

---

[1] The earlier, and less successful, experiences of Carnegie and Rockefeller with support of economics are discussed in Grossman (1982) and Fisher (1993).

Those involved, both in the foundations and in the social scientific community, clearly saw and could agree on the pressing need for improved social science research, particularly research aimed at the investigation and solution of the numerous social problems that were besetting America after the war. In this manner, the major foundations and institutional economists could, and did, form an alliance based on the shared values of an investigative science directed towards improved social control. As agued by Donald Fisher:

> What brought the social scientists and the foundations together was the concept of "social control." For sociologists, this concept had become the central theoretical thrust behind their attempts to investigate social problems. ... Institutional economists like Mitchell used the concept as a means of linking together their efforts to improve upon the mechanisms of competition and the marketplace. ... The theoretical and the practical merged as these social scientists and foundation officials ... sought to use social scientific research to solve social problems and thereby increase the degree to which society was socially controlled. (Fisher 1993, p. 58)

What is important to fully realize about this is that in the interwar period, it was institutionalists and institutional research programs that had the best access to external sources of funding. It was their ideals of empirical science and social control that were shared by many at the major foundations.

There was, however, a tension between the ideal of social control and the desire of the foundations to distance themselves from political partisanship. RF's involvement in an earlier (1914) investigation of industrial relations, at a time when companies in which the Rockefeller family were heavily invested were involved in violent strikes, had resulted in the accusation that RF funds were being used to further the family's own business interests (Grossman 1982; Fisher 1993, p. 46). Thus, for those involved with the foundations, an important aspect of the social science research that they were willing to fund was that it appeared to be conducted in an independent manner and be free from any overt taint of bias or political partisanship.[2] One strategy used by the foundations was to fund organizations such as the NBER, Brookings, and the SSRC to provide a "buffer" between themselves and the conduct of the research.

The relationship between the foundations and the agencies they fund is a complex one. Foundation officials have opinions concerning the types of economic research and types of organizations deserving of financial

---

[2] For a discussion of the problem of "advocacy and objectivity" in an earlier phase of American social science, see Furner (1975).

support. These views are not static, but can and do change over time, and foundations alter their views of what they should be funding. In terms of the NBER, it is quite clear that the foundations involved had interests in particular types of economic research and sought to have an effect not only on the exact role of the NBER in the conduct of economic research, but its overall direction, its organization, and, at times, its leadership. Thus, the foundations were "far from being inactive distributors of funds" (Craver 1986, p. 206).

This is not to suggest a simple one-way line of causation from foundations to the nature of economic research, but a fairly complex interaction between academic researchers, those involved in the foundations as staff or as trustees, and the more general "climate of opinion" within which both groups operate (Turner 1999). The boards of trustees of foundations normally include many individuals with business or other nonacademic backgrounds, with relatively little knowledge of particular disciplines, and often with a bias toward the practical; but boards can also contain influential individuals with strong views of the importance of particular lines of research. The views of the trustees may or may not coincide with the existing priorities of those involved in the discipline or disciplines involved. On the other hand, the foundation officers or staff members who make recommendations to the trustees are often individuals with links (and sometimes very close links) to the academic disciplines in their areas of responsibility. In the period under discussion here, it was quite common for individuals to move between senior academic positions and key staff positions with the foundations. Such people, of course, arrive with their own views of funding priorities, and also solicit opinion from (selected) others within the discipline involved. As argued by Richardson and Fisher (1999), foundation officers often have very considerable amounts of discretion over who or what to recommend for funding, and although they are not unconstrained by the overall viewpoint of their boards, they do have input into the formation of that viewpoint. Indeed, the process of establishing priorities is one involving a continuing negotiation between trustees, staff, and key academic researchers on the outside. This process can easily result in unresolved disagreements and tensions, but it can also give rise to a "consensus" view (explicit or tacit), which can result in a degree of "disciplinary hegemony" being negotiated and maintained (Kay 1997). Even when formed, however, such a consensus is subject to disturbances both small and large, leading to periods of disagreement and conflict until the relationship breaks down completely or a new consensus is established.

CARNEGIE, ROCKEFELLER, AND ECONOMIC RESEARCH

In the immediate post–World War I period, the Carnegie Corporation was a leader in the funding of social science research. In 1920, James R. Angell[3] became President of the Carnegie Corporation and brought with him an attitude very much in line with those of younger empirical social scientists such as Wesley Mitchell. Carnegie was to play an important role in the original funding of the Institute of Economics and the NBER, but the Carnegie trustees included some members of conservative views, who were critical of some of the projects funded, and Carnegie's role was to be eclipsed first by the LSRM and then by the RF.

The most remarkable development in funding for the social sciences came from the program developed by Beardsley Ruml and his staff at the Laura Spelman Rockefeller Memorial Foundation (Bulmer and Bulmer 1981). Ruml had worked as an assistant to James R. Angell at Carnegie, but after Angell left Carnegie, Ruml moved to become Director of the LSRM in 1922, while still only in his late twenties. Shortly afterward, Ruml set out his views in a "General Memorandum" that emphasized the importance of the development of the social sciences, particularly the "production of a body of substantiated and widely accepted generalizations as to human capacities and motives and as to the behavior of human beings as individuals and groups." The underlying purpose was the generation of social scientific knowledge that could be used for social improvement. Ruml argued that "all who work toward the general end of social welfare are embarrassed by the lack of that knowledge which the social sciences must provide," the situation being as if "physicians were practising in the absence of the medical sciences" (Beardsley Ruml, General Memorandum by the Director, October 1922, RAC-LSRM, Series 2, Box 2, Folder 31, pp. 9–10).

In 1923, Ruml commissioned Lawrence K. Frank to carry out a review of social science research in universities and independent research organizations. As mentioned in the previous chapter, Frank was an economist of institutionalist persuasion who had trained at Columbia. He was then working as the business manager at the New School for Social Research.[4]

---

[3]   James R. Angell had been a psychologist at the University of Chicago, Acting President of the University of Chicago, and Chairman of the National Research Council. Beardlsy Ruml was a protege of his. Angell's stay at Carnegie only lasted a year, after which he became President of Yale. Carnegie also supplied the initial grant that established the Institute of Economics. James W. Angell of Columbia was the son of James R. Angell.

[4]   For a brief discussion of Frank's work on business cycles, see Chapter 8.

Frank's report deplored the lack of funding for properly scientific social science research, by which he meant work that was "investigational" or "experimental" – terminology that reflected the influence of John Dewey. These scientific methods he contrasted with those of speculative theorizing and library-based research, the dominance of which had resulted in both the "inertia" of the social sciences and its failure to separate itself from political partisanship (Frank 1923a, pp. 20–21). Frank identified five universities with the most active PhD programs in the social sciences (Columbia, Chicago, Harvard, Wisconsin, and Pennsylvania), and among independent research agencies he made the most favorable mention of the Institute of Economics and the National Bureau, commenting particularly on the Bureau's organization designed "to ensure impartiality of findings and to reassure readers of reports that no bias has entered into findings" (Frank 1923a, p. 13). After completing his report, Frank joined the staff of the Memorial.

Among the trustees, and particularly Raymond Fosdick, the concern was with "practical social control" (Fisher 1993, p. 65), but both Ruml and Frank came from social science backgrounds and both were concerned with advancing more "basic" research that might contribute to the solution of social problems over the longer term. Despite these differences, the LSRM did focus on "advancing knowledge" rather than immediate social amelioration, and there was a clear demarcation between the types of social science that were funded by the LSRM and those that were not. The LSRM supported a conception of social science requiring "not the reading of books and abstract thought" but "realistic" and methodical empirical and quantitative research (Bulmer and Bulmer 1981, pp. 347–348), and there can be no doubt that Ruml and the LSRM succeeded in generating "a vast expansion of quantitative empirical economic analysis" (Turner 1999, p. 220).

There was a clear, and quite explicit, consensus of viewpoint between Ruml and Frank at the LSRM and economists such as Gay, Mitchell, and others of similar mind, who worked through the NBER and other organizations to promote a particular concept of "scientific" economics – one that was associated with empirical and quantitative work directed to improved social control.

From 1923 until the end of the LSRM's separate existence in 1928, the Memorial provided almost $21 million of financial support for social science research, with the largest recipients being the University of Chicago, the Brookings Graduate School (for research undertaken in the Institute for Government Research), the Social Science Research Council, Columbia

University, The London School of Economics, Harvard University, and the NBER (Bulmer and Bulmer 1981, p. 368).[5]

In 1929, the LSRM was consolidated into the Rockefeller Foundation. Ruml became Director of the Spelman Fund that concentrated on public administration,[6] and economist Edmund E. Day became Director of the new Social Science Division of the Rockefeller Foundation. Ruml opposed the merger but did manage to secure the place of social science funding within the new RF. The focus of the Social Science Division of the RF remained, as he wished, on the "advancement of knowledge" and not on the charity and welfare work that had dominated before.

Day had been a Professor of Economics at Harvard and later the Chair of Economics and the Dean of Business at Michigan. On being appointed as Chair of the Economics Department at Michigan in 1923, Day wrote to Mitchell concerning possible appointees. He wrote that "Men like Wolman and [Walter] Stewart are the sort I have in mind" (Edmund Day to Wesley Mitchell, 17 May 1923, Wesley Mitchell Papers, Box 8, Edmund Day Folder), so there is no doubt of Day's sympathy with the more quantitative style of institutional economics. Day was hired to the Memorial by Ruml in 1927. Later, in 1932, Day hired Stacy May as Assistant Director of the Division of Social Sciences of the Rockefeller Foundation, in which capacity he served until 1942.[7] Day fully shared Ruml's views on the importance of strengthening the empirical aspect of social sciences, and with the advent of the Great Depression became particularly concerned with funding research on the problem of economic stabilization. In Day's view:

The costs imposed by serious business depression – of demoralization, broken health, disorganized families, neglected children, lowered living standards, permanent insecurity, impaired morale, as well as financial distress – are so appalling when viewed socially as well as individually that no problem of this generation calls more clearly for solution than this of economic stabilization. ... The need for more adequate data, for sustained analysis, for more constructive experiment is all too obvious to require elaboration. (Quoted in Craver 1986, pp. 211–212)

---

[5]   For the history of the LRSM and RF involvement with the SSRC, see Fisher (1993). For Rockefeller support of the LSE, see Rutherford (2007).

[6]   Bulmer and Bulmer (1981) discuss the reorganization and Ruml's role in more detail. Ruml became Dean of Social Science at the University of Chicago between 1931 and 1934, had involvement with the New Deal, and later became treasurer for Macy's department stores. He maintained contacts with the foundations and with the academic world, and served on the Board of Directors of the NBER.

[7]   May had been a student of Walton Hamilton at both Amherst College and at the Robert Brookings Graduate School (see Chapter 6).

The RF under Day became the major source of funding for the NBER. Nevertheless, Day was not without his criticisms of the Bureau, and – as will be seen – he did push for changes in the operation of the NBER.

In 1936, Raymond Fosdick became President of the Rockefeller Foundation. Fosdick had been involved in the hiring of Ruml, but he had since developed a critical view of the Division of Social Science, particularly in its European operations, and had become increasingly skeptical of the results of funding research in the social sciences. Day resigned in 1937 to take the presidency of Cornell University. Craver argues that these and other related events show the social sciences losing favor within the Rockefeller Foundation (Craver 1986, p. 221). This may well be correct, but the NBER managed to maintain a privileged position, thanks largely to the appointment of Joseph Willits to the Directorship of the Division of Social Science in 1939.

Willits was a 1916 PhD from the University of Pennsylvania and had written his dissertation on unemployment in Philadelphia. He became a faculty member at the Wharton Business School, and in 1921, he and Anne Bezanson founded the Industrial Research Department at Wharton, which focused on problems in industrial relations. Both Willits and Bezanson fully accepted the empirical view of scientific investigation and the ideal of pragmatic social reform (De Rouvray 2004). Not surprisingly, Willits had many contacts with people such as Mitchell, Walter Stewart, and Leo Wolman. Willits had close contacts with the NBER. He became a member of the Board, serving as Chairman of the NBER Board of Directors in 1933, and a few years later taking on the job as Executive Director of the NBER until 1939. Willits went straight from that job to the Rockefeller Foundation.[8]

Willits's view of economic research was very similar to that held by Ruml and Day, except that he was an even more unabashed admirer of the NBER than his predecessor. Despite Fosdick's skepticism, Willits was able to create a stable and long-lasting relationship between the RF and the Bureau. This success is all the more surprising considering that when, in 1943, Willits attempted to have the RF undertake a major new commitment in the social sciences (Craver 1986, p. 222, n. 58), Fosdick questioned what advances in knowledge in the social sciences had been made:

Institutions? Yes, i.e., Brookings, the SSRC, The National Bureau etc. Statistics? Yes. But what have *these* accomplished? For example, do we know more about economic

---

[8]   For background on Willits's career at Wharton and his role in developing the School and its research activity, see Sass (1982, pp. 201–231). For his involvement with the SSRC and the RF, see Fisher (1993). Willits was later instrumental in bringing Kuznets to Wharton, while allowing him to continue his work with the Bureau.

laws than we did twenty years ago? Can we point to specific advances in knowledge? Has there really been a "deepening of understanding of social processes and problems?" (Raymond Fosdick, Diary entry 12 November 1943, RAC-RF, quoted by Craver 1986, p. 222)

Of course, Fosdick was not the only important and influential member of the board, and between 1940 and 1950, Walter W. Stewart was Chairman of the Rockefeller Board of Trustees. Stewart had also had close involvement with the NBER, serving on the Board and advising on projects to do with monetary economics. Stewart became close with Arthur F. Burns, and Joseph Willits was described by Burns as being a "dear friend" of Walter Stewart's (Arthur Burns to Helen Stewart, 31 March 1958, Arthur Burns Papers, Box 35, Walter Stewart Folder). There were, therefore, a number of significant personnel at Rockefeller with long-standing and close connections to the National Bureau.

As will be seen from the further discussion, Willits was an unfailing champion for the NBER, its methods, and its research programs. Willits's views remained unaffected by the criticism of the NBER launched by Koopmans of Cowles in his "Measurement without Theory" paper in 1947. In 1951, Willits wrote to Henry Clay in England that he was increasingly separating economists into two groups:

The first I very profoundly respect. It is composed of men who know economics theoretically, empirically, and through experience, and who know a lot besides economics.... The second group is very sharply separated from the first; with respect to them my arrogance of opinion runs free. This group includes various categories of today's conventional economists. It is usually composed of men who are not close to what really happens or why it happens but engage in a most adroit game of formal logic or higher mathematics. I cannot develop enthusiasm about these, yet they are in the great majority. I have brought myself to recommend grants for them because I do not feel that RF grants should be limited to my narrow prejudices, but I must confess that I find it harder and harder to do so. (Joseph Willits to Sir Henry Clay, 18 May 1951, Henry Clay Papers, Box 72, File 1951–53)

What is interesting about this comment is Willits's awareness that the "great majority" of the profession had by that time moved toward the use of more formal techniques, and that despite this awareness, he maintained his own, more empirical view of appropriate approaches in the social sciences, and RF support for the Bureau, to the virtual (but not quite complete) exclusion of what had already become more "conventional." As might be expected, this close consensus of views between the Division of Social Science at the RF and the Bureau did not survive long after Willits's retirement from Rockefeller in 1954.

THE NBER, 1920–1930

The idea for an independent research bureau in economics sprang from discussions between Malcolm Rorty and N. I. Stone in 1916. Rorty was a statistician with AT&T, Stone an economist working as an arbitrator and economic advisor. Their policy views clashed, but they could agree on the need for more reliable information. They involved Wesley Mitchell, Edwin Gay, and John R. Commons (then President of the American Economic Association). World War I interrupted progress, but the experience of the war made the lack of quantitative information concerning the economy even more apparent, and by the AEA meeting of December 1919, all the necessary elements were in place.

The National Bureau of Economic Research was founded early in 1920, with Wesley Mitchell as Director of Research and Edwin Gay as President. The central vision of the Bureau was one of an independent organization with a primary focus on basic research. This focus on basic research was not, however, one of research for its own sake, but one that was founded on the view that an increase in basic knowledge concerning the economy and its functioning was a prerequisite to improved economic policy and social control. The manner in which the NBER was organized, with its commitment to empirical investigation, its large board of directors drawn from many different universities, scientific associations, and business and labor organizations, and its system of manuscript review designed to remove any possibility of bias, was explicitly designed to assure confidence in the scientific objectivity of its work.

The NBER was established with an initial research agenda focused on the estimation of the size and distribution of the national income, and a small research staff consisting of Mitchell, Willford I. King, Frederick Macaulay, and Oswald Knauth. The initial financial support came from a grant from the Commonwealth Fund, but they then shifted their attention to other projects, and the Bureau approached the Carnegie Corporation in considerable need. Carnegie reacted quickly and favorably to the Bureau's request for funding, and late in 1920, Carnegie granted the NBER $45,000 over three years (with $20,000 of that to be matched by funds raised from elsewhere), a grant that was vital to the initial success of the Bureau (Lagemann 1989, pp. 60–65).[9] In 1921 and 1922, the NBER published its first national income estimates: *Income in the United States: Its Amount and Distribution* (Mitchell et al. 1921; 1922)

---

[9] In 1921, the total income of the Bureau was more than $43,000, compared with just $24,000 in 1920.

In 1922, Mitchell launched his project to update and improve his previous work on business cycles through the NBER, and this required additional support. Mitchell applied to the LSRM, and the first grant from the LSRM to the NBER was made in 1923 for an amount of $12,500 per year (this grant also required substantial support from elsewhere). In that year, the Bureau's total income from all sources was slightly more than $60,000.[10] The Bureau also received funding from Carnegie and through the President's Conference on Unemployment. A special NBER staff was assembled to produce *Business Cycles and Unemployment* in 1923 (Mitchell 1923b). This included chapters by Mitchell, Willford King, Frederick Macaulay, Oswald Knauth, N. I. Stone, Paul Brissenden, Leo Wolman, John B. Andrews, and Stuart Rice, among others. The topics included business cycles, cycles in particular industries, the measurement of unemployment, unemployment insurance, employment agencies, underemployment, the costs of unemployment, and various methods of stabilization of production and employment.

Support from the LSRM continued and became somewhat larger, but the Bureau itself grew substantially over the 1920s. By the late 1920s, the senior research staff had expanded to include not only Mitchell, King, and Macaulay but also Harry Jerome ("borrowed" from Wisconsin), W. F. Willcox, Willard Thorpe, Leo Wolman, F. C. Mills, and Simon Kuznets (see Table 9.1). In 1924, Edwin Gay was appointed co-Director of Research, largely to relieve Mitchell of his administrative responsibilities (Fabricant 1984). The bureau's research expanded equivalently to include Wolman's work on trade union membership, a substantial project on the topic of labor migration (undertaken by Harry Jerome and at the request of the National Research Council), F. C. Mills's extensive series of price studies, as well as further work on national income and business cycles. In 1926, the five major projects of the Bureau were stated as business cycles, bond yields and interest rates, the labor market, problems of migration, and the structure and working of the system of prices (NBER *Bulletin*, May 1926).

In 1926, Thorp and Mitchell produced their important work, *Business Annals* (Thorp and Mitchell 1926), and a year later Mitchell produced the first of his projected volumes on business cycles, *Business Cycles: The Problem and its Setting*. This book provided a review of theories of the business cycle,

[10] Figures for the Bureau's total income come from a letter from William J. Carson, Executive Director of the National Bureau to Joseph Willits, then Director of the Social Science Division of the Rockefeller Foundation (16 October 1950, RAC-RF, RG 1.1, Series 200 S, Box 370, Folder 4376).

Table 9.1. *Selected NBER staff members, 1920–1948 (Date of Appointment)*

Wesley Mitchell (1920)	Arthur Burns (1930)
Frederick Macaulay(1920)	Solomon Fabricant (1930)
Willford King (1920)	Milton Friedman (1937)
Oswald Knauth (1920)	Moses Abramovitz (1938)
Willard Thorp (1923)	Ralph Young (1938)
Leo Wolman (1923)	Allen Wallis (1939)
Edwin Gay (1924)	Geoffrey Moore (1939)
Harry Jerome (1924)	George Stigler (1943)
Walter Willcox (1925)	Morris Copeland (1945)
Frederick Mills (1925)	Rutledge Vining (1948)
Simon Kuznets (1927)	

Sources: Arthur Burns Papers, Box 124; NBER *Bulletins*

a discussion of business cycles in relation to business decision making, the system of prices, the monetary mechanism, and a survey of data sources, both from statistics and business annals. The book concluded with a working concept of business cycles and a plan of work toward a second volume, tentatively titled *The Rhythm of Business Activity*:

> The concept of business cycles developed in this volume suggests that the leading question of the second volume be put in the form "How do business cycles run their course?" rather than in the form "What causes business cycles?" What we are seeking to understand is a complex of recurrent fluctuations in numerous interrelated processes. To learn what we can about the workings of these processes in their relations to one another and as a whole is the next step. When we have taken that step, it will be time to see what the question about the cause of business cycles means, and in what sense it can be answered. (Mitchell 1927, p. 470)

The first of Mills's studies of prices, *The Behavior of Prices*, also appeared in 1927. At this point, the various parts of the business cycle project all seemed to be progressing well.

The last grant awarded by the LSRM directly to the Bureau was in 1928 for $25,000 a year for five years, but in that year, the Memorial's $25,000 contribution amounted to only 15 percent of the Bureau's total income of $167,000. Other sources of Bureau income included Carnegie, the Falk Foundation, the American Statistical Association, a very large number of subscriptions from business and labor organizations, as well as government and private agencies, and book sales. The bureau also continued its association with the President's Conference on Unemployment by contributing the research for *Recent Economic Changes in the United States* (1929). The research staff included Gay, Mitchell, Wolman, Mills, and Thorp, as well as Morris Copeland, Edwin Nourse, and Henry Dennison. The Bureau's involvement was to provide the background scientific research and not to directly draw policy conclusions, but the project was explicitly designed to provide a properly scientific basis for policy discussion and improved social control. That this involvement was consistent with the policies then held by the foundations is indicated by the fact that the project was supported by both Carnegie and the LSRM (although not all Carnegie trustees were supportive).

Early in 1929, Edwin Gay applied to the RF for a $750,000 grant to extend over five years. The major items in this ambitious request were for enlarged space, research fellowships and scholarships, the establishment and maintenance of "a laboratory of quantitative economic research," including special laboratory and library facilities, and for two specific projects on the price level and price structure (Edwin Gay to Edmund Day, 16 January 1929, RAC–RF, RG 1.1, Series 200 S, Box 367, Folder 4351). If awarded, this would have provided $150,000 a year when in 1928, the entire income of the Bureau had been $167,000. In fact, the Bureau was awarded half that much, $375,000 over five years beginning July 1, 1929, and with the stipulation that all payments would have to be matched dollar for dollar with funds secured from other sources. Nevertheless, this grant resulted in a huge boost to the Bureau's fortunes, with the total Rockefeller contribution in 1929 jumping to $63,000 out of a total income of almost $169,000, or 37 percent. In 1930, the Bureau also received funding from Carnegie for its program of research fellowships. The level of total income attained at this point would not be consistently surpassed until after 1937.

In other developments, Kuznets took over the work on national income from King in 1931,[11] and from 1933 he was "loaned" to the Department of Commerce to work on the construction of official national income estimates. The initial result of Kuznets's efforts was his report *National Income, 1929–32*, published in 1934.

---

[11] Kuznets replaced Willford King on the national income work of the Bureau. Both Mitchell and Gay had become increasingly concerned about the quality of King's estimates and decided to eliminate him from the Bureau "as soon as it could be decently done." King was ill for a year, which delayed matters. Kuznets was given the job of undertaking a preliminary investigation at the beginning of 1932, with the idea that on Mitchell's return from England, he would take over the general supervision of the work, with Kuznets under

CRISIS AND RECOVERY, 1930–1939

The history of the NBER, Carnegie, and the LSRM from 1920 through to the early 1930s is one in which a close consensus on the type of economic research worthy of funding and on the nature and role of the Bureau in generating this type of research seemed to have been established. This consensus was, however, to be disturbed both by the onset of the Great Depression and by changes of viewpoint within the foundations.

The Great Depression was not anticipated by Mitchell or in any of the Bureau publications. The fact that the economy was in a depression began to be discussed in Bureau *Bulletins* from November 1930, primarily in reports on price and output trends by F. C. Mills, and then by discussions of wages and employment in the depression by Leo Wolman and Meredith Givens. Also in 1930, Leo Wolman took time away from his other Bureau work to complete a study on the *Planning and Control of Public Works* (Wolman 1930), undertaken as an emergency study at the request of the federal government. The work of the Committee on Recent Economic Changes was continued in order to chart the course depression and to relate its onset back to the previous period of prosperity (NBER *Annual Report* 1930). The Bureau also arranged for J. M. Clark to take an independent look at the work on business cycles, work published by the NBER in 1934 as *Strategic Factors in Business Cycles* (Clark 1934; see Chapter 10 in this book).

The Great Depression also had a severely adverse effect on the Bureau's finances and on the financial position of the foundations themselves. Bureau subscriptions from businesses and other organizations fell off sharply, and this had an additional impact in creating difficulties in finding money with which to match foundation grants.[12] The amounts actually collected from Rockefeller fell well below the maximums allowed, and in 1931, only $49,000 out of the possible $75,000 was given by Rockefeller to the Bureau. This resulted in a series of meetings and memos detailing the Bureau's financial plight. In 1931, the Bureau attempted to obtain approval to use $50,000 of a $100,000 grant from the President's Committee on Recent Economic Changes for matching purposes, but

him (Edwin Gay to Edmund Day, 18 March 1932, RAC-RF, RG 1.1, Series 200 S, Box 368, Folder 4353).

[12] Many of the details that follow concerning the Bureau and the Rockefeller Foundation in the 1930s are taken from "National Bureau of Economic Research–History from 1919 to1937" (RAC-RF, RG 1.1, Series 200 S. Box 368, Folder 4359).

was denied on the grounds that special-purpose funds could not be used for matching.[13] The Bureau applied to the Falk Foundation for $150,000 over three years, but was refused. The picture going into 1932 looked grim, with estimated expenses of $144,000 and income in sight of $85,000. Intensive discussions ensued as the Bureau attempted to persuade Rockefeller to waive the matching requirement. Gay indicated to Day that if Rockefeller declined, the Bureau could maintain only a skeleton organization. The NBER staff was cut, salaries reduced, and the research associates program suspended in order to bring 1932 expenditures down by some $30,000.

At the same time, the Bureau was experiencing difficulties with Carnegie and did not expect a renewal of its Carnegie grant. These difficulties stemmed from Carnegie director Russell Leffingwell who had strongly opposed Carnegie involvement with the Committee on Recent Economic Changes. He felt that the project was too political and that the "National Bureau had disgraced itself and the Carnegie Corporation by its work on Recent Economic Changes" (quoted by Biddle 1998b, p. 64). In desperation, Oswald Knauth, then Chairman of the NBER Board, suggested to Leffingwell that if Carnegie supplied some emergency funding, the Bureau would use the funds to complete outstanding projects and then cease operating (Alchon 1985, pp. 162–163).[14]

Carnegie did give an emergency grant of $15,000 to the Bureau for 1932, along with an indication that they would not contribute further, and shortly thereafter Rockefeller agreed to waive the matching requirement on $35,000 in 1932 and $50,000 in 1933. This allowed the Bureau's income to stabilize at $106,000 in 1933, of which some $70,000, or 66 percent, was supplied by Rockefeller. This resolved the immediate crisis, but there were clearly some fundamental issues that needed to be addressed. Mitchell (who had been in England during the time of financial crisis) reaffirmed the Bureau's

---

[13] Although the Committee had produced its report in 1929, it continued in existence and awarded grants to the NBER for the purpose of producing a statistical profile of the depression.

[14] Alchon questions whether Mitchell or Gay knew about this letter, but it seems unlikely that they would not know. It should be noted that although Gay was instrumental in involving the Bureau with the Recent Economic Changes project, he was also unhappy with the way the work had turned out (Heaton 1952, p.202). Leffingwell had also strongly opposed the renewal of Carnegie funding to the Institute of Economics. Robert Brookings wrote to Harold Moulton in 1926 that Leffingwell thought that Carnegie should never have funded the Institute because "it was lending its name to a group of writers who could easily do more harm than good" (Robert Brookings to Harold Moulton, 1 June 1926, Brookings Institution Archives, Item 30, Box 1, Brookings, Robert [1925–1926] Folder).

commitment to basic research and stressed his intent to avoid work dealing with politically charged policy problems (Biddle 1998b, pp. 64–65). He was able to reassure Carnegie sufficiently that in March of 1933 they awarded the Bureau $5,000 a year for five years (although the Bureau had asked for $50,000 a year). Carnegie remained a consistent contributor to the Bureau's funding, notably to the Bureau's associates program, but at levels well below Rockefeller's.

Edmund Day was also facing a changing situation at Rockefeller. The Great Depression resulted in a period of financial retrenchment, but there were also changes in policy taking place, changes that moved in the opposite direction to Carnegie, toward a focus on more concrete policy application related to the current emergency. Late in 1933, the RF established a Committee on Appraisal and Plan, with Raymond Fosdick as Chair. This committee was of the view that the scientific attitude had been successfully established in the social sciences and recommended a movement away from the more general promotion of scientific research to specific research areas and particularly those with policy importance. Day strongly opposed these directions, but the Committee recommendation was accepted, and from 1935, the RF focused on economic security, international relations, and public administration (Fosdick 1952; Fisher 1993, p. 134). The Bureau's research on business cycles could, of course, be fitted into the category of economic security, but the NBER commitment to basic research and its increasing dependence of RF funding became problems for Day. Mitchell was driven to stress repeatedly the link between the Bureau's "basic" research and improved policy.

Shortly before these developments, in February 1933, Mitchell applied for a renewal of Rockefeller funding of $75,000 a year for five years, with $50,000 a year being unconditional. The proposed research was (1) the revision of national income estimates to be undertaken by Simon Kuznets; (2) the completion of Mitchell's business cycle project; (3) an analysis of biennial censuses of manufactures by F. C. Mills; (4) the study of price and price relationships by Mills; (5) a study of the labor market by Leo Wolman; (6) and a study (unassigned) of national savings and investment of capital. The proposal noted some reorganization of the Bureau (Gay had retired as co-Director of Research in 1932), the reduction in overhead costs, the reductions in salaries, and the reduction in the rate of loss of subscriptions. Day's renewal proposal, approved in June, granted the Bureau $225,000 over *three* years, with $50,000 per year unconditional and up to $25,000 per year on a matching basis. The final paragraph of the docket read:

In view of the invaluable work which the Bureau has already done, and in view of its importance as an organization for research in the specific field of economic stabilization, it is recommended that the Foundation continue the present level of support for a period of three years. Before the expiration of the grant a search-ing review will be made to determine whether the results of the Bureau's research justify the continuance of liberal Foundation support, even if substantial contri-butions are not forthcoming from other sources. (National Bureau of Economic Research, History from 1929 to 1937, RAC-RF, RG 1.1, Series 200 S, Box 368, Folder 4359, p. 5)

Over the next few years, Day made his concerns about the Bureau very clear. First, in the view of Day and others of his staff, such as John Van Sickle, the NBER was not a *National* Bureau at all, but basically an adjunct of Columbia University (Mitchell, Mills, and Wolman all being Columbia faculty). Second, the Bureau's research direction was being dictated by the research interests of this permanent staff, rather than what might be regarded as more pressing research topics. The basic rather than applied nature of the Bureau's research was seen as limiting the Bureau's appeal and ability to raise funds from a suitably wide variety of sources. In 1934, for example, the Bureau received $71,000 from Rockefeller, only $10,000 from subscriptions, and only $11,000 in total from Carnegie, Falk, and the Twentieth Century fund. Third, the Bureau was expensive because it paid salaries to research staff members even when they held regular fac-ulty positions. The contrast was made with the Harvard Committee on Economic Research, which did not compensate professors for their research (Edmund Day to Oswald Knauth, 18 October 1935, and JVS [John Van Sickle] Interview with Joseph Willits, 7 December 1935, RAC-RF, RG 1.1, Series 200 S, Box 368, Folder 4356). Day's view was that the Bureau should act more as a national center for economic research in specific areas of economics, coordinating and promoting research conducted primarily by university-based researchers. This was in contrast with the Bureau's own conception of itself as consisting of a battery of "high powered researchers" pursuing their own research agendas, but Day was firm that things had to change in order to avoid, in his nicely turned phrase, "what are likely to prove embarrassments in the Foundation's relationship to the Bureau's fur-ther funding" (Edmund Day to Oswald Knauth, 18 October 1935, RAC-RF, RG 1.1, Series 200 S, Box 368, Folder 4356, p. 3). Day was also concerned that the process of changing the nature of the Bureau would require a com-mitted Executive Director who could devote himself to the task of broad-ening the Bureau's appeal and raising funds. He and Knauth discussed the matter, but Knauth's interests lay in his own research (Oswald Knauth to

Wesley Mitchell and Joseph Willits, 16 October 1935, RAC-RF, RG 1.1, Series 200 S, Box 368, Folder 4356).

The upshot of these differing views on the purpose and design of the NBER was not the elimination of its own research staff or research programs, but a compromise solution involving the creation of the Universities-National Bureau Committee. This Committee was established in 1935 and consisted of two members from the NBER and two members from each of six universities (Yale, Harvard, Pennsylvania, Chicago, Wisconsin, and Columbia). The Committee was charged with examining major problems of research interest, undertaking cooperative projects, and with recommending "that form of continuing organization which study and experience have suggested" by the end of 1937. Out of this Committee came the Conference on Income and Wealth, and the Conference on Prices.[15] Each of these conferences was chaired by a Bureau researcher (Kuznets and Mills), and their function was to work out and implement plans for the systematic cultivation of their research areas. The Universities-National Bureau Committee reported in November of 1937, indicating considerable success and eagerness on the research side and suggesting an organization that would retain the Bureau connection. The Bureau would handle funds for the Conferences and provide sponsorship, facilities, and publication media. Thus the functions of the Bureau were to be divided into two parts: the stimulation of research and the conducting of research. The Universities-National Bureau Committee would also continue but with broader university representation (JVS [John Van Sickle] "National Bureau of Economic Research, 1 July 1936–31 December 1939," RAC-RF, RG 1.1, Series 200 S, Box 368, Folder 4359).

Movement along these lines resulted in the renewal of the Bureau's funding in 1936 for the three years, 1937–1939, at previous levels and with additional funding to provide for the expenses of an office of Executive Director. Joseph H. Willits took on this position on a part-time basis in 1936, and a little later gained assistance from William J. Carson. Willits devoted a very significant amount of effort to establishing the Universities-National Bureau Committee and to active fundraising. He was much involved in the setting up of a Bureau program on financial research, which was supported by the Association of Reserve City Bankers, a project that provided large amounts of funding to the NBER over many years. This project became very applied

---

[15] There is also mention of a Conference on Fiscal Policy, but this does not seem to have survived as long.

in nature, much more so than the Bureau itself originally intended,[16] but the additional revenue allowed Mitchell to significantly expand the number of research associates working with the Bureau.

Despite all this turmoil, the work of the Bureau continued. Arthur Burns had been with the Bureau working with Mitchell since 1930, and had become Mitchell's closest associate. Burns published his *Production Trends in the United States* in 1934. Solomon Fabricant also joined the Bureau in 1930 and began work on trends in corporate profits. Kuznets continued work on national income and also on capital formation. Harry Jerome worked on mechanization in industry, labor displacement, and productivity. Wolman worked on wages and hours under the NRA codes, and then on wages and employment in the recovery. Mitchell and Burns worked to develop the NBER methods of reference and specific cycles (NBER *Bulletin* July 1935) and statistical indicators. Mills produced his *Prices in Recession and Recovery* in 1936 (Mills 1936). Milton Friedman was appointed an assistant to Kuznets in 1936 and took over his project on income from professional practice. Between 1937 and 1939, Moses Abramovitz, Julius Shiskin, Allen Wallis, and Geoffrey Moore, among several others, were added to the staff and allocated sections of the business cycle project. The project, however, was not progressing as originally planned and was becoming ever larger. In 1938, Burns wrote to Mitchell concerning progress on the project. He mentions some thirteen monographs either underway or planned that are to provide the "statistical groundwork for the volume on the Rhythm of Business Activity," but goes on to make numerous suggestions (over almost five pages) of additional information that Mitchell may require for the final "theoretical volume" (Burns to Mitchell, 12 December 1938, Wesley Mitchell Papers, Box 46, Folder B). At some point, the original concept of two volumes changed to three, with the second volume initially titled *Business Cycles: The Analysis of Cyclical Behavior*. It was originally expected that the second volume would be produced by the end of 1935. It was this volume that would eventually appear as Burns and Mitchell's *Measuring Business Cycles* (Burns and Mitchell 1946).

---

[16] Originally the idea was to have James W. Angell of Columbia do a study on monetary aspects of the cycle, but his proposal was turned down by the Falk Foundation. The alternative backers, the Reserve City Bankers, were not keen on Angell because of his support of 100 percent money (James Angell to Wesley Mitchell, 25 June 1936, and Joseph Willits to Wesley Mitchell, 2 July 1936, Wesley Mitchell Papers, Box 46, Folders A and W).

THE WILLITS YEARS, 1939–1954

As noted earlier, Willits moved to Rockefeller from the position of Executive Director of the NBER in 1939. Not surprisingly, the Bureau sought to take immediate advantage and applied for a ten-year grant at $125,000 a year to support both its own research and its cooperative program with the universities. The NBER was awarded $870,000 over ten years, a significant increase in both the annual amount and in the length of the term that had been common up until then (RAC-RF, RG 1.1, Series 200 S, Box 368, Folder 4360). This provided the Bureau with a stability of base funding that it had never previously enjoyed.

At the end of 1939 and with the Bureau about to enter its twentieth year, Mitchell, in his annual Director's Report, sought to survey the achievements of the bureau to date. Mitchell's report strongly defended the Bureau's focus on basic research and its avoidance of short-term policy advocacy. He accuses his critics of "impatience" and calls his supporters "thoughtful." He fully accepts the need for improved "social engineering" but argues that "making useful inventions is not a simple matter." Mitchell's institutionalism is displayed clearly in his argument that economic organization has progressed less than industrial methods. New forms of economic organization are required, but to achieve that end, a more useful type of economics is needed: Not a "speculative" economics, but one that can command the respect and attention of policy makers due to its "well tested knowledge" (Mitchell 1939, pp. 9–14). Mitchell goes on to lay out a program for the early 1940s. The first item, of course, is the business cycles project. Mitchell admits that the Bureau has poured considerable resources into the business cycles project and has not yet obtained proportionate returns (Mitchell 1939, p. 21). The second volume on cycles, now called *Methods of Measuring Cyclical Behavior*, is promised shortly, to be followed by the theoretical volume: "The ultimate aim of our business-cycle program is clearer understanding of the complicated processes that bring about financial crises and industrial depressions. Such knowledge we think prerequisite to intelligent efforts to prevent, or even to mitigate appreciably, these recurring disasters" (Mitchell 1939, pp. 23–24).

Some criticism of NBER work appeared in 1940, with the SSRC-sponsored study of Mills's *Behavior of Prices* that was undertaken by Raymond Bye (Bye 1940) and published with discussion by both supporters and detractors (Marschak 1941). The heavily descriptive nature of Mills's study was attacked, but despite this, the work of the Bureau continued along the established lines. In the 1943 Annual Report, the major areas of research are listed as business cycles, incomes and capital formation, production and productivity, and labor. In addition, there were the conferences on income and wealth and prices, and the financial research program. More major changes occurred in 1945 with Mitchell's retirement and Burns's appointment as Director of Research. At that point, the work on the second business cycle volume was essentially complete, and Burns and Mitchell's *Measuring Business Cycles* finally appeared in 1946.

Burns's major interest was in continuing the work on business cycles. Burns had a more Marshallian orientation than Mitchell, and theoretical capabilities that Mitchell lacked, but he was, if anything, even more of a perfectionist concerning empirical work and could be a demanding critic of the work of his colleagues and staff. Some at the Bureau would have preferred that Kuznets be given the job of director. Moses Abramovitz recalled that some of the staff felt that Kuznets "had a breadth of vision about the scope of the Bureau's possible program that was far wider than Burns's" and would have been "more appealing to economists generally and enlarged the potential contribution of its work" (Abramovitz 2001, p. 101). Burns's interest in maintaining the emphasis on business cycles also led to conflicts with Kuznets who wanted to shift the emphasis of the Bureau toward comparative long-run economic growth. Burns refused, expressing doubts over the reliability of the data. Kuznets pursued his interests through the Conference on Income and Wealth and won the financial support of the Social Science Research Council. By the mid-1950s, he was no longer closely associated with the Bureau, and the work on economic growth that won him the Nobel Prize in 1971 was done largely without Bureau participation (Abramovitz 2001, p. 102).[17] It is also worth noting that Moses Abramovitz's move to Stanford in 1948 was motivated partly by concerns similar to Kuznets's. Burns wanted him to work on business cycles and was not keen to let him pursue his own research agenda on long-run growth. This resulted in compromises that left Abramovitz unsatisfied (Abramovitz 2001, pp. 85–86, 103). Burns stayed as Director of Research until appointed to the Council of Economic Advisers by President Eisenhower in 1953, but returned to the Bureau as its President in 1957.

After assuming the directorship, Burns began discussions with Willits on how further long-term security could be given to the Bureau's operations. The upshot of these discussions was a proposal made by Willits to the Rockefeller Trustees in December of 1947, two years before the expiration of Rockefeller's existing grants, for a further ten years of general

---

[17] Kuznets did not formally resign as a member of the Bureau staff until 1961.

funding (1949–1959) at $240,000 a year plus a $50,000 a year supplement to the existing grant for work on international trade. The date of this application is significant. By the end of 1947, the work of the Bureau and its approach to business cycles had come under attack. Tjalling Koopmans of the Cowles Commission had recently published his critique, "Measurement without Theory" (Koopmans 1947), of Burns and Mitchell's *Measuring Business Cycles* (1946). This critique prompted considerable shock and anger among the NBER staff, and a reply from Rutledge Vining defending the NBER method (Vining 1949). Moreover, Burns had been involved in some sharp exchanges with Alvin Hansen on the issue of the merits of Keynesian economics (Burns 1946; 1947; Hansen 1947), an exchange that included both methodological and theoretical issues (see Chapter 10 in this book). Although the structural approach being pioneered at Cowles had its doubters and, in empirical terms, failed to live up to its early promise (Epstein 1987, pp. 64, 99–113), these disputes must have raised questions at Rockefeller about whether the Bureau was still on the forefront of empirical economic research, or in line with what had, in the postwar period, become mainstream macroeconomics.

Willits was very much aware of these criticisms of the Bureau, and of the views of Fosdick, and he took steps to be prepared. He ensured that the application was extensively documented; he also talked with both Fosdick and Stewart to discuss policy and clear issues. He asked Burns to give him his views on econometric models and on Keynesian economics, and wrote to Milton Friedman to solicit his opinions on the National Bureau's contributions and place in economics (Arthur Burns to Joseph Willits, 5 November 1947 and Milton Friedman to Joseph Willits, 28 November 1947, RAC-RF, RG 1.1, Series 200 S, Box 369, Folder 4371). Burns wrote that "we have recently set one investigator to work on econometric models, not because any member of our group has much faith in them but because we wish to check our judgment and give this approach an opportunity to prove its merits."[18] His reply concerning Keynesian economics contained

---

[18] This is undoubtedly a reference to the impending arrival of Lawrence Klein as a visiting fellow at the NBER in 1948. Klein had been with Cowles and then had spent a year in Oslo with Ragnar Frish and Trygve Haavelmo. Klein states: "My econometric interests were tolerated but not enthusiastically monitored." He also tried to defend Koopmans against "intense anger on the part of NBER staff" and was "treated somewhat as a curiosity – an outsider who might eventually view the NBER approach in a more favorable light" (Lawrence Klein to Malcolm Rutherford, 27 August 2002). After his time with the Bureau, Klein wrote to Burns that he "did not see any real conflict between the econometric work that I or others want to do and the work of the business cycle staff of the Bureau." In this letter, Klein describes most econometric models as "parametric," whereas the "National

a long condemnation of the "religious element" apparent in the work of some Keynesians, and of what he saw as the overly speculative nature of Keynesian theory. For Burns, much of the Keynesian literature was "taking a grand vacation from life and its realities" (Arthur Burns to Joseph Willits, 5 November 1947, RAC-RF, RG 1.1, Series 200 S, Box 369, Folder 4371, p. 4). Friedman's letter claimed that Burns and Mitchell's 1946 book was "the first really significant advance in the field of business cycles since Mitchell's 1913 volume." Friedman supported the Bureau's focus on basic research and its empirical orientation, although he did suggest that this orientation should change over time:

The Bureau should devote more attention in the future than in the past to the construction of generalizations and somewhat less to the accumulation of observations.... This is the one point at which I should be inclined to agree even in part with some of the criticism of the Bureau. Their strictures on the score of "too little theory" – as they very inaccurately put it – were, I think, misplaced and erroneous for the past but would be appropriate if the Bureau continued without change in emphasis. (Milton Friedman to Joseph Willits, 28 November 1947, RAC-RF, RG 1.1, Series 200 S, Box 369, Folder 4371, pp. 3–4)

Willits's presentation of the NBER application to the Rockefeller Trustees is remarkable in a number of respects. It opens with the message that the health of the American economy, and its ability to avoid serious recessions, is vital for "America's fitness to survive" in competition with the Soviet Union and with socialist ideology. What is required is the kind of knowledge "essential to a wise management of our economy," and the kind of knowledge required is exactly the kind supplied by the National Bureau: the kind that substitutes "fact for conjecture and tested conclusion for hypothesis." He argues that the Bureau is "the most significant research organization in the world," and makes special mention of Kuznets's work on national income, Mills's on the behavior of prices, and Burns and Mitchell's *Measuring Business Cycles*. He goes on to present the work of the National Bureau as a bulwark against what he sees as the tendencies within economics to "retreat from science," to "retreat from reality," and to "retreat from humanism." The "retreat from science" he illustrates by the work of Keynes's more ardent disciples and their "tendency to substitute a new dogma for an old with neither based

Bureau technique" is largely "non-parametric." He argues that such nonparametric studies are a necessary first step to a final parametric study. He goes on to observe that "there is actually an econometric school of thought that falls in between the work of the Cowles Commission and the National Bureau." In this connection, he mentions the work of Tintner, Stone, and Wold (Lawrence Klein to Arthur Burns, 23 January 1950, RAC-RF, RG 1.1, Series 200 S, Box 370, Folder 4376).

on systematic verification nor observations." The "retreat from reality" he illustrates with the work of the econometricians who focus too much on the building of mathematical models and too little on the "study of actual situations and the motivations essential to real understanding." The "retreat from humanism" he sees as coming from a loss of historical perspective and the substitution of mathematics for an understanding of the broader institutional setting (Remarks made by JHW in presenting item re National Bureau of Economic Research, 3 December 1947, RAC-RF, RG 1.1, Series 200 S, Box 369, Folder 4371).

In a related communication to Fosdick, Willits explicitly addresses the issue of whether the Bureau will move beyond "measurement and interpretation of those measurements to the application of its rich foundation in fact to the more general issues in economics." He answers:

My conclusion is that under Arthur Burns' directorship it will. Burns does not have the "savoir faire" of Wesley Mitchell, but he has a sharper mind and the courage to face general issues. Witness the present scientific discussion with Alvin Hansen. The problem in economics is always to preserve the marriage of realistic and scientific knowledge and the issues of general theory and value. The Bureau has provided, as no one else has, the elaborate and continuing foundation of scientifically measured factual knowledge. Now, under Burns, it is moving to face the more general issues. His report and article on Keynesian economics are an illustration. (Memo from JHW to RBF, 5 November 1947, RAC-RF, RG 1.1, Series 200 S, Box 369, Folder 4371)

In hindsight, Willits was overly optimistic. Burns was never able to bring the business cycle project to a conclusion. The final theoretical volume on business cycles was never produced. Abramovitz speaks of his sense that "Burns was seriously frustrated and depressed by this failure," and that the invitation to join the Eisenhower administration in 1953 came as "a happy release" (Abramovitz 2001, p. 102).

Willits's arguments on behalf of the Bureau were, however, highly successful. The Bureau received the additional funding requested for its project on international trade and was given $240,000 in each year from 1950 through 1954, a total commitment of $1,300,000, and the largest grant ever made in the field of economics by the Rockefeller Foundation. In addition, the Bureau was invited to make applications five years in advance for further one-year extensions beyond 1954. The Bureau applied for additional funding as suggested, although the amounts awarded for 1955 to 1957 fell to $200,000 a year.

This very close concordance in vision between Willits and the Bureau obviously created a high degree of hegemony that left those pursuing other approaches on the outside. Willits frequently solicited Mitchell's, and later Burns's, opinions on the research proposals he had before him,[19] and Willits and those at the Bureau shared considerable skepticism as to the potential contribution of more formal theoretical and econometric methods.[20] The most obvious example of this is to be found in the case of the Cowles Commission.

As early as 1937, Cowles himself had attempted to obtain the support of Mitchell and Willits for Rockefeller funding, stressing Mitchell's position on the Cowles Advisory Council, the avoidance of duplication, and the Commission's focus on econometrics and mathematical statistics.[21] Mitchell did write a moderately supportive letter, but no funding was forthcoming (Alfred Cowles to Wesley Mitchell, 2 June 1937 and 15 October 1937; Alfred Cowles to Joseph Willits, 16 October 1937, Wesley Mitchell Papers, Box 46, Folder B; Wesley Mitchell to Miss Walker (Rockefeller), 11 October 1937, Wesley Mitchell Papers, Box 46, Folder W). The first Rockefeller grant to the Cowles Commission did not come until 1942, for a study of wartime price controls conducted for the NBER Conference on Prices.[22] Willits did later provide continuing support for Cowles, but only to the extent of around $10,000 a year. Early in 1947, Jacob Marschak approached Willits for increased funding, arguing that Cowles "is the only institute in the world formulating economic theories precisely and submitting them to mathematical tests." While Cowles relied on NBER data, and there was, in that respect, a "good" division of labor between the organizations, Marschak pointedly argued that the NBER "is only telling what occurred" and "is

---

[19] I have not found any comments by Mitchell on grant applications from the Cowles Commission in his papers, but they do contain Mitchell's comments to Willits on proposals from Adolf Berle, The Brookings Institution, and the Harvard Business Cycle Research Group. Willits did solicit Arthur Burns and Milton Friedman's opinions on a 1947 application from Cowles (see the materials in RAC-RF, RG 1.2, Series 216 S, Box 4, Folder 26).

[20] For a comparison of the Mitchell/Burns approach to measuring business cycles and the Cowles Commission attempt to build and test structural models, see Morgan (1990, pp. 51–70, 251–253). Morgan argues that for Mitchell, "statistical work was concerned with constructing representations of the cycle itself," although this was "a prelude to later understanding." Those using the econometric approach, in contrast, were less concerned with defining the cycle because "their theories told them what facts or data to study and their aim was to explain what caused the cycle" (Morgan 1990, pp. 68–69).

[21] In the earlier years of the Cowles Commission, before the move to Chicago, Mitchell visited Colorado Springs, and people such as F. C. Mills, Isador Lubin, and Mordecai Ezekiel attended Cowles conferences. There seems to have been little of the direct conflict between Cowles and the NBER that came to characterize their later relations.

[22] This project received funding both from Rockefeller and the National Bureau, although in fairly small amounts: Rockefeller contributed slightly more than $17,000, and the National Bureau $6,000.

not trying to pose theories and then test them" (Joseph Willits memo and attached notes of interview with Jacob Marschak, 21 January 1947, RAC-RF, Record Group 1.2, Series 216 S, Box 4, Folder 26).

Willits's reaction was to ask Arthur Burns and Milton Friedman to give an appraisal of the Cowles program. As Marschak suspected, Willits was being advised by members of "the other school" (Epstein 1987, p. 64; Mirowski 2002, p. 219), but it must be said that Willits himself was no admirer of formal methods. Burns replied that he was "not confident" that their method would lead to significant results, although he did allow that "they are able people and should have a chance to try out their method to the full" (Joseph Willits to Frederick Stephan, 5 June 1947, RAC-RF, Record Group 1.2, Series 216 S, Box 4, Folder 26). Friedman, who was famous for his criticisms of work presented at Cowles seminars at Chicago (Epstein 1987, pp. 108–110), expressed similar opinions, recognizing the intellectual caliber of those involved at Cowles but rejecting their basic "articles of faith" and expressing "considerable confidence that their experiment will fail" (Milton Friedman to Joseph Willits, November 1947, Milton Friedman Papers, Box 89). Willits also solicited from Burns a series of questions that might be posed to the people at Cowles. Burns provided a lengthy list that raised such thorny issues as discriminating between conflicting economic theories, the exogenous or endogenous nature of specific variables, the possibilities of various structural relationships and functional forms, the stability of relationships and of leads and lags over time, and many other points. He also suggested that they be asked for "an example of an economic theory of practical relevance" that they had developed (attachment to Joseph Willits to Frederick Stephan, 5 June 1947, RAC-RF, Record Group 1.2, Series 216 S, Box 4, Folder 26). As pointed out by Mirowski (2002, pp. 215–220), this is the background to the measurement without theory dispute.

The period from the mid-1940s through until Willits's retirement from Rockefeller in 1954 was a mixed time for the Bureau's research. Some excellent projects were undertaken. Milton Friedman and Anna Schwartz began their work on U.S. monetary history in 1948, a project that took until 1963 to publish. Walter Stewart advised on this project, giving Friedman a reading list to start him off (Milton Friedman to Walter Stewart, 12 January 1949, Milton Friedman Papers, Box 33). Friedman, however, went his own way in the interpretation of the monetary history of the Great Depression, focusing on quantity-of-money issues, as opposed to Stewart's concern with the lending and investing activities of banks and quality-of-credit issues (Milton Friedman to Arthur Burns, 3 May 1949, Milton Friedman Papers, Box 15). Friedman did other important work, particularly on consumption theory. Abramovitz worked on inventories and business cycles. George Stigler, who had joined the bureau staff in 1943, worked on output and employment trends. Geoffrey Moore refined the system of leading indicators for business cycles, and, as discussed in Chapter 4, Morris Copeland developed the analysis of money flows, later to become flow of funds accounts. All the same, the focus of the bureau's efforts had become less sharp; it was conducting much work of lesser value and continuing to run into financial difficulty.

ROCKEFELLER BOWS OUT

In the previous chapters on Wisconsin and Columbia, the decline in institutionalism's position can be seen in the hiring decisions made after the end of World War II in 1947. In the case of the NBER, the continuation of the relationship with Rockefeller sustained the Mitchell/Burns empirical approach for another ten years.

Fosdick's retirement as president in 1948 changed Rockefeller's policies in a number of important respects. There was a sense that the Foundation had become too set in its ways, was simply continuing to fund the same institutions, and that new initiatives were becoming hard to implement. Chester Barnard, who took over the Presidency, and his successor, Dean Rusk, made an effort to capitalize recurrent requests. In line with this policy, the Bureau applied in 1952 for a $2,000,000 "terminating grant" to help provide a capital fund. This application was approved. The annual support previously awarded was to continue to 1957 and then stop. The Bureau could only take the interest on the capital sum until 1962. After that, the Bureau could also draw on the principal. The idea behind this decision was that the Bureau would be able to raise substantial additional endowments from elsewhere and hence finally secure its future without need for continual recourse to Rockefeller for general operating grants. In July 1952, William Carson wrote to Willits to thank him for his support of the NBER, calling him a "silent partner in an important scientific and scholarly endeavor" (William Carson to Joseph Willits, 18 July 1953, RAC-RF, RG 1.1, Series 200 S, Box 369, Folder 4379). The Bureau did apply elsewhere, and in 1954 received a $200,000 capital grant from Carnegie, and in 1955 an unrestricted grant from the Ford Foundation for $1,250,000. In 1954, Willits left the Rockefeller Foundation and was immediately back on the Board of the National Bureau. With Willits's departure, priorities at the Division of Social Science were reassessed and attention was increasingly turned to problems of international relations and underdevelopment (Geiger 1988, p. 325).

Thanks in good measure to the support of Willits, the Bureau might have been supposed to be on course toward long-term financial stability, but this was not to be the case. Even before the end of the Rockefeller annual grant, Arthur Burns (now President of the NBER) and Solomon Fabricant (who had replaced Burns as Director of Research)[23] were back at Rockefeller asking for more support. This time, however, they did not have Willits's sympathetic ear, but were met by the much more skeptical Dean Rusk, Erskine McKinley, and Leland DeVinney. The expenses of the Bureau had ballooned (mainly due to rising costs of salaries and benefits), leaving the Bureau with a deficit of $200,000 in 1957 and a possible deficit of $400,000 (on estimated total expenditures of $937,000) in 1958 when the annual Rockefeller grant was no more. On top of this, Burns and Fabricant wanted to increase salaries and to decrease the Bureau's dependence on purchased research projects, increasing the possible deficit to $600,000 on a $900,000–$1,100,000 operation.

Rusk and others at Rockefeller insisted that the Bureau think about its focus and efficiency by deciding on its core priorities, trimming marginal projects, reviewing its operating procedures, and developing a plan as to how it might operate at a level consistent with its means (RAC-RF, RG 1.1, Series 200 S, Box 371, Folder 4385). This was not the message Burns and Fabricant wanted to hear. In a long letter to Leland DeVinney, written in May 1958, Fabricant stressed the importance of the Bureau's projected work in (1) developing and interpreting new data, (2) economic growth, (3) economic fluctuations and stabilization policies, and (4) the economic impact of the rising trend of government activity. This list shows the adaption of the Bureau's previous business cycle project to the economic issues of the 1950s, and, despite the references to developing and collecting new data, Fabricant made it clear that the Bureau was moving toward a greater interest in the analysis of current policy issues – a shift that was very likely due to Burns's experience with the CEA. Fabricant then laid out what he proposed as a solution to the Bureau's financial problems: That the Bureau would cut its operations by 20 percent (although without really specifying what would be cut) and balance the budget over the next five years by a combination of drawing on its capital reserves and obtaining new funding

---

[23] Previous to Burns becoming President, the presidency of the NBER had rotated among the Board. The Director of Research was really the person in charge (along with the Chairman of the Board, and, later, the Executive Director – as with Knauth and Willits). After Burns stepped down as Director of Research, Fabricant took over that position. After his period with the CEA, Burns returned to the Bureau as President and regained a good deal of control.

from foundations. This would still leave the Bureau in the years beyond 1962 with an ongoing deficit of $250,000 a year. At this point, they "would be able to review [their] situation calmly," with time to make adjustments (Solomon Fabricant to Leland DeVinney, 19 May 1958, PA55–66, Ford Foundation Archives).

The reaction at Rockefeller was one of horror. In a series of internal memos, Burns and Fabricant were called "blind and irresponsible" and "administratively irresponsible," and the NBER the "National Bureau of Expensive Research" (RAC-RF, RG 1.1, Series 200 S, Box 371, Folder 4385). The administration and Board were chastised for doing little to raise funds from other sources, but the problems discussed extended to the extremely long time it took the Bureau's work to be completed and published,[24] and the quality of much of the Bureau's research, a great deal of which concerned relatively minor topics. Also, some of the outside criticism of the Bureau was clearly filtering through. It was noted that no proper review of Bureau programs had been undertaken, that the Universities-National Bureau Committee seemed not to be consulted as to the most worthwhile research directions, and that the oft-repeated assertion that the NBER was "the foremost economic research institution in the world" was wearing thin and might be questioned by many economists. McKinley wrote to DeVinney: "I really believe that both Burns and Fabricant are so convinced of the rectitude of their methodology and of their own excellence as directors of the 'foremost, etc.', that it would be impossible to bring them to realize that a good many other reasonably able professional people cannot accept this appraisal but regard their work as pedestrian both in design and result" (EWM to LCD, 23 May 1958, RAC-RF, RG 1.1, Series 200 S, Box 371, Folder 4385). DeVinney also spoke to Kuznets who indicated that he thought the Bureau had lost direction that had originally been supplied by his work on national income and Mitchell's on business cycles (Leland DeVinney, Interview with Simon Kuznets, 17 April 1958, RAC-RF, RG 1.1, Series 200 S, Box 371, Folder 4385).

In June, DeVinny wrote to Fabricant signaling the end to the close NBER-RF relationship. He and his colleagues, he said, "are forced to conclude that the Bureau envisages no long-term solution which we could assist significantly through any recommendation we feel we can make to our trustees" (Leland DeVinney to Solomon Fabricant, 16 June 1958, RAC-RF, RG 1.1, Series 200 S, Box 371, Folder 4385). This, however, was not the end of the Mitchell/Burns NBER. The Bureau made a successful shift to the Ford Foundation and was able to continue in its accustomed mode for many more years. It was not until 1966 that the Ford Foundation forced changes to the senior staff and pushed the Bureau in a direction more in line with what had become mainstream economics and econometrics. That part of the story will be told in Chapter 11.

CONCLUSION

What has been said about the history of the Bureau through to the end of the 1940s demonstrates a number of important points. The Bureau and its financial backers in the 1920s and 1930s shared the ideals of empirical science and social control. It was this shared ideology that brought the foundations and research organizations such as the NBER together, and held them together through the interwar period. This is not to say that there were no periods of disagreement and tension. There seem to have been periods of close consensus in the vision of economic research held by the Bureau and its major financial supporters, divided by periods of disagreement and conflict. The first period of close agreement occurred in the 1920s, with the clear concordance of view between Mitchell and Gay at the NBER and Angell, Ruml, and Frank at Carnegie and the LSRM. Both sides in this relationship shared a vision of social science based upon the development of empirical knowledge with a view to improved social control.

At this point, the type of economics that had the best access to funding from the LSRM and Carnegie was associated with the more empirical end of the institutionalist movement. As I have argued previously, it was the institutionalists who had adopted the empirical natural science model, not the neoclassicals, and "social control" was a standard term in the institutionalist literature. The success and prestige of institutionalism within American economics of the 1920s was very much related to its place within this consensus.

This particular consensus, however, began to run into some difficulty in the 1930s, with the foundations taking differing views on the issue of "basic" versus more policy-oriented research, with Edmund Day's efforts to involve university-based researchers and alter the role of the Bureau, and with Raymond Fosdick's increasing skepticism concerning what had actually been achieved by the LSRM and RF general support of the social sciences. In the late 1930s, there was clearly a general backing away from the support of the social sciences within Rockefeller, but the Bureau was able to maintain, and even improve, its funding situation owing largely to the arrival of Joseph Willits as Director of the Division of Social Science at Rockefeller in 1939.

The second period of close consensus existed from that time to the early 1950s, and was very largely negotiated and maintained between Joseph Willits and Wesley Mitchell and later Arthur Burns. Despite the growing difficulties in Mitchell's business cycle project, Willits continued to defend the Bureau from criticism and was undoubtedly responsible for the program of research surviving as long as it did. Whereas at Wisconsin and Columbia universities, there was a move away from institutionalism in the immediate postwar hiring undertaken around 1947, the criticisms made of the Bureau's research positions, by Cowles and by Hansen, by econometricians and Keynesians, did not result in a loss of financial support or in any effective pressure to for the NBER to change directions.

All the same, with Mitchell's retirement, the NBER research agenda lost much of the explicitly institutionalist underpinning that was a feature of Mitchell's vision. It should be emphasized that it was exactly this institutionalist underpinning that gave the business cycle project as conceived by Mitchell its coherence and its link to an overall (if only very generally stated) theoretical vision. Without this basis, the business cycles project inevitably lost focus. Burns did, however, maintain a number of the key aspects of Mitchell's approach: his careful empiricism, his concern with complexity and multiple hypotheses, and his view of cycles as nonuniform and changing over time. These preconceptions gave rise to a critical view of what might be achieved by alternative, mathematical and econometric modeling, methods (Morgan 1990, p. 69), and one that was fully shared by Willits. This particular consensus resulted in organizations such as Cowles being denied all but small amounts of support. The NBER's privileged position with respect to funding, even after it had come under attack, and even after its approach was no longer so widely accepted in the profession, was very much due to Willits's continued support of the Bureau and his (admitted) biases against more mathematical and econometric approaches. This, however, was a situation that could not continue indefinitely.

PART FOUR

CHALLENGES AND CHANGES

10

The Institutionalist Reaction to
Keynesian Economics

It is a common argument that one of the factors contributing to the decline of institutionalism as a movement within American economics was the arrival of Keynesian ideas and policies. That thesis is not disputed here. Keynesian economics, and the subsequent macroeconomic debates between Keynesians and monetarists, did displace the various institutionalist research programs on cycles and depressions and played a significant part in the marginalization of institutional economics in the post–World War II period. What will be disputed, however, is the common view that institutionalists were somehow left helpless by the phenomenon of the Great Depression, so that Keynesian economics was "welcomed with open arms by a younger generation of American economists desperate to understand the Great Depression, an event which inherited wisdom was utterly unable to explain, and for which it was equally unable to prescribe a cure" (Laidler 1999, p. 211).[1]

As work by William Barber (1988) and David Laidler (1999) has made clear, there is something very wrong with this story. In the 1920s, there was, as Laidler puts it, "a vigorous, diverse, and distinctly American literature dealing with monetary economics and the business cycle" – a literature that had a central concern with the operation of the monetary system, gave great attention to the accelerator relationship, and contained "widespread faith in the stabilizing powers of counter-cyclical public-works expenditures"

This chapter is based on an article coauthored with Tyler DesRoches (Rutherford and DesRoches 2008).

[1] Examples of this line of argument can be found in Myrdal (1972, pp. 6–7) and Ross (1991, p. 419). The same line of argument is repeated most recently by Hodgson (2004, p. 384). Ross argues "Institutionalism as a movement ... fell victim to the Great Depression and its Keynesian remedy. For self proclaimed experts in historical change, their inability to come to any better understanding of the Depression than their neoclassical colleagues was a considerable deficit."

(Laidler 1999, pp. 211–212). As should be obvious from previous chapters of this book, contributions by institutionalists such as Wesley C. Mitchell, J. M. Clark, and others were an important part of this literature.

Institutionalists had consistently recommended countercyclical public works programs as a part of an appropriate response to business depressions. They had also consistently advocated unemployment insurance programs and policies to help stabilize the private sector. The experience of the Great Depression quickly led some institutionalists to place a greater emphasis on expenditure policies. Wolman's 1930 book on public works was produced by the NBER as a response to the emergency (Wolman 1930), and in 1933, Mordecai Ezekiel was estimating that about 12 million people out of the 40 million previously employed in the "industrial sector" were unemployed, and that unemployment relief, to be effective, "must start with a large scale and vigorous program of construction and public works" (Ezekiel Papers Box 1, Folder: Agriculture, US Dept of 1932–33). From the early 1930s J. M. Clark was working on his own version of the multiplier,[2] and published on the cumulative effects of changes in aggregate spending in 1935 in research conducted for the National Planning Board (Clark 1935a; 1935b). Others within the New Deal administration, particularly Lauchlin Currie, were also developing and promoting a consistent program of government expenditures from 1935 onward. Currie's ideas found support from institutionalists such as Ezekiel and Isador Lubin. The Keynesian Revolution in America, then, had many of its roots in the work of New Deal economists, both institutionalist and otherwise (Barber 1996; Laidler 1999).

It is also worth reemphasizing the institutionalist background of the person who became the leading American Keynesian – Alvin Hansen. Hansen completed his PhD dissertation, "Cycles of Prosperity and Depression, 1902–1908," in 1918 at Wisconsin, his supervisors including R. T. Ely and J. R. Commons.[3] Although Hansen did not associate himself with the institutionalist movement, and initially developed more of an interest in European cycle theories,[4] he maintained a close concern with the problems

---

[2] There has been some debate over how fully Clark had developed his thinking on the multiplier prior to seeing Kahn's famous 1931 paper. For this debate, see Fiorito (2001) and Dimand (2002). For further discussion on Clark and his role in the American Keynesian Revolution, see Fiorito and Vernengo (2009).

[3] Hansen retained a great respect for Commons. See Chapter 7 in this book.

[4] There is a nice letter from Mitchell to Hansen concerning his work on cycles dating from 1924. Mitchell states that "in view of the very large amount of purely empirical investigation that is now being done I think you are setting a good example in making use of general economic theory in your cycle studies. We ought gradually to get to a point where economists will turn from analytic to statistical work and back again in economics as

of unemployment, unemployment compensation, and social security. As pointed out in Chapter 7, when Hansen took to Keynesian economics, he married a Keynesian "full employment program" to a broad social reform program with obvious Wisconsin roots.

The relationship between institutionalism and what became Keynesian economics is, however, a complex one. Parts of what was institutionalism were taken over into the American Keynesianism of the 1940s, and there were certainly aspects of that Keynesianism that institutionalists could and did approve of. This, however, should not be taken to mean that institutionalists simply adopted Keynesian ideas wholesale, because they most certainly did not. Hodgson's recent statement that "institutionalists such as Mitchell, Commons, Clark, Copeland, and Ayres were very sympathetic to Keynes's theories and policies" (Hodgson 2004, p. 385) represents a significant overstatement. What will be argued further is that the institutionalist response to Keynes was a varied one[5] and involved some substantial criticisms of Keynesian economics on methodological, theoretical, and empirical grounds. These lines of criticism grew out of the several institutionalist research agendas on business cycles and unemployment that were active in the 1930s. Keynesianism did not simply arrive and sweep the board, but met challenges and criticism, and not just from more orthodox economists,[6] but also from the more empirical and reform-minded institutionalist contingent.

INSTITUTIONALIST RESEARCH AGENDAS OF THE 1930S

Within institutionalist research on depressions and unemployment in the 1930s, there are a number of strands visible. The first of these is the program of empirical research on business cycles conducted primarily by

habitually as physicists turn from mathematical to experimental work and back again." (Mitchell to Hansen, March 19, 1924, Hansen Papers, 3.10, Box 2, Folder M). For discussion of Hansen's career, see Barber (1987) and Mehrling (1997).

[5] As will be seen further in this chapter, this variation can be attributed to the different institutionalist lines of research that were operating in the 1930s, to some differences in methodological viewpoint, and to the degree of involvement with the policy making process within the New Deal Administration. The two main strands of institutionalist work on cycles and depressions were those based on the idea of business profit seeking combined with the working of the credit and price system, and those based on underconsumptionist ideas. Both strands can be found in Veblen (1904, pp. 177–267).

[6] These more orthodox critics included Frank Knight, Henry Simons, Jacob Viner, Joseph Schumpeter, A. C. Pigou, Denis Robertson, Ralph Hawtrey, and Alvin Hansen (until his conversion to Keynesian ideas). See Laidler (1999, pp. 277–295). Criticism also came from F. A. Hayek, of course.

Wesley Mitchell, Arthur Burns, and others such as Simon Kuznets and
F. C. Mills at the National Bureau of Economic Research. This research was
built on Mitchell's earlier studies of business cycles (Mitchell 1913; 1927).
In broad terms, Mitchell saw business cycles as involving the functioning
of an advanced "money economy" and deriving from the interaction of
business decision making based on profit expectations, the banking and
financial system, and the leads and lags in the adjustment of prices and
wages.[7] Mitchell also thought of the business cycle as a complex multicausal
phenomenon, and even with certain lines of causation changing over the
course of the cycle. Mitchell was certainly familiar with Keynes's work and
the work of other monetary theorists such as Cassel and Wicksell, and saw
Keynes's *Treatise on Money* as a work that sought to make money a "larger
element in general economics," and in that sense marking an important
advance over the "real exchange" focus of earlier economists (Mitchell
1967/1969, Vol 2, p. 826), but these developments in theory did not deflect
Mitchell from his own empirical approach.

    As was seen in the previous chapter, the business cycle project at the
NBER had expanded by the late 1930s to include a vast array of studies of
national income and its composition, cycles in particular industries and
lines of activity, the structure of prices over the cycle, inventories over the
cycle, employment and incomes over the cycle, cycles in stock prices, bond
yields, and much more. Out of this developed the "NBER method" of specific and reference cycles. The NBER approach was not to work with highly
aggregated data, and their investigations discovered a considerable amount
of variation between cycles, leading to a great deal of caution in the making of generalizations or in assuming the stability of certain relationships.
In terms of policy, Mitchell saw the empirical work of the NBER as linked
to improved decision making in both the private and public sectors, and
holding out the prospect of stabilization via improved forecasting, indicative national planning, and countercyclical public works programs (Laidler
1999, pp. 221–222; see also Alchon 1985, pp. 71–90).

    One aspect of this research program deserves special emphasis in the
present context: F. C. Mills's work on prices, begun in the 1920s (1927;
1929) and continued into the 1930s. Mills's research found growing productivity in manufacturing industry over the 1920s combined with large
increases in profits and increasing price inflexibility. In his 1936 book, he
explicitly linked this price inflexibility to problems in "the wide and prompt

---

[7]   Mitchell's emphasis on the role of pecuniary institutions and profit seeking in business
    cycles is taken from Veblen's discussion of cycles (Veblen 1904, pp. 177–212).

diffusion of purchasing power" (Mills 1936, p. 440). Of course, Mills was not the only person concerned with the relative inflexibility of industrial prices; Gardiner Means published his first work on the subject in 1935 and continued throughout his career to stress the significance of administered pricing. During the Great Depression, farm prices had fallen much more than industrial prices, leading to a general concern with "price balance," but Mills's work linking productivity gains and price inflexibility to a rise in the share of profits was widely cited by other institutionalists and, as will be seen further in this chapter, was often used as part of an underconsumptionist argument.

A more theoretical strand of institutionalist work, although still relying heavily on the empirical work on business cycles done by the NBER, was that produced by J. M. Clark. Clark's *Strategic Factors in Business Cycles* (1934) was an attempt "to chart a course between the extremes of theoretical study, which gave causes too far and too simple on the one hand, and inductive studies, which revealed "so many factors at work, so completely interrelated, that we are likely to come to the conclusion that everything is both cause and effect" and present too many complications to be of practical use, on the other hand (Shute 1997, p. 92). The "short cycle" is described by Clark in terms that have their origin in Mitchell's 1913 volume, but with an emphasis on the accelerator mechanism, now expanded to include not merely capital goods but durable goods more generally. Clark also points to a number of other strategic factors including "movements of credit" and cyclical shifts in the proportionate distribution of income between different groups. These shifts, together with diverse habits of consumption and saving between the groups involved, lead to "instability in the proportions of the national income saved and consumed over the course of the cycle" (Clark 1934, p. 198). Findings, such as those by Mills, Clark discussed in terms of longer-term trends, with increased price inflexibility making the recovery process more difficult. At the same time, Clark was developing his version of the multiplier, and his *Economics of Planning Public Works* (1935b) is an extended examination of the promise and problems of public works programs as a means of countering depression and unemployment.

Clark certainly favored a public works program to help the recovery, but in Clark's view, the exact effects of any such program would also depend on the method of financing, what is happening to public expenditures more generally, and on the effect on private capital formation. Clark expressed himself in favor of public deficit spending for purposes of stimulating private sector investment, but he explicitly warned against the dangers of "unlimited" deficit spending, particularly its likelihood to crowd out private investment or have adverse effects on business confidence by creating a fear of inflation: "A fair conclusion seems to be that public-deficit spending cannot bear the burden of lifting production from the level of a serious depression without going so far as to bring about ... deferring effects on private business" (Clark 1935a, p. 19; 1935b, pp. 110–112):

If public expenditures are so handled as to tend to bring about a condition in which the volume of production and employment will become dependent on a perpetual continuation of such expenditures, then it will defeat the end of revival as that is commonly conceived, and will tend to bring us that much nearer the point at which the task of producing goods and maintaining the livelihood of the population could not be successfully handled by private business as now constituted. (Clark 1935b, p. 112)

It is important to understand that in Clark's hands, neither the accelerator nor the multiplier concepts were ever applied in a mechanistic fashion, but always with caution, and a concern for the other factors that may play a role in determining the final outcome.

Somewhat similar views can be found in the work of other institutionalists, such as Sumner Slichter. In 1932, Slichter strongly supported the public works programs and deficit spending suggested by Senator Wagner (Barber 1988, p. 225), a position he continued to maintain in later work dealing with the depression (Slichter 1934; 1937). Like Clark, Slichter saw such deficit spending on public works as being a part of a "market supporting program" designed to "lift business out of the depression" (Slichter 1934, p. 175). Nevertheless, he was concerned that deficits be neither too large (as that may create business uncertainly) nor continued too long (as that may produce a fear of inflation), and was also concerned about possible adverse effects on relative prices (Slichter 1934, pp. 179–182). Slichter also emphasized the possible stabilizing role of unemployment reserves, and the importance of maintaining industrial research so that new technologies and investment opportunities may be created to produce a revival in private investment (Slichter 1934, p. 183; 1937).

A different strand of institutionalist thinking took to an explicitly underconsumptionist position, derived either from the work of John A. Hobson or from W. T. Foster and W. Catchings,[8] and often making significant

---

[8] Mariner Eccles is often regarded as one of the pioneers of a Keynesian approach within the New Deal administration but his ideas were more in the nature of those of Foster and Catchings, and he probably never read Keynes. Eccles was first invited to visit Washington by Rexford Tugwell (Barber 1996, pp. 85–86). Underconsumptionist ideas were also strongly promoted by Paul Douglas (1935). In his earlier work, he referenced Foster and Catchings, but later he tended to refer more to Hobson (Laidler 1999, pp. 225–226).

reference to the work by F. C. Mills mentioned previously. Hobson's work had attracted considerable attention in the United States, and he taught at the Robert Brookings Graduate School in the 1924–1925 academic year. Students at Brookings, who included Mordecai Ezekiel and Isador Lubin, were given significant exposure to Hobson's ideas (see Chapter 6).

A good example of this line of institutionalist thinking can be found in the work of Rexford Tugwell. Tugwell's position grew out of what was originally a highly optimistic view of the possibilities opened by new technology, holding out the promise of improved living standards for all (Tugwell 1927). A problem in the realization of this promise was a tendency to oversaving on the part of corporations (Tugwell 1931; 1932b; 1935b). Tugwell made explicit use of Mills's empirical work, arguing that firms with high overheads tended to try to build up reserves and so did not reduce prices as costs fell. The 1920s were thus seen as a period of technological change but with little reduction in selling prices, raising profits and corporate savings, and a failure to enhance consumer purchasing power in proportion to productive potential. Tugwell, along with Mordecai Ezekiel and Gardiner Means, formed a group supporting a "structural" or planning approach to the depression. The planners supported a joint program of recovery and reform and favored some type of direct government intervention in order to increase purchasing power, allocate investment, and establish minimum standards. Many of the planners were in the Department of Agriculture, and their ideas were most clearly displayed in the policies of the Agricultural Adjustment Administration (Hawley 1966; Barber 1996). Despite their emphasis on planning, it should be remembered that a key ingredient of their programs was to enhance the stream of consumer purchasing power.[9]

Quite closely related in spirit was the series of books produced by the Brookings Institution by Edwin Nourse, Harold Moulton, and others between 1934 and 1935: *America's Capacity to Produce* (Nourse and Associates 1934), *America's Capacity to Consume* (Levin, Moulton, and Warburton 1934), *The Formation of Capital* (Moulton 1935a), and *Income and Economic Progress*

Veblen's discussion of chronic economic depression contains underconsumptionist elements (Veblen 1904, pp. 257–254; see also Vining 1939), and he refers to Hobson. The underconsumptionism found in the institutionalist literature of the 1930s is focused very much on the distribution of income and is clearly Hobsonian in nature (Rutherford 1994b).

[9] It is of course true that for the "planners," enhancing consumer purchasing power was only one aspect of their broader program. For the "Keynesians" such as Currie, increasing expenditure was the program. For an excellent discussion of the work on consumption and its relation to institutionalism and the program of the "planners" during the New Deal, see Stapleford (2006).

(Mouton 1935b). Nourse has stated that J. A. Hobson was "the intellectual daddy of what we did at Brookings on the Price and Income Books" (Knapp 1979, pp. 470–471). The main thrust of this study was summarized by A. F. Burns in the following way: "The central argument of the work is simple. The chronic retardant of economic progress is our method of distributing incomes. As national income has risen expenditures on consumption goods have failed to keep pace. ... The proper remedy for our economic difficulties is to increase the purchasing power of the masses, and this may be best achieved by passing on to consumers the benefits of technical progress thru price reductions" (Burns 1936, p. 477).

The first volume of the series, *America's Capacity to Produce*, was an attempt by Nourse to estimate the productive capacity of the United States between 1900 and 1930. Nourse estimated a capacity to produce significantly in excess of actual production but found no evidence of a build-up of excess capacity immediately prior to the depression.[10] The second volume of the series, *America's Capacity to Consume*, was written primarily by Moulton and sought to assemble "a number of estimates relating to the volume of national income, its distribution by size among families, and the relation between income and savings" (Kuznets 1936, p. 301). Moulton's study argued that consumption had not kept up with potential output due largely to a growing inequality in its distribution. Too much was going into savings rather than consumption. The third volume dealt with capital formation and presented capital formation as depending on consumer expenditure rather than on the volume of saving. Excess savings had, according to Moulton, gone into the bidding up of stock prices and other asset values. The final volume, *Income and Economic Progress*, included a summary and a discussion of policy:

Our study of the productive process led us to a negative conclusion – no limiting factor or serious impediment to a full utilization of our productive capacity could there be discovered. Our investigation of the distribution of income, on the other hand, revealed a maladjustment of basic significance. Our capacity to produce consumer goods has been chronically in excess of the amount which consumers are able, or willing, to take off the markets; and this situation is attributable to the increasing proportion of the total income which is diverted to savings channels.

---

[10]   The idea that the economy might be characterized as having a chronic tendency to excess capacity is a theme that can be found in Veblen (1921) and in the work of others such as Stuart Chase's *The Tragedy of Waste* (1925). This was also a major motivating theme for the Report of the Columbia University Commission, *Economic Reconstruction* (1934), although many contributors, such as J. M. Clark, placed more stress on the problem of stabilization and control of fluctuations.

The result is a chronic inability ... to find market outlets adequate to absorb our full productive capacity. (Moulton 1935b, p. 16)

Moulton's solution to this problem ran in terms of a "price policy" to ensure that productivity advances were passed on to the mass of consumers through declining prices, but no real mechanism for doing this was suggested other than one of persuading large corporations to adopt a low-price policy.[11] As a part of this, Moulton argued that his price policy would not reduce profits because firms could achieve lower costs with increased output. Moulton did consider other possible solutions, including redistribution of income and public expenditures, but found them too limited in effect. He was in favor of public works programs to counter the depression, but was clearly not in favor of continued deficit financing of public expenditure. Government is not a "Santa Clause," and accumulated indebtedness ultimately involves higher taxes or a breakdown of government credit (Moulton 1935b, pp. 99–100).

The Brookings studies were widely discussed among institutionalists, and the first two books of the series had a particular impact. On one side, the Brookings studies elicited critical responses from both Arthur Burns and Simon Kuznets of the NBER. Kuznets complained that Moulton's analysis of capital formation was one sided, his empirical evidence sketchy, and his policy conclusions arbitrary and inconsistent (Kuznets 1936). Burns produced a very lengthy and detailed critique of the methods used, statistics produced, and inferences made (Burns 1936). Burns expressed much skepticism concerning the Brooking diagnosis of the problem as one of *chronic* over saving, although he conceded a lack of adequate research on consumption and saving to that date. He also expressed bewilderment that the policy proposal did not seem to follow from the diagnosis. If maldistribution of income and oversaving are the problem, then redistribution would be the solution, not a price policy that it is claimed will benefit all consumers and profit makers alike.

On the other side, more positive responses came from some of those involved in the National Resources Board (later the National Resources Committee). Several commentators on the work on production and consumption undertaken by the Industrial Committee of the NRC have pointed to the impact of the Brookings studies, *Capacity to Produce* and *Capacity to Consume*, in providing a significant part of the inspiration for

---

[11] The Moulton/Nourse policy suggestions were therefore quite corporatist in nature. On Mouton and Brookings, see Lee (1997). For a discussion of types of "planning" in America between 1930 and 1950, see Balisciano (1998).

the Committee's work on industrial capacity and consumption patterns (Lee 1990; Stapleford 2006). Gardiner Means supervised extensive studies on industrial capacity and Hildegarde Kneeland supervised studies on consumption (including a large-scale survey of family expenditure). This work culminated in Means's *The Structure of the American Economy* (1939), which he saw as a step toward developing a system interindustry planning (Lee 1990; Lee and Samuels 1992). More directly, Mordecai Ezekiel used the Brookings studies on production and consumption (as well as points from Gardiner Means) in his books *$2,500 A Year* (1936) and *Jobs For All* (1939a), which contained versions of his "Industrial Expansion Plan," modeled on aspects of the AAA.[12] This plan was designed to produce a coordinated increase in output and final demand and raise real incomes. Ezekiel wrote that these books represented an attempt to provide a mechanism to carry "into action the general economic recommendations which Dr. Moulton had proposed in his book *Income and Economic Progress*" (Ezekiel to Leverett Lyon, January 11, 1939, Ezekiel Papers, Box 11; Ezekiel 1936, pp. 272–276). In the hands of Means and Ezekiel, the problems pointed to in the Brookings studies indicated the need for some form of planning rather than a price policy to be adopted voluntarily by corporations.

INSTITUTIONALISTS AND KEYNESIAN ECONOMICS

In 1935, the U.S. Supreme Court found aspects of the National Recovery Act unconstitutional, and a year later made a similar finding with respect to certain provisions of the Agricultural Adjustment Act. Virtually no economists, including the planners, approved of the way the NRA had worked in practice. Those in favor of planning argued for a reformulated NRA, and Ezekiel continued to present versions of his Industrial Expansion Plan through to 1939, but over the next few years, the New Deal effectively moved into a second phase based predominantly on expansionary fiscal policy and more vigorous antitrust enforcement. This move was also promoted by the experience of the recession of 1937, caused, it was thought, by a sharp reduction in government expenditures (Barber 1996, pp. 108–112), and the congruence of the continuing work of Lauchlin Currie with the publication of

---

[12] Ezekiel received his training in statistics from the USDA. A combination of sophisticated statistics and institutional economics was to become a feature of the USDA Graduate School training through the New Deal years (see Rutherford forthcoming). Ezekiel himself taught at the School (Archive of the USDA Graduate School, Box 1, National Agricultural Library).

Keynes's *General Theory of Employment Interest and Money* in 1936. Ezekiel has described his own transition to Keynesian ideas as follows:

Both Currie and we [Ezekiel and Louis Bean] were working with elements of what later become known as the Keynesian theory. But although Keynes' book had been published in 1936, I myself didn't really catch up with it and absorb it fully until about 1939 or 1940. So, we were groping in the same direction that Keynes was working in England. Currie, as a matter of fact, who was the financial economist, came the nearer of any American economist to preceding Keynes in the discovery of the effect of the possibility of under-employment equilibrium and the way in which government programs worked to offset it. Of course, at the beginning of the New Deal, it was felt that the pump could be primed by public works to get activity going and then, after awhile, that could be withdrawn and they would keep on going by themselves. But when they were withdrawn in 1936–1937, that led to a new recession. And that led to an awareness that however pump-priming worked, it didn't work as a primer. Something had to be kept up if conditions were such as to call for it. Later, Keynes' analysis gave a very clear and eloquent exposition of just how it worked. (Ezekiel 1957, p. 96)

Also, sometime between 1936 and 1938, Alvin Hansen made his transition to a Keynesian position (Barber 1987). Hansen's version of Keynesianism connected the idea of unemployment equilibrium to a stagnationist (or "mature economy") thesis; that is, that insufficient investment opportunities were keeping investment below the level of full employment savings. The government would thus have to play a more permanent role in maintaining aggregate demand, not merely act to "prime the pump" for private investment. Of course, the Keynesian program could also be connected to a policy of progressive taxation and redistribution through programs such as social security, designed to increase the buying power of the poor. This would reduce the need for deficit financing of public expenditures. This version of the Keynesian program was perhaps most evident in work by Currie, but Hansen also favored tax and social policies involving redistribution (Barber 1987).

The Currie-Hansen program had been pretty much worked out by 1940, and it did gain institutionalist adherents. Isador Lubin gave his support and, according to Barber, Ezekiel had fully transitioned to a similar position by 1941 (Barber 1996, p. 128). In the late 1930s and early 1940s, Ezekiel did considerable amounts of empirical work on consumption, savings, and investment, with many references to *America's Capacity to Consume*, but with increasing reference to Keynes (Ezekiel 1937; 1942). This transition to Keynesian ideas can also be seen very nicely in Ezekiel's 1939 paper, "Keynes versus Chamberlin" (Ezekiel 1939b), which presents a clearly Keynesian analysis of full employment saving exceeding investment, although with an added concern with monopolistic competition, and still with one reference to his Industrial Expansion Plan.

The larger history of the shift in view within the NRC from Means's structural planning to a Keynesian style fiscal policy has been told elsewhere (Lee 1990), but it is certainly the case that both Lubin and Ezekiel were a part of that shift. Leon Keyserling, a former student of Tugwell who became closely associated with Senator Wagner and a leading proponent of the 1945 Full Employment Bill, also adopted a set of ideas very similar to Currie's that he combined with some of Tugwell's planning perspective. Keyserling would, however, downplay the specifically Keynesian contribution to his advocacy of public expenditure and redistribution, and it is noticeable that Keyserling complained that many Keynesians neglected the distributional aspects of Keynes teachings (Keyserling 1972).[13] For Keyserling, the problem was the maldistribution of income and savings, and this maldistributionist and redistributive interpretation of Keynesian economics was also adopted by Clarence Ayres, who became an advocate of guaranteed minimum incomes (Ayres 1938; 1966). Thus, a number of younger institutionalists, and particularly those most closely involved with the policy discussions in Washington, did make a transition to Keynesian views, although the inspiration for this shift came as much or more from Currie than from Keynes himself.

More critical discussions of Keynes and Keynesian economics (particularly the Keynesianism of Alvin Hansen), however, came from J. M. Clark, Sumner Slichter, A. F. Burns, Edwin Nourse, Harold Moulton, and Morris Copeland. Gardiner Means also remained a critic of Keynesian analysis, continuing to emphasize the role of administered pricing and developing his own monetary theory of aggregate demand (Lee and Samuels 1992).[14] Some relevant material can also be found in the debates over the funding of Social Security involving E. E. Witte, other Wisconsin institutionalists, and the "Keynesians."[15]

---

[13] Keyserling was a member of the first Council of Economic Advisers and succeeded Edwin Nourse as Chairman. For a discussion of Keyserling, see (Brazelton 1997).

[14] Means's work on administered prices led him to the view that the "appearance of an oversaving problem" was really product of price inflexibility. Attacking administered pricing in the sectors where it appeared most prevalent would, according to Means, stimulate investment (Means 1939; Barber 1996, p. 127).

[15] Commons does not say much about Keynes. In *Institutional Economics* (Commons 1934a), he refers very occasionally to Keynes's monetary theory work. *The General Theory* is mentioned briefly in Commons's discussion of Mouton and the Brookings books. Commons presents Keynes as supporting a price stabilization policy rather than Mouton's price reduction policy, but says little about the Keynesian analysis of unemployment equilibrium or fiscal policy proposals (Commons 1937). Commons was always of the view that monetary policy should be conducted with a view to price stabilization.

Within this institutionalist literature on Keynesian economics, there are a number of common themes. There is a concern about dogmatism, about the too-mechanical use of simplified models, about the factors omitted from the model, about the empirical foundations of some key aspects of the model, about the thesis of "economic maturity," and the wisdom of continued deficit financing of government expenditure. Of those previously mentioned, J. M. Clark was probably the most generously disposed toward Keynes and Keynesian economics, but even Clark expressed substantial reservations. Clark willingly conceded that "certain central problems cannot be successfully handled without the use (which does not imply exclusive reliance) of the income-flow method of analysis of which Keynes's studies are the most prominent form" (Clark 1942, p. 9). Yet in the next breath, he states: "Keynes offers a revised Ricardianism, of similar power and exposed to similar dangers, including that of undue dogmatism of the part of disciples" (Clark 1942, p. 9) – a clear reference to the "Ricardian vice" of deriving policy recommendations from highly simplified models. Clark even wrote to Keynes using similar language:

It has seemed to me that what I call the "income-flow analysis", of which yours is the most noted presentation, has done something which has not been done in comparable degree since Ricardo and Marx: namely, constructed a coherent logical theoretical system or formula, having the quality of a mechanism, growing directly out of current conditions and problems which are of paramount importance and furnishing a key for working out definitive answers in terms of policy. On this a "school" has grown up. All that has tremendous power; and is also exposed to the dangers of too-indiscriminating application.... I am myself enough of an "institutionalist" (whatever that may mean) to have more than a lurking distrust of formulas and equations! But not enough of an institutionalist to ignore their importance: merely to want to think all around them and reckon with the imponderables that modify their action; and the other factors which no single formula can comprehend – for instance, the long-run incidence of continued large deficit spending.[16]

Clark also complained of the tendency of Keynesians to wish to intervene at any point short of "something called full employment," representing a position that may not be achievable through the policies advocated, their "obliviousness" to the importance of wage and price adjustments, their "philosophy of unlimited deficit spending as the one tested and reliable way to secure full employment," and their "dogma" that such spending will not tend to be dissipated in wage or price increases until full employment is

---

[16] Clark to Keynes, 24 July 1941, J. M. Clark Papers, Box 2. Keynes replied to this letter saying, "I agree with what you say about the danger of a 'school', even when it is one's own" (Keynes 1941).

achieved. These ideas, for Clark, were "unsupported by reason" and flew "in the face of experience" (Clark 1942, p. 9). In a letter to Hansen, he argued that "indefinite deficit spending is not an enduringly workable solution for chronic partial stagnation of an economic system like our own" (Clark to Hansen, February 13, 1939, Hansen Papers, 3.10, Box 1).

Slichter also expressed concerns involving the possible inflationary effects of the Employment Act combined with the increased power of unions, and he strongly rejected Hansen's stagnationist thesis, emphasizing instead the possibilities for private investment opened up by new technological advances (Slichter 1961, p. xiv; Leeson 1997, p. 447n).[17]

Mitchell and Burns had greater difficulties with Keynesian economics. Mitchell himself did not write on the *General Theory*, but he did discuss it in some of his seminars at Columbia. Keynes's work is presented as an attempt to integrate monetary theory and general economic theory, although largely within the "orthodox tradition" (Mitchell 1967/1969, vol. 2, p. 826). Mitchell saw a need for such an integration, but also a need to "work on a deeper level than do Keynes and his disciples" (Mitchell 1967/1969, vol. 2, p. 826). Mitchell's response to Keynesian enthusiasm on the part of students made it clear that he was not overly impressed (Interview with Eli Ginsberg, 17 March 2000). It was Arthur Burns who mounted the principal NBER criticism of Keynesian economics, although the correspondence from Burns to Mitchell concerning this critique makes it clear Burns thought he had Mitchell's general agreement with his position.[18]

Some of Burns's language is strikingly similar to Clark's. He compares Keynes to Ricardo. Both had produced "bold and vigorous theoretical speculation" related to the pressing problem of the time, but both were subject to "serious error if the premises accepted for purposes of reasoning are contrary to fact" (Burns 1946, pp. 4, 8). He was also concerned with the "religious" element he finds among Keynes's "more zealous followers." Although Burns admits that Keynes had an important liberating effect on those brought up within orthodox theory, "he failed to teach economists that economic truth cannot be firmly reached by speculation alone" (Burns 1947).

Burns also argues that Keynesians tend to assume that the consumption function is stable, that savings increase with income, and that private

---

[17] Slichter moved from a position in the 1940s that showed a great deal of concern with the possibility of inflation to one in the 1950s and early 1960s that strongly downplayed the significance of inflation (see Leeson 1997).

[18] Burns to Mitchell, 18 December 1936, Mitchell Papers, 1998 Addition, Box 46, Folder B. As noted previously, Burns's empiricism was very much in line with Mitchell's. Burns succeeded Keyserling as Chairman of the Council of Economic Advisers.

investment opportunities are too limited to assure full employment. Burns points out that equilibrium in a Keynesian model is at the aggregate level and does not imply that all markets or firms are in equilibrium, so that the final position may be not as predicted by the model. Furthermore, he points out that the research undertaken or being undertaken by the NBER suggests that the consumption function is far from stable,[19] that the secular trend of savings in relation to income has been downward, and that there is little clear evidence of secular stagnation as suggested by Hansen (Burns 1946).[20] Burns also complained of Keynes's focus on the level of employment as opposed to the business cycle (Burns 1952; see also Wells 1994). Hansen replied to Burns, disputing the characterization of Keynesian economics as "Ricardian" in character, pointing to the empirical component in Keynesian macroeconomic work, and questioning Burns's understanding of Keynesian theory (Hansen 1947). Burns in turn wrote a lengthy rejoinder, backing down not at all:

I suspect that Hansen is troubled because my essay conveys the impression that the Keynesians are excessively mechanical in their thinking, that they gloss over the turbulent life that goes on within aggregates, that they give little heed to adjustment processes in our society, that they subject *ceteris paribus* to excessive strain, that they slight in particular the instability of the consumption function; and that while Keynes is guilty on all these counts, the Keynesians – among whom Hansen is outstanding – are guiltier still. (Burns 1947, p. 260)[21]

Morris Copeland also criticized Keynesian analysis, his most considered response coming in the early 1950s, after the language of "models" and "model building" had begun to find its way into the literature. Copeland admitted the popularity of the Keynesian model and found the causes of this popularity in the facts that it was aggregative in nature, embedded in the neoclassical tradition, did not attempt to deal with the entrepreneur or consumer on an individual level, and lent itself to empirical investigation.

---

[19] Simon Kuznets had already produced work concerning the longer-run relationship between income and consumption (Kuznets 1942). Kuznets and Friedman's (Friedman 1945) work on income from professional practice also has significance here, particularly because the work had been completed many years before the final publication date. This work was followed by a series of studies at the NBER and through the Conference on Income and Wealth (Burns 1953) that were to culminate in the development of the permanent-income hypothesis (Friedman 1957).

[20] A major critic of Hansen's stagnationist thesis was George Terborgh (1945). Terborgh had been a student at the Brookings Graduate School and had worked as an assistant to Lauchlin Currie (Barber 1996, pp. 166–167).

[21] It is worth repeating that this exchange with Hansen was occurring at the same time as the NBER came under attack from Tjalling Koopmans at Cowles for "Measurement without Theory" (Koopmans 1947; see also Rutherford 2005a).

This last point was one to which Copeland, as a statistical economist himself, attached considerable importance. It is also the case that Copeland's own work on unemployment and expenditure policy came to utilize Keynesian terms and ideas (Copeland 1944; 1966). Nevertheless, Copeland complained about the number of factors omitted from Keynesian models, argued that the Keynesian contribution was one of "model analysis" alone, and that model analysis had serious limitations (Copeland 1951; 1952b). Keynes's *General Theory* was too selective, "it omitted points that ought not to have been omitted" (Copeland 1952b, p. 7). Being aggregative, it omitted the detail of the cyclical process that had been such a central feature of the work of the NBER. Copeland argued the *General Theory*, in addition to ignoring relations with political and social theory, "... added not to what we know about macroeconomics but our ability to express what we know in terms of model analysis" (Copeland 1951; 1952b, p. 26).

Upholding the methods of institutionalism, Copeland aimed criticism at the limitations of model analysis, affirming it to be only a *part* of economic analysis: "Model analysis has thus far been confined to quantitative relationships and it has invariably involved a great oversimplification of the real world. Institutionalism has been concerned to emphasize the complexity of reality and the importance of qualitative as well as quantitative facts" (Copeland 1951, p. 57). Not only was the *General Theory* limited to model analysis, for Copeland, Keynesian models were lacking key factors and details; they were an "expurgated" version of Mitchell's theory of business cycles. It is quite clear that Copeland felt that any such simplified model would have limited applicability and predictive capacity (Copeland 1951; 1952b).

Nourse and Moulton had particular difficulties with Keynes and Hansen on the policy front. Moulton wrote in 1949 that "Keynes's analysis has little kinship with that of the Brookings Institution. It diverges sharply at critical points, and the ultimate implications with respect to the future of private enterprise are fundamentally at variance from ours" (Moulton 1949, p. 128). Neither Moulton nor Nourse appear to have been impressed by Keynes and were suspicious of solutions to the depression that substituted government expenditure for private investment. Nourse held a highly skeptical view of the original 1945 Full Employment Bill, but was happy enough with the Employment Act of 1946 to accept the position of Chairman of the Council of Economic Advisers (Knapp 1979, p. 201). Nourse's concept of the role of the council and his reluctance to adopt the kinds of policies being advocated by Keyserling, however, led to his eventual resignation. Nourse continually expressed concern over the building up of government indebtedness and criticized government for "slipping back into deficits as a way of life in a period when production and employment are high" (Knapp 1979, p. 327). He also doubted the effectiveness of macro-level policy tools on their own: "even fiscal and monetary policy cannot be adequately analyzed and formulated in isolation from the processes of the private business world – collective wage bargaining, administrative price setting, capital formation and investment" (Knapp 1979, p. 405). Those who believed in the certain ability of monetary and fiscal policy alone to control the level of economic activity he called "a cult of economic magicians" (Knapp 1979, p. 405). He also very pointedly rejected Hansen's stagnationist views and continued to promote a "price policy" (Nourse 1944).

Not surprisingly, Moulton held similar views of Keynesian economics. In *Capital Expansion, Employment, and Economic Stability*, Moulton and his coauthors argue that the idea of the American economy having reached a mature state is false. They point out that "a primary implication of the conception of economic maturity is that government must increasingly supplant private enterprise" (Edwards, Moulton, Lewis, and Magee 1940, pp. 163–164). The authors reject the thesis and its implication. Moulton's *The New Philosophy of Public Debt* (1943) carries the argument on to a direct criticism of what Moulton took to be the disregard of the problem of government debt by Keynesians such as Hansen. Moulton draws a distinction between the traditional view and the new conception of public debt. He describes the former as the view that "a continuously unbalanced budget and rapidly rising public debt imperil the financial stability of the nation," and the latter as the idea that "a huge public debt is a national asset rather than a liability and that continuous deficit spending is essential to the economic prosperity of the nation" (Moulton 1943, p. 1). Moulton argues that those who adopt the new philosophy believe that "public finance is really only a matter of book keeping, that a rising debt has no adverse consequences, and that without a constantly increasing debt we cannot hope to have full employment and prosperity" (Moulton 1943, p. 3). Hansen's supporters responded with the charge that Moulton was misrepresenting Hansen's position (Wright 1943; 1945), a charge that drew angry denials from Moulton (Hansen Papers, 3.42, Box 7).

That many institutionalists took a much more cautious attitude toward government debt than those on the Keynesian side can also be seen clearly in the debates surrounding the financing of social security. The original Social Security Act of 1937 involved funding from payroll taxes only and included provision for a reserve fund and contemplated working toward a fully funded system of social security. The large Wisconsin contingent involved in Social Security, including Arthur Altmeyer and E. E. Witte, favored creating a full social security reserve fund (Witte 1937). Witte argued that failure to set up a full reserve would only result in higher taxes later on. He wrote, "if the money collected from these younger workers is not in some fashion set up to their credit, there is the grave danger that the entire scheme will become one for taxing the working people for old age assistance extended to aged dependents of the present day" (Witte to Theresa McMahon, October 7, 1937, Witte Papers, Box 34). On the other side of this argument were the "Keynesians," including Currie, Eccles, Hansen, and Keyserling (Keyserling 1972), who favored a pay-as-you-go policy financed by progressive taxation. Others involved in the debate over social security, such as Abraham Epstein and Paul Douglas (Douglas 1936; Epstein 1936, pp. 793–806), were also highly critical of Witte's position. The revisions to the Social Security system made in 1939 moved to a pay-as-you-go system, and the role of the reserves was reduced to that of a contingency fund.

CONCLUSION

Institutionalists had a deep and abiding interest in the problems of unemployment and business cycles that ran back to the very beginnings of the movement immediately after World War I. They supported many types of intervention in the economic system under the rubric of "social control." They were not believers in the adequacy of unregulated markets to achieve the maximum of social welfare, and had often advocated for policies such as countercyclical public expenditures, and unemployment insurance plans. The experience of the Great Depression led to a number of lines of institutionalist research, a variety of policy proposals, and a good deal of debate even within institutionalist ranks.

But because they *did have established research agendas themselves*, their reaction to the "new" economics of Currie, Keynes, and Hansen was far from uniformly enthusiastic. Some institutionalists did take on such Keynesian ideas. Keyserling was an early convert, and he and Ezekiel and Lubin came to support the Currie-Hansen position on expenditure policy. Clarence Ayres also adopted Keynesian ideas. Sumner Slichter, too, became increasingly close to Hansen in his views after 1950, although even then he never accepted Hansen's stagnationist thesis (Leeson 1997). J. M. Clark began to use the language of income-expenditure models, despite his doubts about their adequacy, and even Arthur Burns could applaud the fact that Keynesian economics had made profession at large recognize that the problem of unemployment was "the principal problem in economic theory" (Burns 1946, p. 4).

Nevertheless, the leaders among the interwar generation of institutionalists remained skeptical about key elements of Keynesian economics. They did not like the degree of simplification in Keynesian models and were suspicious of the degree of aggregation and of the microeconomic detail left out. They were, in fact, highly doubtful about the entire "model building" approach to economics that was becoming dominant within the profession and displacing their own style of empirical economics. Their concerns, however, were not only methodological. The NBER business cycle program had shown a high degree of variation between cycles, and work on income and consumption was indicating that the Keynesian consumption function may not be as stable as assumed. They clearly did not accept Hansen's thesis of economic maturity with its implication of a need for ongoing government expenditure to make up for a lack of private investment. They were more concerned with reviving private investment than in finding a permanent substitute for it. Finally, most institutionalists were quite clearly more fiscally conservative than the Keynesians and more concerned with maintaining price stability. They did not approve of ongoing government deficits, arguing that they would create inflation, damage business confidence, or impose long-run burdens in the form of higher taxes.

In the context of the macroeconomic discussions in the immediate post–World War II period, the policy concerns raised by the interwar generation of institutionalist critics of Keynesianism sometimes placed them on the more conservative side of the debate, warning of inflationary pressures and the need to consider microeconomic conditions.[22] With the benefit of hindsight, and experience with Keynesian econometric models, government deficits, inflation, and social security funding problems, their concerns seem to have been more than justified.

It is true neither that criticism of Keynes came only from more orthodox economists, nor that most of the interwar generation of institutionalists adopted Keynesian ideas. What did happen was that many of the leading interwar institutionalists remained quite suspicious of several key aspects of Keynesianism, but Keynesian economics appealed to the type of younger economists who in the early 1920s might have joined the institutionalist

---

[22] See, for example, J. M. Clark's very cautious approach as outlined in his statement in the Report to the UN *National and International Measures for Full Employment* (Clark, et al. 1949). Clark is suggesting that for many times and places, the unemployment rate achievable via macro policy without creating inflation may be much higher than the usual definitions of full employment.

ranks. What institutionalism had promised then was a new, more scientific approach to economics, one that related to the pressing problems of the day and appeared to offer effective instruments for the improvement of economic performance – science and social control. This is exactly what Keynesian economics held out to those beginning their careers in the 1940s. In that respect, Keynesian economics took over the basis of the original appeal of the institutionalist movement and made it its own. Keynesian economics became associated with the new "scientific" tools of econometrics and econometric model building, and both Hansen in the United States and Beveridge in the United Kingdom linked Keynesian economics to a broad array of social programs that effectively adopted and expanded the social reform agenda that had been so central to interwar institutionalism. The institutionalist movement declined after World War II, partly because of this, and the research programs they had initiated were displaced first by Keynesian modeling and then by the monetarist/Keynesian debates.[23]

Those few institutionalists who did come to prominence in the post–World War II period generally adopted a Keynesian style of macroeconomics, stressing the use of fiscal policy to achieve full employment. Institutionalist markers continued to be visible, particularly in the advocacy of additional policy tools including some form of planning or price controls. Perhaps the most obvious example of this is J. K. Galbraith, but the work of others, such as Allan Gruchy, fits the same mold.[24] Nevertheless, it can hardly be maintained that there were identifiable institutionalist research programs dealing with macroeconomic issues in the same sense that they existed in the 1930s.

---

[23] Friedman's attacks on Keynesian economics had their foundations in his work for the NBER. Friedman's work on U.S. monetary history and his quantity theory interpretation, however, represented a break from earlier NBER attitudes that had generally been skeptical about the quantity theory relation, and had placed more emphasis on the operation of the banking system and quality-of-credit issues. Walter Stewart was an important source of institutionalist thinking on monetary issues and his views were more in line with the banking school.

[24] For Gruchy's discussion of the relationship between institutionalism and Keynesian economics, see Gruchy (1950a; 1950b). For Galbraith's views, see (1952). Gruchy includes Gerhard Colm as a member of the post war "neo-institutionalist" group (Gruchy 1972). Colm was associated with the National Planning Association and worked broadly in the areas of public finance and fiscal policy.

11

Neoclassical Challenges and
Institutionalist Responses

When institutional economics first emerged, the state of neoclassical economics was pretty much as J. B. Clark and Alfred Marshall had left it in the 1890s. The theory of the consumer was based on cardinal utility and, for most purposes, assumed given preferences and a constant marginal utility of money. The theory of markets dealt only with perfect competition or with pure monopoly. The theory of labor markets and of distribution also assumed competitive conditions. Marshall's discussion of externalities only applied to external costs or benefits external to firms but internal to industries, and was largely taxonomic in effect. It was easy to question the applicability of this body of theory to a dynamic economic world of corporations, consolidations and mergers, salesmanship, trade unions, labor unrest, business depressions, and so on. Even among the more orthodox American economists themselves, it was rarely claimed that the standard theory provided anything more than a first approximation to a much more complex and dynamic world. Neoclassical economics could claim a consistent body of theory, but the applicability, predictive power, policy usefulness, and empirical testability of that theory were frequently questioned, and not only by institutionalists.

In 1932, Paul Homan launched a major criticism of the progress of institutionalist program since its formation in 1918. Homan was, of course, a knowledgeable critic, having been a student at Brookings. Homan's argument was based on a particular definition of the aims of the institutionalist movement. For Homan, the defining characteristic of institutionalism was its basic acceptance of "Veblen's account of the nature of institutional prescription of conduct in an evolving society," and its related rejection of equilibrium theorizing. If there is an identifiable institutional economics, then it has to consist of a body of knowledge that (1) would not exist but for that particular orientation, and (2) has some "necessary organic relation to that orientation" (Homan 1932, p. 11). Homan argues that of the work commonly thought of as institutionalist, only a "substantial minor fraction" meets the first test and only a "tiny fraction" the second, so "that an institutional economics, differentiated from other economics by discoverable criteria, is largely an intellectual fiction" (Homan 1932, p. 15).

Now, Homan's thesis that the work of people such as Hamilton, Mitchell, Clark, and Commons did not have a clear "organic" relation to the idea of institutions affecting conduct in an evolving society seems to me to be impossible to maintain, but the major impact of Homan's piece was rather in the contrast he drew between institutionalist work as primarily descriptive (although with related analysis) and what he called "systematic theory." What is implicit in Homan's argument is that "an adequate organon of economic thought" must contain a body of systematic theory, and as institutionalists have failed to develop this they simply have "not created an institutional economics" (Homan 1932, p. 16).[1]

On the other hand, Homan's defense of orthodox economics is quite constrained. He admits that the institutionalist criticism of orthodox economics "has caused the whole structure of economic theory to be subject to searching and critical scrutiny." Standard theory "no longer furnishes an economic philosophy. ... Its more comprehensive generalizations are in disrepute, or else are labeled with proper warning of their partial or hypothetical character. ... Its incompleteness as to method and generalized results are not open to question" (Homan 1932, p. 15). Homan maintains, however, that orthodox theory does have a necessary and essential function "that has been made sufficiently plain to all except the blind." That essential function is "of furnishing paths through the jungles of data and tools of thought for the labors of analysis" (Homan 1932, p. 15).

Of course, one might respond that the theory of competitive markets did not provide any very obvious paths or adequate tools for the investigation and analysis of many, if not most, real-world markets, which is exactly why it was often largely neglected in the applied economics of the time. Hamilton's approach, for example, was based exactly on the argument that the standard models failed to identify many of the key factors that affected the performance of markets. One might also respond that Mitchell did

---

[1] Homan had previously critiqued Veblen and institutional economics in his book (Homan 1928) and in his entry on institutional economics in the *Encyclopaedia of the Social Sciences*, first published in 1931 (Homan 1937). The year 1932 also saw an attack on institutionalism in Robbins's *Nature and Significance* (Robbins 1932), but Robbins's attack was a critique of Mitchell's empiricism from an Austrian viewpoint, and although Robbins's book was widely discussed, it had much less impact on later arguments.

explicitly use the available theories of cycles to guide his empirical work, that Clark in no sense ever abandoned theory, and that Commons clearly did develop a theoretical framework in his work on transactions and law and economics. Institutionalism did contain much of the type of "descriptive with related analysis" work Homan points to, but it was never confined to that. The theoretical contributions of institutionalists might not have been highly systematic, but Homan never even attempts to address the reasons for his particular emphasis on the "systematic" in "systematic theory," nor did he really probe the reasons for the relative lack of systematic theory within institutionalism.

In its development of systematic theory or a general theoretical framework, institutionalism was handicapped by the failure of a key part of the program as originally outlined by Hamilton, and by a number of its own methodological convictions. For almost all the original institutionalist contingent, a central part of the program was to base economics on "modern psychology." This, however, turned out both to be a moving target and one that developed in unsuitably behavioristic directions. Institutionalism never developed a theory of individual behavior well defined enough to form the basis of a general theoretical framework – a problem, it might be said, that still plagues attempts to move away from traditional rationality assumptions. The references to habits or to institutional determinants of behavior retained an ad hoc character, and specific, well-defined, psychological theories were rarely embedded in the economic analyses developed. Beyond this, however, institutionalists were always suspicious of high levels of abstraction and took as a methodological desideratum that theoretical work stay close to the facts, and close to the complex and changing nature of the real world. Such methodological commitments do not preclude theoretical work (witness the many theoretical contributions of J. M. Clark) but do require institutional and historical specificity and necessarily place limits on the degree of generalization. One can certainly argue that in some cases, these methodological concerns were taken too far. Mitchell, for example, never completed his final "theoretical volume." Nevertheless, Mitchell's work did result not only in the development of data but also in the development of instruments such as business cycle indicators.

On the other hand, it should be remembered that a body of systematic theory can easily be systematically misleading or unhelpful. The systematic nature of Walrasian general equilibrium theory tells us little about its usefulness or applicability to real-world problems. Similar points might be made concerning Lucas's equilibrium macroeconomics or the efficient markets hypothesis in finance. Systematic theory is not a notable characteristic of other social sciences, or other applied sciences, or indeed of that much of any science outside of physics. System hardly trumps other considerations. Nevertheless, Homan's characterizations, often in a highly stripped down form that did not even recognize the important contributions made by institutionalist work, gradually became widely accepted. Institutionalism became characterized not merely as lacking systematic theory, but as "descriptive" and lacking in theory altogether, and, as such, clearly inferior to the more theoretical work of both Keynesians and neoclassicals.

This viewpoint, how it developed in the years after Homan wrote, the increasing harshness with which it was stated, and its impact on the institutionalist movement are the subjects of this chapter. There are many parts to the story. One of these, the impact of Keynesian economics on institutionalism, was discussed in the last chapter. This chapter will focus on developments in microeconomics, both theoretical and applied, the eventual demise of the empirical Mitchell/Burns methods at the NBER, and the rise of the Chicago school – its methodological and ideological opposition to institutionalism – as well as its application of standard economic tools to topics such as households and the law. In a variety of ways, these developments led to more orthodox economics taking over some significant parts of the content of institutional economics while displacing others. Even more importantly, these developments were accompanied by new ideas of "scientific" economics, based largely on European logical positivism (and some of its variants) and at odds with the institutionalist views of science derived from John Dewey and the American pragmatic tradition. This led to a redefinition of the meaning of "science" in economics. As a result of these developments, institutionalism lost its place in the mainstream of American economics.

DEVELOPMENTS IN MICROECONOMIC THEORY

Homan's critique of institutionalism and his contrast of institutionalist work with the systematic theory provided by orthodox economics preceded most of the important developments in economic theory in the 1930s and 1940s. These developments were to work to enhance the contrast pointed to by Homan. In one earlier development, Pigou had expanded on the Marshallian treatment of externalities, providing a basis for the discussion of market failures in terms of a divergence between private and social costs (Pigou 1912; 1920). In the 1930s, Edward Chamberlin produced his work on monopolistic competition (Chamberlin 1933), and Joan Robinson her book on imperfect competition in the same year (Robinson 1933). These books provided a theoretical language with which to discuss various forms of imperfect competition both in output and in labor markets. In the 1930s, ordinal utility concepts replaced cardinal notions of utility. John Hicks and R. G. Allen (1934) popularized the indifference curve approach to demand theory, which eliminated the need for cardinal conceptions of utility and allowed for the language of preferences to substitute for that of hedonism. Samuelson attempted to remove further unobservable concepts with his revealed preference approach (Samuelson 1938). The research groups associated with World War II were the incubators for operations research and game theory (Mirowski 2002). Finally, Samuelson produced his mathematical formalization of neoclassical theory in 1947 (Samuelson 1947).

Even by the mid- to late 1930s, then, the neoclassical economics faced by institutionalists looked very different from its state twenty years earlier, and institutionalists did respond to the challenges created. In terms of Pigou and externalities, it might seem that this work would immediately appeal to institutionalists with their broad view of market failures and the need for new forms of social control. Indeed J. M. Clark did make use of Pigou's ideas in his *Social Control of Business* (Clark 1926) and elsewhere, but Clark, like other institutionalists, wanted to move beyond Pigou's interest in economic welfare to welfare more broadly considered, and still, to a significant extent, looked back to J. A. Hobson's approach to welfare (Clark 1927, pp. 264–271). The notion of utilizing consumers' surplus measures never had appeal for institutionalists because such evaluations of necessity take existing preferences and the distribution of income as a given. Also, at that time, there had been little development of methods for applying such concepts to nonmarketed goods. In any case, for Clark, as for other institutionalists, the key question was the same as Hobson's: "What is welfare, and how is it affected by existing methods of producing and circulating wealth?" (Clark 1957, p. 59). Clark was to find even less appeal in Paretian welfare economics, arguing that its ban on interpersonal comparisons and the limitation to Pareto improvements meant that it was "welfare economics with the welfare left out" (Clark 1957, p. 5). Clark's views on social value were a direct inspiration for the work on social costs very much in the institutionalist tradition undertaken in the 1950s by K. W. Kapp (1950).

The institutionalist reaction to theoretical work on imperfect competition was not entirely dissimilar to the institutionalist reaction to Keynes – somewhat mixed. Chamberlin's work in particular was subject to a considerable amount of institutionalist discussion by Copeland, Clark, A. R. Burns, and J. K. Galbraith, among others (Fiorito 2010a). Chamberlin's supervisor was Allyn Young, and it is interesting that Chamberlin himself acknowledged the influence on his thinking of Veblen's work on salesmanship and Clark's on overhead costs (Chamberlin 1961; Sawyer 2004). Clark and Chamberlin were on good terms: Chamberlin wrote to Clark on receiving a reprint of Clark's "Soundings in Non-Euclidean Economics" to say that "this exercise in studying 'contrary assumptions' is so congenial to my own spirits that I feel more than ever the link between us." He goes on to say that "an awful lot" of what Veblen had to say about salesmanship "can be fitted into [monopolistic competition] without any trouble at all" (Edward Chamberlin to J. M. Clark, 30 July 1958, J. M. Clark Papers, Box 5).

The general institutionalist reaction to Chamberlin's work is perhaps best indicated by Copeland's review already mentioned in Chapter 4 of this book. Chamberlin was seen as providing a very considerable advance over the previous competitive and pure monopoly models. As Copeland put it, Chamberlin's work "opens up new vistas for what has been called pure, abstract, or deductive economics" (Copeland 1934, p. 249). But this type of praise was generally followed by a list of concerns involving the things that the model did not capture and the much greater variety of market conditions and pricing policies to be found. Copeland, Clark, and A. R. Burns all argued that overhead costs and decreasing costs over large ranges of output were a more important factor in creating monopolistic or imperfect competition that Chamberlin allowed (A. R. Burns 1937; Clark 1940; Copeland 1940b). Copeland taught courses that sought to combine Clark's *Overhead Costs* with the work of Chamberlin (Personal interview with James Millar, 14 February 2000; Letter from Morris Copeland to Arthur F. Burns, 25 May 1953, Morris A. Copeland Papers, Box 4, Morris Copeland Personal Folder). He also toyed with the idea of writing a book to be called "Can Neoclassical Economics Be Made Realistic," which was to construct models including monopolistic competition, credit, overhead costs, and other issues.

Largely in response to Chamberlin, Clark developed his concept of workable competition (Clark 1940). As Clark pointed out, it was only with the development of theories of imperfect competition that the concept of perfect competition became well defined. Given that the conditions of perfect competition were unlikely to be met in the real world, the key policy question became one of defining a concept of "workable" competition. This would not necessarily involve meeting as many of the conditions of perfect competition as possible, but of considering a variety of conditions relating to demand, cost conditions, and barriers to entry (Clark 1940). Clark later sought to combine a great deal of existing theoretical and empirical work into a rich discussion of competition as a dynamic process (Clark 1961).

One might argue that these contributions of Clark lacked "systematic theory," but as Clark was to argue on another occasion:

I suppose the difficulty arises when one takes the evolutionary character of society seriously enough to allow it to enter into his main working concepts. If that necessarily impairs "systematic thought" then I am afraid mine is impaired. But isn't there some systematic thought involved in reaching the evolutionary conclusions, as well as in trying to make terms with it ... I have a theory of competition which argues that any fixed schematic laws must be misleading, because competition is an evolving thing. And I have a theory of human nature which can't be used as a basis for deductive theorizing, because it includes too many various elements and leaves too much room for personal and group differences in values and behavior. But I had an idea that I spent a good deal of systematic thought in reaching that position. (J. M. Clark to Wesley Mitchell, 14 May 1948, J. M. Clark papers, Box 2)[2]

In terms of demand theory, the shift to ordinal utility received relatively little institutionalist discussion, as from an institutionalist viewpoint, little of significance changed. After all, the idea of the utility maximizing individual with given preferences remained entirely intact. J. M. Clark argued that the shift from cardinal to ordinal utility produced only a very minor improvement:

The gain seems to amount to the removal of what is usually a minor element of inaccuracy in an analysis in which much larger elements of inaccuracy inescapably remain. It is, from this standpoint, a curious phenomenon that the removal of these difficulties or inaccuracies should apparently have sufficed to occasion a great revival of what is still essentially utility theorizing which still contains the major psychological elements which were successfully attacked as bad psychology something like thirty years ago, and which brought marginal utility theory into general discredit in this country during the succeeding decades. (Clark 1946, p. 348)

With reference back to his 1918 article, Clark argues that preferences are not stable over time and that attention needs to be given to the "dynamic process of preference formation as a process" (Clark 1946, p. 349).[3]

The ordinal approach did remove some of the more explicitly hedonistic language from economics, and this was undoubtedly a part of its appeal as it seemed to free economic theory from explicit psychological foundations, and in that way from some of the institutionalist criticisms of the "outmoded" psychological assumptions of orthodox economics. As Lewin

[2]   This letter to Mitchell has to do with Mitchell's reaction to Clark's reply to Hayek – *Alternative to Serfdom* (Clark 1948).
[3]   In this discussion of the difficulties of measuring indifference functions, Clark takes as his starting point the well-known paper by Wallis and Friedman (1942).

has argued, "treated historically ... or rhetorically" Hicks and Allen (1934) was clearly a part of the "anti-psychological movement" within neoclassical economics (Lewin 1996, p. 1310). Nevertheless, as Clark argued, Hicks and Allen had provided a basis for "independence from psychological hedonism, but not from psychology proper." Their work still rested on the inherently psychological assumption of ordinal utility (Lewin 1996, p. 1310).

As is well known, Samuelson's revealed preference approach was originally intended to provide a complete break with psychological unobservables. In the earlier phases of his work, Samuelson had a strong commitment to "operationalism." Operationalism is a particular version of logical positivism, which held that, to be meaningful, theoretical terms had to be linked to the empirical domain through a set of correspondence rules, so that "every term in the theoretical vocabulary had to be given an explicit definition in terms of the observational vocabulary" (Hands 2004, p. 955). This program had links to the behaviorist insistence on observables. As seen from the previous discussion, a number of institutionalists such as Mitchell and Copeland had also been attracted by behaviorism's appeal to empiricism in the 1920s (and opposition to references to unobservable and arbitrary sets of instincts), but behaviorism, for most institutionalists, meant little more than general references to the role of institutions in molding behavior. The manner in which behaviorism developed in psychology did not, ultimately, jibe well with pragmatic ideas of the active mind and creative intelligence. Samuelson's revealed preference approach also failed to form the foundation of a behavioristic economics. As soon as it was shown that revealed preference theory could be used to *derive* preference functions from observed choices, the theory was turned on its head and became the basis for the scientific justification of the concepts of preference and utility, rather than of their elimination (Hands, 2004, p. 958).

Other institutionalist concerns with notions of maximizing behavior and the importance of cognitive limitations, decision-making costs, habits, and social norms were generally ignored by more orthodox economists. After the advent of Friedman's methodological essay, criticism of the idea of maximization was countered either by reference to "as if" arguments or by loose appeals to evolutionary selection processes, or both (Friedman 1953). It is only much more recently (and with a significant lag) that the work of Herbert Simon on bounded rationality (1955) and Daniel Kahneman and Amos Tversky on heuristics and biases (1974) have brought such concerns back into the mainstream literature. This work would seem to be a natural extension of things said by Veblen, Mitchell, Commons, and especially by

J. M. Clark in his 1918 essay mentioned several times already, but there does not appear to be any obvious line of direct connection.[4]

The mathematical formalism brought into economic theory during and after World War II, represented by Samuelson's *Foundations* and the work of Kenneth Arrow and many others, was a development quite at odds with institutionalist sensibilities. Copeland's reactions to model building were outlined previously. J. M. Clark also provided an institutionalist response in his 1947 "Plea for Communicability" (Clark 1947). For Clark, the primary difficulties with mathematical economics lay in the highly simplified nature of many models and difficulties of providing empirical verification of premises and results. He argued that these difficulties were more severe in some areas of application than others:

The problem applies in differing degrees to the three major areas of mathematical study. The first is the study of the relations between tangible aggregates in the economy at large. Here mathematics is at its best, verification is most nearly practicable, and the difficulties of other methods at their greatest. The second is the analysis of business relations, assumed to be directed to maximizing profits. Here the assumption is indefinite in meaning, involving arbitrary limitations on the businessman's expectations of consequences, which involve logical dilemmas, and involving also simplification of the environmental conditions. It is also seriously incomplete as an explanation of actual business behavior. The third is the analysis of individuals' choices between qualitatively different values, typically via indifference curves. Here the attempt to avoid psychology excludes major parts of the essential problem, while the remaining psychological implications, minimal as they attempt to be, are sufficient to do violence to the character of economic choices. (Clark 1947, p. 76)

What is particularly interesting about these developments is that to some extent they were prompted by institutionalist criticisms of the state of orthodox theory. These responses, it must be said, only very partially answered the criticisms but they did open up many new lines of theoretical development and revive the neoclassical theoretical project. As a result, institutionalists increasingly found themselves in the position of dissenters from the mainstream of the profession rather than fully a part of that mainstream.

DEVELOPMENTS IN APPLIED MICROECONOMICS

Of course, even after World War II, the vast bulk of economic literature was applied in nature, and there was a very general concern with the

---

[4] There is a line of connection between Commons and some of Simon's work that runs through Chester Barnard. Barnard (1938) makes use of Commons's ideas on "industrial goodwill" and also his notion of strategic and routine transactions (Rutherford 2009).

problems of the empirical application of the newer theoretical ideas. In the more applied areas of the discipline, institutionalist work became gradually absorbed into research programs that were increasingly (although still far from completely) neoclassical in orientation. Two key examples of this will be discussed here: industrial organization and labor economics.

The subdisciplinary area called industrial organization is usually traced back to Harvard and Edward Mason and Joe Bain who developed the "Structure, Conduct, Performance" (SCP) paradigm in the late 1930s and early 1940s (Mason 1939; Bain 1944; 1959). Now, the area of industrial organization in the post–World War II period consisted of much more than work in the SCP program. Gardiner Means continued his work on administered prices, there were all kinds of work on concentration and firm behavior, a large amount of discussion on both sides of the Atlantic concerning full-cost pricing (Mongin 1992), and much more besides. Just mentioning this work indicates the continuation of institutionalist programs and themes into the postwar period, but the development of the SCP program does have some elements of special interest and will be the focus of attention here.

Chamberlin's monopolistic competition model created much discussion concerning the problems of its "statistical verification." The difficulties of statistically verifying Chamberlin's results, in terms of estimating firm level cost and demand functions, were explicitly mentioned by Mordecai Ezekiel, J. M. Clark, A. R. Burns, and others. Burns insisted that Chamberlin's theory would not be able to make advances without "far more adequate data than are now available" (Burns 1937, p. 663), and argued for a close interaction between industry studies and general theory. In 1938, the NBER Conference on Prices established a Committee on Price Determination to investigate exactly the possibilities of empirical research in the area of cost-price relationships and price determination. Members of this committee included both J. M. Clark and Edward Mason (Fiorito 2010a). Again we see the institutionalist emphasis on empirical work having an impact.

Mason clearly wanted to see theoretical economics become more applicable and testable. He then argued that the "classification of market structures" could act as a way past the problem:

We can admit that if cost and demand curves for short, long, and intermediate periods were discoverable rather than assumed, a large part of what is called business policy could be explained without resorting to so crude a device as the classification of market structures. It is, however, precisely because theoretical techniques of price analysis have been constructed without regard to their empirical applicability that such a classification is necessary as a first and important step towards an understanding of business policies and practices. (Mason 1939, p. 66)

Mason then goes on to list the various characteristics that could be used to define and classify market structures, such as the nature of the product, cost conditions, number of size of firms, ease of entry, demand conditions, and distribution channels. These factors involved *both* the internal structure of the firm and the external market structure.

Mason made some interesting comments on the relationship between his approach and institutionalism. He argued that "the theory of oligopoly has been aptly described as a ticket of admission to institutional economics," yet he was critical of the "excessive" institutionalism of Walton Hamilton with its emphasis on the peculiarities of each case. Mason wanted an approach that promised some greater generality. As has been argued, he was per-haps "seeking a compromise between theorists and institutionalists as to the appropriate level of abstraction" (Phillips and Stevenson 1974, p. 338).

Mason's approach formed the basis of the SCP model that was to be much elaborated by Joe Bain and others. In his 1944 work, Bain reiterates many of the points made by Mason. He stresses the problems involved with the empirical verification of Chamberlin's model, which would require a series of observations concerning demand and cost curves and their shifts over time, observations that were not available. At the same time Bain was not keen on the particularist case study style of work produced by Walton Hamilton. According to Bain, "until it adopts some unifying hypothesis, its findings promise no more than an indefinitely long catalogue of apparently unique cases" (Bain 1944, p. 5).

Also, an examination of Bain's methodological pronouncements makes it clear that he had adopted something of a positivist methodological posi-tion. His work is full of references to the importance of "empirical content," to the lack of verifiability as indicating the "sterility" of a hypothesis, and of the significance of theoretical propositions being "verifiable." In this con-nection, it is noteworthy that, thanks to the presence of W. V. Quine and Rudolf Carnap, Harvard in the late 1930s became "suffused" with the teach-ings of logical positivism (Quine 1985; Brown 2008).[5]

In the field of labor economics, work on imperfect competition had also provided new theoretical tools, but with many of the same empirical issues that faced research in industrial organization. It is not uncommon to find reference to a "second generation institutionalist," or "neoinstitutionalist," or "revisionist" labor economists, including such people as John Dunlop, Clark Kerr, Richard Lester, Lloyd Reynolds, and Arthur Ross (Kerr 1988; Boyer and Smith 2001; Kaufman 2004). Their training had brought them

---

[5]   This is before Quine developed his criticisms of positivism.

into close contact with both the institutionalist literature on labor in the Wisconsin tradition and neoclassical theory including Hick's *Theory of Wages* (1932) and Paul Douglas's empirical work on the Cobb-Douglas production function (Cobb and Douglas 1928; Douglas 1934b). Kerr and Dunlop completed PhDs at Berkeley. Kerr's thesis supervisor, and later coauthor, was Paul Taylor. Reynolds was trained at Harvard where he would have had contact with Sumner Slichter.

One way of thinking about the work of these labor economists is that they started from the competitive model, but thought about the competitive forces of the market as only one of a number of factors that could affect wages, and not necessarily the most important ones. Experience with the War Labor Board during World War II led to an awareness of a range of wage differentials difficult to reconcile with the competitive model, and the key importance for labor of a variety of nonwage conditions and procedures (Kerr 1988, pp. 7, 24). They also developed an interest in internal labor markets and the wage and salary structures within firms. Kerr argued that the "basic explanations of traditional economics become useful to full understanding only as realistic observations of them are made in operation and as exceptions to them are comprehended" (Kerr 1988, p. 22). Of course, the exceptions can mount up to pretty much overwhelm the "traditional theory." As Boyer and Smith note, the attitude to the neoclassical model was often highly "ambivalent." The textbooks produced by Lester (1941) and Reynolds (1949) contained very little on the competitive determination of wages. Instead the emphasis was on trade union bargaining, employer practices, and government regulations, all institutionalist themes (Boyer and Smith 2001, pp. 203–204).

One of the most interesting episodes in this literature concerned Richard Lester's critique of the marginal productivity theory in the context of the effect of minimum wage laws (Lester 1946; 1947). Lester's critique was based on interviews with business decision makers and strongly indicated that they did not think in terms of marginal productivity and, in any case, could not calculate it from the data available to them. Lester concluded that the marginal productivity theory of labor demand was "invalid" and that a new approach was required. As is well known, Lester's critique was in turn attacked both by Fritz Machlup and George Stigler, essentially on the grounds that the neoclassical model was a formal representation of what decision makers did even if they were not consciously aware of all the steps. Machlup's reply to Lester had a heavily subjectivist orientation (Machlup 1946), whereas Stigler resorted to the rhetoric of accusing Lester of "an attack on economic theory" (Stigler 1947b; Prasch 2007). One upshot of this was Milton Friedman's great unease at Machlup and Stigler's responses because they verged on denying that any empirical evidence could refute marginal productivity theory (Leeson 1998; Prasch 2007). This became one element in Friedman's development of his own methodological position as expressed in his famous essay on positive economics (Friedman 1953).

What this brief discussion of industrial organization and labor economics demonstrates is that through the 1940s and for some time beyond, applied microeconomics was still much affected by the institutionalist emphasis on empirical relevance and the realism of theories. This can be seen not only in the two field areas dealt with here, but in many areas of applied economics and policy analysis as well. Development economics and international affairs would be other cases in point where more institutional forms of analysis continued to exist. In all of these areas, however, any explicit identification with institutionalism was clearly on the decline. The institutionalist critique of neoclassical theory and the acceptance of the need for an empirical and institutional component were accommodated in a particular way. If Mason, Bain, and Kerr are taken as examples, there was a tendency to characterize previous institutionalist work as nontheoretical; a greater willingness to accept neoclassical theory at least as a starting point, although requiring modification in the light of empirical observations and institutional considerations; and an acceptance of a positivist methodological position with its emphasis on empirical content and verifiability. Further moves toward neoclassicism in these areas were to come with the development of the Chicago School and its related methodological position, as discussed further.

COWLES AND THE FURTHER HISTORY OF THE NBER

Another important development came with what has been called the "probabilistic revolution in econometrics" occasioned largely by the work of Trygve Haavelmo (Morgan 1990). The probabilistic approach combined with the use of simultaneous equation models became the basis of the Cowles Commission approach in its Chicago years, particularly at the hands of Jacob Marschak and Tjalling Koopmans. It was this approach that provided the basis of Koopmans' critique of Burns and Mitchell's *Measuring Business Cycles* as mentioned in Chapter 9 (Koopmans 1947). Koopmans opposed the NBER approach on the grounds that it lacked a well-specified structural economic model and so constituted "measurement without theory." As pointed out by Carl Christ, "the Cowles Commission approach to econometrics was built on the premise that a correct a priori specifications were already available for the models that were to be estimated by its methods" (Christ 1994, p. 53), and the Cowles group used a Walrasian model "based on the aggregation of individual economic agents as units and in which the cycle was seen as a deviation from an underlying equilibrium level" (Morgan 1990, p. 56). Koopmans also argued that the NBER work lacked a proper theory of statistical inference, and that theories "should be explicitly formulated as statistical hypotheses, so that methods of inference based on probability theory could be used to measure and test the relationships" (Morgan 1990, p. 56). The defense of the NBER was made by Rutledge Vining, who argued that the NBER methods were designed to *discover* hypotheses, and that the economic theory used by Cowles was at best thin and unsatisfactory. As Vining put it, "in seeking for interesting hypotheses for our quantitative studies we might want to wander beyond the classic Walrasian fields" (Vining 1949, p. 85). Vining, however, did not reject the probability approach to empirical work in economics and himself cited Haavelmo in support of his contentions.

Although work from the NBER did use a variety of techniques, including hypothesis testing and the use of probability inference,[6] those associated with the NBER continued to be critical of the work by Cowles, on the grounds that it took a stochastic Walrasian model "as the essence of economic reasoning" (Hastay 1951), and those in charge at the NBER remained decidedly suspicious of the method of econometric model building. As discussed in Chapter 9, the NBER was able to maintain adherence to its own methodological ideas for a very long period of time after Koopmans's attack, and this despite the fact that the profession as a whole was moving in different directions.

The reasons for the long survival of the Mitchell-Burns approach to empirical work at the NBER are to be found in the strong support given to the NBER by Joseph Willits until his retirement from Rockefeller, followed by a long period of benign neglect from the Ford Foundation (FF). Rockefeller only bowed out of providing funding for the NBER in the late 1950s, and at that point, the NBER turned to the Ford Foundation. In the period after World War II, Ford provided "the most generous patronage of economics by any foundation" (Goodwin 1998, p. 77) and came very largely to displace Carnegie and Rockefeller in the support of social science (Geiger 1988). Ford's philosophy was similar to Carnegie's and Rockefeller's in that it also envisaged the improvement of human welfare through the best that social

---

[6] In NBER work, hypothesis testing tended to be of specific hypotheses within the investigation and not of an overall model.

science had to offer, but the attitude at Ford tended to be much more critical of the then-existing state of social science, regarding it as insufficiently "scientific," but with "science" now defined in terms of the development of a theory of human behavior and a closer integration of theory with application to social and economic problems. The direction of the Ford Foundation was established by a committee of consultants chaired by H. Rowlan Gaither Jr., who was then President of the RAND Corporation.[7] Gaither would serve as President of the FF between 1953 and 1956. As argued by Geiger:

At the Ford Foundation the critique of the current state of the social sciences was better informed and more explicit than it had been in the two other foundations. The social science disciplines were not yet fulfilling their basic mission. There was insufficient integration of theory and research, and insufficient continuity and cumulativeness of findings. (Geiger 1988, p. 327)[8]

Despite this, Thomas Carroll at Ford was significantly less horror-struck by Fabricant's proposals than those at Rockefeller had been, and he set about establishing a committee of economists to review the Bureau's work and its financial position. This committee was chaired by Gardner Ackley, with George Stocking and Richard Ruggles as the other members.[9] The Committee reported in February 1959, but the criticism of NBER research contained in the report was quite mild and did not suggest any major changes (Gardner Ackley, Richard Ruggles, and George Stocking, Report to the Ford Foundation on the National Bureau of Economic Research,

---

[7] For a discussion of the work conducted at RAND during and after the war, see Mirowski (2002, chapter 4, pp. 207–222, and chapter 5). RAND was associated with game theory, mathematical economics, and operations research. RAND became a major sponsor of the Cowles Commission.

[8] This attitude toward social science at Ford was perhaps best displayed in the program operated by the Division of Behavioral Sciences that was focused on basic research designed to promote the "scientific study of man" and make the "behavioral sciences more scientific" (Geiger 1988). Most applied economic research, including both Brookings and the NBER, however, was funded through the Division of Economic Development. One of the priority areas for this division, as defined in 1950, was that of promoting research aimed at "achieving a growing economy with high output and employment and a minimum of destructive instability" (Nelson 1966, p. 523), but some of the same Ford attitude prevailed there too, with the conception of good science in economics being much more in line with the emerging postwar "consensual neoclassical mainstream" (Goodwin 1998, pp. 77–78) than with the interwar conceptions of empirical science that had been endorsed by Willits.

[9] Correspondence between Committee members indicates disagreement over the extent to which the criticisms shared with Thomas Carroll in a confidential letter to him should also be plainly stated in the Report. Ruggles seemed the most concerned not to offend anyone at the Bureau, with Stocking arguing that the letter to Carroll and the Report should be made as consistent as possible (George Stocking to Gardner Ackley and Richard Ruggles, nd [February 1959], PA55–66, Ford Foundation Archives).

16 February 1959, and Letter to Thomas Carroll, 16 February 1959, PA55–66, Ford Foundation Archives). On this basis, the Ford Foundation awarded the Bureau $2.5 million in June 1959 (paid as a lump sum).

The various points made by the Committee appointed by Ford seem to have had only a slight impact at the Bureau. Crucially, Ford did not insist on further progress reports, and the Bureau was allowed to continue to follow its own lights. Criticisms of the Bureau's research or methods tended to be dismissed as due to a failure to "comprehend the majesty of the achievements of the Bureau" (Joseph Willits to Arthur Burns, 26 February 1963, Arthur Burns Papers, Box 134).

The next step came at the initiative of Ford. In early 1964, Marshall Robinson of Ford invited a number of research organizations, including the NBER, to look ahead and make proposals for further long-term grants. After some preliminary investigations, Robinson reduced the field of possible candidates to Brookings and the National Bureau. A large grant was made to Brookings in December 1965.[10] Things did not go so smoothly for the Bureau. Fabricant wrote an initial response to Robinson, but shortly thereafter tendered his resignation as the Bureau's Director of Research, in order to focus on his own work, and the Bureau launched into a major effort to select a successor. As a part of this, the Bureau also reviewed its research direction (Committee on Arrangements to Meet Problem of Retirement of Director of Research, Report to the Executive Committee, 8 March 1965, Arthur F. Burns Papers, Box 126), but the candidate chosen was Geoffrey Moore, who had been with the Bureau since the late 1930s and had been the Associate Director of Research for many years. The choice of Moore was seen as a decision by the Bureau to stay very much on its existing track. Paul Samuelson, on the Board, later said that Moore's selection seemed somehow inevitable, the "basic assumption being that the Bureau would continue pretty much the pattern of the past" (Marshall Robinson to McGeorge Bundy, June 15, 1966, PA 69–707, Ford Foundation Archives). Moore did establish an Advisory Committee consisting of both Bureau Board members and outside academics to consider the Bureau's research direction. Several members of this Committee argued that what the Bureau needed was a "nucleus of econometricians," but Moore's own comment on this was that "not too much attention was paid to what the econometricians would do,

---

[10] It might be noted here that Brookings had already shifted away from its earlier institutionalist ideas and connections and moved in a more Keynesian direction. Harold Moulton retired in 1952 and was succeeded by Robert Calkins and then Kermit Gordon. The Brookings-SSRC econometric modeling project involving Lawrence Klein began in the early 1960s.

why they needed the Bureau in order to do it, or even that the superior power of econometric techniques had been demonstrated" (Geoffrey Moore to Arthur Burns, 26 May 1966, Arthur F. Burns Papers, Box 125).

Burns sent a formal proposal to Ford in May 1965, followed up in March 1966 with documents relating to the Bureau's history and financial position. Robinson followed Ford precedent and established an Advisory Committee, but this time to report in confidence. This Committee consisted of Emile Despres (Stanford), R. A. Gordon, (Berkeley), Lawrence Klein (Wharton), Lloyd Reynolds (Yale), Theodore Schultz (Chicago), George Shultz (Chicago) and James Tobin (Yale). Many Committee members had experience with the NBER either as members of the Board or as Visiting Fellows, but the group as a whole was clearly representative of the mainstream applied economics of the time. Although this Committee thought highly of the Bureau's earlier work and the accomplishments of the Conference on Income and Wealth, they expressed a number of serious concerns: The Bureau's research program was too diffuse and not carefully thought out; many of the Bureau's studies were too narrow and lacked adequate analytical content; Moore lacked sufficient academic stature, and his appointment was reflective of poor selection processes; Burns lacked sufficient vigor and breadth for leading the institution; the Board of Directors was obsolete and provided insufficient direction; the resident staff, with some notable exceptions, were not first rate; the Bureau's role as a middleman between foundations and the academician was no longer required; and the Bureau had not kept up to date with "modern research methodology and techniques" (R. A. Gordon, Comments on the National Bureau of Economic Research; Marshall Robinson, The National Bureau Meeting – 4 June 1966, 7 June 1966; Marshall Robinson to McGeorge Bundy, The NBER-FF: Recent History, 8 June 1996; Lloyd Reynolds to Marshall Robinson, 10 June 1966, PA69–707, Ford Foundation Archives).

With the explicit intent of forcing changes at the Bureau, Marshall Robinson informed Burns that the Foundation had decided to "take no action at this time" on the Bureau's proposal (Marshall Robinson to Arthur Burns, 24 June 1966, PA69–707, Ford Foundation Archives). Shortly after the Ford decision, on 20 June, Burns indicated to the NBER Board his wish to step down as President of the NBER. A Search Committee for a new President was established under the Chairmanship of Joseph Willits (other members included Crawford Greenewalt, Robert Roosa, Paul Samuelson, Theodore Schultz, and Boris Shishkin) to find a successor. The issue of econometrics came up in this context too, R. A. Gordon expressing regret that the Bureau had not maintained an involvement in the large-scale econometric modeling project at Brookings. Others expressed some skepticism "about the contributions to economic knowledge that were being made by econometricians" (G. E. Moore, Position of the National Bureau of Economic Research Re Econometric Studies, 13 June 1966, Arthur Burns Papers Box 139).

In mid-1967, John Meyer of Harvard was appointed as President of the National Bureau, Burns became Chairman of the Board, and internal conflict was not long in coming. Meyer presented a reorganization plan to the Executive Committee in February 1968. This reorganization would give the president responsibility for the overall formulation of research programs and setting guidelines for research design. The guidance of groups of research programs would be given to two or more Vice Presidents for Research who would have under them directors of specific research programs. The president would be responsible for "bringing the best people together with the best possible project," and evaluating the results of each program. He would also assume responsibility for submission of proposed new research to the Board and submission of reports to the Board for review prior to publication (Minutes of Meeting of Executive Committee of the National Bureau of Economic Research, 15 February 1968, Arthur F. Burns Papers, Box 125). Meyer's plans also involved a reduction in the emphasis given to business cycles, a new emphasis on human resource economics and urban economics, and a build-up of staff "committed to assorted highly mathematical tools of analysis" (Marshall Robinson, National Bureau of Economic Research, 25 June 1968, PA69–707, Ford Foundation Archives). As might be expected, both Burns and Moore were upset and attempted to reverse Meyer's plans. Meyer, however, insisted and was ultimately to get his way (John Meyer to The Executive Committee, 14 March 1968, Arthur F. Burns Papers, Box 125). Moore left the Bureau in 1969 to become Commissioner of Labor Statistics,[11] and Burns became an "Honorary Chairman" of the Bureau.

Meyer resumed discussions with Ford in mid-1968, and Robinson did invite an application for a proposal that "would give the Bureau a degree of freedom with which it could demonstrate what the new administration can do – something like a five-year grant providing some annual support funds." In due course, an application for $2 million in general support over five-to-seven years was submitted. In the preceding correspondence, Meyer had emphasized the changes brought to the organization of the Bureau, the changes to the Board, the new staff appointments, the new research

---

[11] Moore was later at New York and Columbia Universities, where he continued to work on business cycles, particularly on forecasting, using the old-style National Bureau methods.

programs started in human resources, urban economics, and law and economics, the increase in conference activity, the need for more extensive computer facilities, the success in bringing promising young scholars to the Bureau as research fellows, and the introduction of student subscriptions and *The National Bureau Report*.

Ford's own subsequent view of this grant was that it exactly achieved its purpose. It had allowed Meyer to shift the focus of the Bureau, bring in able young scholars, modernize the Bureau's research methods, and recapture the Bureau's image and prestige (Irma Bischoff to M. K. Chamberlain, 30 June 1980, PA69–707, Ford Foundation Archives).

Meyer's Presidency of the Bureau is significant in that it represented a clear break away from the attitudes and priorities of the Bureau's previous "establishment" and the creation of a new consensus between Ford and the Bureau based around the application of neoclassical theory and econometric methods. This consensus had, of course, been developing within the profession and its financial patrons ever since the end of World War II, but with Meyer's presidency, the Bureau became aligned with the dominant postwar mainstream consensus.

CHICAGO ECONOMICS AND INSTITUTIONALISM

The development of the Chicago School of Economics has importance in the history of institutional economics in at least three of its aspects. First, in the effort to reformulate a defense of free markets as opposed to institutionalist and other lines of criticism; second, in the methodological defense of abstract theoretical models produced by Friedman; and third, in the application to neoclassical models to a variety of areas that had previously been outside of the scope of standard economic analysis.

Simons's desire to create at Chicago a center that would maintain adherence to traditional liberal values has already been noted. Simons's wish began to bear fruit with the establishment at Chicago of the "Free Market Project" that commenced in 1946. This project was funded by the Volker Foundation, organized by Fredrick Hayek, led by Aaron Director, and involved Milton Friedman and many others at Chicago (Van Horn 2009; Van Horn and Mirowski 2009). As the project developed, those involved came to adopt a viewpoint that was relatively unconcerned with the problem of monopoly. Particularly important in this respect was Warren Nutter's study of monopoly that took direct aim at A. R. Burns's "decline of competition" thesis (Nutter 1951). The upshot was a view that innovation in products and techniques tended to undermine monopoly positions provided that such monopoly was not supported by government regulations or licensing requirements. This in turn led to revised views on appropriate antitrust policies and policies toward patents and intellectual property.

The Free Market Project broadened into Friedman's wide-ranging defense of markets, most obviously in his *Capitalism and Freedom* (Friedman 1962), but even before that, Friedman had taken the leadership in promoting the Chicago View, particularly in his price theory course, and his work on macroeconomic and monetary economics. Friedman's main targets were Keynesian economics, the Cowles Commission, and the imperfect competition theories of Edward Chamberlin and Joan Robinson. Stigler, who joined Friedman at Chicago in 1958, also mounted many attacks – "Demolition Derbies," to use Thomas Sowell's phrase (Sowell 1993) – on monopolistic competition theory, on Paul Sweezy's kinked demand curve (Stigler 1947a), on Richard Lester's challenge to marginalism (Stigler 1947b), on J. K. Galbraith's countervailing power (Stigler 1954), on Gardiner Means's work on administered prices (Stigler and Kindahl 1970), and on Berle and Means on corporate ownership and behavior (Stigler and Friedland 1983). Stigler was openly contemptuous of institutionalist work, saying: "Institutional economics is dying out at a fantastic rate – though still not fast enough to suit me" (Sowell 1993, p. 788).

Very closely related to the defense of the competitive model was Friedman's methodological position. Friedman's methodology owed something to his contact with Henry Schultz as a student at Chicago, his involvement with the NBER, and his contact with Karl Popper through the Mont Pelerin Society. As noted earlier, Friedman's contact with the NBER began in 1937 when he took over Simon Kuznets's study of professional income. Later, at Arthur Burns's urging, he took on the study of the monetary aspects of the business cycle, a project that resulted in Friedman and Schwartz's *Monetary History* (1963). These studies were very much in the traditional Mitchell-Burns NBER empirical mold. Friedman held both Mitchell and Burns in high regard (Burns had been his teacher at Rutgers).

Friedman's methodological position, as expressed in his famous "The Methodology of Positive Economics" (Friedman 1953), can be seen as a combination of NBER empiricism with various positivist ideas of science and his own interpretation of Karl Popper's emphasis on falsification and the testing of predictions. The key elements in Friedman's essay are the notions that theories should be seen as instruments for prediction, that theories should be tested only on the basis of their empirical predictions, and that the unrealism of a theory's assumptions should not be a matter of concern. Indeed unrealism of assumptions is seen as a necessary characteristic of theories capable of yielding testable predictions. Contained in the essay, implicitly or explicitly, are criticisms of the various attacks then being made on the "unrealism" of the standard neoclassical assumptions, theories of imperfect competition, and the structural modeling approach of the Cowles Commission (Hammond 1996).

Friedman's methodology has been seen as linked back to the instrumentalist philosophy of John Dewey (Hirsch and de Marchi 1990), but there are major differences. Those influenced by Dewey's version of instrumentalism often spoke of theories as tools or as instruments, but in Dewey's view, they are tools for "prediction and control" with the emphasis on the idea of theories as instruments for social control. Prediction and control here means useful for the prediction of the consequences of institutional change for economic behavior and outcomes. Prediction is not narrowly confined to a few economic variables such as price and quantity, and the whole enterprise of prediction and control is seen as an integral part of a process of policy experiments and of learning from trial and error in the application of theories to the solution of social problems. Friedman's methodology, undoubtedly because it allowed economists to leave behind the nagging question of how to make theory more realistic, became quickly and widely accepted within the profession. The important point here is not Friedman's own methodological practice, but the impact of his essay on the profession at large.

Chicago economics, however, developed into much more than a combination of competitive price theory, monetarism, and Friedman's methodology. The Chicago approach to economics was soon to move into a wide variety of areas that were outside of the previous range cultivated by neoclassical economics. Gary Becker led the way with his work on labor economics and the economics of the household. Becker expressed his view that "the combined assumptions of maximizing behavior, market equilibrium, and stable preferences, used relentlessly and unflinchingly, form the heart of the economic approach as I see it" (Becker 1976, p. 5). This attitude, with its stark contrast to institutionalist attitudes, took over the areas of labor economics and industrial organization in the 1970s, but it went much further than that.

The Chicago View, with its strong promarket, antiregulatory emphasis, became the basis of Chicago law and economics (Medema 1998; Van Horn 2009). Simons's teaching in the law school had begun this trend, but it was with Aaron Director and his contribution to teaching of the antitrust course with Edward Levi, and the founding of the *Journal of Law and Economics* in 1958, that brought Chicago law and economics to the fore (Duxbury

1995). Ronald Coase joined the Chicago Law School (from the University of Virginia) in 1964, and much work on the economics of property rights stemmed from Coase, Stigler, and students such as Harold Demsetz. Others, such as James Buchanan and Warren Nutter, developed the area of public choice theory; Buchanan making the important distinction between the constitutional level of rules and the rules that emerge from the decision making within that constitution. In addition, Chicago became associated with the neoclassical approach to the economics of the household in the person of Gary Becker (Becker 1965; 1976). Becker spent 1954–1957 at Chicago, then moved to Columbia where he came into contact with Jacob Mincer, before returning in 1969. Mincer had also had exposure to Chicago as a postdoctoral student (Grossbard-Shechtman 2001). In these ways, Chicago economics moved the analytics of price theory out of its traditional realm and into areas previously cultivated by American institutionalists.

Despite the obvious and substantial differences between old-style American institutional economics and modern Chicago School economics, there are a number of interesting links between them. One connection runs from Margaret Reid to the "new" economics of the household and consumption economics. Both Mincer and Becker were exposed to Reid's work on the household while at Chicago (Reid 1934; Grossbard-Shechtman 2001). Moreover, the empirical work of Margaret Reid, along with others such as Dorothy Brady and Rose Friedman, on income and consumption was instrumental in prompting Milton Friedman's development of the permanent income hypothesis (Friedman 1957, p. ix; Forget 2000). As noted, Friedman had worked on professional income for the NBER, and a significant part of the work of Reid, Brady, and Rose Friedman was conducted through the NBER's Conference on Income and Wealth. A consistent interest in consumption and household economics, running from the institutional approaches of Veblen, Abbott, Kyrk, and Reid to the neoclassicism of Theodore Schultz, Becker, and Friedman, is a notable feature of the history of Chicago economics.

There are some connections between the Chicago law-and-economics movement with the earlier legal realist movement. As we have seen, hiring economists into law schools was not a Chicago invention; it was, in fact, the legal realists who "initiated the interdisciplinary turn in American legal education" (Leiter 2001). Edward Levi was interested in the relationship between law and the social sciences, very much a realist theme, and entirely familiar with the work of Karl Llewellyn and Walton Hamilton. Levi had even worked on antitrust with Hamilton and Arnold, but later transitioned to a Chicago perspective (Van Horne 2009, p. 220). Llewellyn was hired from Columbia to Chicago in 1951, and it was while he was at Chicago that he made many of his major contributions to the formulation of the Uniform Commercial Code. Llewellyn's argument concerning commercial law is relevant in that he claimed that the courts tended to enforce the norms of prevailing commercial practice, including the obligation of "good faith" or the observance of "reasonable commercial standards of fair dealing in the trade" (Leiter 2001). A similar view was expressed by Commons. Schwartz (2000) has argued that this anticipated the more recent law and economics position concerning the efficiency of common law. Efficiency is "an important norm of mercantile practice," thus if judges enforce these norms, "it will turn out that judges will try, among other things, to produce efficient outcomes" (Leiter 2001).

Posner and others have denied that Chicago law and economics owes anything directly to the legal realist movement, and this is a controversial topic (Posner 1995). Posner himself frequently cites Justice Holmes's sociological jurisprudence and refers often to John Dewey's pragmatism, both of which were sources for the legal realist movement. On the other hand, it should not be surprising that Llewellyn himself did not approve of the particular type of neoclassical law and economics being developed by Director and others at Chicago (Kitch 1983). As with other Chicago work, we find here an older institutionalist theme being reworked and modified through the application of neoclassical price theory.

Chicago, through the person of Robert Fogel, also has an association with cliometrics, but this too has some institutionalist connections. As seen in Chapter 8, Fogel was a student of Carter Goodrich, who was working on questions relating to canals and American economic development, but given Fogel's empirical interests, Goodrich suggested he transfer to Johns Hopkins to work with Kuznets.

A final, and fascinating, institutionalist-Chicago connection runs through Rutledge Vining. Vining graduated from Chicago in 1944 with a thesis on regional variation of short-run business cycles, but he had also been taught by Frank Knight. Vining became a research associate at the National Bureau and, as previously noted, it was Vining who wrote the reply to Koopmans, defending the Burns-Mitchell approach to business cycles (Vining 1949). His NBER experience gave him an interest in the institutionalist conception of a "price system" or "economic system" that underlay much of the empirical work of institutionalists such as Mitchell and F. C. Mills, but which had never been made explicit (Rutledge Vining to Arthur Burns, 10 June and 9 October 1963, Arthur F. Burns Papers, Box 35). Vining sought to make a "simple peace" between statistical economists and the methodological writings of Knight. For Vining, quantitative economics was not about solving social problems but about "the behavior properties of population systems" (Vining 1950). Such systems can be thought of as consisting of individuals acting within a set of "laws" or rules that are largely institutional in nature. Such laws he though of as stochastic in nature, producing variations in outcomes. From this he developed a concern with the problem of "diagnosing faultiness in the observed performance of an economic system" (Vining 1963) and an emphasis on ensuring that policy did not merely attack symptoms but operated on the level of the underlying rules or structure of the system. In Vining's view, the policy maker's job was to choose the rules rather than to try to directly regulate outcomes. Vining spent his career at the University of Virginia (from 1945) and recruited Buchanan and Nutter there. For many years, Buchanan and Vining were close, and Vining's emphasis on the underlying institutional rules was a vital factor in the development of Buchanan's own thinking, as Buchanan himself has often acknowledged (Buchanan and Tullock 1965, p. 210).

These links, however, only serve to emphasize the fact that Chicago style economics took over areas of study that had previously been very largely the preserve of institutionalists.

DEFINITIONS OF SCIENCE

As argued at length in Chapter 2, in the interwar period, it was the institutionalists who were claiming to be following a "scientific" method. The notion of science held by institutionalists was empirical, investigative, experimental, involved taking on board work in related disciplines, and very much related to the ideal of social control. These views were taken in large part from the pragmatic and instrumental view of science provided by John Dewey. Theories are seen as instruments for investigation and control to be tested by the consequences of their application.

Also, in Dewey's work, there is no hard distinction made between the methods used to appraise scientific theories and those used to appraise values. Both are appraised on the basis of the consequences of their application. This point of view was accepted even by those such as Mitchell who wanted to keep their scientific investigations separate from political discussion of policy goals and objectives. This was not because Mitchell thought that values could not be appraised instrumentally, but because of his perceived need to keep his (and the NBER's) work clear from any possible accusation of political bias. Mitchell advocated for a National Planning Board that might, "by throwing light upon the consequences that different lines of action would produce," be able to "contribute much towards making social valuations more rational" and help attain a "more valid scale of social values than now prevails among us" (Mitchell 1936b, p. 135).

Neoclassical economists did mount defenses of their more theoretical and deductive approaches, but it is very noticeable that at that time, neoclassicals did not generally claim to be taking their methods from the natural sciences. Raymond Bye (1924), Frank Knight (1924), Jacob Viner (1928), and Allyn Young (1929) all mounted defenses of orthodox theory and methods, but their arguments all contained major qualifications in the attempt to link neoclassicism to natural science. At most, they argue that orthodox theory is like natural science in the sense of *theoretical* or *mathematical* physics, but they cannot deny that most natural science is a good deal more empirical than orthodox economics. As a result, they seek to limit the more general transfer of natural science methods, usually on the grounds of the greater complexity of social phenomena and the inability to conduct controlled experiments. Viner, for example, argues, in response to Mitchell and Mills, that "methodological analogies from physics should not be applied to economics as a whole without the most serious qualifications and reservations" (Viner 1928, p. 31). This demonstrates the justice of Porter's remark that "while neoclassical economists may have derived much of their mathematical theory using analogies with physics, they were very far from accepting the prevailing standards of physics as a practice" (Porter 1994, p. 157).

This situation radically reversed itself in the post-1945 period, mainly owing to the importation of various positivist ideas of science. Positivism in various forms was brought to the United States by Quine and Carnap, and by the many émigré academics who arrived to escape fascism in Europe.[12] Some of the signs of this are to be found in material mentioned earlier, such as Samuelson's operationalism, the methodological rhetoric of verificationism utilized by Bain and others, and the methodology pursued by the Cowles Commission.

It is sometimes claimed that institutionalists (and particularly people such as Mitchell) adopted "positivist" ideas, but such claims require care. As Wade Hands has argued:

---

[12] For discussion of the impact of émigré economists in America, see Craver and Leijonhufvud (1987), Scherer (2000), Hagemann (2005), and Mongiovi (2005). Many of the economists who arrived at the New School (The University in Exile) were left-of-center and skeptical of various aspects of neoclassical thinking. Institutionalists did form some contacts with certain members of the émigré group, such as Adolf Lowe and Gerhard Colm, but less than might have been thought.

Yes, pragmatism, like logical positivism, was a "scientific philosophy"; and, yes, both approaches promote the extension of scientific reasoning ...; and, yes, both are broadly "empirical" and concerned with "experience"; but the similarities essentially stop with these basic points. Dewey in particular had a very "latitudinarian" view of the experimental method of science ... and never exhibited the positivist tendency to view "science" as a narrowly circumscribed endeavor. Dewey was both anti-epistemology and anti-foundationalist and certainly never shared the positivist goal of dictating the proper empirical foundation of all scientific knowledge. Perhaps most importantly, he considered the scientific form of life to be social, linked to democracy, and not a subject for armchair philosophizing about the ultimate character of knowledge. (Hands 2004, p. 959)

The demands of logical positivism and operationalism were, however, extremely onerous, and economists tended to adopt either the less restrictive logical empiricism of Carnap, Carl Hempel, and Ernest Nagel or Friedman's version of instrumentalism. Both of these approaches gave wide range to deductive theorizing with the emphasis only on the empirical testing (by verification or falsification) of the implications of the theoretical model. Logical empiricism, moreover, claimed to be a general description of scientific procedure, applicable to both the natural and physical sciences, and it largely displaced pragmatism as the ruling philosophy of science in the United States.

Logical empiricism emphasizes the "hypothetico-deductive" nature of theories. Theories contain axioms and statements derived from them. The axioms "may refer to either observables or theoretical entities," and the "system is given empirical meaningfulness only when the system is given some empirical interpretation" via the translation of some of the theoretical statements into observational language (Caldwell 1982, p. 25). It is usually the "lower level" deduced consequences of a theory that will describe observables and that are subject to empirical verification. Friedman's methodology is much less formal and simply focuses attention on the testing of a theory's predictions, with no attention being given to the realism of assumptions. Both positions, however, provided a view of science that could counter institutionalist demands for realism. Provided orthodox theory had an empirical component, it could claim the mantle of science while at the same time accusing institutionalists of naïve empiricism. All of the criticism of institutionalism as descriptive, lacking theory, or antitheoretical either explicitly or implicitly adopts one of these views of what constitutes a "scientific economics."

INSTITUTIONALISM IN THE 1940S AND BEYOND

This book is not intended here to give a history of post–World War II institutionalism, but there are some key developments that should be mentioned in terms of institutionalist reactions to the changing nature of orthodox economic mentioned earlier. One of the most important of these involves the emergence of Clarence Ayres as a leading figure within institutionalism.

Ayres arrived at the University of Texas in 1930 and found himself in a department that was already heavily institutionalist. A. B. Wolfe taught at Texas between 1914 and 1923, Max Handman between 1917 and 1930, Robert Montgomery began teaching at Texas in 1922, even before going to Brookings for his PhD, E. E. Hale joined the faculty in 1923, George Stocking was there between 1925 and 1946, and Ruth Allen joined in 1933. Until this time, Ayres had taught philosophy but he transitioned into economics, although always retaining a philosophical orientation. A number of writers on institutionalism have commented on this "Texas School" (see Phillips 1995).

Ayres's fist major work in economics was a book, *The Problem of Economic Order* (1938), a title that harked back to Hamilton's courses at Amherst. Ayres sent copies of this book to all and sundry with a covering note emphasizing the use of the definite article. *The* problem of the economic order, according to Ayres, lay in the unequal distribution of income that was responsible for the economic problem of depressions and more besides. Greater equality would be an instrumentally effective change. This remained a theme in Ayres's work, but he was to broaden his scope considerably in his next major book, *The Theory of Economic Progress* (1944).

Ayres was to argue that one of his concerns in writing this book was to respond to the criticism of institutionalism as lacking in theory (Clarence Ayres to J. M. Clark, 9 August 1944, Ayres Papers, Box 3F286). In the book itself, he seems to agree that institutionalism had been largely descriptive (Ayres 1944, pp. 11–12). To develop his theory of progress, Ayres turned back to Veblen: on the one hand, to Veblen's emphasis on technology as the engine of economic growth and progress, and on the other hand, to Veblen's view of the existing institutional system as often blocking further progress through the power of established ways of thinking and doing. Ayres takes these ideas and gives them a particular interpretation, identifying technology with instrumental ways of thinking and institutions with "ceremonialism" (Ayres 1944). This "dichotomy" between the instrumental and the ceremonial is at the heart of Ayres's system. For Ayres, the institutions of the market and of orthodox economics are ceremonial in nature. Neither is seen as being instrumental in the service of human progress, which in turn is defined very broadly as a life process consisting at base of the growth of instrumental capacities.

The difficulties with Ayres's system are several and serious. He comes dangerously close to simply defining technology as instrumental and institutions as ceremonial. He does not seem to fully recognize the necessary functions of institutions or that institutions can themselves be more or less instrumental. He does not want to recognize the possible adverse consequences of technological advance. He minimizes the problem of distinguishing what is instrumental from what is not with an analogy to a mechanic picking the right tool. When he specifies the values he sees as consistent with progress (freedom, equality, security, abundance, excellence, democracy), he argues that they can all be increased together, thus avoiding the heart of the problem of value (Rutherford 1981). There is little in Ayres's work that is empirical.

Ayres's effort to define institutionalism in terms of his instrumental/ceremonial dichotomy was, at the time, not particularly well received by other institutionalists, and completely failed to make any headway among other economists. Indeed, it could be claimed that Ayres's work only served to increase the marginalization of institutionalism considering that it contained almost nothing to appeal to the generality of postwar economists. Even those who knew Ayres well, such as Dorfman, Clark, and Copeland, were decidedly cool. Clark, who was much admired by Ayres, awkwardly declined Ayres's request that he write a reply to Hazlitt's scathing review of his book (J. M. Clark to Clarence Ayres, 13 August 1944, Ayres Papers, Box 3F286). Ayres's 1945 "Addendum To The Theory of Economic Progress," published in the AER (Ayres 1945), was prompted by word that Clark had been repeating Hazlitt's jibe about "machines to make machines to make machines" in the halls at Columbia (Clarence Ayres to Paul Homan, 21 September 1945, Ayres Papers, Box 2E71). Other old friends, such as Meiklejohn and Copeland, exchanged long and critical correspondences with Ayres concerning his dichotomy, neither becoming convinced by Ayres's arguments.

The disagreements between Ayres and Copeland are particularly interesting given the close connections between them. In 1965, Copeland wrote an introductory text to provide own view of what such a text should contain in place of the usual "principles-of-economics or model-analysis type of statement of our free-enterprise system" (Copeland 1958a, p. 2; 1965). There is a very explicit emphasis on the desirable aspects of the "free enterprise" system in this book that may relate to the context of the Cold War. But the idea is that the system of pecuniary institutions, although flawed in many ways and in need of reform, played an indispensable role and was responsible for much of the historical economic development of the west. Copeland opens his book with chapters concerning the problem of "central management without a central manager" and of the central institutions that perform the management functions, including freedom of calling, trade, the market, the price system, the profit system, and the free enterprise system. This is continued on a more detailed level with discussions of business corporations, property, contract, the debtor-creditor relation, money, the income and money circuit, competition, the wage system, business accounting, capitalism, business mores, private wrongs (including torts), and bankruptcy. The book continues with chapters on improving the theory of the firm, dealing with overhead costs, monopolistic competition, sales effort, and mark-up pricing, and on the capital budgeting decisions of the firm. Copeland then discusses ways of improving the set of pecuniary incentives, including restraints on high finance, depletion of natural resources, unfair competition, antisocial industrial practices, improper discrimination, de facto torts, conflicts of interest, and, following Clark, conversion of overhead costs to direct costs. Copeland also advocates positive action to improve information, encourage technological advance, set minimum standards, and regulate utilities. In certain cases, Copeland approves of public enterprise. The book concludes by discussing the "two major problem areas" in the economy, these being the problems of generating full and stable levels of output and employment and improving labor relations.

Prompted by Copeland's book, Ayres wrote a critical letter to Copeland in March 1966 that resulted in an exchange of correspondence (Clarence E. Ayres Papers, Box 3F286, Morris Copeland Folder). Despite their long friendship, the exchange occasionally had a testy character. The issues were the extent of Copeland's willingness to rely on "free enterprise" and pecuniary incentives, questions of value judgment, and Ayres's instrumental/ ceremonial or technological/institutional distinction. Copeland complains that Ayres's distinction involves a classification of behavioral patterns on the basis of a subjective value judgment and not on an objective, descriptive, basis; that it "is basically one between social structures you consider good in some sense and those you consider bad" (Morris Copeland to Clarence Ayres 24 August 1966 and 7 February 1967, Clarence E. Ayres Papers, Box 3F286, Morris Copeland Folder). Copeland argues that "economists, as far as social objectives are concerned, should confine themselves to questions of how objectives on which there is a good deal of agreement can be implemented and with the extent to which these objectives are consistent" (Morris Copeland to Clarence Ayres, 7 February 1967, Clarence E. Ayres Papers, Box 3F286, Morris Copeland Folder). Ayres, in return, argues that the distinction between the instrumental and the ceremonial is a demonstrable one, and makes it clear that in his view, the "free enterprise" system is a vehicle through which "the power structure" runs the country (Clarence Ayres to

Morris Copeland, 11 February 1967, Clarence E. Ayres Papers, Box 3F286, Morris Copeland Folder). It is this exchange that lies behind Copeland's 1967 paper in the *Journal of Economic Issues* on the role of markets and proper government functions, "Laissez Faire, Pecuniary Incentives, and Public Policy" (Copeland 1967), and Ayres's reply (Ayres 1968).[13]

These arguments outline some of the key differences between Ayres and the institutionalist program as expressed by most of the interwar members of the movement. Hamilton, Mitchell, Clark, Commons, and Copeland always gave the market an important instrumental role, even while suggesting the need for new forms of social control, and none of them would have found Ayres's tendency to see institutions as almost entirely ceremonial as a useful approach. Ayres's attitude toward markets and the price system is much closer to Veblen's than anyone else's. Nevertheless, and despite the criticisms that can be made of Ayres's ideas, he represents in an important way the primary institutionalist reaction to the new situation facing them. This reaction was to turn attention back to the ideas of Thorstein Veblen, as representing a source of more theoretical ideas and a more thorough rejection of orthodox economics. Ayres was able to produce a number of students (such as Fagg Foster, David Hamilton, and many others) who spread his ideas throughout many of the universities of the Southwest, and this Veblen-Ayres version of institutionalism became a major part of the post-1945 institutionalist movement. Of course, not everyone in the movement adopted the Ayresian system. J. K. Galbraith developed a different analysis of American capitalism, although also derived from Veblen (Galbraith 1958; 1967), Allan Gruchy maintained a greater emphasis on the structure of industry and on economic policy issues, and Warren Samuels, Harry Trebing, Allan Schmid, and Dan Bromley carried on in the Commons tradition. Overall, the movement became much less coherent and much more subject to internal disagreement than had previously been the case.

Texas itself remained a center for institutionalism for many years with people such as Wendell Gordon, Walter Neale, and H. H. Liebhafsky.[14] Outside of Texas and the Southwest, small institutionalist groups came

---

[13] Copeland also produced perhaps the most mathematical paper ever published in the *Journal of Economic Issues* – a paper arguing that the Pigou effect may be counteracted by the increasing burden of inflexible charges, such as the service on outstanding debts, as prices fall (Copeland 1970). This paper was badly mangled in the production of the Journal. Copeland received no proofs, a key element in its title was changed from "price and wage flexibility" to "price and wage stability," and there were many errors in the mathematical notation. A corrigenda was published in the June 1971 issue of the Journal.

[14] At this point, there was not only interest in Ayres, but also Polanyi and Commons (interview with John Adams, 15 February 2000).

to exist at Maryland (Allan Gruchy), the University of Massachusetts at Amherst (Ben Seligman), Cornell (Douglas Dowd), and at a few other places, but nothing on the earlier scale. J. K. Galbraith was by far the highest profile institutionalist of the post-1945 period, but he was a lone figure at Harvard and did not produce academic followers. Interestingly, Gruchy, Dowd, and Galbraith all appear to have been introduced to institutionalism at Berkeley.[15] Many economists continued to have concerns with neoclassical economics but became unwilling to associate themselves with "institutional economics."

In 1959, a small group of ten people met at the Windsor Hotel (formerly the Wardman Hotel) during an AEA conference to discuss the future of institutional economics. The meeting had been called by Allan Gruchy. As a clear indication of the disrepute into which the term "institutional economics" had fallen, one of the major items of business was the name that the group should adopt. As an interim measure and in the face of nothing better, the group called itself the Wardman Group. Joseph Gambs undertook to survey American economists with respect to their interest in institutional economics and produced a brief description of his talks with forty-five economists described as "dissenters." The largest group were those in the Veblen-Ayres tradition, but Gambs also noted another group who did not see themselves as in the tradition of Veblen or as institutionalists, but who were interested in the "reconstruction" of economics.[16]

The Wardman Group continued to meet at AEA conferences, growing to about 150 people on the mailing list by 1963. Two years later, the Association for Evolutionary Economics was formed with a broad statement of purpose designed to attract both groups identified by Gambs, and a paid membership for 1966 of 110. Those involved at this point included Clarence Ayres, John Blair, Joseph Dorfman, Douglas Dowd, Fagg Foster, John Gambs, J. K. Galbraith, Meredith Givens, Carter Goodrich, Wendell Gordon, Allan Gruchy, Forest Hill, Louis Junker, William Kapp, Gardiner

---

[15] On Dowd's career, see Keaney (2000). On Galbraith, see Parker (2005), Bruce (2000) and Dimand and Koehn (2008). Gruchy's introduction was in a course given by Homan, then visiting Berkeley. Homan's treatment of Veblen infuriated Gruchy but developed his interest.

[16] It is interesting that Gambs did not travel to those places where he might have found people working in the Commons tradition. Despite the broad statement of purpose it was not long before Gruchy was complaining that the *JEI* was publishing material that was not institutionalist (Gruchy Papers). Debates over this issue (and others) led to disputes over the editorial direction of the JEI and the formation of the Association for Institutional Thought (AFIT) in 1979 (Ransom 1981). For Gambs own take on institutional economics see Gambs (1946).

Means, Walter Neale, Warren Samuels, Ben Seligman, Marc Tool, Harry Trebing, and Theresa Wolfson. With some delay and difficulty, the Association's *Journal of Economic Issues* appeared in 1966. The institutionalist tradition in America continues to exist, but it remains a relatively small heterodox movement existing, for the most part, outside of the mainstream of American economics.

CONCLUSION

From all of the above, it is abundantly clear that as we move into the 1940s and beyond, institutionalism was facing a radically changed academic environment, with neoclassical and Keynesian economics very much on the ascendant. The key elements of institutionalism's original appeal no longer applied. The institutionalist claims to science had been taken over by a combination of Keynesian and neoclassical economics supplemented by econometrics and linked to some type of positivist method. Institutionalists reacted largely by abandoning the more "positivist" aspects of their own previous methodology. Statistical work virtually disappeared, and reference was made instead to ideas of "holism" and "pattern models" (Wilber and Harrison 1978), ideas that were a part of an antipositivist reaction in the social sciences.[17] The other central idea of social control also lost ground, partly through the very success of the New Deal, the arrival of Keynesianism and the welfare state. In the post–World War II environment, too, suggestions of planning or of more far-reaching social reforms could, and did, fall afoul of Cold War witch hunting.[18]

Certain areas such as industrial organization and labor economics increasingly became less hostile to neoclassical ideas, at least as starting points, and orthodox theory had itself become much developed, with many new lines of work opening up. Institutionalism was not renewed at Columbia and Wisconsin and gradually died out at those institutions with the retirement of the interwar generation. The NBER was also eventually realigned along orthodox lines. In the face of all of this, institutionalism could not maintain its previous position. Institutionalism as a movement

[17] Wilbur and Harrison presented their institutionalist methods explicitly as a contrast to Friedman's. There has been considerable debate over their characterization of institutionalist methods. Lind (1993) found little in the way of any distinctive institutionalist methods except a noticeable lack of econometrics and mathematical models.

[18] At Texas, Clarence Ayres was the subject of investigation in 1951 for alleged "tendencies towards communism" (Breit and Culbertson 1976).

became smaller, much more scattered both geographically and in terms of social cohesion, and became marginalized within the profession.

If institutionalism was to survive at all, it required realignment and redefinition. This did not prove to be an easy task, and the many attempts made to define and redefine institutionalism in the period from the 1940s onward are symptomatic of the problems faced by the movement. Ayres's definition rested on the central place of his dichotomy (Ayres 1951); Gruchy argued for the centrality of the "holistic" approach (Gruchy 1947), and then for the policy of planning (Gruchy 1972). None of these provided broad appeal. Many other definitions have been offered and are still being offered to this day,[19] but so far, at least, American institutionalism has not been able to recapture the intellectual excitement and appeal it generated at the time of its founding.

---

[19] Various definitions of institutionalism have been provided by Witte (1954), Kapp (1976), Mirowski (1987), and Hodgson (2004), among others. Two issues of the *JEI* were devoted to "foundational" issues in 1987.

PART FIVE

CONCLUSION

12

Institutionalism in Retrospect

The approach taken in this book is one that leads the historian of economics to think not just about the published literature associated with a particular group, but with a much broader range of issues – the network of individual contacts between members of the group, the university departments that were centers for them, the research organizations and agencies that supported their work, their contacts with government and government agencies, of where they found jobs for their students, their contacts with related disciplines and intellectual developments elsewhere, and, most important of all, the often contested nature of what is to count as good science. Looking back at the history of the institutionalist movement from its inception in around 1918 until 1947 in this way, we can understand the original appeal of the movement and what its primary elements consisted of; we can see the trajectory of the movement, both in general and in detail as reflected in particular careers and at particular institutions; and we can see the reasons for its loss of status and appeal in the 1940s.

INSTITUTIONALISM'S EARLY APPEAL

At its beginning, institutionalism promised much. Hamilton's 1918 manifesto was an ambitious one. At that time, however, "orthodox" economics was relatively weak, seemingly incapable of dealing with the new problems and issues of an industrial America. But institutionalism was more than just a response to orthodox weakness. Institutionalism caught the temper of the times, so much so that even what was in large part only a *promise* of an institutional economics was enough to attract adherents. This temper affected much more than economics. Institutionalism in economics was an expression of a faith in the power of empirical scientific investigation to

345

provide solutions to social and economic problems, a faith that also found expression in the other social sciences, in law, and in philosophy. Both the problems and their potential solutions were seen as matters of institutional arrangements, and what was required was investigation into the institutional sources of failure and a creative search for solutions. These ideas were built on a pragmatic and instrumental view of science as directed toward social control.

An important part of the idea of institutionalism as scientific was the notion that institutionalism could reconstruct economics on the basis of "modern psychology." This was a particularly significant part of the initial appeal of the movement. Reading the literature of the time, one is struck by a sense of the real excitement that this aspect of the institutional program generated.

These core institutionalist ideas were shared not only by others in the social sciences, but also by those in charge at the major foundations. Institutionalists had access to resources and to like-minded individuals in related disciplines. The strength of the institutionalist movement in the 1920s can be seen in the programs they established or populated at Wisconsin, Columbia, the Brookings Graduate School, The New School, The Institute of Economics, the NBER, and the SSRC. Not all of these efforts were successful or survived in the form originally intended, but institutionalists, *because* of their view of science and the need for more empirical work and research training, were early and heavily involved in the attempts to promote and provide for "scientific" social science research and advanced training and were able to find the sources of funding to advance these goals.

A DEFINITION OF INSTITUTIONALISM

That the American institutionalist movement in the interwar period did embody a set of shared core ideas and beliefs should be clear. These beliefs were general in nature and did not define specific research programs or a "school" of economics as narrowly defined. The picture given here is of institutionalism as a movement and as a network of people. For this network to hold together and for the movement to function as a movement, the group had to have a number of ideas in common, enough to provide for group identity and cohesion, but this necessary degree of identity and cohesion did not require uniformity, particularly on matters of detail. The key ideas involved included both positive and negative propositions, and contained an important normative element. They served to differentiate institutionalists both from more orthodox neoclassicals as well as from the earlier generation of progressives. In general terms the institutionalist position included (1) a clear recognition of the *central* analytical importance of institutions and institutional change, with institutions acting both as constraints on the behavior of individuals and concerns and as factors shaping the beliefs, values, and preferences of individuals; (2) a desire to base economics on a social psychology consistent with this emphasis on the role of institutions, and a related rejection of hedonistic psychology and of the idea of the individual as a utility maximizer; (3) the adoption of a view of correct scientific method in social science as empirical and investigational (including but not limited to quantitative and statistical work), and a related rejection of the highly abstract and overly speculative nature of much orthodox theory; (4) an emphasis on the *critical* examination of the functioning of existing institutions (including issues such as bargaining power, standards of living and working conditions, corporate finance and control, market failures of various types, business cycles, unemployment, and so on), and a related belief in the need for new forms of social control involving greater government regulation of the market and other interventions; and (5) the adoption of a pragmatic and humanistic approach to social value, generally taken from John Dewey, and a related rejection of the standard theories of value and of market efficiency as adequate tools for policy appraisal. The secular nature of this value theory is also significant. Important specific content can be added to this outline as American institutionalists expressed these general beliefs through particular theories and concepts taken or developed from the work of Thorstein Veblen and/or John R. Commons.

It is also the case that institutionalism can be defined sociologically as a network of individuals within the profession of economics. In this case, members of the institutionalist group can be defined as those who were *active participants* in this movement and were involved in attempting to *promote* what they saw as the institutional approach to economics. Several people either self-identified as institutionalists or were explicitly identified by others as institutionalists, including Clarence Ayres, James Bonbright, J. M. Clark, J. R. Commons, Morris Copeland, Lionel Edie, R. L. Hale, Walton Hamilton, R. F. Hoxie, Wesley Mitchell, Harold Moulton, Edwin Nourse, Sumner Slichter, Willard Thorp, Rexford Tugwell, Thorstein Veblen, and E. E. Witte, and it is no stretch to include Mordecai Ezekiel, David Friday, Carter Goodrich, Isador Lubin, Robert Montgomery, Winfield Riefler, Walter Stewart, Leo Wolman, as well as others. This group made up a definite network of people with specific institutional connections, and the links between members of the group were important in affecting such things as appointments, research projects, and financing.

To be sure, there were differences in view between institutionalists, and a shading-off from institutionalist to more orthodox positions.
Institutionalism involved adopting a *complex* of ideas and positions, some
positive, some negative, and some normative. This is not a one-dimensional
definition. Individuals who shared some but not all of these ideas would
have contact with institutionalists along those particular dimensions or on
those issues, and would normally have some degree of sympathy (varying
substantially) with those aspects of the institutionalist movement, but were
also sometimes critics of other aspects of institutionalism, and did not act
as, and therefore cannot properly be seen as, members of the American
institutionalist movement themselves (for example Allyn Young, Frank
Knight, Alvin Johnson, and Paul Douglas, to name a few).

Institutionalism was a program that certainly took a number of its key
ideas from Veblen. Veblen's criticism of hedonism and of the static nature
of orthodox economics, his critique of the consumption habits of the leisure class, his distinction between the institutions of business and the
technology of industry, and his major lines of criticism of business institutions fed directly into the work of institutionalists. But neither Veblen's
biological analogies nor his specific theory of institutional change based
on habituation to new technological "disciplines" carried much weight
in the institutionalist literature that followed. Early on, Hoxie used such
terminology, as did Copeland in some of his methodological writing, but
Hoxie explicitly abandoned Veblen's theory, and Copeland's references to
biological analogy do not appear to be carried over into his substantive
work.

Much the same can be said about the various references to "behaviorism"
to be found, especially in Mitchell and Copeland. Early in the history of
institutionalism, the term behaviorism was used quite loosely; even Dewey
could use the term. Institutionalists of a quantitative bent, in particular,
were drawn to the empiricism of behaviorism and its rejection of unobservable such as instincts. It must be said, however, that neither Mitchell nor
Copeland actually removed references to motivations and goals from their
economic writing. Again, the attachment to behaviorism was evident more
in their methodological writing than in their economics, and in practice
was limited to statements about the importance of institutions in conditioning behavior. Indeed, it is clear that behaviorism, as it developed in the
psychological literature, would be just as susceptible to Veblen's critique of
the picture of man as being pushed around by external forces as was hedonism. Stimulus and response replaces pleasure and pain, but both are at
odds with the pragmatic conception of mind.

Institutionalism, in practice, was neither particularly Darwinian nor behaviorist. The central appeal of the movement lay in its promises of science and social control, and in the kind of rhetoric used by Hamilton in the promotion of the institutional approach and his educational programs. This picture of institutionalism, with its focus on the interwar movement rather than on Veblen as founding father, differs significantly from the picture presented both traditionally, by writers such as Dorfman, and more recently by Geoff Hodgson. Hodgson in particular places Veblen's Darwinism at the center of his discussion (Hodgson 2004) and appraises the successes and failures of institutionalism largely in terms of the place of Veblenian Darwinism within the movement.

THE TRAJECTORY OF INSTITUTIONAL ECONOMICS

The discussions of the careers of Hamilton and Copeland give detail and life to the picture of institutionalism. Hamilton and Copeland exemplify different aspect of the movement, Hamilton qualitative in his approach, Copeland quantitative. But their careers interlace, and they are both informed and inspired by the same set of overall ideals. It is also evident from these chapters that neither man had a "marginal" career, and that each was a part of an extensive network of fellow institutionalists. Moreover, given Hamilton's work on the coal industry, medicine, price formation, patents, antitrust, and on law and economics, and Copeland's on national income, government statistics, and flow-of-funds accounting, it is hardly possible to claim that institutionalism was nothing but dissent from orthodox theory. Hamilton's shift to Yale law school in 1928 was an important loss to the institutionalist movement. Copeland's comments on Keynes and the model-building approach accurately locate some of the changing circumstances facing institutionalism after World War II.

The material on institutionalism at particular institutions gives further detail and shape to the picture of the trajectory of the institutionalist movement. Chicago can be seen as its point of formation in the period around World War I, with Veblen and Mitchell early on and Hoxie, Hamilton, Clark, and Moulton later. Chicago retained an institutional presence much later than usually thought, only really disappearing in the 1930s. From Chicago, institutionalism was taken to Amherst, Brookings, Berkeley, Columbia, the Institute of Economics, and to the NBER by Hamilton, Mitchell, Clark, and Moulton. Veblen also gathered a group at Missouri. Wisconsin was the other starting point, developing from the work of John R. Commons and his students and with much less of a Veblenian input. These two strands of institutionalism connected at a variety of points, most obviously in the campaigns for labor legislation, work on public utility regulation, and on law and economics, and in the New Deal.

The analysis of institutionalism at specific institutions shows how institutionalism grew, outlines the teaching and research programs followed, and the students produced. Again the close network of individuals involved is evident, as are the positive contributions made by those working within institutionalist programs, both in terms of academic work and in terms of policy contributions. The story of Brookings and the program pioneered by Hamilton is a remarkable one, but it was short-lived. Wisconsin and Columbia developed their institutionalist contingent largely through the hiring of their own graduates. Wisconsin's focus on labor issues is noteworthy, as is the large numbers of Commons's students who became involved with social security legislation. Commons developed both a theory of the labor movement and an analysis of law and economics. Columbia institutionalism had a broader focus on business cycles, corporations, declining competition, public utilities, and law and economics. Mitchell's NBER became the center of his efforts to pursue his program on business cycles with extensive Rockefeller support. Clark developed the accelerator, did important work on decision making, the structure of costs, business cycles, public works, and workable competition. Berle and Means developed the analysis of the separation of ownership and control, and Means his theory of administered pricing. Tugwell, Means, and others were to become major figures in the group of New Deal planners.

All of this seems to indicate the strength of the institutionalist movement. Well established at leading universities and research institutes, with excellent access to external funding sources, involved with important government legislation and programs, and linked to recent developments in related disciplines. In all of these respects, institutionalism had as much or more strength than neoclassical economics. At least that was the position in the 1930s. The institutionalist group at both Wisconsin and Columbia peaked in the early 1930s, with little hiring being done between then and the end of World War II. Nevertheless, when Wisconsin and Columbia resumed hiring in 1946–1947, it was not institutionalists who were hired, but Keynesians and neoclassical economists, indicating that some very significant shifts in the academic environment must have taken place between the 1930s and 1946–1947 when hiring resumed. The Mitchell-Burns program lasted, but only due to Willits at Rockefeller and then the attitudes at Ford.

INSTITUTIONALISM AND ORTHODOX ECONOMICS

It is relevant to observe at this point that in the 1920s and 1930s, there was little in the way of any overt "struggle" between institutionalists and others. To be sure, there were disagreements, particularly on the occasions of explicit methodological debate such as at AEA roundtables. Homan's 1932 piece was part of such a roundtable. But Mitchell and Clark were among the most respected of American economists, the NBER had a high reputation, and there appears to have been a very considerable amount of mutual respect and "live and let live" attitudes. This is a somewhat different picture than that presented by Yonay (1998). The timing of the real conflict between institutionalists and others is better indicated by Koopmans's attack on Mitchell and Burns and the sharp exchanges between Burns and Hansen in 1947.

It should also be understood that institutionalist ideas did have an impact on more orthodox economics, so the history of American economics in the 1930s and early 1940s is not only one of institutionalism reacting to the new developments elsewhere, but also one of more orthodox economists reacting to institutionalist criticisms. The attacks on hedonistic language and the "outmoded" psychological assumptions of orthodox theory had an effect, as did institutionalist concerns with sales efforts and marketing, and the various forms of markets other than competitive and monopoly. Institutionalist criticisms of the untestable or untested nature of standard theory also found a sensitive spot. One can see in both the theoretical and applied work of the late 1930s and 1940s a recognition of and reaction to certain lines of institutionalist criticism.

What one observes with the history of more orthodox economics (both Keynesian and neoclassical) in the period around World War II and after is a very considerable technical development, both in theory and in econometric methods. This formalization of economics was accompanied by important shifts in the ideas of scientific method. Logical empiricism or Friedman's version of positivism provided a view of science compatible with the emphasis on abstract model building. This is not to say that post-1945 orthodox economics was all of a piece. As Mirowski has pointed out, there are a number of different strands to be found in postwar American economics (Mirowski 2002), identified respectively with Chicago, Cowles/RAND, and MIT/Harvard. All of these strands, however, pursued programs methodologically (and, in the case of Chicago, ideologically) sharply at odds with the institutionalist tradition. At this point, the conflict between more orthodox and institutional economics becomes much sharper and the history of institutionalism becomes the obverse of the history of orthodox economics.

THE MARGINALIZATION OF INSTITUTIONALISM

By the late 1930s and 1940s, institutionalism was beginning to display a number of internal problems and weaknesses. At the beginning, institutionalism promised an economics based on "modern psychology." This was both a promise that played an important role in its original appeal and a promise that was not fulfilled. Psychology itself shifted to behaviorism of an increasingly narrow type that did not provide an attractive, or even feasible, foundation for a discussion of economic behavior. The psychological foundations for institutionalism remained in a vague and underdeveloped state, and this in turn meant that the theoretical developments produced by institutionalists tended to have an ad hoc rather than a systematic character.

In addition, Mitchell's research program on business cycles was not carried through to its planned conclusion in a "theoretical volume," giving an obvious stock of ammunition to institutionalism's critics. Moreover, no one produced a synthetic statement of the institutionalist view. Hamilton produced numerous drafts of a book on "The Economic Order" but never completed it, and Clark planned a major general treatise, but was deflected by taking on the project on competition for Brookings (J. M. Clark to Carter Goodrich, 13 December 1946, J. M. Clark Papers, Box 5; J. M. Clark to Robert Calkins, 31 December 1961, J. M. Clark Papers, Box 2). These failures were important elements in dissipating the optimism that had originally surrounded the prospects for institutionalism. Homan was correct in his argument that the institutionalist program had not lived up to its original promise (Homan 1932).

The changing attitudes toward institutionalism, however, derived not just from institutionalist weaknesses, but from the growing strength of the more orthodox alternatives. One of the key developments was, of course, the arrival of Keynesian economics. The picture given here is not one of befuddled institutionalists swept away by the new Keynesian theory, but there is no doubt that Keynesian analysis and the later Keynesian/monetarist debates absorbed some institutionalist work (that based on underconsumptionist ideas) and displaced other approaches (the NBER business cycle program). Other developments in microeconomic theory, applied economics, and econometrics also played important roles, as did the reemergence of a strong defense of markets from Chicago, and the Chicago-based "neoclassification" of areas outside of the traditional range of micro theory. What one finds in all of this is a process that is partly one of institutionalist concerns and lines of research being *absorbed* into more orthodox programs, and partly one of institutionalist concerns and lines of research being *displaced* by more orthodox programs. Perhaps the most important displacement of all was that produced by the arrival of positivist ideas of science. These ideas allowed Keynesian and neoclassical economists to successfully adopt the mantle of scientific method while characterizing institutionalism as naïve empiricism.

The new ideas of science displaced the pragmatism of Dewey. Institutionalism also lost other supports. The attitudes of the Ford Foundation toward economics differed from Rockefeller's, and this shift eventually caught up with the NBER. Legal realism declined as a force in American legal scholarship (Medema 1998), and sociology and economics grew further apart (Hodgson 2001). New academic programs in industrial relations and public administration took some of the content of institution-alism out of economics departments (while preserving it elsewhere in the academy). World War I gave a boost to empirical economics, World War II to operations research and other mathematical tools (Mirowski 2002). Neoliberalism emerged as a reaction against both Keynesian economics and the institutionalist ideology of social control (Van Horn and Mirowski 2009).

Under these circumstances, institutionalism could maintain little of the appeal that it had in the early 1920s. The rhetoric of science had been taken over by Keynesian and neoclassical economics supported by econometric methods, and the ideas of social control had been adapted and rebranded by those associated with Keynesian policy and the welfare state. Indeed, the appeal of Keynesian economics in the 1940s was, at base, exactly the same appeal to science and social control that institutionalism had held out previously, and generated similar enthusiasm and success.

Without being renewed by fresh blood, the institutionalist contingents at Wisconsin and Columbia withered away, the Mitchell-Burns program at the NBER was eventually replaced by more orthodox approaches, and institutionalism gradually became marginalized in the profession at large. Institutionalism struggled to redefine itself. It largely abandoned those meth-ods that smacked too much of what had become orthodox positivism, and turned back to theoretical ideas taken primarily from Veblen. These lines of development can be found in a variety of ways: in Ayres's instrumental/cer-emonial dichotomy derived from Veblen and Dewey, in Gruchy's attempt to define institutionalism in terms of holism, and in Galbraith's decidedly Veblenian discussions in *The Affluent Society* and *the New Industrial State*.

For quite a time, Texas remained heavily institutionalist, although that too eventually changed.

Institutionalism has continued to exist and has even had a degree of revival of late. Many of the complaints that institutionalists had of orthodox economics in 1920 still seem to apply, and these concerns continue to feed heterodox traditions. The history of post-1945 American institutionalism and the emergence of other forms of institutionalism, both neoclassical and heterodox, are, however, other stories for other times.[1]

---

[1]   Of special interest are the emergence of the New Institutional Economics and the growth of interest in a heterodox institutionalism in Europe. See Rutherford 1994a; 2001.

Archive Collections Consulted

Henry Carter Adams Papers, Bentley Historical Library, University of Michigan
Clarence E. Ayres Papers, Center for American History, University of Texas
Brookings Institution Archives, Brookings Institution, Washington DC
Arthur F. Burns Papers, Dwight D. Eisenhower Library, Abilene, Kansas
John M. Clark Papers, Butler Library, Columbia University
Henry Clay Papers, Nuffield College, Oxford
John R. Commons Papers, Wisconsin Historical Society
Morris A. Copeland Papers, Butler Library, Columbia University
Ira B. Cross Interview, University of Washington Special Collections
Joseph Dorfman Papers, Butler Library, Columbia University
Richard T. Ely Papers, Wisconsin Historical Society
Mordecai Ezekiel Papers, Franklin D. Roosevelt Library, Hyde Park, New York
Mordecai Ezekiel Interview, Columbia University Oral History Collection
Ford Foundation Archives, New York. (FF)
Milton Friedman Papers, Hoover Institution, Stanford University
Martin G. Glaeser Papers, University of Wisconsin Archives
Carter Goodrich Papers, Butler Library, Columbia University
Allan G. Gruchy Papers, in the possession of Malcolm Rutherford
Robert Hale Papers, Butler Library, Columbia University
Walton H. Hamilton Papers, Tarlton Law Library, University of Texas
Alvin H. Hansen Papers, Harvard University Archives, Pusey Library, Harvard University
Albert G. Hart Papers, Butler Library, Columbia University
Leon Henderson Papers, Franklin D. Roosevelt Library, Hyde Park, New York
Frank Knight Papers. Joseph Regenstein Library, University of Chicago
Willian M. Leiserson Papers, Wisconsin Historical Society
Isador Lubin Papers, Franklin D. Roosevelt Library, Hyde Park, New York
Charles McCarthy Papers, Wisconsin Historical Society
Theresa S. McMahon Papers, University Of Washington Special Collections
Gardiner Means Papers, Franklin D. Roosevelt Library, Hyde Park, New York
Wesley Mitchell Papers, Butler Library, Columbia University
Edward W. Morehouse Papers, Wisconsin Historical Society
Walter Morton Interview, University of Wisconsin Archives, Oral History Project
NBER, Historical Archives, http://www.nber.org/nberhistory/

John U. Nef Papers, Joseph Regenstein Library, University of Chicago
Kenneth H. Parsons Interview, University of Wisconsin Archives, Oral History Project
Rockefeller Foundation Archives, Rockefeller Archive Center, Sleepy Hollow, New York (RAC-RF)
Laura Spelman Rockefeller Foundation Archives, Rockefeller Archive Center, Sleepy Hollow, New York (RAC-LSRM)
David J. Saposs Papers, Wisconsin Historical Society
I. Leo Sharfman papers, Bentley Historical Library, University of Michigan
George J. Stigler Papers, Joseph Regenstein Library, University of Chicago
Frank Taussig Papers, Harvard University Archives, Pusey Library, Harvard University
Rexford G. Tugwell Papers, Franklin D. Roosevelt Library, Hyde Park, New York
USDA Graduate School Archives, National Agricultural Library, Beltsville, Maryland
University of Wisconsin Archives, Oral History Project
Graham Wallas Papers, British Library of Economics and Political Science, London
War Labor Policies Board Records, National Archives, College Park, Maryland
Edwin E. Witte Papers, Wisconsin Historical Society
Allyn Young Papers, Harvard University Archives, Pusey Library, Harvard University

References

Abramovitz, Moses. 2001. *Days Gone By: A Memoir for my Family*. http://www.econ.stanford.edu/abramovitz/abramovitzM.html

Adams, Henry C. 1887. On the Relation of the State to Industrial Action. *Publications of the American Economic Association* 1, No 6.

Adams, Thomas S. and Helen L. Sumner. 1905. *Labor Problems*. New York: Macmillan.

Alchon, Guy. 1985. *The Invisible Hand of Planning: Capitalism, Social Science and the State in the 1920s*. Princeton: Princeton University Press.

Altmeyer, Arthur J. 1966. *The Formative Years of Social Security*. Madison, WI: University of Wisconsin.

Anderson, Theodore W. 1955. The Department of Mathematical Statistics. In R. Gordon Hoxie et al. *A History of the Faculty of Political Science, Columbia University*. New York: Columbia University Press.

Arnold, Thurman. 1937. *The Folklore of Capitalism*. New Haven, CT: Yale University Press.

Arrow, Kenneth J. 1975. Thorstein Veblen as an Economic Theorist. *American Economist* 19 (Spring): 5–9.

Asso, Pier Francesco and Luca Fiorito. 2004a. Human Nature and Economic Institutions: Instinct Psychology, Behaviorism, and the Development of American Instituionalism. *Journal of the History of Economic Thought* 26 (December): 445–477.

  2004b. Lawrence Kelso Frank's Proto-Ayresian Dichotomy. *History of Political Economy* 36 (Fall): 557–578.

Atkins, Willard, E., Donald W. McConnell, Corwin D. Edwards, Carl Raushenbush, Anton A. Friedrich, and Louis S. Reed. 1931. *Economic Behavior: An Institutional Approach*. Boston: Houghton Mifflin.

Ayres, Clarence E. 1918. The Epistemological Significance of Social Psychology. *Journal of Philosophy, Psychology and Scientific Methods* (January 17): 35–44.

  1921a. Instinct and Capacity–I. *Journal of Philosophy* 18 (October 13): 561–565.

  1921b. Instinct and Capacity–II. *Journal of Philosophy* 19 (October 27): 600–606.

  1936. Fifty Years Developments in Ideas of Human Nature and Motivation. *American Economic Review* 26 (March): 224–236.

1938. *The Problem of Economic Order*. New York: Farrar and Rinehart.

1944. *The Theory of Economic Progress*. Chapel Hill, NC: University of North Carolina Press.

1945. Addendum to *the Theory of Economic Progress*. *American Economic Review* 35 (December): 937–942.

1951. The Co-ordinates of Institutionalism. *American Economic Review* 41 (May): 47–55.

1966. Guaranteed Income: An Institutionalist View. In Robert Theobald, ed., *The Guaranteed Income*. New York: Doubleday, pp. 161–174.

1968. The Price System and Public Policy. *Journal of Economic Issues* 2 (September): 342–344.

Ayres, Edith. 1938. What Shall We Do with Economic Science? *International Journal of Ethics* 48 (January): 143–164.

Backhouse, Roger E. 1998. The Transformation of American Economics, 1920–1960, Viewed Through a Survey of Journal Articles. In Mary S. Morgan and Malcolm Rutherford, eds., *From Interwar Pluralism to Postwar Neoclassicism*, Annual Supplement to Volume 30 of *History of Political Economy*. Durham, NC: Duke University Press, pp. 85–107.

Bain, Joe S. 1944. *The Economics of the Pacific Petroleum Industry*. Berkeley, CA: University of California Press.

1959. *Industrial Organization*. New York: Wiley.

Balisciano, Marcia. 1998. Hope for America: American Notions of Economic Planning Between Pluralism and Neoclassicism, 1930–1950. In Mary S. Morgan and Malcolm Rutherford, eds., *From Interwar Pluralism to Postwar Neoclassicism*, Annual Supplement to Volume 30, *History of Political Economy*. Durham, NC: Duke University Press, pp. 153–178.

Barber, William J. 1987. The Career of Alvin H. Hansen in the 1920s and 1930s: A Study in Intellectual Transformation. *History of Political Economy* 19 (Summer): 191–205.

1988. *From New Era to New Deal: Herbert Hoover, the Economists, and American Economic Policy, 1921–1933*. Cambridge: Cambridge University Press.

1994. The Divergent Fates of Two Strands of "Institutionalist" Doctrine during the New Deal Years. *History of Political Economy* 26 (Winter): 569–587.

1996. *Designs within Disorder: Franklin D. Roosevelt, the Economists, and the Shaping of Economic Policy, 1933–1945*. New York: Cambridge University Press.

Barnard, Chester. 1938. *The Functions of the Executive*. Cambridge, MA: Harvard University Press.

Bateman, Bradley W. 1998. Clearing the Ground: The Demise of the Social Gospel Movement and the Rise of Neoclassicism in American Economics. In Mary S. Morgan and Malcolm Rutherford, eds., *From Interwar Pluralism to Postwar Neoclassicism*, Annual Supplement to Volume 30 of *History of Political Economy*. Durham, NC: Duke University Press, pp. 29–52.

Becker, Gary S. 1965. A Theory of the Allocation of Time. *Economic Journal* 75: 493–515.

1976. *The Economic Approach to Human Behavior*. Chicago: Chicago University Press.

Beller, Andrea H. and D. Elizabeth Kiss. 2001. Kyrk, Hazel. In Rima L. Schultz and Adele Hast, eds., *Women Building Chicago 1790-1990*. Bloomington, IN: Indiana University Press, pp. 482-485.

2003. On the Contribution of Hazel Kyrk to Family Economics. Paper Presented at the ASSA/HES Meetings, Washington DC.

Berle, Adolf. A. and Gardiner C. Means. 1932. *The Modern Corporation and Private Property*. New York: Macmillan.

Bernasek, Alexandra and Douglas Kinnear 1995. Ruth Allen: Frontier Labor Economist. In Ronnie J. Phillips, ed., *Economic Mavericks: The Texas Institutionalists. Political Economy and Public Policy* 9. Greenwich, CT: JAI Press, pp. 75-106.

Beveridge, William H. 1909. *Unemployment: A Problem of Industry*. London: Longmans, Green.

Biddle, Jeff. 1998a. Institutional Economics: A Case of Reproductive Failure? In Mary S. Morgan and Malcolm Rutherford, eds. *From Interwar Pluralism to Postwar Neoclassicism*. Annual Supplement to Volume 30, *History of Political Economy*. Durham, NC: Duke University Press, pp.108-133.

1998b. Social Science and the Making of Social Policy: Wesley Mitchell's Vision. In Malcolm Rutherford, ed., *The Economic Mind in America: Essays in the History of American Economics*. London: Routledge, pp. 43-79.

Blaug, Mark. 1978. *Economic Theory in Retrospect*, 3rd. edition. London: Cambridge University Press.

1999. The Formalist Revolution or What Happened to Orthodox Economics after World War II? In Roger Backhouse and John Creedy, eds., *From Classical Economics to the Theory of the Firm: Essays in Honour of D. P. O'Brien*. Aldershot: Edward Elgar, pp. 257-280.

Bonbright, James C. 1937. *The Valuation of Property*. New York: McGraw Hill.

Bonbright, James and Gardiner C. Means. 1932. *The Holding Company*. New York: McGraw Hill.

Boyer, George and Robert Smith. 2001. The Development of the Neoclassical Tradition in Modern Labor Economics. *Industrial and Labor Relations Review* 54 (January): 199-223.

Bratton, William W. 2001. Berle and Means Reconsidered at the Century's Turn. *Journal of Corporation Law* 26: 737.

Brazelton, Robert. 1997. The Economics of Leon Hirsch Keyserling. *The Journal of Economic Perspectives* 11 (Autumn): 189-197.

Breit, William and William P. Culbertson Jr. 1976. Clarence Edwin Ayres: An Intellectual's Portrait. In William Breit and William P. Culbertson Jr., eds., *Science and Ceremony: The Institutional Economics of C. E. Ayres*. Austin, TX: University of Texas Press, pp. 3-22.

Brissenden, Paul F. 1919. *The IWW: A Study of American Syndicalism*. New York: Columbia University Press.

Bronfenbrenner, Martin. 1993. Wisconsin 1947-1957-Reflections and Confessions. In Robert J. Lampman, ed., *Economists at Wisconsin, 1892-1992*. Madison, WI: Board of Regents of the University of Wisconsin System, pp. 130-138.

Brookings Institution. 1931. *Essays on Research in the Social Sciences*. Washington DC: Brookings Institution.

Brown, John Howard. 2008. Where Did Industrial Organization Come From? Mimeo.

Bruce, Kyle. 2000. Conflict and Conversion: Henry S. Dennison and the Shaping of J. K. Galbraith's Economic Thought. *Journal of Economic Issues* 34 (December): 949–967.

Buchanan, James M. and Gordon Tullock. 1965. *The Calculus of Consent*. Ann Arbor, MI: University of Michigan Press.

Bulmer, Martin and Joan Bulmer. 1981. Philanthropy and Social Science in the 1920s: Beardsley Ruml and the Laura Spelman Rockefeller Memorial, 1922–1929. *Minerva* 19 (3): 347–407.

Burns, Arthur F. 1934. *Production Trends in the United States since 1870*. New York: NBER.

1936. The Brookings Inquiry into Income Distribution and Progress. *Quarterly Journal of Economics 50 (May):* 476–523.

1946. *Economic Research and the Keynesian Thinking of Our Times*. Twenty-Sixth Annual Report of the National Bureau of Economic Research. New York: National Bureau of Economic Research.

1947. Keynesian Economics Once Again. *Review of Economic Statistics* 29 (November): 252–267.

1952. Hicks and the Real Cycle. *Journal of Political Economy* 60 (February): 1–24.

1953. *The Instability of Consumer Spending*, 32nd Annual Report, National Bureau of Economic Research. New York: NBER.

Burns, Arthur F. and Wesley C. Mitchell. 1946. *Measuring Business Cycles*. New York: National Bureau of Economic Research.

Burns, Arthur R. 1936. *The Decline of Competition: A Study of the Evolution of American Industry*. Westport, CT: Greenwood Press.

1937. The Organization of Industry and the Theory of Prices. *Journal of Political Economy* 45 (September): 662–680.

Burns, Eveline M. 1931. Does Institutional Economics Complement or Compete with "Orthodox" Economics. *American Economic Review* 21 (March): 80–87.

1936. *Toward Social Security*. New York: McGraw Hill.

Bye, Raymond T. (1924) 1971. Some Recent Developments of Economic Theory. In Rexford G. Tugwell, ed., *The Trend of Economics*. Port Washington, NY: Kennikat Press, pp. 271–300.

1940. An Appraisal of F. C. Mills *The Behavior of Prices: Critiques of Research in the Social Sciences II*. New York: Social Science Research Council.

Caldwell, Bruce J. 1982. *Beyond Positivism: Economic Methodology in the Twentieth Century*. London: George Allen and Unwin.

Camic, Charles. 1991. Introduction: Talcott Parsons before *The Structure of Social Action*. In Charles Camic, ed., *Talcott Parsons, the Early Essays*. Chicago: University of Chicago Press, pp. ix–xix.

1992. Reputation and Predecessor Selection: Parsons and the Institutionalists. *American Sociological Review* 57 (August): 421–445.

Forthcoming. Veblen's Apprenticeship: On the Translation of Gustav Cohn's *System der Finanzwissenschaft*. *History of Political Economy*.

Camic, Charles and Yu Xie. 1994. The Statistical Turn in American Social Science: Columbia University, 1890–1915. *American Sociological Review* 59 (October): 773–805.

Campbell, Persia. (1940) 1968. *Consumer Representation in the New Deal.* New York: AMS Press.

Cauley, Troy J. 1964. Max Handman. *Bulletin of the Wardman Group* 1 (April): 2–3.

Central Statistical Board. 1939. The Central Statistical Board and its Work. Prepared for the use of the Committee on Expenditures in the Executive Departments, House of Representatives, in Connection with consideration of HR 5917, 76th Congress. April 25, 1939. Morris A Copeland Papers, Box 3, Central Statistical Board Folder, Butler Library, Columbia University.

Chamberlin, Edward H. 1933. *The Theory of Monopolistic Competition.* Cambridge, MA: Harvard University Press.

⸻. 1961. The Origin and Early Development of Monopolistic Competition Theory. *Quarterly Journal of Economics* 75 (November): 515–543.

Chase, Stuart. 1925. *The Tragedy of Waste.* New York: Macmillan.

Chasse, John Dennis. 1986. John R. Commons and the Democratic State. *Journal of Economic Issues* 20 (September): 759–784.

⸻. 1991. The American Association for Labor Legislation: An Episode in Institutional Policy Analysis. *Journal of Economic Issues* 15 (September): 799–828.

⸻. 1994. The American Association for Labor Legislation and the Institutionalist Tradition in National Health Insurance. *Journal of Economic Issues* 28 (December): 1063–1090.

⸻. 2004. John R. Commons and His Students: The View from the End of the Twentieth Century. In Dell P. Champlin and Janet T. Knoedler, eds., *The Institutionalist Tradition in Labor Economics.* Armonk, NY: M. E. Sharpe, pp. 50–74.

Christ, Carl F. 1994. The Cowles Commission's Contributions to Econometrics at Chicago, 1939–1955. *Journal of Economic Literature* 32 (March): 30–59.

Clapham, J. H. 1922. Of Empty Economic Boxes. *Economic Journal* 32 (September): 305–314.

Clark, John M. 1915. The Concept of Value. *Quarterly Journal of Economics* 29 (August): 663–673.

⸻. 1916. The Changing Basis of Economic Responsibility. *Journal of Political Economy* 24 (March): 209–229.

⸻. 1917. Business Acceleration and the Law of Demand: A Technical Factor in Business Cycles. *Journal of Political Economy* 25 (March): 217–235.

⸻. 1918. Economics and Modern Psychology, I and II. *Journal of Political Economy* 26 (January, February): 1–30, 136–166.

⸻. 1919. Economic Theory in an Era of Social Readjustment. *American Economic Review,* 9 (March): 280–290.

⸻. 1921. Soundings in Non-Euclidean Economics. *American Economic Review,* 11 (March): 132–143.

⸻. 1923. *Studies in the Economics of Overhead Costs.* Chicago: University of Chicago Press.

⸻. (1924) 1971. The Socializing of Theoretical Economics. In Rexford G. Tugwell, ed., *The Trend of Economics.* Port Washington, NY: Kennikat Press, pp. 73–102.

⸻. 1926. *Social Control of Business.* Chicago: University of Chicago Press.

⸻. 1927. Recent Developments in Economics. In Edward C. Hayes, ed., *Recent Developments in the Social Sciences.* Philadelphia: Lippencott, pp. 213–306.

1931. Wesley C. Mitchell's Contribution to the Theory of Business Cycles. In Stuart Rice, ed., *Methods in Social Science: A Case Book*. Chicago: University of Chicago Press.

1932. Round Table Conferences – Institutional Economics. *American Economic Review* 22 (March): 105–106.

1934. *Strategic Factors in Business Cycles*. New York: National Bureau for Economic Research.

1935a. Cumulative Effects of Aggregate Spending as Illustrated by Public Works. *American Economic Review* 25 (March): 14–20.

1935b. *Economics of Planning Public Works*. Washington DC: US Government Printing Office.

1936. *Preface to Social Economics: Essays on Economic Theory and Social Problems*. Edited and with an Introduction by Moses Abramovitz and Eli Ginzberg. New York: Farrar and Rinehart.

1940. Towards a Concept of Workable Competition. *American Economic Review* 30 (June): 241–256.

1942. The Theoretical Issues. *American Economic Review* 32 (March): 1–12.

1946. Realism and Relevance in the Theory of Demand. *Journal of Political Economy* 54 (August): 374–353.

1947. Mathematical Economists and Others: A Plea for Communicability. *Econometrica* 15 (April): 75–78.

1957. *Economic Institutions and Human Welfare*. New York: Alfred A. Knopf.

1961. *Competition as a Dynamic Process*. Washington, DC: Brookings.

Clark, John M., Walton H. Hamilton, and Harold G. Moulton, eds. 1918. *Readings in the Economics of War*. Chicago: University of Chicago Press.

Clark, John M., et al. 1949. *National and International Measures for Full Employment*. Lake Success, NY: United Nations.

Clay, Henry. 1916. *Economics: An Introduction for the General Reader*. London: Macmillan.

Coase, Ronald H. 1984. The New Institutional Economics. *Journal of Institutional and Theoretical Economics* 140 (March): 229–231.

1993. Law and Economics at Chicago. *Journal of Law and Economics* 36 (April): 239–254.

Coats, A. W. 1960. The First Two Decades of the American Economic Association. *American Economic Review* 50 (September): 555–574.

Cobb, Charles W. and Paul H. Douglas. 1928. A Theory of Production. *The American Economic Review* 18 (March): 139–165.

Cohen, Jacob. 1972. Copeland's Moneyflows after Twenty-Five Years: A Survey. *Journal of Economic Literature* 10 (March): 1–25.

Cohen, Wilbur J. 1960. Edwin E. Witte (1887–1960): Father of Social Security. *Industrial and Labor Relations Review* 14 (October): 7–9.

Commission of Inquiry, Interchurch World Movement. (1920) 1971. *Report on the Steel Strike of 1919*. New York: Da Capo Press.

Committee on the Costs of Medical Care. 1932. *Medical Care for the American People*. Chicago: University of Chicago Press.

Committee on Government Statistics and Information Services. 1933. The Statistical Services of the Federal Government in Relation to the Recovery Program.

Report Addressed to Hon. John Dickinson, Assistant Secretary of Commerce and Dr. Alexander Sachs, Chief of Research and Planning, Industrial Recovery Administration, Washington DC, July 1933. Morris A Copeland Papers, Box 3, Central Statistical Board Folder.

Committee on Recent Economic Changes. 1929. *Recent Economic Changes in the United States*. New York: McGraw-Hill.

Commons, John R. 1899–1900. A Sociological View of Sovereignty. *American Journal of Sociology* 5 (July-November): 1–15, 155–171, 347–366; (January to May): 544–552, 683–695, 814–825; 6 (July): 67–89.

1901. A New Way of Settling Labor Disputes. *American Monthly Review of Reviews* 23 (March): 328–333.

1907. The Wisconsin Public-Utilities Law. *American Review of Reviews* 36 (August): 221–224.

1908. *Races and Immigrants in America*. New York: Macmillan.

1909. American Shoemakers, 1648–1895: A Sketch of Industrial Evolution. *Quarterly Journal of Economics* 24 (November): 219–266.

1910. How Wisconsin Regulates Her Public Utilities. *American Review of Reviews* 42 (August): 215–217.

1921. Unemployment: Compensation and Prevention. *The Survey* 42 (October 1): 5–9.

1924a. *The Legal Foundations of Capitalism*. New York: Macmillan.

1924b. The Delivered Price Practice in the Steel Market. *American Economic Review* 14 (September): 505–519.

1925a. The Stabilization of Prices and Business. *American Economic Review* 15 (March): 43–52.

1925b. The True Scope of Unemployment Insurance. *American Labor Legislation Review* 15 (March): 33–44.

1925c. Reasonable Value. Reprinted and edited by Malcolm Rutherford, Warren J. Samuels, and Charles J. Whalen, in *Research in the History of Economic Thought and Methodology* 26-B (2008): 235–307.

1925d. Law and Economics. *Yale Law Journal* 34 (February): 371–382.

1925e. Marx Today: Capitalism and Socialism. *Atlantic Monthly* 136 (November): 682–693.

1927. Price Stabilization and the Federal Reserve System. *The Annalist* 29 (April 1): 459–462.

1931. Institutional Economics. *American Economic Review* 21 (December): 648–657.

1932. The Problem of Correlating Law, Economics and Ethics. *Wisconsin Law Review* 8 (December): 3–26.

1934a. *Institutional Economics: Its Place in Political Economy*. New York: Macmillan.

1934b. *Myself*. New York: Macmillan.

1936. Institutional Economics. *American Economic Review* 26 (March): 237–249.

1937. Capacity to Produce, Capacity to Consume, Capacity to Pay Debts. *American Economic Review* 27 (December): 680–697.

Commons, John, R. and John B. Andrews. 1916. *Principles of Labor Legislation*. New York: Harper & Brothers.

1936. *Principles of Labor Legislation*, Fourth Revised Edition. New York: Harper & Brothers.

Commons, John, R., H. L. McCracken, and W. E. Zeuch. 1922. Secular Trend and Business Cycles: A Classification of Theories. *Review of Economic Statistics* 4 (October): 244–263.

Commons, John, R. and E. W. Morehouse. 1927. Legal and Economic Job Analysis. *Yale Law Journal* 37 (December): 139–178.

Commons, John, R., Ulrich B. Phillips, Eugene A. Gilmore, Helen L. Sumner, and John B. Andrews. 1910–1911. *A Documentary History of American Industrial Society*. Cleveland, OH: Arthur H. Clark.

Commons, John, R., D. J. Saposs, H. L. Sumner, E. B. Mittleman, H. E. Hoagland, J. B. Andrews, and Selig Perlman. 1918 and 1935. *History of Labor in the United States*, 4 vols. New York: Macmillan.

Cookingham, Mary E. 1987. Social Economists and Reform: Berkeley, 1906–1961. *History of Political Economy* 19 (Spring): 47–65.

Cooley, Charles H. 1913. The Institutional Character of Pecuniary Valuation. *American Journal of Sociology* 18 (January): 543–555.

Copeland, Morris A. 1920. Seasonal Problems in Financial Administration. *Journal of Political Economy* 28 (December): 793–826.

1921. Some Phases of Institutional Value Theory. PhD Thesis, University of Chicago. Morris A. Copeland Papers, Box 8, Manuscripts by M. A. Copeland Folder.

(1924) 1971. Communities of Economic Interest and the Price System. In Rexford G. Tugwell, ed., *The Trend of Economics*, pp. 105–150. Port Washington, NY: Kennikat Press.

1925a. The Economics of Advertising – Discussion. *American Economic Review* 15 (March): 38–41

1925b. Review of John M. Clark *Studies in the Economics of Overhead Costs*. *Political Science Quarterly* 40 (June): 296–299.

1925c. Professor Knight on Psychology. *Quarterly Journal of Economics* 40 (November): 134–151.

1926. Desire, Choice, and Purpose from a Natural-Evolutionary Standpoint. *Psychological Review* 33 (July): 245–267

1927. An Instrumental View of the Part-Whole Relation. *Journal of Philosophy* 24 (February 17): 96–104

1928. An Estimate of Total Volume of Debts to Individual Accounts in the United States. *Journal of the American Statistical Association* 23 (September): 301–303.

1929a. Two Hypotheses Concerning the Equation of Exchange. *Journal of the American Statistical Association* 24, Supplement (March): 146–148.

1929b. Special Purpose Indexes for the Equation of Exchange for the United States, 1919–1927. *Journal of the American Statistical Association* 24 (June): 109–122.

1929c. Money, Trade, and Prices – A Test of Causal Primacy. *Quarterly Journal of Economics* 43 (August): 648–666.

1929d. The National Income and its Distribution. In *Recent Economic Changes in the United States*, vol. 2., New York: National Bureau of Economic Research.

(1930) 1973. Psychology and the Natural Science Point of View. Reprinted in *Fact and Theory in Economics*. Westport, CT: Greenwood Press, pp. 11–36.

1931a. Economic Theory and the Natural Science Point of View. *American Economic Review* 21 (March): 67–79.

1931b. Some Suggestions for Improving our Information on Wholesale Commodity Prices. *Journal of the American Statistical Association* 26, Supplement (March): 110–115.

1932a. Some Problems in the Theory of National Income. *Journal of Political Economy* 40 (February): 1–51.

1932b. How Large Is Our National Income? *Journal of Political Economy* 40 (December): 771–795.

(1934) 1973. The Theory of Monopolistic Competition. In Morris A. Copeland, *Fact and Theory in Economics*. Westport CT: Greenwood Press, pp. 247–251.

1935. National Wealth and Income – An Interpretation. *Journal of the American Statistical Association* 30 (June): 377–386.

1936. Commons's Institutionalism in Relation to Problems of Social Evolution and Economic Planning. *Quarterly Journal of Economics* 50 (February): 333–346.

1937. Concepts of National Income. In *Studies in Income and Wealth*, vol. I. New York: National Bureau of Economic Research.

1939a. Public Investment in the United States. *American Economic Review* 29 (March): 33–41.

1939b. Aims and Purposes of the United States Central Statistical Board. *The Controller* 7 (July): 236–237, 255.

1940a. Examining for Professional Positions. *Personnel Administration* 2 (January): 1–4.

(1940b) 1973. Competing Products and Monopolistic Competition. In Morris A. Copeland, *Fact and Theory in Economics*. Westport, CT: Greenwood Press, pp. 251–300.

1941. Economic Research in the Federal Government. *American Economic Review* 31 (September): 526–536.

1942a. Production Planning for a War Economy. *Annals of the American Academy of Political and Social Science* 220 (March): 94–105.

1942b. The Defense Effort and the National Income Response Pattern. *Journal of Political Economy* 50 (June): 415–426.

1944. How Achieve Full and Stable Employment. *American Economic Review* 34 (March): 134–147.

(1948) 1973. Authority and Reason as Instruments of Coordination in the United States. In Morris A. Copeland, *Fact and Theory in Economics*. Westport, CT: Greenwood Press, pp. 119–129.

1951. Institutional Economics and Model Analysis. *American Economic Review* 41 (May): 56–65.

1952a. *A Study of Moneyflows in the United States*. New York: National Bureau of Economic Research.

1952b. *The Keynesian Reformation: Three Lectures*. Delhi: Delhi School of Economics.

(1955) 1973. Statistics and Objective Economics. In Morris A. Copeland, *Fact and Theory in Economics*. Westport, CT: Greenwood Press, pp. 67–91.

1958a. Institutionalism and Welfare Economics. *American Economic Review* 48 (March): 1–17.

1958b. On the Scope and Method of Economics. In Douglas F. Dowd, ed., *Thorstein Veblen: A Critical Reappraisal*. Ithaca, NY: Cornell University Press.

1965. *Our Free Enterprise System*. New York: Macmillan.

1966. *Toward Full Employment in Our Free Enterprise Economy*. New York: Fordham University Press.

1967. Laissez Faire, Pecuniary Incentives, and Public Policy. *Journal of Economic Issues* 1 (December): 335–348.

1970. On Unemployment and Overemployment, Assuming Wage and Price Stability [Flexibility]. *Journal of Economic Issues* 4 (June-Sept): 40–59. Corrigenda, *Journal of Economic Issues* 5 (June 1971): 134–136.

Copeland, Morris A. and Edwin M. Martin. 1938. The Correction of Wealth and Income Estimates for Price Changes. In *Studies in Income and Wealth*, vol II. New York: National Bureau of Economic Research.

1939. National Income and Capital Formation. *Journal of Political Economy* 47 (June): 398–407.

Craver, Earlene. 1986. Patronage and the Direction of Research in Economics: The Rockefeller Foundation in Europe, 1924–1938. *Minerva* 24 (2–3): 205–223.

Craver, Earlene and Axel Leijonhufvud. 1987. Economics in America: The Continental Influence. *History of Political Economy* 19 (Summer): 173–182.

Cross, Ira B. 1935. *A History of the Labor Movement in California*. Berkeley, CA: University of California.

Curti, Merle. 1980. *Human Nature in American Thought*. Madison, WI: University of Wisconsin Press.

Curti, Merle and Vernon Carstensen. 1949. *The University of Wisconsin: A History 1848–1925*. Madison, WI: University of Wisconsin Press.

Cutler, Addison T. 1938. The Ebb of Institutional Economics. *Science and Society* 2 (Fall): 448–470.

Davidson, Audrey B. and Robert B. Ekelund. 1994. America's Alternative to Marshall: Property, Competition, and Capitalism in Hadley's *Economics* of 1896. *Journal of the History of Economic Thought* 16 (Spring): 1–26.

Dawson, John C. 1991. Copeland as Social Accountant. In John C. Dawson, ed., *Flow of Funds Analysis: A Handbook for Practitioners*. Armonk, NY: M. E. Sharpe, 1996.

ed. 1996. *Flow of Funds Analysis: A Handbook for Practitioners*. Armonk, NY: M. E. Sharpe, pp. 93–100.

Degler, Carl N. 1991. *In Search of Human Nature: the Decline and Revival of Darwinism in American Economic Thought*. New York: Oxford University Press.

De Rouvray, Cristel. 2004. "Old" Economic History in the United States: 1939–1954. *Journal of the History of Economic Thought* 26 (June): 221–239.

Dewey, John. 1926. The Historic Background of Corporate Legal Personality. *Yale Law Journal* 35: 665–673.

1929. *The Quest for Certainty*. New York: Minton, Blach.

1931. Social Science and Social Control. *New Republic* 67 (29 July): 276–277.

Dimand, Robert W. 2000. Theresa Schmid McMahon (1878-1961). In Robert W. Dimand, Mary Ann Dimand, and Evelyn L. Forget, eds., *A Biographical Dictionary of Women Economists*. Cheltenham: Edward Elgar, pp. 304–305.

2002. John Maurice Clark's Contribution to the Genesis of the Multiplier Analysis: A Response to Luca Fiorito. *History of Economic Ideas* 10 (1): 85–91.

Dimand, Robert W. and Robert H. Koehn. 2008. Galbraith's Hexerodox Teacher: Leo Rogin's Historical Approach to the Meaning and Validity of Economic Theory. *Journal of Economic Issues* 41 (June): 561–568.

Donohue, Kathleen G. 2003. *Freedom from Want: American Liberalism and the Idea of the Consumer.* Baltimore: Johns Hopkins University Press.

Dorfman, Joseph. 1934. *Thorstein Veblen and His America.* New York: Viking.

1949. *The Economic Mind in American Civilization,* vol 3. New York: Viking.

1955. The Department of Economics. In R. Gordon Hoxie, et al., *A History of the Faculty of Political Science, Columbia University.* New York: Columbia University Press, pp. 161–206.

1958. Walter Winne Stewart (1815–1958). *Year Book of the American Philosophical Society.* Philadelphia: American Philosophical Society, pp. 155–159.

1959. *The Economic Mind in American Civilization,* vols. 4 and 5. New York: Viking.

1963. The Background of Institutional Economics. In *Institutional Economics: Veblen, Commons, and Mitchell Reconsidered.* Berkeley, CA: University of California Press, pp. 1–44.

1967. Introduction. Wesley C. Mitchell, *Types of Economic Theory,* vol 1. New York: Augustus M. Kelley.

1973. New Light on Veblen. Introduction to Thorstein Veblen, *Essays Reviews and Reports,* edited by Joseph Dorfman. Clifton, NJ: Augustus M. Kelley, pp. 5–326.

1974. Walton Hale Hamilton and Industrial Policy. Introduction to Walton H. Hamilton, *Industrial Policy and Institutionalism: Selected Essays.* Clifton, NJ: Augustus M. Kelley, pp. 5–28.

Douglas, Paul H. 1934a. The Role of the Consumer in the New Deal. *Annals of the American Academy of Political and Social Science* 172 (March): 98–106.

1934b. *The Theory of Wages.* New York: Macmillan.

1935. *Controlling Depressions.* New York: Norton.

1936. *Social Security in the United States.* New York: McGraw Hill.

1971. *In the Fullness of Time.* New York: Harcourt Brace Jovanovich.

Dowd, Douglas F. ed. 1958. *Thorstein Veblen: A Critical Reappraisal.* Ithaca, NY: Cornell University Press.

1994. Against Decadence: The Work of Robert A. Brady (1901–63). *Journal of Economic Issues* 28 (December): 1031–1061.

Downey, E. H. 1910. The Futility of Marginal Utility. *Journal of Political Economy* 18 (April): 253–268.

1924. *Workmen's Compensation.* New York: Macmillan.

Duncan, Joseph W. and William C. Shelton. 1978. *Revolution in United States Government Statistics, 1926–1976.* Washington DC: U. S. Department of Commerce.

Duxbury, Neil. 1995. *Patterns of American Jurisprudence.* Oxford: Oxford University

Edie, Lionel D. 1922. *Principles of the New Economics.* New York: Thomas Y. Crowell.

1926. *Economic Principles and Problems.* New York: University of Chicago.

1927. Some Positive Contributions of the Institutional Concept. *Quarterly Journal of Economics* 41 (May): 405–440.

Edwards, George W., Harold G. Moulton, Celona Lewis, and James D. Magee. 1940. *Capital Expansion, Employment, and Economic Stability.* Washington, DC: Brookings Institution.

Eisner, J. Michael. 1967. *William Morris Leiserson: A Biography.* Madison, WI: University of Wisconsin Press.

Ekelund, Robert B. and Robert F. Hebert. 1990. *A History of Economic Theory and Method.* New York: McGraw-Hill.

Ely, Richard, T. 1914. *Property and Contract in Their Relation to the Distribution of Wealth.* New York: Macmillan.

   1932. Round Table Conferences: Institutional Economics. *American Economic Review* 22 (March): 114–116.

Ely, Richard T., Thomas A. Adams, Max O. Lorenz, and Allyn Young. 1908. *Outlines of Economics,* revised edition. New York: Macmillan.

Emmett, Ross B. 1999. Introduction. In Ross B. Emmett, ed., *Selected Essays of Frank H. Knight.* Chicago: University of Chicago Press, pp. vii–xxiv.

   2009. *Frank Knight and the Chicago School in American Economics.* London: Routledge.

   Forthcoming. Specializing in Interdisciplinarity: The Committee on Social Thought as Chicago's Antidote to Specialization in the Social Sciences. *History of Political Economy.*

Epstein, Abraham. 1936. *Insecurity: A Challenge to America.* New York: Random House.

Epstein, Roy J. 1987. *A History of Econometrics.* Amsterdam: North Holland.

Everett, Helen. 1931. Social Control. *Encyclopaedia of the Social Sciences,* vol. 4. New York: Macmillan, pp. 344–349.

Ezekiel, Mordecai. 1930. *Methods of Correlation Analysis.* New York: J. Wiley.

   1936. *$2,500 a Year: From Scarcity to Abundance.* New York: Harcourt Brace.

   1937. An Annual Estimate of Savings by Individuals. *Review of Economic Statistics* 19 (November): 178–191.

   1938. The Cobweb Theorem. *Quarterly Journal of Economics* 52 (February): 255–280.

   1939a. *Jobs for All through Industrial Expansion.* New York: A. A. Knopf.

   1939b. Keynes versus Chamberlin. *Report of the Fifth Annual Conference on Economics and Statistics.* Colorado Springs, CO: Cowles Commission for Research in Economics, pp. 54–57.

   1942. Statistical Investigations of Saving, Consumption, and Investment, Parts I and II. *American Economic Review* 32 (March): 22–49 and (June): 272–307.

   1957. *Reminiscences of Mordecai Ezekiel.* Columbia University Oral History Research Office Collection.

Fabricant, Solomon. 1984. *Toward a Firmer Basis of Economic Policy: The Founding of The National Bureau of Economic Research.* http://www.nber.org/nberhistory/

Fetter, Frank A. 1932. The Economists' Committee on Anti-Trust Law Policy. *American Economic Review* 22 (September): 465–469.

Field, James A. 1917. The Place of Economic Theory in Graduate Work. *Journal of Political Economy* 25 (January): 48–57.

Fiorito, Luca. 2001. John Maurice Clark's Contribution to the Genesis of the Multiplier Analysis (With Some Unpublished Correspondence). *History of Economic Ideas* 9 (1): 7–37.

   2009. Frank H. Knight, Pragmatism and American Institutionalism: A Note. *European Journal of the History of Economic Thought* 16 (September): 475–487.

2010a. The Institutionalists' Reaction to Chamberlin's *Theory of Monopolistic Competition*. Mimeo.

2010b. John R. Commons, Wesley N. Hohfeld and the Origins of Transactional Economics. *History of Political Economy* 42 (Summer): 267–295.

Fiorito, Luca and Matias Vernengo. 2009. The Other J. M.: John Maurice Clark and the Keynesian Revolution. *Journal of Economic Issues* 43 (December): 899–916.

Fisher, Donald. 1993. *Fundamental Development of the social Sciences: Rockefeller Philanthropy and the United States Social Science Research Council*. Ann Arbor, MI: University of Michigan.

Fisher, Irving. 1919. Economists and the Public Service. *American Economic Review* 9 (March): 5–21.

Fisher, William W., Morton J. Horwitz, and Thomas A. Reed, eds. 1993. *American Legal Realism*. New York: Oxford University Press.

Fishman, L. 1958. Veblen, Hoxie, and American Labor. In D. F. Dowd, ed., *Thorstein Veblen: A Critical Reappraisal*. Ithaca, NY: Cornell University Press, pp. 221–236.

Fitch, John A. (1910) 1989. *The Steel Workers*. Pittsburgh, PA: University of Pittsburgh.

Florence, P. Sargant. 1927. *Economics and Human Behavior: A Reply to Social Psychologists*. New York: Norton.

Forget, Evelyn L. 2000. Margaret Gilpin Reid (1896–1991). In Robert W. Dimand, Mary Ann Dimand and Evelyn L. Forget, eds., *A Biographical Dictionary of Women Economists*. Cheltenham: Edward Elgar, pp. 357–361.

Fosdick, Raymond B. 1952. *The Story of the Rockefeller Foundation*. New York: Harper.

Frank, Lawrence K. 1923a. The Status of Social Sciences in the United Sates. RAC-LSRM, Series 3.6, Box 63, Folder 679.

1923b. A Theory of Business Cycles. *Quarterly Journal of Economics* 37 (August): 625–642.

1924. The Emancipation of Economics. *American Economic Review* 14 (March): 17–38.

1925. The Significance of Industrial Integration. *Journal of Political Economy* 33 (April): 179–195.

Friday, David. 1919. Maintaining Productive Output – A Problem in Reconstruction. *Journal of Political Economy* 27 (February): 117–126.

1920. *Profits, Wages, and Prices*. New York: Harcourt, Brace and Howe.

Fried, Barbara H. 1998. *The Progressive Assault on Laissez Faire: Robert Hale and the First Law and Economics Movement*. Cambridge, MA: Harvard University Press.

Friedman, Milton. 1945. *Incomes from Independent Professional Practice* (With Simon Kuznets). New York: NBER.

1953. The Methodology of Positive Economics. *Essays in Positive Economics*. Chicago: University of Chicago Press.

1957. *A Theory of the Consumption Function*. Princeton, NJ: Princeton University Press.

1962. *Capitalism and Freedom*. Chicago: University of Chicago Press.

Friedman, Milton and Rose Friedman. 1998. *Two Lucky People*. Chicago: University of Chicago Press.

Friedman, Milton and Anna J. Schwartz. 1963. *A Monetary History of the United States: 1867-1960*. Princeton, NJ: Princeton University Press.

Froman, Lewis A. 1942. Graduate Students in Economics, 1904-1940. *American Economic Review* 32 (December): 817-826.

Furner, Mary O. 1975. *Advocacy and Objectivity: A Crisis in the Professionalization of American Social Science, 1865-1905*. Lexington, KY: University of Kentucky Press.

2005. Structure and Virtue in United States Political Economy. *Journal of the History of Economic Thought* 27 (March): 13-39.

Galbraith, John Kenneth. 1952. *A Theory of Price Control*. Cambridge, MA: Harvard University Press.

1958. *The Affluent Society*. Boston: Houghton Mifflin.

1967. *The New Industrial State*. Boston: Houghton Mifflin.

1981. *A Life in Our Times*. Boston: Houghton Mifflin.

Gambs, John S. 1946. *Beyond Supply and Demand: A Reappraisal of Institutional Economics*. New York: Columbia University Press.

Geiger, Roger L. 1988. American Foundations and Academic Social Science, 1945-1960. *Minerva* 26 (3): 315-341.

Gillin, John L. 1921. *Poverty and Dependency*. New York: Century.

1926. *Criminology and Penology*. New York: Century.

Ginzberg, Eli. 1990. Economics at Columbia: Recollections of the Early 1930s. *American Economist*: 14-19.

1997. Wesley Clair Mitchell. *History of Political Economy* 29 (Fall): 371-390.

Givens, Meredith. 1934. An Experiment in Advisory Service: The Committee on Government Statistics and Information Services. *Journal of the American Statistical Association* 29 (December): 394-404.

Glaeser, Martin G. 1927. *Outlines of Public Utility Economics*. New York: Macmillan.

Gonce, Richard A. 2006. John R. Commons' Successful Plan for Constitutional, Effective, Labor Legislation. *Journal of Economic Issues* 40 (December): 1045-1067.

Goodrich, Carter L. 1920. *The Frontier of Control: A Study of British Workshop Politics*. New York: Harcourt, Brace and Howe.

1925. *The Miner's Freedom: A Study of the Working Life in a Changing Industry*. Boston: Marshall Jones.

Goodwin, Craufurd. 1998. The Patrons of Economics in a Time of Transformation. In Mary S. Morgan and Malcolm Rutherford, eds., *From Interwar Pluralism to Postwar Neoclassicism*, Annual Supplement to Volume 30, *History of Political Economy*. Durham, NC: Duke University Press, pp. 53-81.

Graduate School of Economics and Government, Washington University. 1924-1925. Preliminary Announcement 1924-1925. Laura Spelman Rockefeller Memorial Archives, Record Group 3.6, Box 49, Folder 517.

Grossbard-Shechtman, Shoshana. 2001. The New Home Economics at Columbia and Chicago. *Feminist Economics* 7 (November): 103-130.

Grossman, David M. 1982. American Foundations and the Support of Economic Research, 1913-1929. *Minerva* 20 (1-2): 59-82.

Groves, Harold M. 1964. Institutional Economics and Public Finance. *Land Economics* 40 (August): 239-246.

Grimmer-Solem, Erik. 2003. *The Rise of Historical Economics and Social Reform in Germany 1864-1894*. Oxford: Oxford University Press.

Gruchy, Allan G. 1947. *Modern Economic Thought*. New York: Prentice Hall.

1950a. Keynes and the Institutionalists: Some Similarities. In C. Lawrence Christensen, ed., *Economic Theory in Review*. Bloomington, IN: Indiana University Press, pp. 96–100.

1950b. Keynes and the Institutionalists: Important Contrasts. In C. Lawrence Christensen, ed., *Economic Theory in Review*. Bloomington, IN: Indiana University Press, pp. 101–126.

1972. *Contemporary Economic Thought: The Contribution of Neo-Institutionalist Economics*. Clifton, NJ: Augustus M. Kelley.

Gunning, J. Patrick. 1998. Herbert J. Davenport's Transformation of the Austrian Theory of Value and Cost. In Malcolm Rutherford, ed., *The Economic Mind in America*. London: Routledge, pp. 99–127.

Hagemann, Harald. 2005. Dismissal, Expulsion, and Emigration of German-Speaking Economists after 1933. *Journal of the History of Economic Thought* 27 (December): 405–420.

Hale, Robert L. 1921. The "Physical Value" Fallacy in Rate Cases. *Yale Law Journal* 30: 710–731.

1922. "Rate Making and the Revision of the Property Concept." *Columbia Law Review* 22: 209–216.

1923. Coercion and Distribution in a Supposedly Non-Coercive State. *Political Science Quarterly* 38 (September): 470–494.

Hall, Randal L. and Ken Badgett. 2009. Robinson Newcomb and the Limits of Liberalism at UNC: Two Case Studies of Black Businessmen in the 1920s south. *North Carolina Historical Review* 86 (October): 373–403.

Hamilton, Walton H. nda. Control of Industrial Development. Walton Hamilton Papers, Box J4, Folder 6.

ndb. The Control of Industry. Walton Hamilton Papers, Box J3, Folder 3.

1915. Economic Theory and "Social Reform." *Journal of Political Economy* 23 (June): 562–584.

1916a. The Development of Hoxie's Economics. *Journal of Political Economy* 24 (November, 1916): 855–883.

1916b. Tendencies in Economic Theory – Discussion. *American Economic Review* 6 (March): 164–166.

1917. Problems of Economic Instruction. *Journal of Political Economy* 25 (January): 1–13.

1918a. The Price System and Social Policy. *Journal of Political Economy* 26 (January): 31–68.

1918b. The Place of Value Theory in Economics, I and II. *Journal of Political Economy* 26 (March, April): 217–245, 275–407.

1918c. The Requisites of a National Food Policy. *Journal of Political Economy* 26 (June): 612–637.

1919a. The Institutional Approach to Economic Theory. *American Economic Review* 9 (March): 309–318.

ed. 1919b. *Current Economic Problems*, revised edition. Chicago: University of Chicago Press.

1919c. The Rate of Demobilization and the Labor Market. *Proceedings of the Academy of Political Science* 8 (February): 323–329.

1919d. The Lapse to Laissez-Faire. *The Dial* 66 (April 5): 337–340.

1921. Review of *Labor and the Common Welfare*; *Labor and the Employer*. *Political Science Quarterly* 36 (June): 326–329.

1922. A Theory of the Rate of Wages. *Quarterly Journal of Economics* 36 (August): 581–625.

1923. Education – Ritual or Adventure? *The Nation* 116 (June): 720–721.

1924. The Educational Policy of "A Labor College." *Social Forces* 2 (January): 204–208.

1926a. Report to the Board of Trustees, The Robert Brookings Graduate School of Economics and Government, April 30, 1926. Appendix 3 to Harold G. Moulton, The History of the Organization of the Brookings Institution, June 1928. Brookings Institution Archives, Item 17, Formal and Informal Histories of the Brookings Institution, 1928–1966, Box 1, File: Memoranda on the Early History of the Brookings Institution.

1926b. The Problem of Bituminous Coal. *American Labor Legislation Review* 16: 217–229.

1927. Memorandum to Abraham Flexner: The Brookings Ventures at Washington. Appendix 12 to Harold G. Moulton, The History of the Organization of the Brookings Institution, June 1928. Brookings Institution Archives, Item 17, Formal and Informal Histories of the Brookings Institution, 1928–1966, Box 1, File: Memoranda on the Early History of the Brookings Institution.

1928a. The Plight of Soft Coal. *The Nation* 126 (April 4): 367–369.

1928b. The Regulation of Employment Agencies. *Yale Law Journal* 38 (December): 225–235.

1929a. Charles Horton Cooley. *Social Forces* 8 (December): 183–187.

1929b. Judicial Tolerance of Farmers' Cooperatives. *Yale Law Journal* 38 (May): 936–954.

1930a. An Economist Audits His Costs. *The Survey* 63 (January 1): 380–383.

1930b. Affectation with Public Interest. *Yale Law Journal* 39 (June): 1089–1112.

1931a. Competition. *Encyclopaedia of the Social Sciences*, Volume 4. New York: Macmillan, pp. 141–147.

1931b. The Jurist's Art. *Columbia Law Review* 31 (November): 1073–1093.

1931c. The Ancient Maxim Caveat Emptor. *Yale Law Journal* 40 (June): 1133–1187.

1931d. The Legal Philosophy of Justices Holmes and Brandeis. *Current History* 33 (February): 654–660.

1931e. *The World-Wide Depression: Ways Out*. Pamphlet No. 71. New York: Foreign Policy Association.

1932a. The Control of Big Business. *The Nation* 134 (May 25): 591–593.

1932b. The Anti-Trust Laws and the Social Control of Business. In Milton Handler, ed., *The Federal Anti-Trust Laws: A Symposium*. Chicago: Commerce Clearing House.

1932c. The Problem of Anti-Trust Reform. *Columbia Law Review* 32 (February): 173–178.

1932d. Statement by Walton H. Hamilton. In Committee on the Costs of Medical Care, *Medical Care for the American People*. Chicago: University of Chicago Press, pp.189–200.

1932e. Property According to Locke. *Yale Law Journal* 41 (April): 864–880.

1933a. In Re The Small Debtor. *Yale Law Journal* 42 (February): 473–486.

1933b. The Credo of Recovery. *New Republic* 75 (June 28): 185.

1934. Consumers' Interest in Price Fixing. *Survey Graphic* 23 (February): 76–80, 95–96.

1935a. Black Justice. *The Nation* 140 (May 1): 497.

1935b. The Consumer's Front. *Survey Graphic* 24 (November): 524–528, 565, 567.

1935c. Testimony of Walton Hamilton. Hearings before the Committee on Finance, U.S. Senate, 74th Congress, 1st. Session. Washington, DC: Government Printing Office.

1936a. Why the Price Studies? *The Consumer* 1 (January 15): 6–9.

1936b. The Constitution as an Instrument of Public Welfare. *American Labor Legislation Review* 26: 103–107.

1937. The Living Law. *Survey Graphic* 26 (December): 632–635, 735.

1938a. The Path of Due Process of Law. *Ethics* 48 (April): 269–296.

1938b. Cardozo the Craftsman. *University of Chicago Law Review* 6 (December): 1–22.

1938c. Price – By Way of Litigation. *Columbia Law Review* 38 (June): 1008–1036.

1938d. The Doctors' "Union." *New Republic* 96 (September 7): 117–118.

1939a. Preview of a Justice. *Yale Law Journal* 48 (March): 819–838.

1939b. Industrial Inquiry and Sectarian Dogma. *American Economic Review* 29 (March): 102–106.

1940a. Common Right, Due Process, and Antitrust. *Law and Contemporary Problems* 7 (Winter): 24–41.

1940b. *The Pattern of Competition*. New York: Columbia University Press.

1941a. *Patents and Free Enterprise*. Temporary National Economic Committee, Monograph No. 31. Washington, DC: Government Printing Office.

1941b. On Dating Mr. Justice Holmes. *University of Chicago Law Review* 9 (December):1–29.

1941c. Coal and the Economy – A Demurrer. *Yale Law Journal* 50 (February): 595–621.

1943a. Whitewashing the Patent System. *New Republic* 109 (August 30): 278–279.

1943b. Property Rights in the Market. *Journal of Legal and Political Sociology* 2 (April): 10–33.

1944. Review of *The Great Transformation, England's Service, Bureaucracy, and The Road to Serfdom. Yale Law Journal* 53 (September): 805–811.

1946a. On the Composition of the Corporate Veil. Brandeis Lawyers' Society, Publication No 6. Philadelphia: Brandeis Lawyers' Society.

1946b. The Economic Man Affects a National Role. *American Economic Review* 36 (May): 735–744.

1949a. A New Patent Policy. *Current History* 17 (December): 338–341.

1949b. The Genius of the Radical. In John W. Chase, ed., *Years of the Modern*. New York: Longmans, Green.

1953. The Law, the Economy, and Moral Values. In A. Dudley Ward, ed., *Goals of Economic Life*. New York: Harper & Brothers.

1957. *The Politics of Industry*. New York: Alfred A. Knopf.

1958. Veblen – Then and Now. In Douglas Dowd, ed., *Thorstein Veblen: A Critical Reappraisal*. Ithaca, NY: Cornell University Press.

Hamilton, Walton H. and Douglass Adair. 1937. *The Power to Govern*. New York: Da Capo Press, 1972.

Hamilton, Walton H. and Associates. 1938. *Price and Price Policies*. New York: McGraw Hill.

Hamilton, Walton H. and George D. Braden. 1941. The Special Competence of the Supreme Court. *Yale Law Journal* 50 (June): 1319–1375.

Hamilton, Walton H. and Stacy May. 1923. *The Control of Wages*. New York: Augustus M. Kelley, 1968.

Hamilton, Walton H. and Irene Till. 1940a. *Antitrust in Action*. Temporary National Economic Committee, Monograph No. 16. Washington, DC: Government Printing Office.

1940b. Antitrust – The Reach after New Weapons. *Washington University Law Quarterly* 26 (December): 1–26.

1948. What Is a Patent? *Law and Contemporary Problems* 13 (Spring): 245–259.

Hamilton, Walton H. and John C. White. 1926. *A Book of Book Reviews*. Washington DC: np.

Hamilton, Walton H. and Helen R. Wright. 1925. *The Case of Bituminous Coal*. New York: Macmillan.

1928. *A Way of Order for Bituminous Coal*. New York: Macmillan.

Hammond, Claire H. 2000a. Edith Abbott (1876–1957). In Robert W. Dimand, Mary Ann Dimand, and Evelyn L. Forget, eds., *A Biographical Dictionary of Women Economists*. Cheltenham: Edward Elgar, pp. 1–7.

2000b. Sophonisba Breckinridge (1866–1948). In Robert W. Dimand, Mary Ann Dimand and Evelyn L. Forget eds., *A Biographical Dictionary of Women Economists*. Cheltenham: Edward Elgar, pp. 81–88.

Hammond, J. Daniel. 1996. *Theory and Measurement: Causality Issues in Milton Friedman's Monetary Economics*. Cambridge: Cambridge University Press.

2001. Columbia Roots of the Chicago School: The Case of Milton Friedman. Paper Presented at the ASSA Meetings, New Orleans, January 2001.

Hands, D. Wade. 2004. On Operationalism in Economics. *Journal of Economic Issues* 38 (December): 953–968.

2006. Frank Knight and Pragmatism. *European Journal of the History of Economic Thought* 13 (December): 571–605.

Hansen, Alvin H. 1927. *Business Cycle Theory, Its Development and Present Status*. Boston: Ginn.

1932. The Contributions of Professor John R. Commons to American Economics. Alvin Hansen Papers, Harvard University Archives, HUGFP – 3.42, Box 1.

1947. Two Interpretations of Keynesian Economics: Dr. Burns on Keynesian Economics. *Review of Economic Statistics* 29 (November): 247–252.

Hansen, Alvin H. and Merrill G. Murray. 1933. *A New Plan for Unemployment Reserves*. Minneapolis: Employment Stabilization Research Institute, University of Minnesota.

Harris, Abram L. 1932. Types of Institutionalism. *Journal of Political Economy* 40 (December): 721–749.

1934. Economic Evolution: Dialectical and Darwinian. *Journal of Political Economy* 42 (February): 34–79.

Harter, Lafayette G. 1962. *John R. Commons: His Assault on Laissez-Faire*. Corvallis, OR: Oregon State University.

Hastay, M. 1951. Review of T. C. Koopmans, ed., *Statistical Inference in Dynamic Economic Models. Journal of the American Statistical Association* 46 (September): 388–90.

Hawley, Ellis W. 1966. *The New Deal and the Problem of Monopoly*. Princeton, NJ: Princeton University Press.

Hayes, Edward C., ed. 1927. *Recent Developments in the Social Sciences*. Philadelphia: Lippencott.

Heaton, Herbert. 1952. *A Scholar in Action: Edwin F. Gay*. Cambridge, MA: Harvard University Press.

Herbst, Jurgen. 1965. *The German Historical School in American Scholarship*. Ithaca, NY: Cornell University Press.

Hicks, John R. 1932. *The Theory of Wages*. London: Macmillan.

Hicks, John R. and R. G. D. Allen. 1934. A Reconsideration of the Theory of Value. *Economica* NS 1 (February and May): 52–76, 196–219.

Hirsch, Abraham and Neil DeMarchi. 1990. *Milton Friedman: Economics in Theory and Practice*. Ann Arbor, MI: University of Michigan Press.

Hirschfield, Mary L. 1998. Methodological Stance and Consumption Theory: A Lesson in Feminist Methodology. In John B. Davis, ed., *New Economics and its History*. Annual Supplement to Volume 29 *History of Political Economy*. Durham, NC: Duke University Press, pp. 191–211.

Hirshfeld, Daniel S. 1970. *The Lost Reform: The Campaign for Compulsory Health Insurance in the United States from 1932 to 1943*. Cambridge, MA: Harvard University Press.

Hodgson, Geoffrey M. 2001. *How Economics Forgot History: The Problem of Historical Specificity in Social Science*. London: Routledge.

2004. *The Evolution of Institutional Economics*. London: Routledge.

Homan, Paul T. 1928. *Contemporary Economic Thought*. New York: Harper.

1932. An Appraisal of Institutional Economics. *American Economic Review* 22 (March): 10–17.

1937. The Institutional School. *Encyclopaedia of the Social Sciences*, volume 5, New York: Macmillan.

Howlett, Charles F. 2003. David J. Saposs. *American National Biography Online*. http://www.anb.org/articles/14/14–01131.html

Hoxie, Robert F. 1901. On the Empirical Method of Economic Instruction. *Journal of Political Economy* 9 (September): 481–526.

1907. The Trade Union Point of View. *Journal of Political Economy* 15 (June): 345–363.

1908. President Gompers and the Labor Vote. *Journal of Political Economy* 16 (December): 693–700.

1915. *Scientific Management and Labor*. New York: D. Appleton.

1917. *Trade Unionism in the United States*. New York: D. Appleton.

Hurley, Jack F. 1972. *Portrait of a Decade: Roy Stryker and the Development of Documentary Photography in the Thirties*. Baton Rouge, LA: Louisiana State University.

Innis, Harold A. 1929. A Bibliography of Thorstein Veblen. *Southwestern Political and Social Science Quarterly* 10 (June): 56–68.

Ise, John. 1932. Recent Textbooks on Economics and Their Trend. *Quarterly Journal of Economics* 46 (February): 385–397.

Johnson, Alvin. 1952. *Pioneer's Progress*. New York: Viking.

Jorgensen, Elizabeth and Henry Jorgensen. 1999. *Thorstein Veblen: Victorian Firebrand*. Armonk, NY: M. E. Sharpe.

Kahneman, Daniel and Amos Tversky. 1974. Judgment under Uncertainty: Heuristics and Biases. *Science* 185 (September): 1124–1131.

Kantor, J. R. 1922. An Essay Toward an Institutional Conception of Social Psychology. *American Journal of Sociology* 27 (March): 611–627; (May): 758–779.

1924. The Institutional Foundation of a Scientific Social Psychology. *American Journal of Sociology* 29 (May): 674–687.

Kapp, William K. 1950. *The Social Costs of Private Enterprise*. Cambridge, MA: Harvard University Press.

1976. The Nature and Significance of Institutional Economics. *Kyklos* 29 (2): 209–232.

Kates, Steven. 2008. The American Roots and Origins of the *General Theory*. Paper Presented at the History of Economics Society Meetings.

Kaufman, Bruce E. 1993. *The Origins and Evolution of the Field of Industrial Relations in the United States*. Ithaca, NY: ILR Press.

2003. John R. Commons and the Wisconsin School on Industrial Relations Strategy and Policy. *Industrial and Labor Relations Review* 57 (October): 3–30.

2004. The Institutional and Neoclassical Schools in Labor Economics. In Dell P. Champlin and Janet T. Knoedler, eds., *The Institutionalist Tradition in Labor Economics*. Armonk, NY: M. E. Sharpe, pp. 13–38.

Kay, Lily E. 1997. Rethinking Institutions: Philanthropy as an Historiographic Problem of Knowledge and Power. *Minerva* 35 (3): 283–293.

Keaney, Michael. 2000. The Radical Political Economics of Douglas F. Dowd. *Journal of Economic Issues* 34 (March): 117–142.

Keezer, Dexter M. 1934. The Consumer under the National Recovery Administration. *Annals of the American Academy of Political and Social Science* 172 (March): 88–97.

Keezer, Dexter M., Addison T. Cutler, and Frank R. Garfield. 1928. *Problem Economics*. New York: Harper.

Keezer, Dexter M. and Stacy May. 1930. *The Public Control of Business*. New York: Harper.

Kerr, Clark. 1988. The Neoclassical Revisionists in Labor Economics (1940–1960) – R.I.P. In Bruce E. Kaufman, ed., *How Labor Markets Work: Reflections on Theory and Practice by John Dunlop, Clark Kerr, Richard Lester, and Lloyd Reynolds*. Lexington, MA: Lexington Books.

Keynes, John M. 1936. *The General Theory of Employment, Interest and Money*. London: Macmillan.

1941. Letter to J. M. Clark. In Donald Moggridge, ed., *The Collected Writings of John Maynard Keynes, Vol. XXIII*. London: Macmillan, pp. 192–193.

Keyserling, Leon H. 1972. The Keynesian Revolution and Its Pioneers – Discussion. *American Economic Review* 62 (1/2): 134–138.

King, Willford I. 1923. *Employment, Hours, and Earnings in Prosperity and Depression*. New York: National Bureau of Economic Research.

Kitch, Edmund W., ed. 1983. The Fire of Truth: A Remembrance of Law and Economics at Chicago, 1923–1970. *Journal of Law and Economics* 26 (April): 163–234.

Knapp, Joseph G. 1979. *Edwin G. Nourse: Economist for the People*. Danville, IL: Interstate Publishers.

Knight, Frank, H. 1920. Review of *The Place of Science in Modern Civilization* by T. Veblen. *Journal of Political Economy* 28 (June): 518–520.

1921. *Risk, Uncertainty, and Profit.* Boston: Houghton Mifflin.

(1924) 1935. The Limitations of Scientific Method in Economics. In *The Ethics of Competition and Other Essays.* Chicago: University of Chicago Press, pp. 105–147.

(1928) 1956. Historical and Theoretical Issues in the Problem of Modern Capitalism. In *On The History and Method of Economics.* Chicago: University of Chicago Press, pp. 89–103.

1932. The Newer Economics and the Control of Economic Activity. *Journal of Political Economy* 40 (August): 433–476.

1935. Review of John R. Commons's *Institutional Economics. Columbia Law Review* 35 (May): 803–805.

1951. *The Economic Organization.* New York: A. M. Kelley.

Koopmans, Tjalling C. 1947. Measurement without Theory. *Review of Economic Statistics* 29 (August): 161–172.

Kuznets, Simon. 1934. *National Income: 1929–1932.* New York: NBER.

1936. Review of *the Formation of Capital* by Harold G. Moulton and *Income and Economic Progress* by Harold G. Moulton. *Political Science Quarterly* 51 (June): 300–306.

1937. *National Income and Capital Formation, 1919–1935: A Preliminary Report.* New York: National Bureau of Economic Research.

1942. *Uses of National Income in Peace and War.* New York: NBER.

1963. The Contribution of Wesley C. Mitchell. In Joseph Dorfman, et al., *Institutional Economics.* Berkeley, CA: University of California Press, pp. 95–122.

Kyrk, Hazel. 1923. *A Theory of Consumption.* Boston: Houghton Mifflin.

1933. *Economic Problems of the Family.* New York: Harper and Brothers.

Lagemann, Ellen C. 1989. *The Politics of Knowledge: The Carnegie Corporation, Philanthropy, and Public Policy.* Middletown, CT: Wesleyan University Press.

Laidler, David. 1999. *Fabricating the Keynesian Revolution: Studies of the Inter-war Literature on Money, the Cycle, and Unemployment.* Cambridge: Cambridge University Press.

Lampman, Robert J., ed. 1993. *Economists at Wisconsin, 1892–1992.* Madison, WI: Board of Regents of the University of Wisconsin System.

Landreth, Harry and David C. Colander. 1994. *History of Economic Thought*, 3rd. edition. Boston: Houghton Mifflin.

Lange, Dorothea and Paul S. Taylor. 1939. *An American Exodus.* New York: Reynal and Hitchcock.

Lee, Frederic S. 1990. From Multi-Industry Planning to Keynesian Planning: Gardiner Means, the American Keynesians, and National Economic Planning at the National Resources Committee. *Journal of Policy History* 2 (2): 186–212.

1997. Philanthropic Foundations and the Rehabilitation of Big Business, 1934–1977: A Case Study of Directed Economic Research. *Research in the History of Economic Thought and Methodology* 15: 51–90.

Lee, Frederic S. and Warren J. Samuels, eds. 1992. *The Heterodox Economics of Gardiner C. Means.* Armonk, NY: M. E. Sharpe.

Leeson, Robert. 1997. The Eclipse of the Goal of Zero Inflation. *History of Political Economy* 29 (Fall): 445–496.

1998. The Early Patinkin-Friedman Correspondence. *Journal of the History of Economic Thought* 20 (December): 433–448.

2000. *The Eclipse of Keynesianism: The Political Economy of the Chicago Counter-Revolution.* New York: Palgrave.

Leiter, B. 2001. Llewellyn, Karl Nickerson (1893–1962). *International Encyclopedia of the Social and Behavioral Sciences.* Amsterdam: Elsevier, pp. 8999–9001.

Lerner, Max. 1931. The Social Thought of Mr. Justice Brandeis. *Yale Law Journal* 41 (November): 1–33.

1935. What Is Useable in Veblen? *New Republic* 83 (May): 7–10.

1948. *The Portable Veblen.* New York: Viking.

Lescohier, Don D. 1919. *The Labor Market.* New York: Macmillan.

Lester, Richard A. 1941. *Economics of Labor.* New York: Macmillan.

1946. Shortcomings of Marginal Analysis for Wage-Employment Problems. *American Economic Review* 36 (March): 63–82.

1947. Marginalism, Minimum Wages and Labor Markets. *American Economic Review* 37 (March): 135–148.

Levin, Maurice, Harold Moulton, and Clark Warburton. 1934. *America's Capacity to Consume.* Washington, DC: Brookings Institution.

Lewin, Shira. 1996. Economics and Psychology: Lessons for Our Own Day from the Early Twentieth Century. *Journal of Economic Literature* 35 (September): 1293–1323.

Lewinson, Paul. 1932. *Race, Class and Party: A History of Negro Suffrage and White Politics in the South.* New York: Oxford University Press.

1947. *A Guide to Documents in the National Archives for Negro Studies.* Washington, DC: The American Council for Learned Societies.

Lind, Hans. 1993. The Myth of Institutionalist Method. *Journal of Economic Issues* 27 (March): 1–17.

Llewellyn, Karl N. 1925. The Effect of Legal Institutions upon Economics. *American Economic Review* 15 (December): 665–683.

1930. A Realistic Jurisprudence – The Next Step. *Columbia Law Review* 30: 431–465.

1931. What Price Contract? – An Essay in Perspective. *Yale Law Journal* 40: 704–751.

Lobdell, Richard A. 2000. Helen Laura Sumner Woodbury (1876–1933). In Robert W. Dimand, Mary Ann Dimand, and Evelyn L. Forget, eds., *A Biographical Dictionary of Women Economists.* Cheltenham: Edward Elgar, pp. 46–48.

Lubin, Isador. 1924. *Miner's Wages and the Cost of Coal.* New York: McGraw Hill.

Lubin, Isador and Helen Everett. 1927. *The British Coal Dilemma.* London: Allen and Unwin.

Lynd, Robert. 1934. A New Deal for the Consumer? *New Republic* 177 (January 3): 220–222.

1936. Democracy's Third Estate: The Consumer. *Political Science Quarterly* 51 (December): 481–515.

1939. *Knowledge for What?* Princeton, NJ: Princeton University Press.

Lyon, Leverett S. 1927. Report to the Board of Trustees, The Robert Brookings Graduate School of Economics and Government, April 30, 1926. Appendix 10 to Harold G. Moulton, The History of the Organization of the Brookings Institution, June 1928. Brookings Institution Archives, Item 17, Formal and Informal Histories of the

Brookings Institution, 1928–1966, Box 1, File: Memoranda on the Early History of the Brookings Institution.

Lyon, Leverett S., et al. 1935. *The National Recovery Administration: An Analysis and Appraisal*. Washington, DC: The Brookings Institution.

Machlup, Fritz. 1946. Marginal Analysis and Empirical Research. *American Economic Review* 36 (September): 519–554.

Marschak, Jacob. 1941. A Discussion on Methods in Economics. *Journal of Political Economy* 49 (June), 441–448.

Marshall, Leon C. 1918. *Readings in Industrial Society*. Chicago: University of Chicago Press.

Marshall, Leon C., Chester W. Wright, and James A. Field, eds. 1913. *Materials for the Study of Elementary Economics*. Chicago: University of Chicago Press.

Mason, Edward S. 1939. Price and Output Policies of Large Scale Enterprise. *American Economic Review* 29 (March): 61–74.

Mayhew, Anne. 1998. How American Economists Came to Love the Sherman Antitrust Act. In Mary S. Morgan and Malcolm Rutherford, eds., *From Interwar Pluralism to Postwar Neoclassicism*, Annual Supplement to Volume 30, *History of Political Economy*. Durham, NC: Duke University Press, pp. 179–201.

McAllister, Breck P. 1930. Lord Hale and Business Affected with a Public Interest. *Harvard Law Review* 43 (March): 759–791.

McCarthy, Charles. 1912. *The Wisconsin Idea*. New York: Macmillan.

McCracken, H. L. 1933. *Value Theory and Business Cycles*. New York: Falcon Press.

McDougall, William. 1908. *An Introduction to Social Psychology*. London: Methuen.

   1924. Can Sociology and Social Psychology Dispense with Instincts? *American Journal of Sociology* 29 (May): 657–673.

McMahon, Theresa S. 1912. *Women and Economic Evolution*. Madison, WI: University of Wisconsin Bulletin no. 496.

   1925. *Social and Economic Standards of Living*. Boston: D. C. Heath.

McNulty, Paul J. 1973. Hoxie's Economics in Retrospect: The Making and Unmaking of a Veblenian. *History of Political Economy* 5 (Fall): 449–484.

Means, Gardiner C. 1934. The Consumer and the New Deal. *Annals of the American Academy of Political and Social Science* 173 (May): 7–17.

   1935. Industrial Prices and Their Relative Inflexibility. Senate Document 13, 74th Congress, 1st Session. Washington, DC: Government Printing Office.

   1939. *The Structure of the American Economy: Part I, Basic Characteristics*. Washington, DC: National Resources Committee.

Medema, Steven G. 1998. Wandering the Road from Pluralism to Posner: The Transformation of Law and Economics in the Twentieth Century. In Mary S. Morgan and Malcolm Rutherford, eds., *From Interwar Pluralism to Postwar Neoclassicism*, Annual Supplement to Volume 30, *History of Political Economy*. Durham, NC: Duke University Press, pp. 202–224.

Mehrling, Perry G. 1997. *The Money Interest and the Public Interest: American Monetary Thought 1920–1970*. Cambridge, MA: Harvard University Press.

Millar, James R. 1980. Institutionalism from a Natural Science Point of View: An Intellectual Profile of Morris A. Copeland. In John Adams, ed., *Institutional Economics: Essays in Honor of Allan G. Gruchy*. Boston: Martinus Nijhoff, pp. 105–124.

Mills, Frederick, C. (1924a) 1971. On Measurement in Economics. In Rexford G. Tugwell, ed., *The Trend of Economics*. Port Washington, NY: Kennikat Press, pp. 37–70.

1924b. *Statistical Methods*. New York: Holt.

1927. *The Behavior of Prices*. New York: National Bureau of Economic Research.

1929. Price Movements and Related Industrial Changes. In *Recent Economic Changes*, Report of the Committee on Recent Economic Changes of the President's Conference on Unemployment. New York: National Bureau of Economic Research.

1932. *Economic Tendencies in the United States*. New York: National Bureau of Economic Research.

1936. *Prices in Recession and Recovery*. New York: National Bureau of Economic Research.

Mirowski, Philip. 1987. The Philosophical Bases of Institutionalist Economics. *Journal of Economic Issues* 21 (September): 1001–1038.

1990. Problems in the Paternity of Econometrics: Henry Ludwell Moore. *History of Political Economy* 22 (Winter): 587–609.

2002. *Machine Dreams: Economics Becomes a Cyborg Science*. Cambridge: Cambridge University Press.

Mitchell, Lucy Sprague. 1953. *Two Lives: The Story of Wesley Clair Mitchell and Myself*. New York: Simon and Schuster.

Mitchell, Wesley C. 1910a. The Rationality of Economic Activity, I. *Journal of Political Economy* 18 (February): 97–113.

1910b. The Rationality of Economic Activity, II. *Journal of Political Economy* 18 (March): 197–216.

1910c. Money Economy and Modern Civilization (Paper Read Before the Cross-Roads Club of Stanford, May 6, 1910). Edited by Malcolm Rutherford, *History of Political Economy* 28 (Fall 1996): 329–357.

1912. The Backward Art of Spending Money. *American Economic Review* 2 (June): 269–281.

1913. *Business Cycles*. Berkeley CA: University of California Press.

1914. Human Behavior and Economics: A Survey of Recent Literature. *Quarterly Journal of Economics* 29 (November): 1–47.

(1915) 1950. Wieser's Theory of Social Economics. In Wesley C. Mitchell, *The Backward Art of Spending Money*. New York: Augustus M. Kelley, pp. 225–257.

1916. The Role of Money in Economic Theory. *American Economic Review* 6 (March): 140–161.

(1918) 1950. Bentham's Felicific Calculus. In Wesley C. Mitchell, *The Backward Art of Spending Money*. New York: Augustus M. Kelley, pp. 177–202.

ed. 1919. *History of Prices During the War*. War Industries Board Price Bulletins Nos. 1–57. Washington DC: Government Printing Office.

(1919) 1950. Statistics and Government. In Wesley C. Mitchell, *The Backward Art of Spending Money*. New York: Augustus M. Kelley, pp. 42–57.

(1923a) 1950. Making Goods and Making Money. In Wesley C. Mitchell, *The Backward Art of Spending Money*. New York: Augustus M. Kelley, pp.137–148.

ed. 1923b. *Business Cycles and Unemployment*. New York: McGraw-Hill.

1924a. Commons on the Legal Foundations of Capitalism. *American Economic Review* 14 (June): 240–253.

(1924b) 1971. The Prospects of Economics. In Rexford G. Tugwell, ed., *The Trend of Economics*. Port Washington, NY: Kennikat Press, pp. 1–34.

1925. Quantitative Analysis in Economic Theory. *American Economic Review* 15 (March): 1–12.

1927. *Business Cycles: The Problem and Its Setting*. New York: National Bureau of Economic Research.

(1928a) 1936. Letter from Wesley C. Mitchell to John M. Clark. In J. M. Clark *Preface to Social Economics*. New York: Farrar and Rinehart, pp. 410–416.

1928b. The Present Status and Future Prospects of Quantitative Economics. *American Economic Review*, Supplement,18 (March): 39–41.

1929a. Sombart's Hochkapitalismus. *Quarterly Journal of Economics* 43 (February): 303–323.

1929b. Thorstein Veblen, 1857–1929. *New Republic* 60 (September 4), 66–68.

1935. Foreword. In Ewald T. Grether, et al., eds., *Essays in Social Economics in Honor of Jessica Blanche Peixotto*. Berkeley, CA: University of California Press, pp. 1–4.

1936a. Thorstein Veblen. In Wesley C. Mitchell, ed., *What Veblen Taught*. New York: Viking, pp. vii–xlix.

(1936b) 1950. Intelligence and the Guidance of Economic Evolution. In *The Backward Art of Spending Money*. New York: Augustus M. Kelley, pp. 103–136.

1939. *The National Bureau's Social Function*. NBER Annual Report. New York: NBER.

1944. Facts and Values in Economics. *Journal of Philosophy* 41 (April): 212–219.

1949. *Types of Economic Theory*, 2 vols., (stenographic notes from 1934/35). New York: Augustus Kelley.

1967/1969. *Types of Economic Theory*, 2 vols., edited by Joseph Dorfman. New York: Augustus M. Kelley.

Mitchell Westley C., Willford I. King, Frederick R. Macaulay, and Oswald W. Knauth. 1921. *Income in the United States: Its Amount and Distribution, 1909–1919, Volume I: Summary*. New York: NBER.

1922. *Income in the United States: Its Amount and Distribution, 1909–1919, Volume II: Detailed Report*. New York: NBER.

Mongin, Philippe. 1992. The "Full Cost" Controversy of the 1940s and 1950s: A Methodological Assessment. *History of Political Economy* 24 (Summer): 311–356.

Mongiovi, Gary. 2005. Émigré Economists and American Neoclassical Economics, 1933–1945. *Journal of the History of Economic Thought* 27 (December): 427–437.

Moore, Harry H. 1927. *American Medicine and the Peoples' Health*. New York: Appleton.

1933. Health and Medical Practice. In *Recent Social Trends in the United States*. President's Research Committee on Social Trends. New York: McGraw-Hill.

Moore, Henry L. 1908. The Statistical Complement of Pure Economics. *Quarterly Journal of Economics* 23 (November): 1–33.

Moore, W. Underhill and Theodore S. Hope. 1929. An Institutional Approach to the Law of Commercial Banking. *Yale Law Journal* 38 (April): 703–719.

Morehouse. E. W. 1923. Development of Industrial Law in the Rochester Clothing Market. *Quarterly Journal of Economics* 37 (February): 257–290.

Morgan, Mary S. 1990. *The History of Econometric Ideas*. Cambridge: Cambridge University Press.

Morgan, Mary S. and Malcolm Rutherford, eds. 1998. *From Interwar Pluralism to Postwar Neoclassicism*, Annual Supplement to Volume 30 of *History of Political Economy*. Durham, NC: Duke University Press.

Moulton, Harold G. 1928. The History of the Organization of the Brookings Institution, with 24 Appendices, June 1928. Brookings Institution Archives, Item 17, Formal and Informal Histories of the Brookings Institution, 1928–1966, Box 1, File: Memoranda on the Early History of the Brookings Institution.

1935a. *The Formation of Capital*. Washington, DC: Brookings Institution.

1935b. *Income and Economic Progress*. Washington, DC: Brookings Institution.

1943. *The New Philosophy of Public Debt*. Washington, DC: Brookings Institution.

1949. *Controlling Factors in Economic Development*. Washington, DC: Brookings Institution.

Mund, Vernon. 1938. Review of Hamilton and Associates *Price and Price Policies*. *American Economic Review* 28 (December): 818–820.

Myrdal, Gunnar. 1972. *Against the Stream: Critical Essays in Economics*. New York: Pantheon Books.

National Bureau of Economic Research. 1926. *Bulletin* (May 10). http://www.nber.org/newsbulletin/

1930. *Annual Report of the President and Director of Research*. http://www.nber.org/nberhistory/annualreports.html

1935. *Bulletin* (July 1). http://www.nber.org/newsbulletin/

Nef, John U. 1934. James Laurence Laughlin (1850–1933). *Journal of Political Economy* 42 (February): 1–5.

1973. *Search for Meaning: The Autobiography of a Nonconformist*. Washington DC: Public Affairs Press.

Neill, Robin. 1972. *A New Theory of Value: The Canadian Economics of H. A. Innis*. Toronto: University of Toronto Press.

Nelson, Ralph L. 1966. Economic Research Sponsored by Private Foundations. *American Economic Review* 56 (May): 519–529.

Nourse, Edwin G. 1944. *Price Making in a Democracy*. Washington, DC: Brookings Institution.

Nourse, Edwin G. and Associates. 1934. *America's Capacity to Produce*. Washington, DC: Brookings Institution.

Nutter, G. Warren. 1951. *The Extent of Enterprise Monopoly in the United States, 1899–1939*. Chicago: University of Chicago Press.

Nyland, Chris. 1996. Taylorism, John R. Commons, and the Hoxie Report. *Journal of Economic Issues* 30 (December): 985–1016

Ogburn, William F. 1919. The Psychological Basis for the Economic Interpretation of History. *American Economic Review* 9 (March): 291–308.

1922. *Social Change with Respect to Culture and Original Nature*. New York: Huebsch.

Ogburn, William F. and Alexander Goldenweiser, eds. 1927. *The Social Sciences and Their Interrelations*. Boston: Houghton Mifflin.

Oser, Jacob and Stanley L. Brue. 1988. *The Evolution of Economic Thought*, 4th. edition. San Diego, CA: Harcourt Brace Jovanovich.

Panunzio, Constantine, M. 1927. *Immigration Crossroads*. New York: Macmillan.

Parker, Carleton H. 1920. *The Causal Laborer and Other Essays*. New York: Harcourt, Brace and Howe.

Parker, Cornelia S. 1919. *An American Idyll*. Boston: Atlantic Monthly Press.

1922. *Working with the Working Woman*. New York: Harper.

1934. *Wanderer's Circle*. Boston: Houghton Mifflin.

Parker, Richard. 2005. *John Kenneth Galbraith: His Life, His Politics, His Economics*. New York: Farrar, Straus and Giroux.

Parrish, John B. 1967. The Rise of Economics as an Academic Discipline: The Formative Years to 1900. *Southern Economic Journal* 34 (July): 1–16.

Parsons, Kenneth H. 1942. John R. Commons' Point of View. *Journal of Land and Public Utility Economics* 18 (August): 245–266.

1976. Interview by Laura Small. University of Wisconsin-Madison Archives, Oral History Project, interview #081.

Parsons, Talcott. 1928/1929. Capitalism in Recent German Literature: Sombart and Weber: Parts I and II. *Journal or Political Economy* 36 (December): 641–664, 37 (February): 31–51.

1934. Some Reflections on "The Nature and Significance of Economics." *Quarterly Journal of Economics* 48 (May): 511–545.

1935. Sociological Elements in Economic Thought. *Quarterly Journal of Economics* 49 (May): 414–453.

1959. A Short Account of my Intellectual Development. *Alpha Kappa Delta* 29 (Winter): 3–12.

1976. Clarence Ayres's Economics and Sociology. In William Breit and William Patton Culbertson, eds., *Science and Ceremony: The Institutional Economics of C. E. Ayres*. Austin: University of Texas Press, pp. 175–179.

Parsons, Talcott and Addison T. Cutler. 1923. A Word From Amherst Students. Reprinted in Charles Camic, ed., *Talcott Parsons, The Early Essays*. Chicago: University of Chicago Press, 1991, pp. 287–292.

Peck, Gustav and George B. Galloway. 1928. On the Dissolution of the Robert Brookings Graduate School. *The Survey* (May 15): 229–231.

Peixotto, Jessica B. 1927. *Getting and Spending at the Professional Standard of Living*. New York: Macmillan.

Perkins, A. J. G. and Theresa Wolfson. 1939. *Frances Wright, Free Enquirer*. New York: Harper.

Perkins, B. B. 1998. Economic Organization of Medicine and the Committee on the Costs of Medical Care. *American Journal of Public Health* 88: 1721–1726.

Perlman, Mark, ed. 1971. *Carter Goodrich, 1897–1971*. Np.

2001. Two Phases of Kuznets' Interest in Schumpeter. In Jeff E. Biddle, John B. Davis, and Steven G. Medema, eds., *Economics Broadly Considered: Essays in Honor of Warren J. Samuels*. London: Routledge.

Perlman, Selig. 1928. *A Theory of the Labor Movement*. New York: Macmillan.

Persky, Joseph. 2000. The Neoclassical Advent: American Economics at the Dawn of the 20th Century. *Journal of Economic Perspectives* 14 (Winter): 95–108.

References

Phillips, Almarin and Rodney E. Stevenson. 1974. The Historical Development of Industrial Organization. *History of Political Economy* 6 (Fall): 324–342.

Phillips, Ronnie J. 1995. *Economic Mavericks: The Texas Institutionalists*. Greenwich, CT: JAI Press.

Pigou, Arthur C. 1912. *Wealth and Welfare*. London: Macmillan.

1920. *The Economics of Welfare*. London: Macmillan.

Pittenger, Mark. 1997. A World of Difference: Constructing the "Underclass" in Progressive America. *American Quarterly* 49 (March): 26–65.

Polanyi, Karl, Conrad Arensberg, and Harry Pearson, eds. 1957. *Trade and Market in Early Empires*. Glencoe, IL: Free Press.

Porter, Theodore M. 1994. Rigour and Practicality: Rival Ideas of Quantification in Nineteenth Century Economics. In Philip Mirowski, ed., *Natural Images in Economic Thought*. Cambridge: Cambridge University Press, pp. 128–170.

Posner, Richard A. 1995. *Overcoming Law*. Cambridge, MA: Harvard University Press.

Prasch, Robert E. 2007. Professor Lester and the Neoclassicals: The "Marginalist Controversy" and the Postwar Academic Debate Over Minimum Wage Legislation: 1945–1950. *Journal of Economic Issues* 41 (September): 809–825.

President's Research Committee on Social Trends. 1933. *Recent Social Trends in the United States*. New York: McGraw Hill.

Quine, W. V. 1985. *The Time of My Life*. Cambridge, MA: MIT Press.

Rader, Benjamin G. 1966. *The Academic Mind and Reform: The Influence of Richard T. Ely in American Life*. Lexington, KY: University of Kentucky.

Raushenbush, Paul A. and Elizabeth Brandeis Raushenbush. 1979. *Our "U. C." Story*. Madison, WI: np.

Reder, Melvin W. 1982. Chicago Economics: Permanence and Change. *Journal of Economic Literature* 20 (March): 1–38.

Reid, Margaret G. 1934. *The Economics of Household Production*. New York: Wiley.

Report of the Columbia University Committee. 1934. *Economic Reconstruction*. New York: Columbia University Press.

Reynolds, Lloyd. 1949. *Labor Economics and Labor Relations*. Englewood Cliffs, NJ: Prentice-Hall.

Rice, Stuart A., ed. 1931. *Methods in Social Science: A Case Book*. Chicago: University of Chicago Press.

1933. Committee on Governmental Statistics and Information Services. *Journal of the American Statistical Association* 28 (September): 333–334.

Richardson, Theresa and Donald Fisher. 1999. Introduction: The Social Sciences and Their Philanthropic Mentors. In Theresa Richardson and Donald Fisher, eds., *The Development of the Social Sciences in the United States and Canada: The Role of Philanthropy*. Stamford, CT: Ablex.

Riefler, Winfield W. 1930. *Money Rates and Money Markets in the United States*. New York: Harper.

Rima, Ingrid H. 1996. *Development of Economic Analysis*, 5th. edition. London: Routledge.

Ripley, William Z. 1927. *Main Street and Wall Street*. Boston: Little, Brown.

Robbins, Lionel. 1932. *The Nature and Significance of Economic Science*. London: Macmillan.

Robert Brookings Graduate School of Economics and Government. 1928. General Catalogue 1923–1928. Washington, DC. Appendix 23 to Harold G. Moulton, The History of the Organization of the Brookings Institution, June 1928. Brookings Institution Archives, Item 17, Formal and Informal Histories of the Brookings Institution, 1928–1966, Box 1, File: Memoranda on the Early History of the Brookings Institution.

The Institute of Economics, The Institute for Government Research. 1924–1925. Personnel. Walton H. Hamilton Papers, Box J9, Folder 5.

The Institute of Economics, The Institute for Government Research. 1927–1928. Personnel. Walton H. Hamilton Papers, Box J9, Folder 5.

Robinson, Joan. 1933. *The Economics of Imperfect Competition*. London: Macmillan.

Ross, Dorothy. 1991. *The Origins of American Social Science*. Cambridge: Cambridge University Press.

Ross, Edward A. 1901. *Social Control*. New York: Macmillan.

1920. *Principles of Sociology*. New York: Century.

Ross, Joseph S. 2002. The Committee on the Costs of Medical Care and the History of Health Insurance in the United States. *The Einstein Quarterly Journal of Biology and Medicine* 19: 129–134.

Rostow, Eugene V. 1941. Bituminous Coal and the Public Interest. *Yale Law Journal* 50 (February): 543–594.

Rutherford, Malcolm. 1981. Clarence Ayres and the Instrumental Theory of Value. *Journal of Economic Issues* 15 (September): 657–673.

1987. Wesley Mitchell: Institutions and Quantitative Methods. *Eastern Economic Journal* 13 (1): 63–73.

1994a. *Institutions in Economics: The Old and the New Institutionalism*. Cambridge: Cambridge University Press.

1994b. J. A. Hobson and American Institutionalism: Underconsumption and Technological Change. In John Pheby, ed., *J. A. Hobson after Fifty Years*. London: Macmillan, pp. 188–210.

1997. American Institutionalism and the History of Economics. *Journal of the History of Economic Thought* 19 (Fall): 178–195.

1998. Thorstein Veblen's Evolutionary Programme: A Promise Unfulfilled. *Cambridge Journal of Economics* 22 (July): 463–477.

1999. Institutionalism as "Scientific" Economics. In Roger Backhouse and John Creedy, eds., *From Classical Economics to the Theory of the Firm: Essays in Honour of D. P. O'Brien*. Aldershot: Edward Elgar, pp. 223–242.

2000a. Institutionalism between the Wars. *Journal of Economic Issues* 34 (June): 291–303.

2000b. Understanding Institutional Economics: 1918–1929. *Journal of the History of Economic Thought* 22 (3): 277–308.

2001. Institutional Economics: Then and Now. *Journal of Economic Perspectives* 15 (Summer): 173–194.

2002. Morris A. Copeland: A Case Study in the History of Institutional Economics. *Journal of the History of Economic Thought* 24 (September): 261–290.

2003. On the Economic Frontier: Walton Hamilton, Institutional Economics and Education. *History of Political Economy* 35 (Winter): 611–653.

2004. Institutional Economics at Columbia University. *History of Political Economy* 36 (Spring): 31–78.

2005a. 'Who's Afraid of Arthur Burns?' The NBER and the Foundations. *Journal of the History of Economic Thought* 27 (June): 109–139.

2005b. Walton H. Hamilton and the Public Control of Business. In Steven Medema and Peter Boettke, eds., *The Role of Government in the History of Political Economy*, Supplement to volume 37, *History of Political Economy*. Durham, NC: Duke University Press, pp. 234–273.

2006. Wisconsin Institutionalism: John R. Commons and His Students. *Labor History*, 47 (May): 161–188.

2007. American Institutionalism and Its British Connections. *European Journal of the History of Economic Thought* 14 (June): 291–323.

2009. Did Commons Have Few Followers? *Journal of Economic Issues* 43 (June): 441–448.

Forthcoming. The USDA Graduate School: Government Instruction in Statistics and Economics, 1921–1945. *Journal of the History of Economic Thought*.

Rutherford, Malcolm and Tyler C. DesRoches. 2008. The Institutionalist Reaction to Keynesian Economics. *Journal of the History of Economic Thought* 30 (March): 29–48.

Rutherford, Malcolm, Warren J. Samuels, and Charles J. Whalen. 2008. Introduction to John R. Commons's *Reasonable Value*. *Research in the History of Economic Thought and Methodology* 26-B: 223–233.

Samuels, Warren J. 1967. Edwin E. Witte's Concept of the Role of Government in the Economy. *Land Economics* 43 (May): 131–147.

1973. The Economy as a System of Power and Its Legal Bases: The Legal Economics of Robert Lee Hale. *University of Miami Law Review* 27 (Spring and Summer): 261–371.

Samuels, Warren J, ed. 2004. Wisconsin "Government and Business." *Research in the History of Economic Thought and Methodology* 22-C.

Samuelson, Paul A. 1938. A Note on the Pure Theory of Consumer's Behaviour. *Economica* 5 (February): 61–71.

1947. *Foundations of Economic Analysis*. Cambridge, MA: Harvard University Press.

Saposs, David J. 1926. *Left-Wing Unionism: A Study of Radical Policies and Tactics*. New York: International Publishers.

1931. *The Labor Movement in Post-War France*. New York: Columbia University.

1960. The Wisconsin Heritage and the Study of Labor – Works and Deeds of John R. Commons. *School for Workers 35th Anniversary Papers*. Madison, WI: University of Wisconsin, University Extension Division, School for Workers.

Sass, Steven A. 1982. *The Pragmatic Imagination: A History of the Wharton School, 1881–1981*. Philadelphia: University of Pennsylvania Press.

Sawyer, Steven. 2004. The Influence of Thorstein Veblen's *Theory of Business Enterprise* on the Economic Theories of Edward Chamberlin. *Journal of Economic Issues* 38 (June): 553–561.

Scherer, F. M. 2000. The Emigration of German-Speaking Economists after 1933. *Journal of Economic Literature* 38 (September): 614–626.

Schlabach, Theron F. 1969. *Edwin E. Witte: Cautious Reformer*. Madison, WI: State Historical Society of Wisconsin.

2001. *Rationality and Welfare: Public Discussion of Poverty and Social Insurance in the United States 1875–1935.* http://www.ssa.gov/history/reports/schlabach.html

Schlegel, John H. 1995. *American Legal Realism and Empirical Social Science.* Chapel Hill, NC: University of North Carolina Press.

Schmid, A. Allan. 2004. The Spartan School of Political Economy at Michigan State University. *Research in the History of Economic Thought and Methodology* 22-C, pp. 207–243.

Schultz, Henry. 1928. *Statistical Laws of Demand and Supply.* Chicago: University of Chicago Press.

1935. Correct and Incorrect Methods of Determining the Effectiveness of the Tariff. *Journal of Farm Economics* 17 (November): 625–641.

(1937) 2000. The Quantitative Method with Special Reference to Economic Inquiry. Lecture given to the Division of Social Sciences, 1937. Edited by Luca Fiorito and Warren Samuels, *Research in the History of Economic Thought and Methodology: Twentieth Century Economics* 18-C: 343–355.

Schwartz, A. 2000. Karl Llewellyn and the Origins of Contract Theory. In J. Kraus and S. Walt, eds., *The Jurisprudential Foundations of Corporate and Commercial Law.* New York: Cambridge University Press.

Seager, Henry R. 1910. *Social Insurance.* New York: Macmillan.

Seager, Henry R. and Charles A. Gulick. 1929. *Trusts and Corporation Problems.* New York: Harper.

Shute, Laurence. 1997. *John Maurice Clark: A Social Economics for the Twenty-First Century.* New York: St. Martin's.

Simon, Herbert. 1955. A Behaviorial Model of Rational Choice. *Quarterly Journal of Economics* 69 (February): 99–118.

Simons, Henry C. 1934. *A Positive Program for Laissez Faire: Some Proposals for a Liberal Economic Policy.* Chicago: University of Chicago Press.

Skidelsky, Robert. *John Maynard Keynes: The Economist as Saviour, 1920–1937.* London: Macmillan, 1992.

Slichter, Sumner H. (1924) 1971. The Organization and Control of Economic Activity. In Rexford G. Tugwell, ed., *The Trend of Economics.* Port Washington, NY: Kennikat Press, pp. 303–355.

1928. The Price of Industrial Progress. *New Republic* 53 (February 8): 316–318.

1931. *Modern Economic Society.* New York: H. Holt.

1934. The Economics of Public Works. *American Economic Review* 24 (March): 174–185.

(1937) 1961. Safeguards Against Depression: An Analysis of Depression Cures. In *Potentials of the American Economy: Selected Essays of Sumner H. Slichter.* Cambridge, MA: Harvard University Press.

1961. *Potentials of the American Economy: Selected Essays of Sumner H. Slichter.* Cambridge, MA: Harvard University Press.

Soule, George. (1924) 1971. Economics – Science and Art. In Rexford G. Tugwell, ed., *The Trend of Economics.* Port Washington, NY: Kennikat Press, pp. 359–367.

Sowell, Thomas. 1993. A Student's Eye View of George Stigler. *Journal of Political Economy* 101 (October): 784–792.

Stapleford, Thomas A. 2006. Market Visions: Liberal Reform and the Study of Consumption in the New Deal. Mimeo.

Sternsher, Bernard. 1964. *Rexford Tugwell and the New Deal*. New Brunswick, NJ: Rutgers University Press.

Stewart, Walter W. 1917. Social Value and the Theory of Money. *Journal of Political Economy* 25 (December): 984–1002.

——— 1919. Economic Theory – Discussion. *American Economic Review* 9 (March): 319–320.

Stigler, George J. 1947a. The Kinky Oligopoly Demand Curve and Rigid Prices. *Journal of Political Economy* 55 (June): 432–449.

——— 1947b. Professor Lester and the Marginalists. *American Economic Review* 37 (March): 154–157.

——— 1954. The Economist Plays with Blocs. *American Economic Review* 44 (May): 7–14.

Stigler, George J. and Gary S. Becker. 1977. De Gustibus non est Disputandum. *American Economic Review* 67 (March): 76–90.

Stigler, George J. and C. Friedland. 1983. The Literature of Economics: The Case of Berle and Means. *Journal of Law and Economics* 26 (January): 237–268.

Stigler, George J. and James K. Kindahl. 1970. *The Behavior of Industrial Prices*. New York: Columbia University Press for the National Bureau of Economic Research.

Stigler, Stephen M. 1994. Some Correspondence between Milton Friedman and Edwin B. Wilson; November-December 1946. *Journal of Economic Literature* 32 (September): 1197–1203.

Stocking, George Ward. 1925. *The Oil Industry and the Competitive System: A Study in Waste*. Boston and New York: Houghton Mifflin.

Stocking, George Ward and Myron W. Watkins. 1946. *Cartels in Action*. New York: Twentieth Century Fund.

——— 1948. *Cartels or Competition*. New York: Twentieth Century Fund.

Stone, Richard. 1947. Definition and Measurement of the National Income and Related Topics. Appendix to *Measurement of National Income and the Construction of Social Accounts, Report of the Sub-Committee on National Income Statistics of the League of Nations Committee of Statistical Experts*. Geneva: United Nations.

Street, James H. 1988. The Contribution of Simon S. Kuznets to Institutional Development Theory. *Journal of Economic Issues* 22 (June): 499–509.

Swisher, Carl Brent. 1930. *Stephen J. Field: Craftsman of the Law*. Washington DC: Brookings Institution.

——— 1943. *American Constitutional Development*. Boston: Houghton Mifflin.

Tannenbaum, Frank. 1929. *The Mexican Agrarian Revolution*. New York: Macmillan.

——— 1933. *Peace by Revolution: An Interpretation of Mexico*. New York: Columbia University Press.

——— 1946. *Slave and Citizen: The Negro in the Americas*. New York: Vintage Books.

Tawney, Richard. H. 1921. *The Acquisitive Society*. London: G. Bell.

Taylor, Horace. 1928. *Making Goods and Making Money*. New York: Columbia University Press.

——— 1938. *Contemporary Economic Problems and Trends*. New York: Harcourt, Brace.

Taylor, Timothy. 2010. Recommendations for Further Reading. *Journal of Economic Perspectives* 24 (Summer): 251–258.

Terborgh, George W. 1945. *The Bogey of Economic Maturity*. Chicago: Machinery and Allied Products Institute.

Thorp, Willard L. 1928. *Economic Institutions*. New York: Macmillan.

——— 1947. Entry in *Current Biography 1947*. New York: H. W. Wilson.

Thorp, Willard L. and Wesley C. Mitchell. 1926. *Business Annals*. New York: National Bureau of Economic Research.

Tugwell, Rexford G. 1921. The Economic Basis for Business Regulation. *American Economic Review* 11 (March): 643–658.

1922a. *The Economic Basis of Public Interest*. New York: Agustus M. Kelley, 1968.

1922b. Human Nature in Economic Theory. *Journal of Political Economy* 30 (June): 317–345.

(1924a) 1971. Experimental Economics. In Rexford G. Tugwell, ed., *The Trend of Economics*. Port Washington, NY: Kennikat Press, pp. 370–422.

ed. (1924b) 1971. *The Trend of Economics*. Port Washington, NY: Kennikat Press.

1927. *Industry's Coming of Age*. New York: Harcourt, Brace.

1930. Human Nature and Social Economy, I and II. *Journal of Philosophy* 17 and 18 (August 14 and 28): 449–457, 477–492.

1931. The Theory of Occupational Obsolescence. *Political Science Quarterly* 46 (June): 171–227.

1932a. Flaws in the Hoover Economic Plan. *Current History* 35 (January): 525–531.

1932b. The Principle of Planning and the Institution of Laissez Faire. *American Economic Review* 22 (March): 75–92.

1933. *The Industrial Discipline and the Governmental Arts*. New York: Columbia University Press.

1935a. Consumers and the New Deal. In *The Battle for Democracy*. New York: Columbia University Press, pp. 268–286.

1935b. When Corporations Save. In *The Battle for Democracy*. New York: Columbia University Press, pp. 187–192.

1937. Wesley Mitchell: An Evaluation. *New Republic* 92 (October 6): 238–240.

1982. *To the Lesser Heights of Morningside*. Philadelphia: University of Philadelphia Press.

Tugwell, Rexford G. and Howard C. Hill. 1934. *Our Economic Society and its Problems*. New York: Harcourt, Brace.

Tugwell, Rexford G., Thomas Munroe, and Roy E. Stryker. 1925. *American Economic Life and the Means of Its Improvement*. New York: Harcourt, Brace.

Turner, Stephen P. 1999. Does Funding Produce its Effects? The Rockefeller Case. In Theresa Richardson and Donald Fisher, eds., *The Development of the Social Sciences in the United States and Canada: The Role of Philanthropy*. Stamford, CT: Ablex.

Van Horn, Rob. 2009. Reinventing Monopoly and the Role of Corporations: Chicago School of Law and Economics. In Philip Mirowski and Dieter Plehwe, eds., *The Road from Mont Pelerin: The Making of the Neoliberal Thought Collective*. Cambridge, MA: Harvard University Press, pp. 204–237.

Van Horn, Rob and Philip Mirowski. 2009. The Rise of the Chicago School of Economics and the Birth of Neoliberalism. In Philip Mirowski and Dieter Plehwe, eds., *The Road from Mont Pelerin: The Making of the Neoliberal Thought Collective*. Cambridge, MA: Harvard University Press, pp. 139–178.

Vaughn, Gerald F. 1999. Veblen's Possible Influence on the New Deal Land-Utilization Program as Evidenced by His Student Claud Franklin Clayton. *Journal of Economic Issues* 33 (September): 713–727.

2001a. Veblen, Camp, and the Industrial Organization of Agriculture. *Journal of Economic Issues* 35 (March): 139–152.

2001b. The Influence of Veblen's Theory of the Leisure Class on Rural Sociologist Fred Roy Yoder. *Journal of Economic Issues* 25 (December): 979–993.

Veblen, Thorstein. 1898. Why Is Economics Not an Evolutionary Science? *Quarterly Journal of Economics* 12 (July): 373–397.

1899. *The Theory of the Leisure Class*. New York: Macmillan.

1899–1900. The Preconceptions of Economic Science, I, II and III. *Quarterly Journal of Economics* 13 (January): 121–150; (July): 396–426; 14 (February): 240–269.

1901. Gustav Schmoller's Economics. *Quarterly Journal of Economics* 16 (November): 69–93.

1904. *The Theory of Business Enterprise*. New York: Scribners.

1906. The Place of Science in Modern Civilization. *American Journal of Sociology* 11 (March): 585–609.

1907. The Socialist Economics of Karl Marx and His Followers, II. *Quarterly Journal of Economics* 21 (February): 299–322.

1908a. Professor Clark's Economics. *Quarterly Journal of Economics* 22 (February): 147–195.

1908b. On the Nature of Capital, I and II. *Quarterly Journal of Economics* 22 (August): 517–542; 23 (November): 104–136.

1909. The Limitations of Marginal Utility. *Journal of Political Economy* 17 (November): 620–636.

1914. *The Instinct of Workmanship*. New York: Macmillan.

1915. *Imperial Germany and the Industrial Revolution*. New York: Macmillan.

1917. *An Inquiry into the Nature of Peace*. New York: Macmillan.

1918. *The Higher Learning in America*. New York: B. W. Huebsch.

1919a. *The Vested Interests and the State of the Industrial Arts*. New York: B. W. Huebsch.

1919b. *The Place of Science in Modern Civilization*. New York: B. W. Huebsch.

1921. *The Engineers and the Price System*. New York: B. W. Huebsch.

1925. Economic Theory in the Calculable Future. *American Economic Review* 15 (March): 48–55.

1934. *Essays in our Changing Order*. New York: Viking.

Viner, Jacob. 1928. The Present Status and Future Prospects of Quantitative Economics. *American Economic Review, Papers and Proceedings* 18 (March): 30–36.

Vining, Routledge. 1939. Suggestions of Keynes in the Writings of Veblen. *Journal of Political Economy* 47 (October): 692–704.

1949. Methodological Issues in Quantitative Economics: Koopmans on the Choice of Variables to Be Studied and on Methods of Measurement. *Review of Economics and Statistics* 31 (May): 77–86.

1950. Methodological Issues in Quantitative Economics: Variations upon a Theme by F. H. Knight. *American Economic Review* 40 (June): 267–284.

1963. On the Problem of Recognizing and Diagnosing Faultiness in the Observed Performance of an Economic System. *Journal of Law and Economics* 6 (July): 165–184.

Wallas, Graham. 1908. *Human Nature in Politics*. London: Archibald Constable and Co.

1914. *The Great Society*. London: Macmillan.

Waller, Spencer W. 2000. The Language of Law and the Language of Business. Working Paper, Institute for Consumer Anti-Trust Studies, Loyola University Chicago School of Law.

Wallis, W. Allen. 1980. The Statistical Research Group, 1942–1945. *Journal of the American Statistical Association* 75 (June): 320–335.

Wallis, W. Allen and Milton Friedman. 1942. The Empirical Derivation of Indifference Functions. In Oscar Lange, ed., *Studies in Mathematical Economics and Econometrics*. Chicago: University of Chicago Press, pp. 175–189.

Wells, Wyatt C. 1994. *Economist in an Uncertain World: Arthur F. Burns and the Federal Reserve, 1970–78*. New York: Columbia University Press.

Whalen, Charles J. 2008. John R. Commons and John Maynard Keynes on Economic History and Policy. *Journal of Economic Issues* 42 (March): 225–242.

Wilber, Charles K. and Robert S. Harrison. 1978. The Methodological Basis of Institutional Economics: Pattern Model, Storytelling, and Holism. *Journal of Economic Issues* 12 (March): 61–89.

Williamson, Oliver E. 1998a. The Institutions of Governance. *American Economic Review* 88 (May): 75–79.

1998b. Transaction Cost Economics: How It Works: Where It Is Headed. *De Economist* 146 (April): 23–58.

Witte, Edwin E. 1932. *The Government in Labor Disputes*. New York: McGraw-Hill.

1937. Old Age Security in the Social Security Act. *Journal of Political Economy* 45 (February): 1–44.

1952. The Teacher and Guide. *John R. Commons: Teacher, Economist, and Administrator*. Madison, WI: Sate Historical Society of Wisconsin.

1954. Institutional Economics as Seen by an Institutional Economist. *Southern Economic Journal* 21 (October): 131–140.

1960. Selig Perlman. *Industrial and Labor Relations Review* 13 (April): 335–337.

Woirol, Gregory R. 1984. Observing the IWW in California, May–July 1914. *Labor History* 25 (Summer): 437–447.

1992. *In the Floating Army: F. C. Mills on Itinerant Life in California*, 1914. Urbana, IL: University of Illinois Press.

1999. The Contributions of Frederick C. Mills. *Journal of the History of Economic Thought* 21 (June): 163–185.

2006. New Data, New Issues: The Origins of the Technological Unemployment Debates. *History of Political Economy* 38 (Fall): 473–496.

Wolfe, A. B. (1924) 1971. Functional Economics. In Rexford G. Tugwell, ed., *The Trend of Economics*. Port Washington, NY: Kennikat Press, pp. 443–482.

1936. Institutional Reasonableness and Value. *Philosophical Review* 45 (March): 192–206.

Wolman, Leo. 1919. The Statistical Work of the War Industries Board. *Publications of the American Statistical Association* 16 (March): 248–260.

1924. *The Growth of American Trade Unions, 1880–1923*. New York: National Bureau of Economic Research.

1927. The Frontiers of Social Control. *American Labor Legislation Review* 17: 233–241.

1930. *Planning and Control of Public Works*. New York: NBER.

Wolman, Leo and Gustav Peck. 1933. Labor Groups in the Social Structure. *Recent Social Trends in the United States*. New York: McGraw Hill.

Worcester, Kenton W. 2001. *Social Science Research Council, 1923–1998*. New York: Social Science Research Council.

Wright, David McCord. 1943. Moulton's The New Philosophy of Public Debt. *American Economic Review* 33 (September): 573–590.

1945. The Future of Keynesian Economics. *American Economic Review* 35 (June): 284–307.

Yohe, William P. 1982. The Mysterious Career of Walter W. Stewart, especially 1922–1930. *History of Political Economy* 14 (Winter): 583–607.

1990. The Intellectual Milieu at the Federal Reserve Board in the 1920s. *History of Political Economy* 22 (Fall): 465–488.

Yonay, Yuval P. 1998. *The Struggle over the Soul of Economics: Institutionalist and Neoclassical Economists in America Between the Wars*. Princeton, NJ: Princeton University Press.

Young, Allyn A. 1918. National Statistics in War and Peace. *Publications of the American Statistical Association* 16 (March): 873–885.

(1925) 1927. The Trend of Economics as Seen by Some American Economists. Reprinted in Allyn A. Young, *Economic Problems Old and New*. Boston: Houghton Mifflin, pp. 232–260.

1929. Economics. In Wilson Gee, ed., *Research in the Social Sciences: Its Fundamental Methods and Objectives*. New York: Macmillan, pp. 53–80.

Index